MW01485815

The Dying City

Studies in United States Culture

Grace Elizabeth Hale, *series editor*

EDITORIAL BOARD

Sara Blair, University of Michigan

Janet Davis, University of Texas at Austin

Matthew Guterl, Brown University

Franny Nudelman, Carleton University

Leigh Raiford, University of California, Berkeley

Bryant Simon, Temple University

Studies in United States Culture publishes provocative books that
explore U.S. culture in its many forms and spheres of influence.
Bringing together big ideas, brisk prose, bold storytelling, and
sophisticated analysis, books published in the series serve as an
intellectual meeting ground where scholars from different
disciplinary and methodological perspectives can build common
lines of inquiry around matters such as race, ethnicity, gender,
sexuality, power, and empire in an American context.

The Dying City

Postwar New York and the Ideology of Fear

....

BRIAN TOCHTERMAN

The University of North Carolina Press   Chapel Hill

This book was published with the assistance of the Anniversary Fund of the
University of North Carolina Press.

© 2017 The University of North Carolina Press
All rights reserved
Set in Charis and Lato by Westchester Publishing Services
Manufactured in the United States of America

The University of North Carolina Press has been a member
of the Green Press Initiative since 2003.

Library of Congress Cataloging-in-Publication Data
Names: Tochterman, Brian, author.
Title: The dying city : postwar New York and the ideology of fear /
    Brian Tochterman.
Other titles: Studies in United States culture.
Description: Chapel Hill : The University of North Carolina Press, [2017] |
    Series: Studies in United States culture | Includes bibliographical
    references and index.
Identifiers: LCCN 2016047325| ISBN 9781469633053 (cloth : alk. paper) |
    ISBN 9781469633060 (pbk : alk. paper) | ISBN 9781469633077 (ebook)
Subjects: LCSH: New York (N.Y.)—Intellectual life—20th century. |
    New York (N.Y.)—In literature. | New York (N.Y.)—In motion pictures. |
    New York (N.Y.)—History—1951- | New York (N.Y.)—History—
    1898–1951. | Fear—Social aspects—New York (State)—New York.
Classification: LCC F128.52 .T59 2017 | DDC 974.7/104—dc23
    LC record available at https://lccn.loc.gov/2016047325

Cover illustration: Skyline of New York City (photograph by author).

Portions of the Introduction, Chapter 4, and the Epilogue were
previously published in a different form in "Theorizing Neoliberal Urban
Development: A Genealogy from Richard Florida to Jane Jacobs,"
Radical History Review 112 (2012): 65–87. Used here with permission
of the Duke University Press (http://www.dukepress.edu).

For Ana

New York, anyone? Come and get it before it is too late. This seems like a death-wish city.

—Ada Louise Huxtable (1970)

Contents

Acknowledgments, xi

Introduction, 1

Part I
Highbrow versus Hard-Boiled
Literary Visions of New York, 1947–1952

1 E. B. White's Cosmopolis, 17

2 Mickey Spillane's Necropolis, 37

Part II
Cancer and Death
New York Narratives in Planning Theory, 1953–1961

3 The Case for Municipal Surgery, 59

4 On Planning Necropolis, 80

Part III
The Other New York
Intellectuals in Necropolis, 1961–1967

5 Farewell to the Universal City, 101

6 Untangling the Pathologies of Ungovernability, 122

Part IV
Detour to Fun City
Cultural Responses to the Death of New York, 1967–1985

7 Fear City on Film, 145

8 The Lure of Decay, 172

Epilogue, 199

Notes, 211
Bibliography, 243
Index, 269

Figures

1 Queensboro Bridge at dusk from *Manhattan* (1979), 33

2 Museum tableau from *Manhattan* (1979), 34

3 Mickey Spillane in *The Girl Hunters* (1963), 38

4 End credits from *The Girl Hunters* (1963), 43

5 Jon Voight and Dustin Hoffman in *Midnight Cowboy* (1969), 146

6 Tiffany & Co. sidewalk in *Midnight Cowboy* (1969), 149

7 Attempted muggings in *Death Wish* (1974), 155

8 Media coverage of vigilantism in *Death Wish* (1974), 156

9 Charles Bronson in *Death Wish* (1974), 162

10 Bodega scene in *Taxi Driver* (1976), 163

11 Florida billboard in *Midnight Cowboy* (1969), 166

12 Suburban Tucson landscape in *Death Wish* (1974), 168

13 Sleaze Sisters concert from *Times Square* (1980), 186

14 Graffiti in *Wild Style* (1983), 190

15 South Bronx landscape in *Wild Style* (1983), 194

Acknowledgments

This is my first book, and there have been many times throughout the process of putting it together where I felt like a traveler on a journey to some unknown, constantly shifting destination. At those points where I found myself with neither a compass nor an atlas, I was fortunate to fall back on the guidance and support of numerous helpful and skilled practitioners whose geographical positioning systems placed me on the path toward completion. While some of the figures profiled in this history would have been wont to claim full responsibility for their accomplishments, it is imperative to recognize the extensive network of collaborators whom I have solicited for directions along the way. Any mistakes and limitations within this work, however, are categorically my own.

I wish to thank the University of North Carolina Press for the commitment they have shown my work since 2014. Mark Simpson-Vos in particular has been a ceaseless advocate for this book, and he was patient as the drafts went from rough to finalized. Lucas Church and Jessica Newman answered countless questions and have been instrumental in ensuring the work's skilled production. I am also indebted to the feedback I received from blind reviewers throughout this process.

As a graduate student at the University of Minnesota, I received invaluable support from Kevin P. Murphy, who pushed me to delve deeper into sources; challenged superficial interpretations; read, edited, and reread various earlier versions of these chapters; and championed my work. I am forever grateful for his selfless guidance. Seminar courses with Elaine Tyler May sparked my interest in the post–World War II culture, and conversations with Lary May encouraged my research on Mickey Spillane and New York City in film. Monthly workshops at their home were instrumental in shaping this book over the past decade. Jeffrey Manuel, Caley Horan, Daniel LaChance, and Andy Urban, among several others, read and critiqued the embryonic stages of this research.

This book would not have been possible without the extensive analog archive of bound periodicals and microfilm at the University of Minnesota's Wilson Library and the library's helpful staff. In addition, Jay Barksdale at the New York Public Library provided me with a reading space in the Wertheim Study and thus access to the main branch's innumerable treasures. At Northland College, Elizabeth Madsen-Genszler and Julia Waggoner secured vital texts and sources from other institutions, and without their help this manuscript would not have been completed in a timely manner.

While living and writing in New York City, I had the pleasure of engaging an incredible group of intellectual and cultural historians at New York University. Thank you to Thomas Bender for inviting me to participate in your writing seminar and to Camille Amat, Natalie Blum-Ross, Rebekah Friedman, Paul Kershaw, Julia Kraut, Tracy Neumann, Atiba Pertilla, Helen Tuttle, David Weinfeld, Peter Wirzbicki, and Dylan Yeats for your constructive feedback on chapter 5 and on additional selections found throughout the book.

The opportunity to publish an article on neoliberal urban development in the *Radical History Review*, encouraged by issue editors Jason Stahl and Mark Soderstrom, allowed me to clarify and refocus chapter 4. Elizabeth Tandy Shermer offered extensive feedback on chapter 6, and Amanda Seligman read and critiqued an abbreviated version of chapter 8. I can only hope that the final product, guided by their constructive criticism, lives up to their respective standards.

The unseasonably warm community of Northland College and Ashland, Wisconsin, has nurtured this project in countless ways. Leslie Alldritt graciously offered me time and space to research and write. Friends, colleagues, and students here have encouraged and broadened my interdisciplinary understanding of the world in ways that are clearly unique to the small liberal arts college environment. I am grateful that a hunger for intellectual nourishment extends beyond college walls and into the Chequamegon Bay region as a whole. In particular I wish to thank Julie Buckles and Charmaine Swan for inviting me to talk about my research at the local tavern. I am not sure how many scholars have had that opportunity, but for me it was a distinct pleasure.

On the subject of taverns, I doubt that this former New York City park inspector would have ever written a book, much less become a scholar, if it were not for the community of organic and inorganic intellectuals that used to huddle around the bar at 1020 Amsterdam Avenue in the early 2000s. Perhaps unbeknownst to that crowd of former regulars, the space is responsible, in a social and not financial sense, for my decision to pursue this line of labor and inquiry. Christopher Lamping, with his boundless font of knowledge, deserves special recognition in this respect.

Reaching back deeper into history, I am indebted in ways that I can never personally repay to my parents, Barbara and Matthew P. Tochterman, who have supported me unconditionally on this long and winding road. I also think back nostalgically on fragments of unfettered childhood street life with my siblings, Barry and Matthew E. Tochterman, and wonder how it shaped my love of urban life, even in our small corner of world on Green Bay's near west side.

I imagine that the most captivating works within the humanities tend to be the product of profound suffering and pain, but over the course of putting this book together I have found much inspiration in joy. The arrival of my two children, Eugenia and Margaret, amid the stress of junior faculty life has provided innumerable moments of pure, unabashed delight. If I have any wish for the impact of this book, it is that in some way, however small, it makes their world less willing to yield to artificial fears. No one has been subjected to more commentary on past artificial urban fears than my partner and spouse Ana Zanger Tochterman. She has shouldered the burden of this book for nearly as long as I have, and has been a constant loving companion during the moments of doubt and triumph. She once risked her life to save my notes and drafts from our burning tenement, and I cannot imagine this book or my life without her in it. To me she is the quintessential cosmopolitan Big Apple migrant—part model citizen and part muse. One who made it in New York and proved willing to test the limits of the city's unofficial anthem by trying to make it in northern Wisconsin. For these reasons and many, many others, I dedicate this book to her.

The Dying City

Introduction

· ·

In July 1975, with the threat of bankruptcy looming, the *New York Times* asked eighteen "urban experts," mostly prominent economists, social scientists, and theorists, "What should be done to solve New York City's dilemma?"[1] Since 1969 the city had lost nearly 500,000 jobs, and twice as many middle-class taxpayers had left New York in the decade prior. The city's woes were indicative of broader trends, as the national economy foundered as a result of geopolitical conflict with countries in Southeast and Middle East Asia, deindustrialization, and the fitful transition to a postindustrial order at home. In this context, New York's generous social democracy, structured around inclusive unionized public employment and equal access to public services, struggled to survive. In the spring of 1975, as Saigon fell, New York effectively defaulted on its debts, unable to pay its bills and with nary a willing lender.[2]

The state intervened, keeping the city afloat through limited bailouts in the first half of the year and later establishing the Municipal Assistance Corporation to control the city's finances. In October 1975, New York City would turn to the federal government for additional support, culminating in a public shaming on the part of President Gerald Ford and the infamous, period-defining *Daily News* headline, FORD TO CITY: DROP DEAD. Citing New York as the exemplar of problematic management, economist Robert Zevin diagnosed the state of the city in the promptly assembled examination of the calamity, *The Fiscal Crisis of American Cities* (1977): "New York's virtual default confirms long apparent trends: a collapsing private economy, a growing and perversely smothering public economy, a city whose populace and government had rapidly decreasing control over its political economy. New York is not quite dead, but death is clearly inevitable." Such was the prevailing narrative of the city by the 1970s.[3]

The "urban experts" willing to "advise, castigate and console the city on its problems" in the pages of the *Times* offered a few key prescriptions. But no respondent, not even renowned architect Buckminster Fuller, could articulate a holistic vision of a thriving future metropolis as prophets and planners like Robert Moses had a mere quarter-century earlier. Some economists, taking their cues from Moses's era, suggested a dose of Keynesianism to stave off bankruptcy. "I think it's fair to say that no problem associated with New York City could not be solved by providing more money," answered John Kenneth Galbraith. Galbraith and his ilk sought accountability from upper- and middle-class metropolitans who "enjoy the proximity of the city while not paying their share," calling for a commuter tax on those accessing city services without the fiscal responsibility. Antiestablishment voices, too, implored fiscal relief through government intervention, particularly at the federal level. Michael Harrington, identified as the "chairman of the Democratic Socialist committee," advocated for three federal laws to end the trouble and to spread the burden of the city's costly public services: "federalization of welfare, the Kennedy-Corman health-security bill and the Hawkins-Humphrey full-employment bill."[4] At a time when New York's health-care costs accounted for 75 percent of the budget gap, health-care reform would have gone a long way in stemming the crisis. Of course, such policies faced a significant uphill battle in an increasingly neoliberal milieu.[5]

Most of those polled disagreed with such proactive remedies, especially social scientists and critics subscribing to market-oriented theory or an influential strand of conservatism emphasizing social and cultural decay. To them, New York City's prospects appeared dim. Jane Jacobs, the famed urban theorist and former New Yorker, was not sure "New York can recover now . . . [for it] stopped being creative a long time ago." Industry withered away and white-collar financial services took over—a political economy she found unexceptional and unsustainable. Milton Friedman offered little but laissez-faire recommendations, signaling the ascendency of neoclassical economic dogma. New York must set an example for overtaxed municipalities: "Go bankrupt. That will make it impossible for New York City in [the] future to borrow any money and [will] force New York to live within its budget." He presented a second, less harsh, plan—"tighten its belt, pay off its debt, live within its means and become an honest city again"—but reminded readers that only the former functioned as a "politically feasible solution."[6]

Respondents also suggested that New York's public sector fostered a culture of entitlement and dependence. Sociologists Nathan Glazer and Edward C. Banfield decried municipal unions as an unfair burden on the management classes. Glazer insisted that the city "figure out a way of providing more services with less highly paid employees," an analogue to the neoliberal austerity paradigm of doing more with less. Indulgent and overpaid municipal workers, from sanitation laborers and token-booth toll-takers to doctors of philosophy and medicine at city universities and hospitals, were expendable. In a mood reminiscent of his cultural interpretation of urban decline, *The Unheavenly City* (1970), Banfield noted that "if the people of New York will tolerate strikes by public employees, against the law, and not tolerate politicians who crack down on strikes, then I can't see that it will be possible to get New York to live within its budget." Even Roy Wilkins, the veteran civil rights activist and then executive director of the NAACP (National Association for the Advancement of Colored People), advanced the austerity argument, despite the notable upward mobility that unionized public sector employment provided an increasing number of African American New Yorkers after World War II. "I know that I'm treading on a lot of toes," Wilkins offered, "but what New York needs in common with most cities of over 25,000 population is a reduction in the number of municipal employees."[7]

Lewis Mumford, garden city designer, regional planner, and author of two landmark explorations of the urban experience, the celebratory *Culture of Cities* (1938) and less than sanguine follow-up *The City in History* (1961), had the final word. He had long given up on New York City, and it showed. "Make the patient as comfortable as possible," he said; "it's too late to operate."[8] Without doubt, the reality of the city's political economy informed the advice, castigation, and consolation offered by the largely white male experts like Mumford, but the prevailing stories told about New York were also influential. Many of these critics, New Yorkers then or once themselves and thus invested in some future for the city, had contributed to the problematic image of New York City throughout the previous three decades. In Jacobs's *Death and Life of Great American Cities* (1961), for instance, "death" signified the trajectory of New York in the age of urban renewal. Banfield and Glazer described a moral decline resulting from an increasingly diverse city and its dependent minority citizens. Even Harrington's *The Other America* (1962) highlighted New York's vicious "cycle of poverty" in an attempt to foster the type of policies he outlined above, which acolytes of Friedman seized on in their attack on welfare capitalism.[9] When he reviewed Jacobs's book in 1962, Mumford cited an "increasing pathology" within the "very conditions she vehemently upholds as marks of urban vitality," a pathology that epitomized New York's descent toward "Necropolis," a term coined by Patrick Geddes, the Scottish planning theorist and Mumford's mentor, to denote the "city of the dead."[10]

······

Following World War II, critics and commentators like Mumford began to suggest that great American cities in the Northeast and Midwest possessed a problematic social order and an antiquated urban form unfit for a nation wedded to modern principles of progress through redevelopment and the triumph of capitalism over communism. Such complaints were indicative of the charged rhetoric of the "urban crisis," a dynamic postwar episode wrought by a variety of political, economic, social, and cultural factors. The 1949 Housing Act, crafted in response to household and urban congestion after the war and a product of Cold War modernism, transformed the physical nature of metropolitan areas by solidifying single-family homeownership policies introduced during the New Deal and driving suburbanization. For cities, Title I of the act endorsed a program of slum clearance. Municipal governments received federal funding to help demolish physically decaying or declining infrastructure, or, in the parlance of the time, blighted slum districts. The addition of more federal funds in 1953 for redevelopment (i.e., urban renewal), and later for interstate highway arterials, projected the postwar vision of a modern, decentralized, and segregated utopia. The goal appeared just, as modern construction favoring natural light, fresh air, and green space replaced crowded and aged tenement communities. However, the failure of that utopia to materialize, and the overt racial and class contingencies of suburban growth and slum clearance, armed critics of the welfare state and destabilized cities.[11] Deindustrialization and capital moves to the suburbs or the South and West further exacerbated the sense of crisis even as surrounding metropolitan areas surged and southern blacks migrated into northern cities in search of economic opportunity and social equity. Without annexation powers, intrametropolitan municipalities were thrown into cutthroat competition over revenue and services, and older cities lost out. Demographic change, declining tax bases, and the loss of industry pushed several cities to the brink, including Detroit, Pittsburgh, Philadelphia, Cleveland, Youngstown, Gary, Milwaukee, Minneapolis, and St. Louis, among others.[12]

New York City's postwar dalliance with decline and death was at once familiar and exceptional. In this period of dramatic spatial and political transformation, New York played a critical role in both shaping the image of crisis and outlining responses to it. Contending with the perceived "cancer" of the slums, Robert Moses, the city's master planner, initiated a targeted clearance and renewal program and influenced similar redevelopment strategies in Boston, New Haven, and Philadelphia. The swift development of Levittown in 1947 on former Long Island potato farms ushered in an exurban construction boom and inspired the suburban components of the 1949 Housing Act.[13] In 1957, the loss of two of the city's three beloved major league baseball teams—the Giants and the Dodgers—to California signaled the increasing allure of western markets. New York City also lost a significant percentage of its total population by 1980—approximately 20 percent—from a height of 7.8 million in 1950, even as the surrounding metropolitan area population grew by over 6 million persons in the same time period. Puerto Ricans and southern blacks filled the vacuum left by departing middle- and working-class whites, sparking a racial and ethnic turf war that grabbed headlines and inspired productions like *West Side Story* (1961). In 1950, white New Yorkers outnumbered blacks nine to one. By 1980 the city's demographic picture shifted to 70 percent white, 25 percent black, and the remaining 5 percent composed of an expanding combination of Asians and Latino/as (in 1950 they had constituted just 0.3 percent of the city's population). In raw numbers, New York City's white population shrunk by over 2.5 million in those three decades while the number of black citizens doubled, quantitative data that do not take into account an intracity migration by whites from unstable enclaves in Manhattan, the Bronx, and northern Brooklyn to newly developed neighborhoods and subdivisions connected by Moses's beltline parkways, bridges, tunnels, and arterial expressways in southern Brooklyn, eastern and southern Queens, and Staten Island.[14]

Violent and property crimes rose swiftly and steadily in New York after World War II. Annual murders more than doubled between 1945 and 1965 (292 and 681 for those respective years). During that time period, robbery and automobile theft increased fivefold and burglary and theft tenfold. The city's crime rate, however, peaked in 1990 with 2,245 murders, 3,126 reports of rape, 100,000 robberies, 120,000 burglaries, 268,000 reports of theft, and 147,000 stolen automobiles. Crime fears did not necessarily correlate with actual crime rates; rather, anxiety surged in the 1960s and peaked in the 1970s with high-profile violent crimes and sensational reporting on the seeming randomness of criminal acts and increasing white victimization.[15] A polarized city, segregated by race and class, also allowed for simplistic interpretations of the perceived epidemic and its scapegoats. Fear of crime transformed the metropolitan political economy as, beginning with I.B.M. in the 1950s, industry and white-collar firms joined the suburban exodus, seizing on the images of disorder as an excuse for relocation.[16] Throughout New York's crisis period, local leaders struggled to balance the social democratic experiment introduced under Mayor Fiorello La Guardia in the 1930s with a shrinking tax base, a bloated bureaucracy, and shifting political ideologies.[17]

New York, of course, is an exceptional American city, and as such it presents a fickle case study for broader developments within U.S. urban and political history. On the global stage New York is recognized as the iconic U.S. metropolis, but among its own the city has long been seen as unique and not symbolic of national trends. Vice President Spiro Agnew liked to cite *Times* columnist James Reston, who called New York "the most unrepresentative community in the entire United States."[18] One aspect of New York's exceptionalism, relative to cities recognized as declining in the postwar period, was its robust and extensive culture industry, which framed the city in crisis for a national audience. This was a sector that, along with a strategic commitment to financial services, comprised a major part of the city's malleable economy as it adapted to a postindustrial milieu. Even more than Los Angeles, New York was and still is the media capital of the country, home to publishing, journalism, and television broadcasting empires and expanding film production and digital media sectors. New York's media industry produced goods for local citizens, but its output was also found in bookstores, newsstands, television sets, and motion picture theaters throughout the United States and the world, expanding the reach of the stories told about the city. In the postwar era, consumers of American media had an intrinsic connection to New York and a collective understanding of its place within the political landscape.

Media tropes, like those that fed New York's crime anxiety in the 1960s, worked in concert with policy, deindustrialization, and changing demography to alter the national physical landscape after World War II. Cultural assumptions informed the decision-making processes of individuals, communities, public institutions, and private corporations in a period of spatial flux. Suburban developers like "Big Bill" Levitt and the construction trades initially benefited from Cold War concerns over safety and density in the atomic age and popular culture's packaging of consumption, conformity, and nationalism around the "warm hearth" of the single-family home. In the years that followed, a desire for exclusion from the perceived realities of urban life further encouraged metropolitan expansion for white middle-class Americans.[19] The aforementioned cluster of industrial cities stretching from the Northeast to the Midwest became stamped as the Rust Belt, a dubious honorific that did little to spur postindustrial investment within these communities. Signifying a foundering, declining region, the Rust Belt was set against the burgeoning Sunbelt that stretched from below the

Mason-Dixon Line west to Southern California. The loaded vocabulary of slums and blight framed urban neglect and signaled an implicit culture within segregated minority and poor neighborhoods. Declension narratives functioned ideologically, nourishing an anxious antiurban political culture.[20] As homeownership transformed individual political identity and perpetual sprawl tilted the balance of power to the suburbs, from Boston to Detroit to Charlotte to Atlanta to Dallas to Phoenix to Orange County, California, and points in between, place-based issues fueled by fear of the Other such as forced integration, school busing programs, civil rights activism, and ghetto uprisings forged and galvanized a new conservative consciousness inhospitable to urban cosmopolitanism.[21]

As the consummate twentieth-century American metropolis, at once facing a set of familiar challenges and featuring exclusive productive possibilities, narratives of decline and crisis produced in and scrutinizing New York City carried substantial political and cultural authority. Elicited by a diverse cadre of popular critics, these narratives both molded a postwar political culture hostile to New York and reshaped the city itself through political decision-making inspired by fear. New York's resonant stories assumed their power through a combination of factors that included an ever-expanding market for tales of urban woe, the perceived authority of the sources, and the persistent echo of the theme. Concerns about New York City's mortality after World War II—beyond the Cold War fear of the bomb— emerged from the realm of fantasy. The pulp fiction formula required criminal activity, but with timely new twists on plot elements of old—the vigilante subverting the role of the detective and a decaying and dying urban setting rather than a merely dark mise-en-scène—the work became a call for renewal, a politically charged text seeking to transform the city. Operating within a market the size of Mickey Spillane's in the 1950s, pulp possessed ideological value, casting New York in a negative light and presenting a crude vocabulary for the physical and social aspects of crisis. At the same time, the writings of planners and urban theorists operated within a feedback loop.[22] The city's master planner utilized the image of decline and death to likewise push for reform and renewal. When that vision failed to address New York's problems, the narrative of decline persisted but with an adjusted target and new voices joining the fray. Observers critiqued the transformed modern landscape as the new disease, and intellectuals increasingly disillusioned with the city took up the dime-novel template to inform the public and condemn the dying city. In the process, the power of crisis narratives shifted from the world of physical planning and urban design to the political arena. Policymakers took note and cited the increasingly familiar tropes. The vocabulary also migrated from niche venues, such as the black-and-white pages of opinion journals, to the technicolor imagery of film and television and a wider audience, further enhancing its potency and resulting in widespread antipathy toward the city and a fear of its environs.

The most influential of these homegrown narratives amassed around a critical thematic postwar dialectic: New York City as Cosmopolis versus New York City as Necropolis.[23] The narrative of New York as Cosmopolis, grounded in the city's historically cosmopolitan image, denotes the sense of optimism that permeated representations of New York immediately following World War II.[24] Since New Amsterdam distanced itself from fellow Atlantic European colonies through diversity and tolerance, New York maintained a reputation of openness, inclusion, and inspiration. It was a goal to which waves of immigrants and internal migrants aspired, a safety valve for the oppression, poverty, and conformity that defined their previous existence. E. B. White, in particular, highlighted Cosmopolis at an important turning point for the city and the nation as a whole. In a critical yet celebratory essay published in *Holiday* magazine as "Here Is New York" (1949), White detailed three different New Yorks: that of the native, that of the commuter, and that of the migrant. Referencing the last, "the greatest" was "the city of final destination, the city that is a goal." Open acceptance of newcomers accounted for New York's "incomparable achievements," as migrants electrified it through virtues of passion, confidence, and ambition. At a time when Cold War tensions posed a threat to New York City's eminence, White held fast to the belief that New York's resilience and verve would persevere, transcending the calls for small-town convention and suburban decentralization. His was an enduring vision of the city (and it has endured), and it defined much of the media culture around New York during the 1950s, even if that openness and cosmopolitanism were, in practice, fraught with structural limitations for marginalized citizens.[25]

In the 1960s and 1970s, however, the vision of hope and optimism for the city eroded in a deluge of poor publicity. Potential migrants or visitors in search of Cosmopolis might encounter in its stead a chorus of voices warning of Necropolis. In 1975, "Welcome to Fear City" became the city's literal greeting as the Council for Public Safety, a front for police and fire unions challenging proposed austerity measures, put it in their timely pamphlet. Emblazoned with a hooded skull and subtitled "A Survival Guide for Visitors to the City of New York," the pamphlet reported that "incidence of crime and violence in New York City is shockingly high, and is getting worse every day." For personal safety and security reasons, the council instructed newcomers to "stay off the streets after 6 P.M . . . do not walk . . . avoid public transportation . . . remain in Manhattan. . . . [and] protect your property."[26] "Welcome to Fear City" offered visitors and migrants disembarking at the city's major entry points—La Guardia Airport, John F. Kennedy International Airport, Pennsylvania Station, Grand Central Station, and the Port Authority Bus Terminal—a dose of seeming reality that validated the New York City depicted in concurrent popular culture. In contrast with Cosmopolis, the pamphlet's coded vocabulary signified identifiable tropes of Necropolis, including physical deterioration, moral decay, racial pathology, and rampant crime at the hands of New Yorkers of color. Necropolis represented a decline in vision from E. B. White's optimistic modernism to postmodern fragmentation, embodied in a collection of narratives nostalgic for some earlier golden age. The postwar interplay of Cosmopolis versus Necropolis nurtured a localized culture war around the idea of what New York represented as the nation's preeminent metropolis. This ideological struggle had profound implications for the national political culture and the planning and development of cities in our own time.

Tales of Necropolis from seemingly credible, primarily white, sources participated in the shaping of ascendant conservative and liberal ideologies as the era's political consensus unraveled. In a collection of essays cataloguing the city's millennial rebirth, scholar Marshall Berman recalled national television coverage at the height of the fiscal crisis, specifically a southern congressman asking constituents about what should be done for New York. The questions elicited a common refrain: "New York is a parasite, it contributes nothing to America, it is noisy and dirty, it is full of foreigners and disgusting sex, every kind of sinfulness, hippies and homosexuals and Commie degenerates, a blot upon America, and now God has given America the chance to rise up and destroy New York forever, wash it down the drain." One asked, "Should New York live or die?" The crowd "jumped to their feet, grinned obscenely at each other in a classic lynch-mob photo, and screamed, 'Die! Die! Die! Die!'"[27] In addition to lacerating monologues like this, and with pens rather than pitchforks, neoconservative thinkers criticized proposed social policy cures for the city in crisis, arguing that it squashed the ambition at the heart of Cosmopolis. Budding think tanks like the Manhattan Institute helped craft an antiurban message through tales of decay. Researchers pointed to Necropolis as an example of welfare capitalism's failure, thus opening the door for market-driven approaches to rehabilitation and redevelopment across the country.[28] Historians of the New Right often frame the movement's rise as a place-based backlash against northern urban liberalism emanating from suburbs and Sunbelt cities, but, via the fears embedded within Necropolis, New York City constituted a major front in the intellectual development of conservative ideology.[29]

While the fate of New York City provided fodder for reactionary politicians from Spiro Agnew to Rudolph Giuliani, the narrative of Necropolis did not fall easily along partisan lines.[30] Images of decline and death emerged from a variety of perspectives, influencing neoliberal urban visions as much as neoconservative and New Right attacks. Instead, intimate connections to New York and whiteness marked the unifying bonds among the most powerful narrative purveyors, and for most a hawkish masculinity reigned, exemplified in a repeated push for vengeance. At an intensity unseen since George Templeton Strong, Jacob Riis, and other nativists condemned the immigrant masses in the nineteenth century, homegrown cultural boosters fretted that "New York could die" if the containment of decline's various symptoms failed.[31] The disparate voices in this chorus included the pragmatic bureaucrat (as he portrayed himself) Moses and his jeremiads against the slums as well as Jacobs, a successful migrant in the tradition of Cosmopolis, who blamed Moses for the death of great American cities like New York. The cultural history of postwar New York, however, extends beyond this popular and mythic Goliath-versus-David tale.[32] The Necropolis canon comprised Trotskyist intellectuals saying good-bye and good riddance to their formative, universal city alongside Republican Party operatives offering "an angry view" of New York from the comfort of East Egg.[33] Each commentator appeared reluctant to acknowledge the city's previous resilience or embrace E. B. White's postwar vision. Their singular images of the city coalesced around limiting difference, whether racial, ethnic, class, gender, or sexual; an attempt to honor, preserve, or reconstruct the great city of yesterday, the once transformative physical, social, and economic place(s) that drew them to New York or defined their corner of the city. To paraphrase Mickey Spillane's less than diplomatic terms, purveyors of Necropolis resisted cosmopolitanism and demographic change, longing to get back to their "kind of people again"—that place of comfort, familiarity, and security.[34] This theme transcended ideological boundaries, and at considerable social cost. Contemporary culture's positioning of neoliberal and New Right stakeholders in opposition has masked the failure of either constituency to adequately address social and economic problems such as racial discrimination in housing, disparities in wages and hiring practices, access to public services, and adequate welfare programs that have festered since the urban crisis.

While emergent political factions avoided these issues, the competing narratives of New York, and Necropolis in particular, had policy and planning implications for the city and beyond. Some officials recognized potential economic contingencies of Necropolis in real time. A municipal magistrate, for example, halted the distribution of the "Welcome to Fear City" pamphlet citing its threat to New York's economy.[35] A decade prior, Mayor John Lindsay sought to employ media cultures to counteract the image of decline and to market New York as "Fun City" (i.e., a version of Cosmopolis defined by hope, opportunity, and harmless thrills).[36] In the wake of the fiscal crisis, power brokers took the prescriptions of neoconservative critics and neoclassical economists to heart, instituting dramatic austerity measures within the public sector and nurturing a service-oriented economy. Along with elites and bureaucrats, a series of business-friendly mayors, beginning with the postcrisis administration of Edward Koch, helped lay the groundwork for the ascendant service sector and foster the changing image of New York City.[37] In the postindustrial "space of flows," now fluid firms learned they could pit cities, towns, and suburbs against each other in a struggle for the most favorable tax incentives and other detrimental giveaways. New York was no stranger to this, as companies like the New York Stock Exchange threatened to relocate to tax-friendly New Jersey in order to mug city agencies into acquiescing on perceived burdens of Manhattan existence.[38] New theories of urban governance—George L. Kelling and James Q. Wilson's "broken windows" theory of policing, for example—emerged from the ruins of Necropolis as well.[39] Public policy had constructed the postwar city through suburban and highway development, slum clearance and urban renewal, and Great Society reforms, and the image of that city shrouded in fear and crisis rendered the failed urban political response an easy scapegoat.[40]

Analysis of the postwar narratives of New York also reveals the increasing significance of culture not only as a source of decline but as a catalyst for urban regeneration and economic growth.[41] Cultural producers disseminating narratives of New York functioned in concert with power brokers, informally citing their work to ensure future limitations on the state to rectify urban problems such as economic inequality and uneven development. This alliance between culture and political economy molded the recent urban renaissance that at once grew out of the decline debate and now situates culture and cultural infrastructure at the locus of urban vitality. When, for example, New Yorkers deployed culture in order to appropriate the city from prophets of decline and death, new real estate development strategies were born. Public and private agents capitalized on the commodification of hip new frontiers—discovered, claimed, settled, and branded.[42] Renewal schemes that grew out of the city's wrestling with Necropolis, including tourist-focused development and unfettered gentrification, have played a significant role in the city's transformation since the 1970s. In this sense, New York City became a proving ground for neoliberal economic development and planning strategies. Its resilient cosmopolitan ethos along with its political and economic decisions in the wake of the fiscal crisis forestalled its death and hastened its resurgence, but cities and towns lacking in similar resilience narratives have been forced to confront their own mortal fears—or the fears perpetuated by the culture industry. The cautionary tales of Detroit's recent bankruptcy and the ascendant rural crisis resulting from the "hollowing out" of the "Heartland" highlight the persistent power of spatial narratives in the competitive arena of the postindustrial economy.[43]

· · · · · ·

The following eight chapters support these arguments through four distinctive parts. Part 1 defines the competing narratives of Cosmopolis and Necropolis via brief biographies of E. B. White and Mickey Spillane, respectively, along with textual analysis of some of their most important works immediately following World War II. This study originates in this period because, as White suggested, atomic fears should have been paramount in an American city with the political and economic significance of New York, hence his emphasis on Cosmopolis continuing to draw in migrants amid the lure and pull of decentralization. In contrast, White's hard-boiled contemporary, Spillane, presented a profound and original Necropolis narrative of New York. In six formulaic, mass-produced pulp novellas starring neofascist Mike Hammer, Spillane crafted an image of the city as physically decaying, demographically in flux, and overrun by violent criminals. These problems required an authoritarian like Hammer, a private investigator by trade, to restore order and demand conformity. While Spillane's work featured a distinct lowbrow dime-store quality, his incredible success and broad reach commanded a diverse audience and offered a template for homegrown critics of New York—like the writer himself—to dismantle the image of Cosmopolis in periods of perceived crisis.

Part 2 highlights the interplay of the competing narratives in influential planning theory. Reexamining familiar figures within the Title I debate, chapters 3 and 4 offer a fresh analysis of the theories of Robert Moses and Jane Jacobs, respectively. Moses wrote extensively for popular publications, framing the need for slum clearance and redevelopment through a Necropolis lens. Much has been made of Jacobs's love of neighborhoods and New York, but her theorizing, as that of Moses, relied heavily on a fear-laden image of the city. Their use of fear to justify their respective visions of Cosmopolis reveals a key contingency of declension narratives: that policy prescriptions, whether directly informed by texts in the case of Moses or indirectly influenced in the case of Jacobs, addressed the simplistic fears at the expense of the complex problems at the root of those concerns. In addition, their mutual apprehension about New York's fate endured. Leading conservatives embraced Moses's suburban-friendly redevelopment priorities and drew upon Jacobs's image of the dying city as an outcome of liberalism, foretelling the weakening of public redevelopment mechanisms.

Part 3 reveals how impressions of the city by prominent New York–based intellectuals and cultural critics participated in the molding of a new political culture. Images of the city in decline played an important role in the nascent ideological schisms among the influential "New York Intellectuals," who came of age in the 1930s and by the 1960s huddled around niche journals like *Dissent*. New York, now measured in terms of social disorder, crime, and moral decline, had in reality mugged, to borrow Irving Kristol's dividing line between neoconservatism and liberalism, rightward-drifting intellectuals. Even when *Dissent* contributing editor and New Left voice Michael Harrington published *The Other America*, a book hailed for highlighting the persistence of indigence in an otherwise affluent era, it mostly ignited a debate on "urban pathologies" centered on New York—an unfortunate contingency of Harrington's efforts to expand government support for the poor. While Harrington's New Left fleshed out a platform of community development and identity politics, conservative commentators in New York perpetuated the narrative of the pathological "underclass," undermining the prospect of a more equitable Cosmopolis.

Part 4 considers how popular films produced in New York played to this new political culture and how underground media cultures offered an alluring counternarrative of the city. With crime and disorder as the feature antagonist in the New York film cycle of the late 1960s and the 1970s, the vigilante became a vital counterpoint to the perceived incompetence of municipal police departments and other state security apparatuses. Escaping a dying New York City also served as a powerful motif in the period's films. Still, some remaining natives—many marginalized in the culture as the "underclass"—and intrepid migrants drawn by the lure of decay appropriated neighborhoods in the spirit of White's Cosmopolis. The explosion of cultural production and community development amid the fog of Necropolis represented the seeds of regeneration. The moment epitomized what Henri Lefebvre called "the right to the city," a more radical interpretation of White's vision defined by claims of autonomy within and a collective reshaping of urban space.[44] New York in the 1970s was an open, culturally vibrant city for those bold enough to seize it.[45]

The story that follows does not seek to diminish New York's postwar political economy and its tangible consequences for innumerable citizens, including a rising violent crime rate, deindustrialization, decaying infrastructure, unemployment and job loss, homelessness, and inequality. Nor does it wish to silence the varied minority voices that challenged the narratives of power in this period, or to dishonor the memory of those victimized by unspeakable, abhorrent violent acts like Katherine Genovese or even the anonymous victims of what Dick Schaap and Jimmy Breslin termed "lonely crimes." Rather, it considers the power of meditation on these events and the fate of postwar New York, whether real, imaginary, or speculative, to shape the political culture and destroy hope. In New York that speculation evolved into exploitation, exaggeration, and sensation, creating what sociologist Barry Glassner calls a "culture of fear," whereby mass media narratives obscure the roots of serious social problems and thus prevent deliberate social policy aimed at alleviating said ills, including racial and economic inequality.[46] As with various historical fears, once the fog lifts a sterile, elite-accessible version of the once-transgressive culture has been coopted.[47] In New York, the postindustrial service economy staked a claim on the new Cosmopolis fostered by those undeterred by fear. Nostalgia for the lures and snares of the city in crisis would remain, but the new urban panopticon—composed of a mixture of Jacobs's "eyes on the street" sentimentality and *Death Wish*–style policing of difference—preserved the security of back-to-the-city pioneers in quest of the order and conformity preached by Spillane. Among the city's power brokers, any vision of an exceptional New York, once highlighted by E. B. White, and how that might translate into its physical and social realms seems to have died with the escape of Necropolis from the national imagination. As such, the epilogue considers the cultural and political response to the city's brush with death, and how the New York of today intersects with the dying city of old.[48]

Part I **Highbrow versus Hard-Boiled**

Literary Visions of New York, 1947–1952

· ·

1 E. B. White's Cosmopolis

....

In New York City, the postwar era began with a moment of triumph, euphoria, and optimism. After the A-bomb's revelations and the end appeared near, a crowd gathered in Times Square to follow the inevitable surrender on the wires and news tickers at the intersection of Broadway, Seventh Avenue, and Forty-Second Street. The revelers danced to the stylings of a big band, and at sunset Mayor Fiorello LaGuardia announced that surrender had indeed been reached. It was August 15, 1945, V-J Day, when the lights of the square glowed at night for the first time in four years, and New York City was full of collective elation and celebration. Alfred Eisenstadt captured the story and the sense of relief and promise in his iconic photograph of a sailor forcing a kiss upon a woman in a white nurse's uniform. Appearing on the cover of the next *Life* magazine, the photograph conveyed a narrative, one that was not the full story: as the nation's leaders brokered a deal that salvaged Japan's dignity, Americans celebrated like mad on the "crossroads of the world," the most famous corner in the country. It captured the exaltation of the United States at the end of World War II, when New York City was a symbol of national power and economic progress—the assured metropole of what *Life*'s publisher Henry Luce termed the "American Century" and a beacon of modernity that contrasted with the rest of the war-ravaged world.[1]

Three years later, in the summer of 1948, and perched in a steamy hotel room off Times Square, essayist E. B. White penned a literary snapshot of New York City as it negotiated its place within the postwar landscape. In many respects, White's text defined the moment after World War II when, as historian Thomas Bender has noted, New York "was finally recognized . . . as an international cultural metropolis."[2] In "Here Is New York," published in the April 1949 issue of *Holiday* magazine, White questioned New York's sustainability in the atomic age: "The city, for the first time in its long history, is destructible. . . . A single flight of planes no bigger than a wedge of geese can quickly end this island fantasy, burn the towers, crumble the bridges, turn the underground passages into lethal chambers, cremate the millions." The allies emerged victorious, but in the process the United States unleashed the mysterious and omnipotent power of the hydrogen atom on Hiroshima and Nagasaki, demonstrating its might to the rest of the world. White's fear of New York's nuclear annihilation was legitimate in the burgeoning Cold War between the United States and the U.S.S.R. As the country's densest, most populated city as well as its center of finance, New York was a certain target in any imagined atomic battle between the world's two superpowers. In this respect "Here Is New York" functioned as White's warning about the potential cost of losing the city, a cost measured by the exceptional gift of dense, primal, and vibrant urbanism that White witnessed in meditative drifts around the "island fantasy" of New York.[3]

"Here Is New York" put forth a narrative of New York City as a safe harbor for fearless migrants after the horrors of war. By 1948, White foresaw that changes in the metropolitan region were set to alter the city's demographics for years to come. The year prior, builder William Levitt opened his model postwar suburb Levittown in Nassau County, ushering in decades of ceaseless suburban development. The Taylorist, assembly-line style construction of single-family homes on former farmland provided a much-needed safety valve for the postwar housing crisis. Returning veterans found themselves in cramped urban quarters, and Levitt's efficient home-building along with the GI Bill provided them modest homes with no down payment. The homebound fifties were still a few years away, and suburban living would soon prove more affordable and more attractive than the city for many Americans. For citizens fearing the intrinsic correlation between density and destruction, leaving the city had to be attractive to many New Yorkers, and White's celebratory narrative sought to ensure that cosmopolitan newcomers filled the vacuum.[4]

Like the millions of Americans who absorbed early representations of postwar suburbanization, White was not immune to the lure of the rural. As such, he had a complicated and deliberate view of the city, yet nothing less than unbridled enthusiasm carried "Here Is New York." After spending a childhood in the vicinity of the city's northern reaches, White longed to reside within New York proper from the moment he graduated from college. He hit a few snags over the course of achieving that goal, but his perseverance and some fortuitous encounters with an upstart magazine, the *New Yorker*, contributed to that achievement. At the *New Yorker* White honed his craft in the pages of "Talk of the Town," yet he hungered for the life of the national syndicated columnists he admired. *Harper's* offered him greater liberty in his writing, and a chance to reside in his other preferred setting: rural Maine. At the *New Yorker* and *Harper's* White displayed a keen knack for observing and capturing in print the natural and unnatural world. His competing interests in the rural and urban shaped much of his most popular writings, from the children's books *Stuart Little* (1945), about a mouse in the city, and *Charlotte's Web* (1952), a barnyard tale, to his essays on the "Death of a Pig" and the hyperurban "City of Tomorrow." As the United States joined the world at war, however, White returned to the city, carrying with him a thirst for more overt political commentary and a growing obsession with international cooperation and world governance.[5]

Preserving liberty and democracy in the postwar era framed White's interest in a new world order, and the intensity he brought to this subject wrought "Here Is New York." The city for White encapsulated these virtues like no other place, and nowhere were there more citizens and migrants "yearning to breathe free" than in New York. It served as a destination first for the castoffs of colonialism, war, economic decline, and religious persecution across the seas. In the early twentieth century, it became a sanctuary for Americans hobbled by Jim Crow, sex or gender discrimination, and undemocratic conformity in smaller cities and towns across the country. The resilient city and its citizens survived fire, war, riot, crime, discrimination, and poverty through its persistent accommodation of difference and its cultivation of ambitious and enthusiastic youth. For these outcasts, New York City advertised itself in various media cultures as a safe harbor. To White, then, New York was a goal that these intrepid migrants sought to achieve, and as long as it remained such a destination, the city's resilience would be preserved. In the midst of a great fear about its sustainability in the atomic age, the city too would remain.[6]

This narrative of New York as Cosmopolis had been a chapter in the city's story from time immemorial, and manifested itself in a variety of cultural forms. In the postwar era it would help frame the debate over the city at a crucial moment for the political economy of urban governance. White's publication of "Here Is New York" coincided with the implementation of federal policies meant to aid cities in acclimating to the atomic age. Arguments in favor of slum clearance and urban renewal similarly sought the preservation of the city and its values in the postwar era. Meanwhile, fellow writers and cultural producers carried on the narrative of Cosmopolis in their works, even though White resisted many requests to revisit the topic. Over the following three to four decades, White's image of New York and its legacy in the culture would function as a bulwark against an increasingly hegemonic discourse of decline that imagined the city as Necropolis. Purveyors of declensionist narratives made the preservation of New York a goal in their arguments, but only White and his acolytes prioritized the city's reputation for individual freedom and mass democracy, its integration of the natural into an unnatural environment, and its mix of savory and unsavory elements over the desire for order at their sacrifice.

· · · · · ·

Born in 1899, E. B. White spent his younger years just outside New York City, growing up in a large house in suburban Westchester—Mount Vernon, to be exact—as his father oversaw a piano manufacturing firm in Harlem. From Mount Vernon he followed family tradition upstate to Cornell University. He demonstrated a talent for writing from an early age, and had his first formal publication at age nine. It was his vocation of choice from then on. Along with writing, living and working in New York City were White's foremost passions. However, New York City's cutthroat information and cultural sector proved a barrier to White's goals, and instead of working in the city he spent his initial postbaccalaureate years traveling across the country via Model T, eventually terminating in Seattle, where he took a job as a reporter with the local *Times*. In 1923 he returned east and boarded with his parents in Mount Vernon as he searched for employment. Unabashed persistence described White's enthusiasm for the New York culture industry, and he pestered editors around town for a level entry into the publishing world. While waiting for a letter of acceptance, he settled rather uneasily into the field of advertising and the life of a commuter.[7]

White was freed from the shackles of these unfulfilling worlds soon enough, and his early career development offered themes that he would return to throughout his life in letters. He illustrated the mundane repetition of a daily routine organized by the time discipline of the metropolitan railroads in an early poem, to wit: "Commuter—one who spends his life / In riding to and from his wife; / A man who shaves and takes a train / And then rides back to shave again." White also understood the coercive impulses of marketing and the power of culture in general to shape the decision-making processes of an ill-informed public. As he later put it, "advertisers are the interpreters of our dreams. . . . Like the movies, they infect the routine futility of our days with purposeful adventure. Their weapons are our weaknesses: fear, ambition, illness, pride, selfishness, desire, ignorance. And these weapons must be kept as bright as a sword." Sentiments such as these were affected not only in his writing but in the way he lived. He consistently fought against the use of his intellectual property and likeness in the marketing of others' products and publicity materials, and he never lived in a suburban place again—settling for New York City and the rural confines of coastal Maine.[8]

In 1925 a new magazine that would change White's fortunes burst onto the city's literary scene. From its inaugural issue, he was as enchanted with the *New Yorker*—a publication dedicated to satire, humor, and highbrow reportage and literature—as publisher Harold Ross was with him. White submitted short pieces to the magazine, and soon Ross and editor Katherine Angell pushed White to join the staff. In 1927 he accepted their offer and spent his time writing the anecdotal sections that commenced each issue, "Comment" and "Talk of the Town." For the most part, "Talk of the Town" offered just that, brief interludes and observations about everyday moments in New York City. The magazine's editors expected authors to have an ear for urban life and the epistolary acumen to ensure their descriptions transcended the mundane reality of sidewalks and parlors. Within a few years, White was instrumental in the evolution of these departments from humorous vignettes employing the editorial *we* to a mix of opinionated bylined sketches, a transition that also paralleled the writer's own professional development into the long-form essayist that marks his legacy. It was also around this time that White achieved his goal of migrating from his parents' home into the city, taking an apartment with college friends in Greenwich Village, then the epicenter of literary bohemianism. His concurrent marriage to divorcee Katherine Angell—his coworker and occasional editor—spoke to White's cosmopolitan enlightenment in a world often policed by prejudice and taboo. White's father, for instance, expressed private shame regarding his son's coauthored (with fellow humorist James Thurber) send-up of the era's sexual handbooks, *Is Sex Necessary?* (1929), because it mocked suburban upper-class mores.[9]

In 1938, White left New York City and the *New Yorker* for his farm in North Brooklin, Maine, and the pages of *Harper's Magazine*. As literary scholar Robert Root suggests, "throughout the 1930s occasional hints of dissatisfaction appeared in White's Notes and Comment writing, and evidence in his letters reinforces the sense that the anonymity, tone, and format of Comment writing were becoming increasingly difficult for him to live with."[10] Instead of sweating the stressful grind of weekly production, confined to the shallow depths of minute brevity in the pages of the *New Yorker*, the monthly *Harper's* offered deliberate respite and a column of his own in which to hone the essay craft. Under the title "One Man's Meat," and inspired by the popular columns he read as a young adult, White wrote some of his most enduring pieces, including "Once More to the Lake," a travelogue about returning to the upstate home where the White family decamped during summer. He also visited New York City for the 1939 World's Fair and published a column titled "The World of Tomorrow." During his encounter with the General Motors (GM) exhibit of the same name, White was seduced by the utopian vision of the United States in 1960, one "of complete religious faith in the eternal benefaction of faster travel." As he was quick to point out, the future city and its harmonious highways failed to consider the seemingly mundane yet rewarding aspects of urban and rural life in GM's master plan. He wrote of the "strong, sweet poison" of Futurama's advertisement for automobile utopia, but "it wasn't till I passed an apple orchard and saw the tree, each blooming under its own canopy of glass, that I perceived that even the GM dream, as dreams so often do, left some questions unanswered about the future. The apple tree of Tomorrow, abloom under its inviolate hood, makes you stop and wonder. How will the little boy climb it? Where will the bird build its nest?"[11]

The passage illustrated both his disillusion with the vision of paternal urbanism in the automobile age and the primacy of nature and wilderness to White's worldview. This latter impulse drove him into the country in the late 1930s. According to confidant Dorothy Lobrano Guth, "White's feelings about New York were mixed: he loved the city (a love he celebrated in many of his writings), but he often felt unfulfilled by urban life."[12] His bestselling and beloved children's books—*Stuart Little* and *Charlotte's Web*—spoke to White's primary literary settings: the city and the farm, respectively. His ability to observe the natural world around him was central to White's development as an essayist. The "One Man's Meat" period was filled with tales of rural life. Although these pieces did not personify varmints and farm animals as did his children's books, giving voice to the voiceless seemed to be one of White's gifts as a writer, and his knack for the observational yet editorial essay served him well in the country. The onset of total war, however, weighed heavily on the former city dweller, and as Root notes, "by August 1942 White's columns had begun to express dissatisfaction with his writing and to foreshadow his eventual return to the city." The *New Yorker*'s war-thinned ranks and the opportunity to compose lengthier pieces within its pages brought White back to the city in 1943, taking an apartment in the Turtle Bay section of Manhattan—a neighborhood soon poised to house the postwar era's monument to internationalism, the United Nations complex.[13]

While White's decampment to Turtle Bay—at the time an area of residences and declining slaughterhouses—was coincidental, internationalism and the promise of a new world order proved vital themes in his optimistic postwar vision. White had already earned a reputation as a humorist and an earnest observer, but as he returned to the *New Yorker* and the horrors of world war once again set in, his commentary took on a more overt political tone. From 1942 until the mid-1950s, commentary was White's dominant genre, and through careful deliberation on the causes, consequences, and contingencies of World War II, he formulated a vision for world government after the war. Harold Ross was somewhat conflicted about the utopian nature of postwar internationalism, but White forged ahead with the arguments nonetheless, and Ross acquiesced on many of them. White noted that Ross "also regarded world government as a Utopian idea, but it struck me that absolute national sovereignty was about as impractical as anything that could be dreamed up." The idea of a world-governing body was nothing new or unique, as the rise of fascism brought into clear focus the poor handling of the post–World War I global restructuring, but for White it proved timely. As the plan for the United Nations governing body emerged from the ashes of war, he followed its development from San Francisco to Lake Success, New York, to its provisional and permanent homes in New York City via columns in the *New Yorker*. The United Nations never emerged as the utopian savior that White theorized during the war, but its creation offered the author a sense of optimism in an uncertain postwar milieu.[14]

White's Cold War fears of nuclear annihilation and the decline of democracy tempered that optimism. The possibility of instantaneous atomic destruction, perhaps without warning, reframed the sense of global mortality already shaken by two world wars. The bomb threatened his consummate values: liberty, democracy, and the sustainability of the rural and urban environments his work celebrated. To him, the humiliating conformity and anticommunist witch hunts birthed at the onset of the Cold War shook the foundations of American democracy and hindered personal liberty and autonomy. The Cold War U.S. model marketed to the postfascist, postcolonial world appeared hollow. White was not a communist, much less a radical, but he defended citizens' right to possess the political beliefs they wished as long as that choice was preserved for all. In contrast, the anticommunist fervor of Richard Nixon, Joseph McCarthy, and the House Un-American Activities Committee, according to White, endangered personal freedom far more than marginal radicals—legislators, after all, possessed significant political capital. He challenged the *New York Herald Tribune*, an otherwise liberal establishment organ, on loyalty oaths, writing, "I am a member of a party of one, and I live in an age of fear. Nothing lately has unsettled my party and raised my fears so much as your editorial . . . suggesting that employees should be required to state their beliefs in order to hold their jobs." Defending privacy, diversity, and democracy proved a central theme in White's commentary following the war.[15]

Together, White's sense of fear and hope in the immediate postwar period converged in "Here Is New York." While he spent the bulk of the early Cold War at the *New Yorker*, the two essays that constituted the pinnacle of his writing were published in other periodicals. "Death of a Pig" (1948) appeared in the pages of the *Atlantic*, the Boston monthly. White published his celebration of New York City in *Holiday*, which employed his stepson Roger Angell. First appearing on newsstands in 1946, *Holiday* was a monthly tailored to the ascendant postwar leisure industry, or as White put it, "a travel publication based on the perfectly sound idea that everybody in the United States would like to be somewhere else." In the summer of 1948, living in Maine and "very homesick for the heat and stench and tensions of the city," White decamped to the Algonquin Hotel, where he along with *New Yorker* colleagues established the hotel's famed literary salon in the 1920s. In letters to Katherine White during this visit, he wrote of the city's tense nature, "full of tourists" and "less relaxed in the summertime." He had walked the Brooklyn Bridge and took in a concert at the Central Park bandshell. "I must say there is nothing in all the world like Central Park on a summer night," he noted in one piece of correspondence. By April 1949 these observations, along with 7,000 more words about the city, were published. "Here Is New York" was swiftly reproduced in book form, earning a selection by the Book-of-the-Month Club and ensuring its national distribution and consumption. As a result, even the middlebrow consumer from Middletown had access to an informative celebration of a city on the cusp of world capital status.[16]

This, after all, was the intended audience of "Here Is New York." With his brief glimpse of the city's magisterial nature, White, like most of the cultural producers examined below, sought as broad an audience as possible—an attempt to capture the heart of prospective New Yorkers and visitors from both national and international locales. He critiqued the image of Cold War New York, and dwelled on its exceptionalism. He understood that New York City's physical, social, cultural, and economic diversity, its history, its geography, and its pure size separated it from other American cities. It was in a class by itself, and it was this combination of factors that drew people from across the United States and around the world to the metropolis. For White, New York's exceptionalism lay it its ability to attract a kind of dreamer—creative and young ambitious types—that provided the city with its spirit and drive. Invoking recent history, defined in part by the Ellis Island gateway, its immigrant enclaves, and bohemian neighborhoods like Greenwich Village, White reiterated the prevailing narrative of New York City in the first half of the twentieth century as an American island of difference and cosmopolitanism in a sea of otherwise segregated homogenous cultures.[17]

New York City, as White described it, was a safe harbor for individual liberty, offering respite for the parties of one in an era of mandated conformity. His essay began with a key sentence on that theme: "On any person who desires such queer prizes, New York will bestow the gift of loneliness and the gift of privacy." These qualities contrasted with the realities of the physical landscape at the time. Suburban America, as currently understood, was still in its infancy, and U.S. citizens for the most part lived in rural isolation or dense cities and towns. New York was one of the latter, of course, but as White went on to write, its exceptional nature shielded a majority of its lonely and private individuals from the dark psychological problems associated with those qualities. For one, New York was the country's capital of culture, and its citizens possessed the remarkable ability to transform the forlorn and individual into identifiable experiences digested around the nation and the world. This insulation and privacy, then, was "a rare gift" that had "a positive effect on the creative capacities of New Yorkers."[18]

While private, the citizen still feels a part of some great unraveling historical opera. The city "carries on its lapel the unexpungable odor of the long past, so no matter where you sit in New York you feel the vibrations of great times and tall deeds." From his hotel room in Midtown Manhattan, White was "twenty-two blocks from where Rudolph Valentino lay in state, eight blocks from where Nathan Hale was executed, five blocks from the publisher's office where Ernest Hemingway hit Max Eastman on the nose, four miles from where Walt Whitman sat sweating out editorials for the Brooklyn *Eagle*," and so on. Citizens of New York tolerated isolation and loneliness because the city "blends the gift of privacy with the excitement of participation." They "always feel that either by shifting your location ten blocks or by reducing your fortune by five dollars you can experience rejuvenation." Due to its exceptional magnitude, odds were in the favor of residents and visitors being insulated "against all enormous and violent and wonderful events that are taking place every minute." This line of reasoning distinguished White from later purveyors of narratives of New York as Necropolis. He understood that the city had its problems, but the key qualities of personal liberty and opportunity far outweighed the potential for trouble. The possibility of triumph in New York, regardless of the field, was well worth the risk.[19]

The three faces of New York shaped the social, cultural, and physical city in distinct ways. The native New Yorker, like the denizens of Anytown, U.S.A., "takes the city for granted and accepts its size and its turbulence as natural and inevitable" while providing "solidity and continuity" amid continual demographic change. The city of the commuter "is devoured by locusts each day and spat out each night." Having intimate knowledge of that existence, White understood that suburban life was central to the city's economic well-being, but that was the extent of it; the commuter was not the dominant image of New York's vitality. The suburbanite lacked the sense of curiosity and intensity that characterized those who took up residence in the city. Unlike the migrant or the native, they took no time to dwell on its cosmopolitan nature. There was little deliberate contemplation in a world of commercial motivation. They have no time to stroll in Central Park. They lack the patience to study and observe the great human flows along the avenues and streets, much less the time to grab a drink at the corner bar with a friend. In essence, the commuter ignored the awe and wonderment that came with inhabiting the urban spectacle day and night. Commuters' primary instinct, as his earlier poems suggested, was to make the morning train, work, and then return to Grand Central or Pennsylvania Station to catch the earliest departure back from where they came. Commuters may put on a lot of miles, but their travels did not necessarily translate into enthusiasm for the city and its inhabitants.[20]

Those inhabitants that beheld the wonder of New York, and provided it with passion and energy, according to White's narrative, had pulled up stakes elsewhere and arrived in the city in search of personal fulfillment and economic opportunity. "Whether it is a farmer arriving from Italy to set up a small grocery store in a slum or a young girl arriving from a small town in Mississippi to escape the indignity of being observed by her neighbors, or a boy arriving from the Corn Belt with a manuscript in his suitcase and a pain in his heart, it makes no difference: each embraces New York with the intense excitement of first love, each absorbs New York with the fresh eyes of an adventurer, each generates heat and light to dwarf the Consolidated Edison Company." For these white migrants (recent African American and Puerto Rican arrivals were notably absent from his roll call), New York was "the city of final destination, *the city that is a goal*."[21]

Migrants understood the city culturally: New York City was a place they heard about through word-of-mouth—perhaps they encountered someone who once lived there and told great stories about the city—or all the more likely the "Big Apple" was a place they encountered in popular culture. National radio broadcasts emanated from New York. Films were set there, and the famous theatrical plays and musicals were first staged on Broadway. The city provided the setting for many a great American novel, or it was the choice setting in which to write said manuscript. Migrants read newspapers and saw the photographs in *Life* magazine, and while they may have been outsiders in Muncie, Des Moines, and Birmingham, or impoverished and maligned in eastern and southern Europe, they acquired the knowledge that New York City was a place where they could fit in, earn a modest living, find success—where they could take a chance and even fail without worrying about loose talk ruining reputations. This was a phenomenon that brought millions from all over the country and the world by 1948. The migrants' passion, drive, and creativity rejuvenated New York City and contributed to its resilience. Manhattan, in particular, was this refreshing kinetic spectacle, a giant snaking isle constantly shedding its skin and growing anew.[22]

The cosmopolitan narrative alluded to New York City's historical reputation as the country's premier entrepôt. The image of New York as a bastion of freedom and economic vitality stretched back to the colonial period, when the settlement harbored Dutch and other international explorers seeking wealth and autonomy in the Atlantic World. In the early nineteenth century, New York City became the primary destination of Irish refugees seeking solace from hunger, so much so that by 1850 the population of native Irish in New York exceeded every city in the world but Dublin. Later the city attracted innumerable immigrants from China and Europe seeking the sort of economic well-being unheard of among men and women of lower-class or -caste status back home. The poor European and Asian immigrants hardly arrived in the Battery to find streets paved with gold, and many were forced to cohabitate in urban squalor on par with or worse than the conditions they faced at home. Yet the sense that the streets may be paved with gold was a decidedly economic goal that the struggling masses carried with them across the sea. This popular narrative suggested that energetic, hardworking, and often low-life immigrants literally and figuratively shaped modern New York.[23]

White's narrative was also drawn from his own experience as a wide-eyed new New Yorker in the 1920s. Even though he spent his boyhood and adolescence mere miles from the city's border, he brought with his move to the Village the passion of the Corn Belt writer with a dream. In "Here Is New York" he recalled "what it felt like as a young man to live in the same town with giants." His most intimate friends were a few roommates from his Cornell days, but, like the isolated New Yorker, his true companions "were a dozen or so columnists and critics and poets whose names appeared regularly in the papers." These "personal giants" like Christopher Morley, Franklin P. Adams, Dorothy Parker, and Ring Lardner buoyed White as an ambitious young man and, as was the case with Morley, offered space in mass-market publications for White to showcase his developing talents as a poet and writer. He recalled standing on a corner near the *New York Sun* thinking "somewhere in that building is the typewriter that Archy the cockroach jumps on at night." While the city "hardly gave [White] a living in that period," the dream of productivity, financial stability, and New York City living "sustained" him. It was an ethos that remained—"a continuing thing" that generated the cosmopolitan allure of New York. "The city is always full of young worshipful beginners—young actors, young aspiring poets, ballerinas, painters, reporters, singers— each depending on his own brand of tonic to stay alive, each with his own stable of giants."[24]

The young were particularly drawn to Cosmopolis. Despite White's middle age, "Here Is New York" did not pine for some past Arcadia. Instead, White recognized that change was New York's only constant. The city "neither looks nor feels the way it did twenty-five years ago." The old elevated trains and the steel infrastructure had been removed. Times Square contained more illuminated signage. White's former haunt, Greenwich Village, was in flux as well. "Big apartments have come in, bordering the square, and the bars are mirrored and chromed." Still, its past lived on in the "lingering traces of poesy, Mexican glass, hammered brass, batik, lamps made of whiskey bottles, first novels made of fresh memories—the old Village with its alleys and ratty one-room rents catering to the erratic needs of those whose hearts are young and gay." He understood physical change and demographic shifts were innate characteristics of New York City. The fact that "first novels made of fresh memories" and the "young and gay" strivers writing them would persist offered White comfort: New York would survive through its youth-oriented allure.[25]

In addition to its youth, White celebrated the city of destination for its acceptance of difference. He wrote in the tradition of earlier chroniclers of the city's democratic sensibility like Walt Whitman and Randolph Bourne, whose essay "Trans-National America" (1916), as historian Thomas Bender notes, "gave ideological expression to the cosmopolitan ideal that would distinguish New York from the provincial values of America." In particular, White cited New York as an exceptional place where "virtually all races, all religions, all nationalities are represented." It was not wholly unique in this respect, but its resiliency in matters of race and ethnicity was worthy of note: "it is a miracle that New York works at all." The city faced racial tumult and mass violence in its past, most notably during the Draft Riots of 1863. It witnessed race and class uprisings, destructive fires, extreme poverty, and economic decline at various points throughout its long history, and the city always bounced back. New York's antidote was the "sense of belonging to something unique, cosmopolitan, mighty and unparallel," the ethos that, according to Bender, "makes New York City uncomfortable with America and America uncomfortable with, even fearful of, New York City." That it survived and continued to survive despite the amount of foresight and energy required to maintain the city was quite unthinkable—New York should have destroyed itself long ago. The city's social history functioned as a beacon in postwar seas, a place where "the collision and the intermingling of these millions for foreign-born people representing so many races, creeds, and nationalities make New York a permanent exhibit of the phenomenon of one world."[26]

White's essay, however, did not skirt the social and economic issues of the time. The Bowery, for example, was still the "street of lost souls" where "pedestrians step along and over and around the still forms as though walking on a battlefield among the dead." White's chief postwar concern was that the city would become a de jure battlefield littered with dead, as the atomic bomb threw New York's unique resilience into question. The conclusion of "Here Is New York" considered the ramifications of this on the fate of Cosmopolis. "The subtlest change in New York is something people don't speak much about but that is in everyone's mind." The bomb made New York mortal "for the first time in its long history." The unique cosmopolitan qualities of the city—culture, architecture, density, power, and riches—also made it the prime target, a "certain clear priority," for the "perverted dreamer who might loose the lightning" on New York. His hope for "clearing the slum called war" was the United Nations, the "greatest housing project of them all" rising in White's neighborhood of Turtle Bay. He christened the complex the "City of Man," the symbol of New York's vibrant internationalism and creativity. It was to be the bulwark "where the planes are to be stayed and their errand forestalled."[27]

The city's potential in a world of international cooperation provoked the poet and naturalist. Not far from the United Nations stood an old willow tree that White admired. "It is a battered tree, long-suffering and much-climbed, held together by strands of wire but beloved of those who know it." Its rings beheld the history of New York: "life under difficulties, growth against odds, sap-rise in the midst of concrete, and the steady reaching for the sun." To have it disappear in a flash of radioactive fire—to have New York reduced to rubble—"would be like death" to the urbanist. When considered in concert, White's cautionary conclusion to the otherwise celebratory narrative of New York was a call to action. It was his attempt to advertise this threatened city as a port of call for the intrepid citizen willing to fight for New York's preservation in uncertain times.[28]

Amid atomic fears and suburban migration, New York was an open city. A sense of hope and optimism embodied in its natural and unnatural environment permeated White's writings on the city throughout his life. In "Here Is New York" it was in the migrant and the scenes he encountered on his flaneur-like drift around the city. It was in the serendipitous encounter with a concert at the Central Park bandshell on a hot summer night, and in the innocent love-making episodes in the cafes and on the sidewalks of Manhattan. In his poems it was the theme of spring, the season where the death and darkness of winter are cast off and life begins anew. "The Lady Is Cold," about the Plaza Hotel fountain in winter, concludes with a stanza about that hope: "The earth is but held in solution / And March will release for long / The lady in brazen ablution, / The trees and the fountain in song!" In "Pigeon, Sing Cuccu!": "Love is alive beneath the pave, / A-pipping at the shell; / Who has the fun that I have, / Or loveth spring so well." New York represented a place that was always on the brink of renewal and rebirth. The city regularly shed its elders and old mansions were torn down, but they were replaced by the verve of newcomers and promise of physical regeneration. On any street, around any corner, and at any moment in its past, present, and future, there existed the potential for wonder—it was, White wrote, the "city of opportunity" for those "willing to be lucky."[29]

"Here Is New York" and its cosmopolitan missive continued to appeal to migrant New Yorkers and media producers alike in the decades that followed, even if its call for an infusion of human capital as urban renewal was soon silenced by plans for slum clearance and large-scale redevelopment. Many publishers begged White to revise and reissue the essay throughout the rest of his lifetime, but in demonstration of his stubbornness (or his stoicism), he never did—the piece included his own self-destruct clause: the notion that what was New York would have to be constantly written about and preserved. Producers scripted plans to adapt the work into a film, one that White entertained for some time, but that too fell through. "Here Is New York" appeared as a television production that featured little to no input from the author. Despite White's unwillingness to return to his narrative of New York, the enduring themes of his essay played out in a variety of texts in the postwar era. When the renewal narratives began to crumble, these productions kept the prevailing voices of New York's decline at bay for the 1950s, for the 1960s, and, in the case of Woody Allen, even into the 1970s.[30]

New York as the alluring Cosmopolis proved an especially potent trope for characterizations of young women in film and television. Blake Edwards's *Breakfast at Tiffany's* (1961), based on the novella by migrant Truman Capote, centered on Holly Golightly (Audrey Hepburn), a Texas transplant who epitomizes the glamour and grace of New York City but achieves it only through shallow ends. The romantic comedy suggested, notwithstanding the "gold-digging" subtext that dominates the film, that true love—one that transcends the exchange value of romantic entanglements before second-wave feminism—was possible only in the big city. The primacy of New York living brings neighbors and unlikely lovers Holly and Paul (George Peppard) together, their mutual adoration for each other matched by their love of New York City. Likewise, the situation comedy *That Girl* (1966–71), starring Marlo Thomas, revolved around a migrant from upstate seeking success in Manhattan. Thomas's Ann Marie represented the struggling actor archetype, but the independent woman making a home for herself in the city marked a groundbreaking shift in gender portrayal on television, despite the doting boyfriend who appears from the pilot onward. (*The Mary Tyler Moore Show*, after all, was soon to follow in Ann Marie's footsteps.) *That Girl* was significant for both its timely feminist implications and its representation of Cosmopolis at a time when other media cultures saw decline and disorder on the streets. Films like *Taxi Driver*, for example, rendered the city inhospitable to single white females. Although the two productions ignored most of the social problems embedded in the city's latent political and economic schisms, due no doubt to their soundstage quality, *Breakfast at Tiffany's* and *That Girl* highlighted New York as a site of opportunity, diversity, and liberation for middle-class whites, including women.[31]

Woody Allen, also working against a tide of fear narratives, brought Cosmopolis back to the streets of New York in the tumultuous 1970s. *Annie Hall* (1977) examined crisis and disorder through a comparative study of

New York and Los Angeles. The plot centered on Alvy Singer (Allen), a co-median and native New Yorker who grew up in the shadows of a Coney Island roller coaster. Friends push him to move to Los Angeles, where the opportunities for a comedian seem limitless. While the prospect of leaving New York City would be similar to death, Alvy articulated the image of sev-enties New York: "Don't you see the rest of the country looks upon New York like we're left-wing, communist, Jewish, homosexual pornographers? I think of us that way sometimes, and I live here." Annie Hall (Diane Kea-ton) represented the yin to Alvy's yang. She was the ambitious migrant from small town Wisconsin following her dream of becoming a singer in the city (in other words, she wants to become a New Yorker like Alvy). They fall in love, but the relationship turns overwhelmingly paternal as Alvy pushes Annie into and out of intellectual pursuits and disrupts her passion for the city. He expresses disgust at her mundane and decidedly migrant foibles. As Annie takes college courses and acquires wisdom, her resent-ment of Alvy and the New York City he represents grows. She tells Alvy that "New York is a dying city," and soon departs for Los Angeles, the ascendant city of opportunity.[32]

Allen's allusion to classic cosmopolitan romantic comedies differentiated *Annie Hall* from other films in the 1970s. The characters were distinctly bourgeois, and they inhabited a world far from concurrent filmic represen-tations of New York. Their neighborhoods (the Village and the Upper East Side) were among the few remaining bastions of white upper-middle-class residence in Manhattan. Alvy and Annie never encountered the crime that 1970s film culture imagined as ubiquitous. In contrast, *Annie Hall* showcased a clean city filled with personal liberty, modest yet attractive apartments, an uber-intelligent citizenry, cultural and professional op-portunity, and open sexuality. Annie and Alvy attended and critiqued art house films. Alvy relished in the ability "to walk out to dinner," and he attended lavish parties that, despite their pomposity, demonstrated rather normative American behavior. In the end, Annie returned to New York and achieved her goal of becoming a singer. The film suggested that de-spite Los Angeles's growing reputation for success and stardom, New York was still a destination for intrepid migrants carrying with them more au-thentic cultural ambitions.[33]

This sensibility extended to Allen's *Manhattan* (1979), his version of "Here Is New York." Like White's essay, Allen's *Manhattan* portrayed a complicated but deliberate view of "his town." As such, New York has its problems, and the film alludes to several tropes found in familiar representations of

FIGURE 1 The iconic scene from Woody Allen's *Manhattan* features Isaac (Allen) and Mary (Diane Keaton) taking in the predawn hours on Sutton Place. At a time when films characterized New York's public spaces as unsavory and unsafe, in particular at night, scenes like this highlighted the romantic allure of the streets in the city that never sleeps.

Necropolis. The script features concurrent complaints about congestion, cost of living, creative destruction, and spiritual decline. But *Manhattan*'s iconic scene offered a simple and sweet echo of "Here Is New York" sparked by a similar drift around the borough. In the city that never sleeps, Isaac (Allen) and Mary (Keaton) sit on a park bench overlooking the East River at dusk. Exhausted by the long night, yet sustained by the adrenaline of newfound love, Isaac opens up about New York. "This is such a great city. I don't care what anybody says. It's just really a knockout, you know?" Once again the benefits outweighed the risks. The message of *Manhattan* featured a sense of optimism about the city long lacking in perpetual narratives of decline. As for the social and moral decay that soothsayers had sensationalized for years, the film's final line offered the most poignant counterargument, couched in New York's universal cosmopolitanism: "You have to have a little faith in people."[34]

Despite the acknowledgment and acceptance of difference at the heart of the Cosmopolis vision, the reality of urban life for the city's racial minorities was largely ignored in cosmopolitan narratives, a critique frequently leveled at Allen's films. New York's African American population was made up of veterans of the Great Migration and their offspring or the descendants of earlier free or enslaved arrivals, who, when confronted with the city, found limits to its tolerance. Ralph Ellison's masterpiece, *Invisible Man*

FIGURE 2 With scenes filmed in museums, bookstores, restaurants, universities, and Lincoln Center, *Manhattan* showcased a white cosmopolitan city in the midst of a culture-driven renaissance.

(1952), which chronicled the stunted mobility of its migrant protagonist, examined White's "gift of privacy" in allegorical terms. "Invisible" escapes the Jim Crow south only to encounter the intolerable cruelty of de facto segregation in the urban north. Shrouded in the narrative of resiliency, "Here Is New York" avoided comment on the tenuous racial politics of the city that had bubbled up into rebellion in Harlem a few years prior. Ellison, however, crafted an image of the New York migrant bestowed the "gift" of privacy with little desire for that "queer prize." Instead, privacy, isolation, and invisibility were branded on the African American migrant seeking liberty and opportunity in spatially segregated New York, arriving only to find the city of discrimination. Invisible's experience highlighted the privilege of White and similar white authors' extolling the value of privacy in Cosmopolis.[35] In contrast to the period's classic race novel, the 1950s teenage masterpiece *Catcher in the Rye* (1951) demonstrated the gift's class privilege. J. D. Salinger's Holden Caulfield rejected the Park Avenue and boarding school "phonies" who made up his social circle, but his class privilege allowed him to carve out a brief private and isolated life within New York mere blocks from his family's Upper East Side home. His adventures mirror the uniquely urban experiences White celebrated in "Here Is New York," but only Holden's cunning intelligence, honed as a native New Yorker, allowed him to navigate and harness the opportunities the city bestowed on him.[36] This sense of urban anomie found a fertile home especially in the period's pulp fiction.

Even E. B. White acquiesced to this prevailing image of the city toward the end of his life. Much like young White pestering New York's publishing houses, the essayist received significant pressure to return to "Here Is New York" throughout his career. In 1968, Eastern Airlines proposed a two-page advertisement, to be run in the *Times*, containing the complete text of the essay. White's response: "a flattering project but not, I think, a sensible one, either for Eastern Airlines or for me." White's once foundational article was now "a period piece." As he explained, "I was writing about a city that has all but disappeared; to publish the piece prominently in the *Times* would be to bewilder or amuse the present inhabitants. When I return to New York, these days, I look around and cry 'Where am I?'—like a frightened child," a comment on the physical and demographic change the city had witnessed. Two years later when a publisher and friend suggested a large-format version with photographs and updated text, White also resisted. The essay was "about a city that no longer exists. . . . To reissue 'Here is New York' in its present text would be unthinkable (the title would have to be 'Here Isn't New York')." White's change of heart signaled both that the provisional city had evolved (or devolved) and that the essayist himself had succumbed to the city's inhospitable nature for the old and infirm.[37]

In the summer of 1948, however, White captured the essence of New York City at an important moment in urban history. New York ascended the ladder of global status and was on the cusp of a massive redevelopment plan that would transform the city over the next few decades. In "Here Is New York" he elegantly captured the two competing narratives that would frame the cultural discourse on the city in the postwar era. On the one hand, the atomic age had rendered the city's viability an uncertainty. This marked his contribution to the host of fears embodied in the image of Necropolis. On the other hand, he refined a narrative that combined the city's tenuous but resilient social history with its significance as a destination for national and global migrants, celebrating the young optimists in particular. Even as his connection to New York soured, he still understood its allure among young migrants. In his last note on the topic, a response to a fan's letter in 1973, he wrote: "I am old now. It is heartening to see by your letter that New York still has the power to enchant and inspire the youth. When a city loses that, it will have lost all that is worth while in a city. I did indeed love it in my day, and it meant a great deal to me as a young man. I loved the little apartments in the Village where I lived and worked. I loved the sounds and the smells. I loved Turtle Bay and its interior garden with its tulips and daffodils and migratory birds in the spring. As far as I know, the old willow tree still stands there, ready to leaf out at the first sign of warmth."[38] White recognized that the city was not for the old and jagged, but unlike the critics who followed, he never gave up on the idea that the city should live on, that it should persist, always in spring, and serve those who embraced it, despite its faults, with the intensity of first love.

2 Mickey Spillane's Necropolis

··

In Mickey Spillane's novel *The Big Kill* (1951), set in New York City, Ellen Scobie is the resident femme fatale, catching the attention of private investigator Mike Hammer. "Miss Scobie" lives in a six-bedroom apartment in the upper Sixties "on the top floor of the only new building in the block." The redevelopment regime then transforming New York wrought this project, as "about a half-dozen brownstones had been razed to clear an area for the new structure." The overt numbers game Spillane plays in this passage marks Scobie as Hammer's bête noire. Her modern apartment, for one, comes packaged with loosened gender roles. When Scobie invites Hammer up to her apartment for a "midnight snack," he is taken aback: "I thought I was supposed to ask that." She replies: "Times have changed." In a less blatant way, the passage alluded to broader issues within New York. The city is hell, Spillane seemed to say. Around every corner, in the slums or on Park Avenue, predators like Scobie sit in wait for their prey.[1] A year earlier, in *Vengeance Is Mine* (1950), Spillane imagined "somewhere in this wild, wild city, there's a guy with a gun who's going to use it again," and while it was "all right for some harmless citizen to forget there were kill-crazy bastards loose," postwar New York needed Mike Hammer.[2] Citizens may have been blissfully "unaware of the tumor breeding in its belly," but the fantastic world of Spillane exposed a physical and social decay lurking beneath the surface of the city with significant implied consequences.[3]

Spillane grew up in and around New York City, and started out as a cultural producer in Manhattan's comic book universe before shuffling off to the south during the war. When he returned he migrated from comics to the pulps, carefully crafting an image of a working-class stiff with a knack for writing. In fact, he stressed the "writer" label so as not to be confused as a scholar or literary highbrow, both were titles that, in Spillane's view, failed to live up to the hard masculine image he wished to project. Between 1947 and 1952, Spillane published six pulp novels, each a best seller and a critical failure, defining the postwar zeitgeist through the exploits of tough-guy Mike Hammer. In his first, *I, the Jury* (1947), Hammer seeks revenge for the murder of his friend and fellow war hero. Its surprising

FIGURE 3 Mickey Spillane playing the role of private detective Mike Hammer in *The Girl Hunters* (1963).

violence and sexuality culminated in a scene where a remorseless Hammer guns down his beloved Charlotte, ultimately exposed as the book's femme fatale, in cold blood, shooting her while she stands naked in front of him. *My Gun Is Quick* (1950) functioned as a critique of high-class morals and a celebration low-class strife. Hammer once again delights in the death of his antagonist, watching as he burns in a Coney Island hotel fire. By *Vengeance Is Mine* Spillane had solidified a successful hard-boiled formula. The novel featured one of his most controversial narrative twists when it climaxed on the revelation that Juno, the beautiful and voluptuous female antagonist over whom Hammer fawns, was transgender. *One Lonely Night* (1951) was Spillane's Cold War treatise, as New York City is overrun by a communist conspiracy that threatens to take over the country. *The Big Kill* operated as a working-class critique of Hollywood in the 1950s, and *Kiss Me, Deadly* (1952)—unlike the film narrative—shone a light on the underworld, exposing the Mafia and its style of organized crime as an urban menace.[4]

While hard-boiled pulp relies on the formulaic, the Spillane oeuvre was original in several ways. Critics, historians, and literary scholars took note of his plots' timeliness, fighting communists and the mob amid a political culture that obsessed over both. Yet in a period of restrictive, homebound gender and sexuality, Spillane's unguarded representations of masculinity, femininity, and casual sex proved shocking and alluring to national audiences. Likewise, Spillane's use of violence and vengeance transcended previous best sellers within the genre, as the writer had no qualms about murdering women in cold blood or meting out punishment to women, corrupt elites, and various low-lifes. In this sense, Spillane's Mike Hammer, unlike his private detective predecessors, operated as a one-man wrecking crew motivated by revenge. Through these literary innovations, Spillane not only achieved great fame and wealth, he shaped and defined the political culture of the 1950s as much as he played off of it. He was a product of a distinct fertile moment for the hard-boiled, and his popularity suffered as the culture shifted in ensuing decades, even though he continued to publish Hammer novels until the 1990s. The early Hammer books were filled with concurrent fears in part of Spillane's making—class unrest, queer suppression, and empowered single women, in addition to communist infiltration and mob power—but the tales' gratuitous violence endures and still holds up in a landscape saturated with sensational coverage of crime and murder. The violence in Spillane's oeuvre was exceptional because of its connection to urban physical space, places he understood as a native of New York City. As such, the often-antagonistic role Spillane offered the city in a period of intense physical and social change demands consideration.

For a city enjoying the spoils of victory after World War II, the representation of New York in Spillane's imaginary seemed far from reality. At the same time E. B. White celebrated the city's resilience and fostered a narrative of Cosmopolis, Spillane employed the pulp formula to envelop New York in fear. In the Mike Hammer novels, New York City was the kind of place where kids thumb their noses at police officers, random murder elicits an apathetic response, and drunks roam the Bowery like zombies. It was a city possessed by an omniscient and omnipotent evil, a collective monster that threatened American civilization. Spillane and White converged at the understanding that New York City sat in a precarious position in the postwar era. Whereas White feared an atomic end to it all, Spillane, via the subjectivity of his protagonist, envisioned a completely different future where murder, crime, and corruption did not happen, a utopian New York wrought by vigilante justice. White saw the city as the solution to its own problems, problems that had plagued it since the beginning. Spillane saw the city as the problem itself, a completely new decline that, while obscured from view, was on the verge of exposing itself and consuming it whole. Spillane's violent representation seemed at odds with the optimistic vision of New York City coming out of depression and war. Nonetheless, Spillane's image stuck.

His new style of hard-boiled writing offered a template for fearful narratives of New York that went beyond White's atomic distress. Spillane's fantastic vision shaped simple yet sensational tropes that New York's homegrown critics would allude to in the ensuing age of perceived crisis. In the novels, the city's problems are obscured but pathological. Amid all the hubbub of the city that never sleeps, a nascent cancer looms. Slum neighborhoods and blighted buildings dominate the physical landscape after years of neglect. Some are cleared, and in their wake sterile modern structures provide cover for the degenerate activities of the upper classes. Physical transformation disrupts the social order, and lower-class ethnic migrants fill the vacuum left by a working-class exodus. To the native—that is, Mike Hammer—the city becomes unrecognizable. Antipathy directed at newcomers and the city's power structure sets in and eventually morphs into apathy toward New York's social and economic circumstances. Decline in engagement and investment in the future of the city devolves into rampant crime wrought by a consortium of organized groups and the weak and permanent underclass whose desperation makes for easy recruitment into the underworld. Unprovoked violence erupts at random, leading to assaults on innocent citizens. In a world of omnipresent crime, only the criminal is safe, leaving the honorable and ethical citizenry to choose escape over the urban war zone. Yet behind the shadows, and seemingly immune to the hail of bullets, lurks a great white hope. He is a strong man, a virile man, one who has as little time for criminals as he does for bureaucratic, ineffective policing. He crafts his own brand of law and order, delivering peace to a thankful and familiar community, and fostering in the process an individualistic urban ethos. This image of Necropolis, predicated on New York's physical and social decay in the postwar world, as well as the selfish assumptions of Hammer's end game, stood in sharp contrast with the sense of collectivity and resilient passion championed by the likes of White.

· · · · · ·

When Mickey Spillane died in 2006, the *Times* described the writer, perhaps in homage, in terse and blunt style: "the creator of Mike Hammer, the heroic but frequently sadistic private detective who blasted his way through some of the most violent novels of the 1940's and 50's."[5] Spillane was a product of the New York City metroplex. He was born in working-class Brooklyn and lived in Elizabeth, New Jersey, before heading off to a short-lived college stint and eventually World War II. Before the war intervened, Spillane found himself working as an editor for a Midtown comic-book firm, Funnies, Inc. When the war came, Spillane enlisted, but much to his dismay he never saw combat overseas. Instead he was relegated to grunt work on the home front, flying planes in the south. Despite his lack of combat action, World War II and its immediate aftermath shaped his politics and the fantastic fictional universe he later created. Returning to Funnies after the war, Spillane began work on a strip called "Mike Danger," planting the seeds of what would become a career in hard-boiled fiction and an antihero that evolved into Mike Hammer, a restless war veteran out to inflict on criminals what Spillane dreamed of doing to Axis enemies. According to crime author Lawrence Block, it was his experience in comic books that made "Spillane Spillane." With proficiency in concise staccato phrasing and dark illustration, Spillane developed a distinct and original literary style. He saw his novels as "comic books for grown-ups"—a more violent and sexually charged version of *Batman*.[6]

The lowbrow pulp magazine *Black Mask* and drugstore dime novels, in particular the work of Carroll John Daly and the vengeful adventures of his protagonist Race Williams, were also key influences. Spillane penned *I, the Jury* in nine days, a novel that sold well once it was published in pulp form. The book introduced the world to Mike Hammer, a hard masculine private investigator with a voracious sexual appetite who preferred vengeance to deliberation. What followed between 1947 and 1952 was the "most violent series of private-eye novels ever written."[7] They were also the most financially successful of this period. Preferring the title of "writer" to "author," Spillane claimed he never wrote for the critics, and only cranked out his novels for financial freedom.[8] "To Mickey an author is a guy who writes one book—a college professor, or a retired general or ex-president," author Max Allan Collins notes. "Writers are blue-collar men and women who pound the keys to make a living and, along the way, entertain the hell out of a hell of a lot of readers."[9] Spillane liked to say that he did not have fans, but "customers."[10] His unblinking conservative working-class identity and vital center masculinity played well in the postwar "consumers republic," with total sales over 150 million copies, including seven of the top twenty-nine best-selling books published between 1895 and 1965.[11]

Spillane's most prolific period, however, lasted only five years. The financial success that came with six of the top-ten best-selling books of the 1950s allowed Spillane some mobility, and he soon settled in the small town of Newburgh, New York, sixty miles north of the city and by the 1960s a major front in the war on welfare and public assistance.[12] He later relocated to rural South Carolina. Nonetheless, Spillane never lost his hometown connection. Each of the original six Hammer novellas were set in New York City and its environs (although Hollywood set *Kiss Me, Deadly* [1955] and *My Gun*

Is Quick [1957] in Los Angeles). His period of greatest success coincided with one of the most abrupt, intense moments in the history of urban development, including the explosion of working- and middle-class suburban growth, federal incentives for slum clearance, and, soon enough, the push for the redevelopment or "renewal" of cities. During this dynamic period, Spillane wrote about geographic locations of which he had working knowledge. As his plotlines, mise-en-scène, characters, and dialogue suggest, he understood the critical metropolitan issues of the time.[13]

Because of his transgressions against social and cultural norms, the literary establishment heaped scorn on Spillane's work. The *Saturday Review of Literature* noted the "lurid action, lurid characters, lurid plot, [and] lurid finish" of *I, the Jury*. The *Times* called it "a spectacularly bad book."[14] Spillane had few defenders among the literati throughout his career, but one loyal acolyte in particular signals the marginal politics of the Hammer novels. Ayn Rand, similarly scorned by the establishment, elucidated an individualistic free-market, and, read through the gender lens of the time, overtly masculine philosophy—"objectivism"—in novels like *Atlas Shrugged* (1957) and *The Fountainhead* (1943). The novelists' mutual allegories and metaphors presented a counterweight to the postwar liberal consensus. For Rand, Spillane was "the only writer today whose hero is a white knight and whose enemies represent evil." Reading his works "gives the feeling of hearing a military band in a public park."[15] According to Rand, Spillane exceeded contemporaries because he resisted moral ambiguity and favored cool, hard facts as well as clear philosophical principles. He was the first famous person Rand recalled meeting who "for once, confirmed and raised, rather than lowered, [my] enthusiasm" for him. If anything, their correspondence and professed mutual affection suggests that Spillane and Rand saw themselves as kindred right-wing literary philosophers, imagining postwar liberalism as soft, weak, effeminate, and therefore a threat to their American vision.[16]

Rand and Spillane were also two fiction writers whose superhuman, isolated protagonists represent ideal reflections of their creators.[17] Like Rand with Howard Roark, Dagny Taggart, and/or John Galt, Spillane's hero also served as an alter ego. Spillane imagined himself every bit as strong and short-fused as his creation. When word got back to him that someone in New York City was passing himself off as Mickey Spillane, he was looking to find the masquerader and "when I make it I'm going to slap that pansy loose from his teeth."[18] Dissatisfied with Ralph Meeker's portrayal of Mike Hammer in *Kiss Me, Deadly* and Darren McGavin's in the *Mike Hammer* (1956–59) tele-

FIGURE 4 "Is" rather than "as." The credit sequence in *The Girl Hunters* emphasized Spillane's identification with his protagonist alter-ego.

vision series, Spillane took the lead role in the film version of *The Girl Hunters* (1963) despite having no previous acting experience.[19] Of these previous cinematic representations, he told Terry Southern: "Everyone was making a mess of it; they were all missing the point," and he ultimately saw his portrayal as the most honest. The principles of Spillane and Hammer were transposable—Hammer's first-person narration seems to embody Spillane's own subjectivity. As Spillane once remarked to a British press agent, "I will tell you this, I *am* Mike Hammer."[20]

Establishing this connection is critical, because Spillane deployed Hammer as his lens onto the early Cold War. Fellow pulp-writer Max Allan Collins highlights Spillane's humanist legacy, arguing that Spillane's work was a reaction to the cultural conformity of the era. "The Hammer novels reveal the darkness underneath that 1950s Norman Rockwell surface particularly the darkness inherent in the archetypal frontier hero, of which Hammer was the modern urban extension." In addition to celebrating Hammer's style of Wild West justice, Collins suggests "Spillane has been a social historian, painting an America whose postwar world did not live up to expectations. . . . Spillane's vision is of a postmodern America, after World War II had destroyed her innocence, when its population woke up screaming from the American dream."[21] Hammer served as Spillane's data recorder and archivist, sensationally chronicling spatial, cultural, and social change in midcentury New York. Author and subject analyzed these processes through first-person narration and participant observation within a dark, violent, liminal city—existing somewhere between reality and pure fiction.

Literary scholar Frederic Jameson cites the private detective's "universal access" within the crime genre, allowing him or her to fluidly navigate the urban space occupied by the various strata of class, race, ethnicity, gender, and sex that characterize city life. Hammer was no different. The privilege of universal access and the observations rendered during his wanderings represent a crucial repository of Cold War thinking on cities and crime from a then fringe political perspective.[22]

Spillane's representation of masculinity, for one, transcended the already overtly "hard" political culture of the Cold War era. The end of World War II and the dichotomous global power structure brought with it obsessive anticommunism at home and abroad. Both Spillane and Hammer embodied this virulent ethic, and the struggle against the Red Menace informed Spillane's repertoire.[23] Amid the domestic anxiety around communism and nuclear annihilation, a sense of conformity and consensus emerged in which paranoid critics perceived a crisis of masculinity. In *The Vital Center* (1949), Arthur Schlesinger Jr. set the tone for Cold War liberalism, railed against postwar conformity, and argued that men went weak in the face of global communism. The resulting political milieu, in the words of historian K. A. Cuordileone, "put a premium on hard masculine toughness and rendered anything less than that soft, timid, feminine, and as such a real or potential threat to the security of our nation." Hammer personified this masculinity, and his "vigilante ethos and contempt for things effete—intellectuals, professionals, homosexuals and the 'pansy' bureaucracy that tied the hands of the police and thus hampered the enforcement of law and order—made him a real *man's man* [sic] in a soft, morally bankrupt world." Through the prism of the United States' Cold War foreign policy, postwar containment and rollback paralleled the vigilante's insistence on judicial omnipotence and distrust in diplomacy, which weakened international governing bodies like E. B. White's celebrated United Nations.[24]

The character of Mike Hammer represented the hypermasculine, anticommunist, near-fascist right wing, marking a crucial turn in the realm of popular American crime fiction. The product of a distinct cultural moment, Hammer served as the agent of Spillane's political agenda regarding not only urbanism but detection and law enforcement as well. Prior to Spillane's postwar arrival, Dashiell Hammett and Raymond Chandler constituted the pinnacle of crime fiction. Shaped by the Popular Front and New Deal liberalism, the two controlled the pulp and celluloid detective genre in the thirties and forties (Chandler, for example, wrote the screen version of Hammett's *The Maltese Falcon* [1941].) Each offered a mode of detection that stood in stark contrast to the vigilante in Spillane's work. Their protagonists, Hammett's Sam Spade and Chandler's Philip Marlowe, were functional detectives going through the realistic process of detection, as Chandler's celebration of Hammett's narratives in "The Simple Art of Murder" (1944) attests. The typical story arc of Hammett or Chandler began with a rather mundane investigative assignment that morphed into some larger, more meaningful web of intrigue. Marlowe and Spade did not exist in a world of inherent violence. Their names suggested identification, or at least empathy, with the underworld: marginalized low-life in the former and shadowy obscurity and otherness in the latter. Spade and Marlowe implied a certain alienation from society at large, and their creators dwelled on their moral ambiguity.[25]

In contrast, Mike Hammer was an avenger, "motivated not by a client who walks in the door, but the murder of a friend."[26] His world is vicious and paranoid; one where random crime originates in the shadows around every corner. He is a private eye in the sense that he must be a watchman, invading unsuspecting citizens' privacy and reacting to transgression accordingly. The name Mike Hammer was blunt and obvious; Spillane, as Rand's praise suggests, had little tolerance for doubt. The character's name referenced Spillane's affiliation with the white working-class tradesman, and the label's abrasive intensity conformed to the character's vicious and destructive worldview. Eschewing justice in social and economic terms, Hammer's ethic featured a definitive totalitarian, vengeful end that distinguished Spillane from the more nuanced morality tales of Hammett and Chandler. Chandler, in fact, found Spillane's work distasteful: "pulp writing at its worst was never as bad as this stuff."[27] Spillane challenged the genre's ethos of justice and morality, offering in turn the antitheses of those virtues: subjective authority and unrepentant violence.[28]

Literary scholars cite Spillane's sadistic turn as a point of devolution within the crime genre and a perversion of the prewar hard-boiled private eye.[29] The character of Mike Hammer marks an evolutionary step from the nascent racist vigilantism of Carrol John Daly, whose work Spillane admired. Sean McCann employs the phrase "Klan Fantasy" to describe the crime and detection universe of Daly and his protagonist. Race Williams, a character who "emerged amidst the frustration and confusion that characterized the turbulent years following World War I [just as] Mike Hammer was created under similar conditions following the end of World War II."[30] According to McCann, "in both Klan ideology and hard-boiled crime fiction, the American city was riven by illicit sexuality, corruption, and crime—

closely linked forms of social disarray that demanded the control of vigilant men."[31] Mike Hammer epitomized the vigilant man, and in Spillane's pages his urban crusade sought the control and eradication of transgressive sex, vice, and organized crime while hypocritically utilizing sex, coercion, and murder to reach that end. "Hammer stood for," in the words of historian Kenneth C. Davis, "in no special order, sexism, racism (blacks are either shuffling genetic defectives or pimps and pushers), anti-intellectualism, homophobia, and a brand of jackbooted fascist vigilantism in the guise of preserving order."[32] At its worst, his vengeance was code for expunging difference from the cosmopolitan city.

On the ground, Spillane's obsession with violence representation similarly squared with Cold War impulses. Victory in World War II, pervasive economic prosperity, collective atomic fear, and unity wrought by compulsive conformity provided fertile ground for representations of rebellious individualism in American culture. As historian Warren Susman notes, "this moment of triumph was accompanied by something disturbing: a new self-consciousness of tragedy and sense of disappointment." While violence has been a defining part of mythic American history, only after the war did it become "a major problem that society needed to solve." Cultural crime narratives surged, structured around a desire to see man as ultimately alienated from society. According to Susman, "that is why film noir and juvenile delinquency films and certain detective stories, particularly Mickey Spillane's popular novels that feature the psychopathic hero, Mike Hammer, flourished." Spillane was one of many critics and commentators who detailed a decaying, violent New York City throughout the Cold War era, but ultimately, he was one of the first to obsess about public disorder in such a sensational manner. In the 1950s, he had the broadest popular audience.[33]

As such, the Mike Hammer novels represent a fertile archive of period-centric cultural concerns and anxieties. Spillane's work provided a setting for meditations on the sociology and psychology of violence and disorder in the postwar city. Participant observation combined with universal access to create a comprehensive geography of the novelist's fantastic New York. Spillane, in particular, highlighted his discontent with the city through transcriptions of Hammer's movement through Manhattan, Brooklyn, and Queens on foot or by automobile. In scholarship on mid-century film noir, pulp fiction's celluloid counterpart, this trope has been dubbed "the walking cure," which chronicles through memory and imagination the state of the city and the character's experience within its space in the spirit of the nineteenth-century flâneur. The noir detective, navigating the streets, became the mid-twentieth-century walker, helping an increasingly sub-urbanized audience grasp the "often-overlooked features of the city" and "endangered urban spaces" in the era of renewal. Spillane's passages elicit such subjectivity, conjuring a certain filmic image. His words established a sense of place, acquainting the reader with the geography of New York and crafting a literary document of a changing city removed from its cosmo-politan sensibility.[34]

As a universal agent absorbing the transforming city through various walking cures, Hammer delighted in White's "gift of privacy." Spillane's un-derstanding of privacy, however, proved far more nefarious and paranoid than his contemporary's. Hammer accepted the privacy gift, and the alien-ation the character experiences functioned at once as a blessing and a source of angst. In the fictional New York mapped by Spillane, the city's anony-mous nature allowed his protagonist to troll the sidewalks unnoticed. When-ever Hammer desired privacy, he took solace among the canyons where the city pulsed but citizens were suspiciously absent. As Hammer narrated in *One Lonely Night*: "The street was mine, all mine. They gave it to me gladly and wondered why I wanted it so nice and all alone." On the flip side, the gift of privacy was also attractive to New York's underworld. When Ham-mer roughed up one informant, the latter reveals that he was drawn to New York for the opportunity to participate in criminal activity. "That's why I moved to the city. Where I was, anyone could get to me. At least here there are other people around." Thus, the shadowy anonymity of Spillane's New York fueled Hammer's paranoia about the violent nature of the city. In Ham-mer's words, 'Sometimes the city is worse than the jungle. You can get lost in it with a million people within arm's length. . . . A guy could roam the streets for a week without being recognized." This gift attracted criminals who utilized their anonymity to blend in with the innocent populace.[35]

In Spillane's New York, the volatile combination of privacy, extreme den-sity, and physical decline foster madness and thus crime. The Bowery, the city's historical skid row, proved a neighborhood of ubiquitous decline. In *Vengeance Is Mine*, Spillane took the reader into the heart of the impover-ished Lower East Side. "The Bowery Inn was off the main line," he writes. "It was a squalid place with half-boarded-up windows, fly-specked beer signs and an outward appearance of something long ago gone to seed."[36] When Hammer travels uptown, he maps a city where decay does not dis-criminate. In Spillane's representation, much of Manhattan has fallen into disrepair. Thirty-Third Street, for example, home to or abutting, in no spe-cific order, the Empire State Building, Herald Square's shopping district, and, soon-to-be New York's most infamous twentieth-century demolition, McKim, Mead and White's Pennsylvania Station was from Hammer's perspective a "cemetery of buildings."[37] Portions of the plot of *Kiss Me, Deadly* occupy Manhattan's east side in the vicinity of the United Nations complex, the construction of which involved the clearance of the area's industrial legacy. Hammer reports that "once you put in time on Second Avenue you never forget it," especially the "human rubble that inhabited the place."[38]

Via Hammer's universal access, Spillane designated blighted and problematic neighborhoods throughout the city. Greenwich Village, the city's iconic twentieth-century bohemian neighborhood, featured prominently in these novels, always as a site of transgressive sexuality. Spillane's representation invoked the standard pop-cultural imagination of bohemian life—jazz emanating from dark and smoky nightclubs, starving artists slumming in "dump" tenements, drunks stumbling home from all-night binges at various watering holes. Spillane also captured the nonnormative sexuality that proliferated in this period of the "Lavender Scare." A few of Hammer's female romances—single, independent, and sexually assertive—reside in the neighborhood. In addition to the neighborhood's open and casual heterosexuality, Spillane recognized the Village's history as a queer enclave. Hammer wanders into "Monica's Bar" which "catered to a well-assorted clientele" of lesbians, gay men, and bohemian straights.[39] It is a neighborhood of "fag joints," as Hammer notes in *The Big Kill*, two decades before the Stonewall uprising. Writing in a period that prized virile masculinity and a political culture that marginalized male homosexuality, Spillane shaded the Village in lavender. His narratives linked deviant sexuality with New York's decline and signaled the Village's risky qualities to heterosexual and homophobic readers. Yet he also gestured, deliberate or not, at queer readers who might find a certain lure in decay, that is, the distinct sexual freedom the Village offered to prospective Cosmopolis migrants.[40]

As the Village anecdotes suggest, Spillane's decaying New York was both a cause and an effect of segregated populations. Associating marginal and minority neighborhoods with urban decline evoked the concurrent practice of "redlining," whereby credit agencies judged dense, congested, poor, and minority neighborhoods too risky for housing investment.[41] Hammer sends his secretary Velda to Brooklyn with a warning: "Remember, it's a rough neighborhood, so be on your toes." In Astoria, Queens, just across the East River from Manhattan, "the people gave way to the rats and the trash that littered the shore." The neighborhood emits "the smell of decay," and residents cruising over the Triborough Bridge on their way to suburban Long

Island "were happily unaware of this other part of New York."[42] When Hammer visits Hell's Kitchen—a neighborhood of working-class Irish and Italians and recent Puerto Rican migrants—he encounters such decay up close. His destination is "a beat-up affair fifty years old bearing the scars only a neighborhood like that can give it. . . . The hall was littered with junk I had to push aside until I came to the door. . . . I shoved it open and the light . . . glistened off the fetid pools of vomit on the floor." These examples affirmed the claims of master planners who designated slums, politicians who railed against blight, and bureaucrats at the Home Owners Loan Corporation who denied investment in "risky neighborhoods," that physical decay wrought social and moral decline. Spillane's geography lesson acknowledged that slums and disorder went hand in hand.[43]

Writing at the height of slum clearance and urban renewal, Spillane incorporated aspects of the city's redevelopment program in his narrative of New York as Necropolis. As Hammer roamed the city, Spillane established a sense of place that emphasized the destruction and reconstruction of New York's urban form. The publication of *The Big Kill* and *Kiss Me, Deadly* in 1952 coincided with the construction of the United Nations complex, and each book includes scenes set in White's Turtle Bay neighborhood. Hammer chronicled the ongoing slum clearance, and his description featured the standard markers of "blight" like unsightliness and unwanted public activity. "The sidewalks were littered with ancient baby buggies, a horde of kids playing in the garbage on the sidewalks and people on the stoops who didn't give a damn what the kids did so long as they could yap and slop beer," for example. Hammer looks down one street's "two rows of tenements . . . and wondered which windows were alive today who wouldn't be alive tomorrow." Later following a lead, Hammer discovers a "brownstone that seemed to tilt out toward the street" and lacking a front door. Shuttered and mostly vacant, the building became Spillane's symbol of a city slouching toward despair.[44]

In Spillane's universe, modernist redevelopment like Ellen Scobie's apartment building failed to resolve the contingencies of New York's decline. Renewal functioned as a façade, obscuring the swelling social problems behind the tall glass-and-steel structures. As he put it in *The Big Kill*, "the city was a little bit cleaner than it was before, but there was still some dirt under the carpet."[45] Spillane's critique of modern design intensified in the 1960s, weighing the costs and benefits of clearance and redevelopment through Hammer's universal access. A lengthy hiatus from writing (1952–61) allowed Spillane to digest Robert Moses's remaking of New York, and the descriptions evoked the criticism of then contemporary Jane Jacobs, whose *Death and Life of American Cities* appeared just as Spillane returned to the writing game. In *The Body Lovers* (1967) Hammer comes across a tenement that "lay in the fringe area adjoining a slum section that was marked for urban renewal when they could figure out where to put the people that were already there. You could feel the depression that hung over the buildings like an emotional smog. . . . It was a place that existed on the gratuity of the city's Welfare Department." Such compassion for displaced slum dwellers, once the face of disorder, would have seemed out of place in the earlier novels. He visits a company in a "new forty story building it had just built on Sixth Avenue, a glass and concrete monument to commercialism with the sterile atmosphere of a hospital." Much of Sixth Avenue (a.k.a. Avenue of the Americas) fell to the bulldozer in the 1950s, as Midtown adapted to both the ascendant postindustrial economy and a new zoning code that prized modern skyscrapers set back amid semipublic plazas. As Spillane put it, the boulevard "had lost its identity over the last ten years. It was an empire now."[46] The makeover was so devastating that Spillane plagiarized himself in *Survival Zero* (1970): "All the old places [on Sixth Avenue] were gone and architectural hangovers towered into the night air, the windows like dimly lit dead eyes watch the city grasping harder for breath every day. New York was going to hell with itself. A monumental tombstone to commercialism." In his nostalgia for the old city, Spillane echoed contemporary narratives in urban criticism that saw New York declining *because* of modern design.[47]

Spillane's late critique of postindustrial white-collar redevelopment stemmed in part from an essential trope in his early Hammer novels—an unease with the shifting demographics of the city. Spillane's narrative implied that New York was different, confusing, at times incomprehensible, and therefore treacherous for the outsider and even the native to navigate. Hammer's internal monologue refers to Harlem as "that strange no-man's-land where the white mixed with the black and the languages overflowed into each other like that of the horde around the Tower of Babel," with "strange, foreign smells of cooking and too many people in too few rooms." He brands the combination of density, overcrowding, and mixed ethnicities as "foreign," despite the fact that, geographically, this other world existed only a few subway stops from his Midtown flat. Such passages illustrated, in his reading of the postwar urban moment, the perpetrators of decay. He offered images of slum life, blight, crime, and abandonment as examples of forces tearing apart the comfortable white working-class city that xenophobes like Hammer cherished. Ultimately, he saw modern development creating bulwarks for capital and suspect upper-class citizens, leaving the remaining working class to fend off an ascendant underclass for limited space.[48]

One key passage from *Kiss Me, Deadly*, the ultimate first-wave Hammer novel, reveals Spillane's discomfort in an increasingly diverse New York City. On a walking cure along Broadway, Hammer separates himself from the crowd of the street, and seeks solace among the shrinking white ethnic population. The private detective turns to the "east where the people talked different and dressed different and were my kind of people. They didn't have dough and they didn't have flash, but behind their eyes was the knowledge of the city and the way it thought and ran." In contrast to E. B. White's enduring spectacle, the city in Spillane's oeuvre was ignorant, segregated by class, increasingly paranoid and antisocial. Out of touch with the surrounding city despite universal access, Hammer has little desire to be a part of the street ballet. His people, in part, were responsible for this decline, migrating in ever-larger numbers to surrounding suburbs like Levittown. As suburban housing became affordable, ethnic neighborhoods in New York broke apart.[49]

In Spillane's imagination, this demographic rupture contributed to the New York–centric violence and disorder that littered his pages. What he terms "the monster" in *Kiss Me, Deadly* denotes a collective force of evil that holds sway over the city. Overtly, the monster refers to the Mafia—the novel's bête noire. Considered within the broader context of the author's oeuvre, however, the monster represents the permanent underclass of criminals that terrorized the city and its inhabitants, both organized and disorganized. According to Hammer, the monster's "voice . . . was a constant drone." It had a "sarcastic sneer that pushed ten million people into bigger and better troubles," and believed "death was the biggest joke of all." This beast was responsible for a remarkable body count: "I sat and heard it and thought about it while the statistic ran through my head. So many a minute killed by cars, so many injured. So many dead an hour by out-and-out violence. . . . It made a long impressive list that was recited at board meetings and assemblies," fanning the flames of fear. The monster could act out violently anywhere and anytime. It preys on innocent victims "scared stiff" and lying "awake nights worrying about things they shouldn't have to worry about," broadcasting "incomprehensible sounds that were the muted whinings of deadly terror . . . [whose] meaning was clear." Spillane's monster was an urban problem that the city's technicians struggled to solve despite good intentions. For the reader, the meaning was clear: urban life was dangerous living. Spillane's incessant terrorized city turned any narrative of collectivism and compassion on its head.[50]

The monster fostered a more public, indiscriminate version of crime and an increasingly apathetic citizenry in tandem. Spillane's mapping of random New York violence commenced in *I, the Jury*, where he stages a drive-by shooting at East Sixty-Seventh Street and Fifth Avenue, right on Central Park and adjacent to one of the wealthiest districts in the country.[51] In *Vengeance Is Mine*, Hammer becomes a target on Broadway, the "busiest street in the world." A simple stroll from Times Square to Thirty-Fourth Street leaves Hammer untouched by the hail of bullets in one of the city's overcrowded districts. The combination of Broadway and random gunplay demonstrated that New York City was a place where "murder wasn't supposed to happen and did all the time."[52] Spillane's explicit and gratuitous violence advised readers that crime could occur at any time and any place in the large metropolis. These graphic representations of public violence in a period that wrought Frederic Wertham's demonization of transgressive popular culture, *Seduction of the Innocent* (1954), along with Spillane's infamous sexual plotlines, earned the novelist the label of, in the eyes of at least one moral critic, "the most dangerous man in America."[53]

Unlike the shocked citizens of suburban America, the denizens of Hammer's city have been desensitized to violence. "This is New York," Spillane wrote in *Kiss Me, Deadly*. "Something exciting happening every minute. After a while you get used to it and don't pay any attention to it. A gunshot, a backfire, who can tell the difference and who cares. A drunk and a dead man, they both look the same."[54] As Spillane was apt to repeat, there were a variety of neighborhoods where "murder isn't uncommon," and where "a killing . . . was neither important nor interesting enough to drag out the local citizenry in a downpour."[55] As violence numbed the population, Hammer worried that if he were to fall victim nary would a witness testify—"that's the way people are."[56] Where murders attracted attention, they became a part of the urban spectacle. A rubbernecking crowd of curiosity seekers battled for access to the body in *One Lonely Night*, and *My Gun Is Quick* and *Vengeance Is Mine* featured similar spectacles.[57] Spillane cordoned off blocks and neighborhoods to stage sensational voyeuristic passages that invoked the famous tableaux of Weegee's crime photography, just as later urban commentators seemed to borrow from Spillane's perilous scenes. The boundless violence in the novellas, along with Spillane's representation of New

Yorkers as apathetic vultures drawn to spilled blood and lifeless bodies, wrapped the treacherous city in yellow "CRIME SCENE" tape.[58]

Spillane presented two options for citizens in the crime-ridden postwar city. Only one was reserved for the lay reader: suburban escape. New York City's burgeoning metropolitan hinterland exemplified an alternative to the physical decay and social violence of the city. While the estates of Westchester County symbolized, in Spillane's plots, old money subversion, perversion, and organized crime, the Levittowns sprouting from old farmland in northern New Jersey and central Long Island appeared within reach of the class of people with whom Hammer, and thus Spillane, identified. The opening scene in *One Lonely Night* (1951), in particular, illustrated the nascent postwar urban and suburban dichotomy. Spurned by a soft "little judge," Hammer takes a long walking cure to the George Washington Bridge, the liminal space between the city and suburban New Jersey. Standing on the bridge and staring down at Manhattan, Hammer considers a lifestyle change. Perhaps he will take his loyal and otherwise platonic secretary, Velda, and "start up in real estate in some small community where murder and guns and dames didn't happen," leaving the "scum that stood behind a trigger and shot at the world" to "organized law and order." For working-class males and single women like Velda, the new suburbs represented a frontier of prosperity, opportunity, and tranquility. While Hammer was not able to cross the bridge—the city's ubiquitous random violence intervenes, in the form of a serendipitous murder-suicide, later tied to the city's communist underground—Spillane's meditation on northern New Jersey and Long Island narrativized the suburb as a goal for working-class strivers like himself, and an appropriate binary for his dying city.[59]

Hammer embodied the more aggressive solution—a hard, vigorous man willing and able to circumvent bureaucratic obstacles in order to uphold rigid morality in an ungovernable city. If Hammer could eliminate crime, violence, communism, and the mob, then it was understood that the sources of New York's decline were eliminated as well. This is evident from the opening of *I, the Jury*, where Hammer appears on the scene "anxious to get some of the rats that make up the section of humanity that prey on people."[60] From the beginning, Spillane faults contemporary police practice for much of the city's problems. Hammer's "investigations" were cases traditionally reserved for New York Police Department (NYPD) detectives or the Federal Bureau of Investigation (FBI), such as hunting murderers, solving burglaries, and underworld surveillance. In lieu of any solicitation for services,

Hammer undertakes unpaid missions of vengeance. On the "job," he operates outside the parameters of civil rights, and his own run-ins with the law become a running trope, often resulting in the loss of his sidearm or private investigator's shield. In *The Big Kill* he complains to his friend and NYPD detective Pat Chambers, "Tell me that I'm interfering in police work and I'll tell you how sick I am of what goes on in this town. I live here, see? I got a damn good right to keep it clean even if I have to kill a few bastards to do it. There's plenty who need killing bad and if I'm electing myself to do the job you shouldn't kick." As a new symbol of investigation, Hammer represented an innovative mode of policing that sought greater law enforcement power, less red tape, and minimal interference from the legal system.[61]

In this sense, Mike Hammer epitomized the Cold War era's "do-it-yourself" ethic, seeking total control of New York City's spatial landscape.[62] As evident from the title, Hammer's authoritarian impulse was also introduced in *I, the Jury*. He informs Chambers: "I'm not letting the killer go through the tedious process of the law. . . . This time I'm the law and I'm not going to be cold and impartial." To Hammer, due process meant lawyers finding loopholes that led to mistrials or cold and impartial juries returning not-guilty verdicts, thus releasing pathological criminals back into society.[63] The character revels in paramilitary fantasy: "Some day I'd stand on the steps of the Kremlin with a gun in my fist and I'd yell for them to come out and if they wouldn't I'd go in and get them and when I had them lined up against the wall I'd start shooting until all I had left was a row of corpses that bled on the cold floors."[64] Spillane ensured that Hammer possessed immeasurable power, including a license to kill. This power combined with Cold War masculinity to transform Hammer into the consummate expert on urban matters. Spillane's vigilante imagined consolidating his authority through violence and manipulation, utilizing his position to destroy and rebuild New York City. Ultimately, the character fulfilled a neofascist authoritarian dream that transcended the "Klan Fantasy" of Race Williams, all in the name of saving the city from some unforeseen yet imminent end. Hammer, then, provided a template for later law-and-order advocates, from the illusory realm of *Dirty Harry* and *Death Wish* to pandering politicians like Richard Nixon. As a response to a perceived rise in street crime, the Miranda ruling, and urban disorder, Nixon and others called for tougher enforcement to salvage the city and "keep it clean" at the height of the urban crisis.[65]

Spillane's utopian New York never revealed itself, but presumably it stood where and when Hammer's work as the one-man wrecking crew concluded. Unlike the power brokers and master planners transforming cities in the age of urban renewal, Spillane made his mark by establishing an indelible narrative of New York in crisis, thus leaving the readers with the impression of decay and danger. In *My Gun Is Quick* he equated citizens and city life with gladiators doing battle with bloodthirsty beasts. Invoking the colossal Roman spectacles where "wild animals rip a bunch of humans apart" while the public revels "in the sight of blood and terror," Spillane wrote that the criminal atrocities occurring in New York "go on every day and night making Roman holidays look like school picnics." Only a hard and vigorous gladiator like Mike Hammer could defeat the beast: "You have to be quick. And able. Or you'll be dead." Without Hammer, New York was Necropolis. Avoid the city or be devoured—a narrative carried forward via a range of critics. Among them, there would be those who wished to save New York, like Hammer, and those, like Hammer too, who sometimes wished to see it devour itself.[66]

· · · · · ·

After *Kiss Me, Deadly,* Spillane seemed to do an about-face, taking a long leave of absence to serve the Jehovah's Witnesses. In 1962 he returned to form with *The Girl Hunters.*[67] In many ways it was the same old Spillane and Hammer. The violence was tempered, but the sex, with the bonds of conformity loosening, became far more graphic. Still, the books never sold anywhere near the record numbers of the six novellas he released from 1947 to 1952. Even the film version of *The Girl Hunters* (1963), starring Spillane as Hammer, failed to reach the popular and critical heights of *Kiss Me, Deadly* (1955), considered by some film historians as the pinnacle of the film noir cycle.[68] Although Spillane continued to work until the 1990s, and Mike Hammer became a regular on television in the 1950s and 1980s, the writer never reached the level of success he achieved in the early postwar period— not even when he tried to piggy-back on the culture's obsession with international espionage à la James Bond. He later pushed his antiquated brand of bravado in beer commercials. Spillane's creation was the consummate Cold Warrior, the product of cultural moment that prized a hard, virile man. It was an era when a housing crunch, mass suburbanization, and the breakup of older ethnic working-class communities, along with the new threat of nuclear annihilation, brought anxiety about the future of American urban life.

Through slum clearance, urban renewal, and modern architectural forms, New York changed dramatically in those nine years. Waking from a long lost weekend, Mike Hammer took in the city's transformation. He noticed that "outside the window was another New York—not the one I had left, because the old one had been torn down and rebuilt since I looked out the window last."[69] In the opening of *The Body Lovers*, Hammer visited a part of New York "that was being gutted to make room for a new skyline. There was nothing but almost totally disemboweled buildings and piles of rubble for three blocks, every scrap of value long since carted away and only the junk wanted by nobody left remaining."[70] He strolled among the rubble of demolition and redevelopment, noting that much of the "general population" had moved to the suburbs. In these later books New York was still very much the dangerous, dark monster of old: there were "open wounds on its surface," it was a "minion of Count Dracula," and "cross-town traffic was like a giant worm trying to eat into the belly of the city." Yet Spillane offered a new narrative imbued with nostalgia and sentimentality for the old New York, one that his contemporaries in the city's intellectual community would echo as well.[71]

By then Spillane had played a significant role in the narrative shaping of New York City. He presented a stark image of an exploding metropolis, and showcased a popular protagonist disgusted by excess, progress, and difference. The thrills Hammer encountered were of the violent variety, casting the city as dangerous, dark, and lacking in public trust. The vigilante was Spillane's authoritarian response to the physical and moral decline he imagined in the postwar city. In contrast to the detective hero Chandler lionized in "The Simple Art of Murder," Spillane's world "has no vestige of the failed American Dream or the redemptive hero in it; his streets don't seem particularly mean—except for the fact they are inhabited by men who resemble Mike Hammer—and his hero is in no way a man of honor."[72] Hammer's foibles with government institutions played to a period-specific impulse that sought great men willing to act alone in the remaking of the urban landscape, ridding society of subjectively defined evils, and doing so without interference from the public. When the need to tame the disorderly city emerged in the 1960s, the vigilante predictably became, at least in popular culture, a practical solution. In the years between, Spillane's image of New York echoed in the words of various commentators, each employing aspects of his Necropolis to enhance their political power or institute a program of slum clearance and urban renewal—a task not unlike Mike Hammer's attempt to purge the criminal underclass. Spillane's posthiatus novels never sold at the same pace as his earlier works, but not only because his moment soured. Rather, his lurid tales of violence and disorder in the naked city were no longer novel. They were commonplace.

Part II **Cancer and Death**

New York Narratives in Planning Theory,
1953–1961

· ·

3 The Case for Municipal Surgery

· ·

As Mike Hammer consolidated power and shunned due process in a fantastic postwar New York, Robert Moses thwarted opponents and bureaucratic red tape through the power of the pen. The impetus of his canon, however, was to highlight a vision of renewal, one that he would strive rather strenuously to put into practice over the course of a decade and a half. By the 1950s, Moses had already mapped, modeled, and in some cases developed an expansive new New York replete with sprawling highway systems; art-deco suspension bridges spanning the East River, New York Harbor, and even Long Island Sound; and tower-in-a-park residential construction inspired by the utopian designs of French architect Le Corbusier. Vital to his success and durability, Moses secured power in park design, first granted by Governor Alfred E. Smith in the 1920s, and parlayed that into revenue-producing bridge and highway construction during the New Deal. His use of quasi-public "authorities" shielded him from the electorate and municipal leaders. He also employed a coterie of trustworthy engineers, planners, and designers who catered to his whims. While blaming Moses solely for the "fall of New York," as biographer Robert Caro first did in 1974, or celebrating him for the "rise of New York" makes for a uniform historical narrative, complexity defines Moses's role in the shaping of the postwar city. He craved power and schemed nonstop to render his vision a reality, employing public transcripts in some of the United States' most widely read periodicals when necessary.[1]

In the age of "urban renewal," commencing with Title I of the 1949 Housing Act, the national narrative of urban decline hinged on, as historian Robert Beauregard notes, "the two most prominent urban problems to be solved": slums and blight. Fused with connotations of race, poverty, and crime, the terms signified an environment to escape, avoid, or destroy. Municipal planners, politicians, and bureaucrats saw slum neighborhoods and blighted areas as spaces to be demolished and replaced with expressways or physical plants on a grand scale. In this milieu, the master planner functioned as an authoritarian figure, and that was Moses in the case of New

York City. If a planner pushed through a plethora of urban renewal projects throughout the 1940s and 1950s, he did so because, despite the protestations of residents living in neighborhoods under slum or blighted designation, there was a certain amount of public support for the enterprise. Moses benefited from the poor image of slum neighborhoods in popular culture, an image that he in part shaped. In the age of Title I, newspapers and magazines, radio and television news, and even fictional representations of urban space, like those found in Mickey Spillane's novels, worked in concert with planners and politicians to develop narratives about New York and other cities possessing the abject qualities coded as slums and blight in this period.[2]

The policies of slum clearance and urban renewal in the 1950s, in fact, coincided with one of the most vital periods of opinion journalism. It was the magazine medium's historical summit before the country turned its eyes to more visual media cultures for its knowledge and news. In "The Article as Art" (1958), the cultural critic and New York Intellectual Norman Podhoretz highlighted the ascendance of magazine reportage. A dearth of great novels along with the recent emergence of so-called Beat writing had sullied the reputation of "traditional" American literary outlets. In their place a new form rose to prominence, one once considered beneath the contempt of the critic. In what poet Randall Jarrell coined the "Age of Criticism," Podhoretz hailed the magazine article as the pinnacle of literary expression and cultural critique. It emerged as an outlet of creativity and power for a number of authors, and their message found its way into the minds of Americans as, according to Podhoretz, "a large class of readers . . . found itself responding more enthusiastically to what is lamely called 'non-fiction' (and especially to magazine articles and even book reviews) than to current fiction."[3]

At the intersection of long-form criticism and urban renewal sat New York City, the torchbearer for large-scale redevelopment planning and practice and the locus of mass-market print culture. From their perches, publishers and bureaucrats spied new parkways, expressways, bridges, and tunnels that granted New Yorkers automobile access to the developing suburban landscape of Long Island, Westchester County, and northern New Jersey. Old tenement districts were bulldozed and residents displaced under the rubric of "slum clearance," as the new "International Style" towers that rose in their place provided light, air, and greenspace. Planners pored over plans for speculative cultural and commercial developments both downtown and uptown. Their cosmopolitan vision was a technocratic and corporate automobile utopia in the vein of General Motors' "Futurama," unveiled to a global audience at the 1939 New York World's Fair (and critiqued by E. B. White in *Harper's*).[4]

Robert Moses also stood at the intersection of planning and publishing. In the 1950s he wrote regularly for the *New York Times Magazine*, among other publications, and understood the necessity of shaping an environment where one could "get things done" with minimal interference. Moses, in large part, echoed the crime fiction fantasies of Spillane, perpetuating an effective narrative of New York City descending into the abyss. To begin with, he outlined Title I of the 1949 Housing Act, vesting himself with the power to remake New York City. Then he took to the pages of magazines to foster an image of pragmatism, bashing both ideology in planning circles and unfounded criticisms of realist plans. As the Title I vision was unfurled to the city's establishment, Moses used his comfortable relationship with the mainstream press to condemn slums as a cancer, outline his clinical solution, and attack opponents—tangible and straw men alike. Employing fear to justify the restoration of Cosmopolis, Moses carved out a space where he and his expert planners could perform municipal surgery immune from critical questioning. The image he constructed served him well for much of the 1950s. Surgeons followed through on most of his prescriptions, laid out in his two- and three-dimensional master plans.

In embracing the magazine article, however, Moses brandished the chosen weapon of his most persistent and powerful critics, and as the planner succumbed to the kind of ideological ad hominem treatises he initially condemned, the writers pounced. When investigative journalists, accomplished fiction authors experimenting with the nonfiction form, and pop-sociologists observed Moses's new city from the street, their deliberate reaction was to fear what the city had and could become. Where Moses saw cancer, critics found communities that municipal surgeons destroyed for cosmetic and corrupt fiscal ends. Collections like *The Exploding Metropolis*, short memoirs by native New Yorkers from neighborhoods ravaged or ignored by Title I, and muckraking pieces such as "The Shame of New York" gave voice to the grassroots resistance that pestered the power broker from the 1940s through the 1960s, opponents Moses had kept at bay through his convincing fear-laden narrative. By the end of the decade, these critics proved instrumental in weakening Moses's sway over New York redevelopment, ushering in a cultural shift on the meaning of blighted slums and limiting the power of municipal surgeons—planners and bureaucrats—to remake the dying city.[5]

· · · · · ·

Moses began his rise to power in the 1920s, and by the 1950s he secured near-omnipotent status, characteristic of what political anthropologist James C. Scott has termed "authoritarian high modernism," at both the city and state levels. Le Corbusier may have been the dreamer, but it was Moses that possessed the power to transform the city by his own design.[6] An urban visionary, he foresaw American culture's love affair with the automobile as well as its general disinterest in public transportation. Beginning with Long Island parkway projects under the reign of Smith, Moses developed much of the New York metropolitan area's arterial highway system. While the early construction focused on the sprawling rural estates of New York's landed families, Moses later rebuilt the city itself by constructing parkways, expressways, and their bridge and tunnel links to and from each of the five boroughs. In the 1960s his infamous Cross Bronx Expressway trench tore apart vital neighborhoods in the borough, and he unveiled plans for three similar cross-Manhattan expressways replete with modern architecture tailoring at Broome Street, Thirty-Fourth Street, and 125th Street in Harlem before community opposition finally squashed Moses's vision. Starting with the Stuyvesant Town/Peter Cooper Village project in the 1940s, a public-private partnership between the city and the Metropolitan Life insurance company, Moses oversaw a slum clearance and redevelopment program that further demolished New York City neighborhoods and landmarks.[7]

As a result of Moses's ability to "get things done" in rather astonishing fashion, New York City's twentieth-century history is inherently tied to him. The amount of ink spilled on the power broker is considerable. He has been blamed for everything that went wrong for New York in the 1960s and 1970s, portrayed as a pawn for the Rockefeller family, and hailed as the city's savior for staving off the urbicide that demoralized the industrial cities of the Northeast and the Midwest. Moses has been the focus of lengthy biographies and a prominent subject of filmmaker Ric Burns's multichapter historical documentary on New York City, and even inspired a nascent Broadway musical and a dissertation-cum-novelization. His use of fear and the image of New York as Necropolis, however, has largely gone unanalyzed. Between 1945 and 1961, Moses submitted articles to the *New York Times,* the *New York Times Magazine, Harper's,* and *Esquire*; completed one edited collection, *Working for the People* (1956); and later published a memoir, *Public Works: A Dangerous Trade* (1970). A close reading of these texts reveals Moses as a thinker and an ideologue, and showcases the centrality of fear and declension narratives to the implementation of his renewal program.[8]

Linking New York's slums to cancer proved Moses's most potent trope, not unlike "the monster" of Mike Hammer's paranoid delusions. The imagery of New York's blighted landscape projected by the cancer metaphor demanded the scale and scope of his program in the 1950s. In humans, cancer, regardless of its origins, ripples throughout the body, often with ease. If blight festered too long in one neighborhood, the narrative went, it would metastasize in the surrounding areas, swiftly reproducing and spreading outward. Slum clearance, according to Moses's practice, was not to proceed in piecemeal (e.g., a few lots on one block and a lot or two on the adjacent block). Only large-scale slum clearance would ensure that all cancerous cells were eliminated. As a result, whole neighborhoods were torn down and excavated piece by piece to make way for the city's grand postwar projects: the "Gashouse District" on Manhattan's east side would become Stuyvesant Town and Peter Cooper Village; Turtle Bay, also on the east side, would become the United Nations complex; Lincoln Square became Lincoln Center and Fordham University's Manhattan campus. The size of these "improvements" fulfilled the modernist "clean slate" ideology, and demonstrated that slums required wholesale eradication to secure the postindustrial Cold War Cosmopolis.[9]

The passage of the aforementioned Housing Act of 1949 expanded Moses's power to alter New York City significantly. Title I of the act initiated the program that came to be known as urban renewal, offering municipalities federal funds to clear slums and, with later legislative enhancements, construct public and private developments in their place. Moses played an active role in the formulation of the Housing Act, working with Senator Robert Taft to draft the bill and fighting for its swift passage. He also convinced New York State to establish the Committee on Slum Clearance Projects to orchestrate the city's urban renewal program, and installed himself as agency head. With his leadership firmly established, Moses based the Committee on Slum Clearance in his isolated office complex on Randall's Island, headquarters of the Triborough Bridge and Tunnel Authority then under his control, insulating his redevelopment vision from the influence of City Hall and Albany. For the next decade Moses, with limited interruption and interference, controlled slum designation and demolition. He also determined the future use of the cleared land, who would rebuild what where, and the distribution of public and private redevelopment funds.[10]

As city construction coordinator (1946–59) and the architect of slum clearance, Moses initiated the planning and supervised the construction of various high-profile projects that transformed whole neighborhoods. Moses's goal for urban renewal was three-pronged: constructing attractive, middle-class housing in order to compete with the emerging suburbs; enhancing New York's reputation as a center of learning, particularly higher education; and maintaining the city's reputation for high culture.[11] Moses built middle-class housing projects—not to be confused with New York City Housing Authority (NYCHA) public housing developments—across Manhattan and in sections of Brooklyn and Queens. Residential construction intersected with university redevelopment in such notable cases as Morningside Heights, Kips Bay, and the Washington Square South project that integrated apartment buildings designed by famed architect I. M. Pei with New York University infrastructure. Housing, education, and culture intersected in the grandest of his urban renewal projects, the aforementioned Lincoln Square. In this development, planned in the 1950s and executed in the early 1960s, the city bulldozed a large swath of Manhattan's Upper West Side for middle-income apartments, Fordham University's extension campus, and Lincoln Center, which would come to house the Metropolitan Opera and the Juilliard School, among other institutions. Other than the Coliseum—a convention center meant to be a symbol and a celebration of public service—Moses's urban renewal aims sought to alleviate public problems (i.e., slums and blight) through state investment in private enterprise. Urban renewal's tenuous public-private partnership, in due course, resulted in heightened tension and conflict between Moses and various actors invested in the future of the city.[12]

To diffuse potential conflict and opposition to New York's massive slum clearance initiative, the city construction coordinator found utility in the vocabulary of Necropolis. Between 1949 and 1960 Moses developed thirty-five slum clearance plans under Title I, of which seventeen were completed. The Committee on Slum Clearance assembled glossy brochures for twenty-six of the plans, featuring the rationale for clearance alongside the proposed site's modern redesign. Each publication included a section titled "Demonstration of Slum Conditions" (altered to "Demonstration of Blight" in 1952), which defined problematic communities through photographic narratives. For planning experts, extensive text was unnecessary. As Moses said, "it's the schedules themselves, the plans and pictures that count with the statement that we mean business." Among the practitioners of Title I, the common visual language of disorder and blight was self-evident. The instructions, according to historian Themis Chronopoulos, "gave the impression that the brochure photographs captured objective slum conditions that could be universally understood and accepted." The preference of photography over text confirmed that Moses saw slums as a physical problem, revealed effortlessly in black-and-white images of old architecture, limited setbacks, and street life. Decaying infrastructure represented the urban illness, and thus Moses's brochures recommended an influx of new modern development as the solution, as opposed to policy considerations aimed at the social and economic issues of lower- and working-class neighborhoods in New York. The audience for the publications appeared to be one conscious of documentary evidence of slums and amenable to a physical rather than a social program: New York City's Board of Estimate, the Planning Commission, Federal Title I and housing officials, politicians at various levels, and any concerned members of the general public.[13]

The audience's niche quality was indicative of the modernist sensibility that governed slum clearance, redevelopment, and master planning. Moses populated his agencies with skilled technicians, experts in the disciplines of planning, transportation, engineering, architecture, and construction charged with fulfilling the goals of modernist design: efficiency, convenience, and order. Expertise assumed schooling in and knowledge of prevailing planning theory, which equated disorder with density, age, and congestion. Each of these variables had been identifiable to the critical eye since Jacob Riis turned his discriminating camera on the side-by-side tenements and street life of "Mulberry Bend" and "Bandits Roost," revealing the symbols of the Progressive Era's Necropolis. The general public, however, lacked such knowledge, at least from the perspective of the omniscient planning establishment. While the experts understood blight when they saw it, citizens willingly occupying such districts were blind to the decay. As such, Moses shifted to less official organs in the 1940s and 1950s to document the growing scourge of the slums. Contrasting with the glossy visual slum clearance brochures, he published text-heavy editorials in some of the country's most important journals. In lieu of photographs and architectural designs, he crafted a literary narrative of slums as cancer. These means justified Moses's ends: utopian modern design and efficient automobile accessibility.[14]

Even before Title I became law, Moses took his concerns about slums and their redevelopment to a national audience. In January 1945 he published

"Slums and City Planning" in the *Atlantic*, an article that defined slums, attacked utopians and "perfectionists" for their lack of pragmatism, critiqued public housing development, and outlined a plan for slum clearance based on the Stuyvesant Town/Riverton model then rising in the Lower East Side and Harlem neighborhoods of New York. Moses observed slums from the perspective of a Progressive Era reformer: dense class-segregated districts exploited by rent-hungry property owners and real estate interests funneling multiple families into quarters where a single family might find comfort. "In the tenements people are packed in like chickens in a coop," he wrote. "Wave after wave of newcomers inhabit these rookeries. As soon as one generation achieves enough prosperity to get out, it moves on and another with lower standards and income takes its place." The description evoked the slum narratives of Riis's *How the Other Half Lives* (1890), whom Moses referenced alongside Jane Addams and Lillian Wald as "pioneers [who] lifted up the tabernacle in the city wilderness and awakened the sleeping conscience of a generation too busy making money and enjoying it to give thought to their less fortunate fellow men." Reformers and the settlement houses they ran triumphed in their time, but the persistence of slums a half-century later indicated that such success came with physical limitations. "We owe thanks to the early social workers" as agents in literal and figurative forms of slum clearance over the course of fifty years of struggle. Yet their work had not extinguished the pathology of slum creation. Moses insisted that the time had come to change course: "the task is now one of engineering and management, and [social workers] must turn the job over to administrators."[15]

He defined blight in public terms, citing various municipal and corporate initiatives as the source of urban illness. On the one hand, "New York's leading real estate operators . . . created our slums of today by selling small lots for big buildings and by preventing zoning, proper building, multiple-family regulations." The lack of rational planning emerged as a scapegoat for slum conditions in overcrowded tenement districts. "Everywhere these men left a slimy trail behind them which eventually had to be mopped up by public offices with money out of the public treasury." Public servants also collaborated with private companies in the creation of infrastructure developments that wrought "central decay." Moses despised mass forms of transit, and refused rights of way for commuter or subway rail lines along his highway routes. As he reported then, "if in New York City we had refrained from building so many miles of subways at twenty million dollars a mile and had put some of this money into rehabilitating and making livable and attractive the older and central parts of town, millions of people would not today be crowded like cattle into hurtling trains during the rush hours." These types of problematic developments had ceased in New York as a result of the control of Moses and his various development hats. The combination of factors, however, had left a number of lingering symptoms that, if not treated, would destroy cities—"high taxes, bad living, economic dry rot, humiliation, disease, and crime."[16]

Despite his authoritarian reputation, Moses strategically situated himself prior to the passage of Title I between the "revolutionaries" advocating decentralization and the "perfectionists" pushing clean-slate master plans. Utopian dreamers in the age of planning enlightenment took on the industrial city in the twentieth century, advocating small but dense mixed-use towns connected via rail and water transit. Ebenezer Howard's "Garden City of Tomorrow" established this two-dimensional vision, which he saddled with communitarian social and economic considerations in order to confront the exploitive practices of real estate interests, industrialists, and machine politics. Moses's contemporary Frank Lloyd Wright offered "Broadacre City," a neo-Jeffersonian vision fusing urban and agrarian design for the automobile age. Despite good intentions, Moses found such "revolutionary plans" of "decentralization by whatever name" lacking in viability, much less practicality. "Habit is too strong," he wrote; "sentiment for the old neighborhoods, which is pooh-poohed by revolutionaries, the pinks and reds who never get their roots down anywhere, will continue to be a great factor in the necessity for gradual and conservative change"—a sentiment that Moses would have significant success in silencing over the next fifteen years.

The "perfectionists," editorialists at *Architectural Forum* invoking the order and clean lines of Le Corbusier's "Radiant City," were also immune to compromise. Engineers, technicians, and planning experts rejected such absolutes in favor of compromise and piecemeal redevelopment—the deliberate and conservative process that Moses deemed necessary for successful slum clearance. In this article he outlined a number of features later codified in Title I: the use of eminent domain; collaboration between federal, state, and local agencies; public-private partnerships in urban renewal; arterial highway construction; and limited public and subsidized housing construction. As he noted, "more slum clearance has been accomplished indirectly than directly" through civic improvements like parks and parkways. "My particular little group of demolition and building demons have without fanfare and social worker abracadabra pulled down more rookeries than all the housing experts and authorities put together. And the best thing about it is that we have substituted nothing for the rookeries but broad highways lined with landscaping and recreation facilities, open to the sun and the elements, and affording the very best incentive to further slum clearance and improvement on their boundaries." Just as critics of urban decay claimed blight rippled outward, Moses argued that sound redevelopment in selective, well-planned, and well-placed doses would cure the disease of the slums.[17]

Following the passage of the 1949 Housing Act, however, Moses's tone changed. He no longer envisioned piecemeal implementation of its prescriptions, and slum clearance by definition eschewed small-scale projects. In one key public transcript, "Problems: Many—and a Program" (1953) published in the *New York Times Magazine*, Moses refashioned himself as a defensive "perfectionist," pooh-poohing the critics of his slum clearance plans. Most of the articles that followed functioned as a defense mechanism against a variety of straw-men opponents that Moses referred to in a typically colorful and serial manner as "bellyachers, Cassandras, cynics, scoffers, timid souls, defeatists and existentialists . . . radical advocates of dispersion and decentralization, back to Walden scribblers, Vestal Virgins of Reform in their thin muslin gowns, ward politicians, myopic statisticians, monarchs of all they survey, inventors of formulas and gadgets, diplomats and protocol boys, prestidigitators, magicians, alchemists and editorial pundits," among others. From this new perspective, a cultural cynicism toward slum clearance and urban renewal had eaten away at the promise of a great public endeavor, as well as overshadowed the "extraordinary accomplishments" of the city's growing redevelopment bureaucracy. "The moral atmosphere and political climate in which we find ourselves at the moment," wrote Moses, "are not conducive to the realization of this main purpose. We have been living in a period of seemingly endless investigation and lurid disclosures. Our newspapers are full of these things and almost everything constructive and optimistic is subordinated to screaming headlines and melodrama on screen, radio and television." For the city construction coordinator, sensationalism and criticism from writers outside of the redevelopment process threatened to stall the progress achieved during four years of Title I.[18]

Simplistic ridicule placed Moses in the tradition of postwar practitioners and critics who employed suggestions of gender and sexual nonnormativity to smear opponents. In "Problems: Many—and a Program" Moses's writing, taking a page from Spillane, was hard and vigorous, like his public personality, while his opponents were soft, effeminate, and lacking the bellicose temperament that allowed an accomplished "builder," as he referred to himself, to get things done. In language befitting the masculine political culture of the era, Moses labeled those who threatened him "goo-goos" or "do-gooders," infantilizing terms that constructed an image of critics as weak and childish and therefore impractical and idealistic. To Moses, the good-government crowd fostered urban decay by stonewalling the Title I process. In contrast, he employed hard masculine rhetoric to position himself within the "vital center," lest he be confused with a revolutionary feeding off the welfare state. As a vital centrist, and thus pragmatist, Moses insisted that he had a practical plan for solving New York City's problems, and sought to validate his own as well as his municipal surgeons' planning expertise as productive and progressive. As he put it, "the time has come to empower experienced practitioners to reach [the major objective of urban renewal], to adjourn mud throwing, cheap politics and professional uplift, stop beefing over our impending demise and wrangling over details of the funeral and get ready for drastic remedies and temporarily painful sacrifices for the common good."[19]

The nameless goo-goos, in the press, at City Hall, and on the streets, had clearly frustrated the planner, and by taking his complaints and ad hominem attacks to the *Times*, Moses endorsed mass media as a key venue for shaping public opinion on policies like slum clearance and urban renewal. Fulfilling New York's massive redevelopment vision required a certain amount of social capital and goodwill. In an inhospitable milieu, one that saw slum clearance and urban renewal as destructive or, worse, a failure, establishing public support and raising necessary revenue would prove difficult. Garnering public empathy was particularly important for the implementation of Moses's Title I projects. As practiced in New York, slum clearance required the demolition and displacement of poor and working-class neighborhoods. Moses understood that dislocation was never popular, but much of his writing asserted that the ends justified the means. As he often said in public and in print, "You cannot make an omelet without breaking eggs," and "we must create a new atmosphere and climate" if New York's renewal was to be successful and the city's future secure. Media culture proved vital to achieving those ends, and Moses sought editorial aid in shaping an environment where his redevelopment policies would be implemented with the least resistance. In combating the critics' "idealistic cynicism," Moses relinquished his earlier moderation in favor of the "perfectionist" image of later biographies.[20]

Discerning the power of a provocative sensational narrative in the media marketplace, Moses confronted idealistic imagery through Spillane's template. Although trained in the classics at Yale, Moses adored the hardboiled genre—"the more lurid the subject matter the better." According to geographer Timothy Mennel, Moses "felt that no physical work would outlast a great piece of literature," and in those rare moments of regret, he "wrote of his secret desire to live the life of a drunken pulp writer." Caro notes too that it was always Moses's "ambition to write cheap pulp stuff" like Mickey Spillane, and to do so for the money.[21] Eschewing ambiguity and flexibility à la Spillane, Moses lumped his critics together in one broadbrush swath. They were "purveyors of pseudoscience and Madison Avenue ballyhoo, editorial pundits, footloose columnists, assorted map makers, market analysts, statisticians gone loco, architects graduated by their own letterheads into planners and poll-parrot imitators." When not resorting to petty name-calling, Moses employed the persuasive literary technique of metaphor to full effect. His urban illness of 1945 evolved into the "cancer of the slums" by 1953. In "Problems" Moses described the city as a patient "not fully aware of his condition," evoking Spillane's "tumor breeding in its belly" and imploring the public to prepare for "long" cures. "They will not be brought about by taking antibiotic pills guaranteeing in a twinkling to fix everything from stuttering to the Chinese rot."[22]

Diagnosed with slum cancer, Necropolis required surgery performed by New York City's most skilled planning practitioners. At the opening of a Lower East Side housing project, for example, Moses pleaded for the power and funds to address New York's malignant tumors, arguing that little good can come from renewal without wholesale slum removal. "There can be no real neighborhood reconstruction, no superblocks, no reduction of ground coverage, no widening of boundary streets, no playgrounds, no new schools, without the unflinching surgery which cuts out the whole cancer and leaves no part of it to grow again, and spread and perpetuate old miseries." Tumor removal was seen as the first step toward the broader regeneration of the city.[23]

Moses's medical analogies appealed to the public's anxiety about not only their own mortality but the mortality of their cities as well. On the one hand, this anxiety stemmed from the political realities of the Cold War, the one highlighted by E. B. White in "Here Is New York." In a *New York Times Magazine* article outlining the implications of civil defense for cities like New York, Moses expressed concern that such plans would become an excuse for idealists to advocate for urban decentralization, and thus the destruction of American cities before the bomb even dropped. Moses suggested that civil defense planning must instead focus on traffic congestion and multipurpose parking garages. In the event of an attack, there would be efficient dispersal of the exiting population and sufficient fallout shelter within the structures for those willing to stay. His allusion to atomic devastation, in this sense, validated a grand arterial plan for the New York City metropolitan area, reiterating the theme that pragmatic civil servants, if provided the space to operate, could solve public problems. That extended to the great Cold War fear of the bomb and the bureaucratic mess of civil defense, which "looks to us like defense against overcrowding in all its aspects—against fright, hysteria and mob psychology—and presents to our crude and practical minds a great opportunity to solve problems we ought to solve anyway, only more completely, with less compromise, favoritism and politics, faster, better and more cheaply than if we wait until we are inexorably driven to it."[24]

On the other hand, Moses's Necropolis superseded the threat of atomic destruction. A number of critics, planners, and utopians in the forties and fifties understood the city as an antiquated spatial form. The middle class exited cities almost en masse for suburbs like Long Island's Levittown—the stand-in for the postwar suburb since. Here Moses cited Wright's decentralized Broadacre. The plan imagined the end of traditional condensed urban forms. Instead, citizens would possess at minimum an acre of land to cultivate as they wished. Moses lashed out at midcentury antiurbanists for their representations of New York and other cities as "overgrown, crazed villages, inhabited by cockroaches who will soon be squashed in their own filthy juices." In the words of Moses, Wright's evocation of urban disorder "was really the death of the city."[25]

Moses understood that a complete and successful urban renewal program had the potential to shift the narrative and end the city's public relations problem, one that caused great detriment to New York's political economy and constrained the builder's power. Moses complained of outsiders, going as far back as Charles Dickens in *American Notes* (1842), who came to the city's welcoming shores only to dwell on the negative aspects of life in "Gotham." As Moses put it, "the citizens of New York have been, in a very special way, the victims of acidulous visitors busily scribbling with pens dipped in acid, partly no doubt because they land here first and promptly and gleefully have their worst fears confirmed before they pass the Statue of Liberty." Such critics often presented any number of fatal prophecies: "We are . . . told that there is too much uncontrolled public housing, too little middle-income housing, intolerable high-rental housing; that only shops and millionaires, banks and Bourbons, will be left in Manhattan; that integration will kill Harlem; that folks are returning to Harlem; that Macy's and Gimbels are going, basements and all, to the suburbs; that the customers are mobbing the old stores; that nobody wants to go to New York any more." As late as 1959, his power waning, Moses complained that critics failed to see the value of technical urban planning, that is, the practical and progressive nature of top-down redevelopment.[26]

The image of decline, along with the vitriol, name-calling, and forceful polemics in Moses's writings, had a purpose: to demonstrate the important role of planning expertise in sustaining New York. His vision originated from a cosmopolitan perspective, expressing concern along with empathy, and demonstrating to New Yorkers through his stated benevolence and pragmatism that he had the city's best interests in mind. He worked obsessively, (slightly) tolerated criticism, and inconvenienced so many because a few "broken eggs" meant a meaningful future for New York City. Jane Jacobs and Robert Caro, among others, later established an image of a man who despised cities: favoring automobiles over mass transit, ripping through neighborhoods with little empathy for the displaced, employing abysmal aesthetics, and lacking knowledge of street-level urban functions. Moses saw the city as whole, favoring an overhead perspective that removed the social and emphasized the physical, in particular the massive circulatory system pumping blood through the metroplex. Yet he adored New York City—at least his vision of New York—and he happily proclaimed it "the most fascinating of all metropolitan areas" and "the most stimulating workshop in the world."[27]

As the quantity and breadth of Moses's publications indicate, the planner enjoyed a favorable relationship with the city's mainstream press through the 1950s. For the most part, magazines and local newspapers delighted in his renewed New York. Some, like Henry Luce's *Time/Life* empire, even moved into the modern Midtown towers that rose in the period. A 1959 issue of *Life* featured a glossy photo essay, titled "A Newer New York," that commemorated the city's commercial construction boom with a visually stunning, almost shocking, contrast of turn-of-the-century versus modern development. The photograph showcased a lone brownstone—its edges serrated from neighboring destruction—amid a field of rubble and empty sidewalks. Behind the brownstone sat a tableau of modern apartment buildings like those that would eventually replace the cleared plot. A caption called it a "solitary survivor on block cleared for 20-story building . . . [that]

forlornly awaits the inevitable." While the caption indicated gloom, the same issue cited the city's unprecedented pace of redevelopment, celebrating modern architecture and Moses's grand accomplishments.[28]

The *New York Times* also fed the narrative that Moses's skilled municipal surgeons had nearly eradicated the cancer of slums. In the summer of 1955, the newspaper published a twenty-part neighborhood-by-neighborhood series called "Our Changing City" that highlighted Moses's projects and expressed optimism in the ability of the state and its planners to solve New York's problems. The series, and similar special publications devoted to the city's makeover, saluted the planning profession's skill in salvaging still-declining neighborhoods. Reporters hoped that future plans would enhance perceived blighted districts still untouched by the surgeons' knife—no slum was deemed beyond remedy. The series also acknowledged New York City's unique modernist moment under Title I. In a milieu where Moses shaped the message, the destruction of landmarks, like the then-proposed bulldozing of Pennsylvania Station for a "skyscraper to be known as the *Palace of Progress*" housing a "world trade center," drew little rebuke. As series editor Meyer Berger put it, the demolition of beloved buildings and neighborhoods was merely a contingency of keeping up with the "changing fashion."[29] In 1957 *Reader's Digest* offered another gushing profile, calling Moses "one of the great public servants of our time," one whose projects inspired "planners from practically every major city in the United States, Canada and Latin American." The country's most popular magazine noted his penchant for "personally breaking bottlenecks, barging through festoons of restrictive red tape, cajoling, exhorting, pleading, pontificating, or just plain raising hell—whichever the occasion demands." Here was a man "who gets things done" and did things right—citing his "instinct and sympathy for the masses," notably without public testimony to support that claim.[30]

Yet at mid-decade, and indicative of the growing understanding of Necropolis within the culture, the *Times* posed a provocative question to Moses: "Has New York a future?" The builder took the inquiry as a personal insult, and fired off a missive: "As to this idea that New York is finished and has no future, I am devoting a good part of my time in [Mayor Robert F.] Wagner's Administration and otherwise to demonstrating that this is not so, and I do not want to do a piece to prove what needs no proof." Moses relented and published a *New York Times Magazine* response. He put forth proof tenfold of the city's sustainability, each point tied to his redevelopment and public works programs of the previous three decades, including parkland reclamation, housing, highways, culture, industry, and education among others. Moses adamantly defended his vision. Contrary to the popular fatalism, he insisted, "No dead or dying community makes such preparation for the future." Affirming the resurrection of Cosmopolis, Moses noted that New York's citizens, especially migrants, would ensure the city's persistence: "The most ambitious come here because they find the greatest opportunities for advancement and success, because they seek the stimulus of an interesting life, because of cultural opportunities." It was a line, in essence, cribbed from E. B. White.[31]

"New York *Has* a Future" encapsulated the foremost theme running through the Moses canon. Behind fear sat an unrelenting modernist faith in progress, a trajectory building toward the ultimate new city. New York City's survival, according to the builder, required a transformation of space on a grand scale, but it also required spaces in which small groups of expert planners and engineers could operate with little interference. Moses sought to both validate the need for that space to exist and establish it at the same time, reaching out to the public to explain, in sometimes esoteric terms, the costs and benefits of Title I. Ultimately, he saw urban renewal as the preeminent solution to urban problems, and parlayed Necropolis into both political and critical success. In recent years, historians have argued that Moses's projects contributed to New York's viability and allowed the city to avoid the fate of other industrial and commercial centers in the Northeast. Others, as noted above, have blamed Moses's program for New York's decline. For certain, his work and writings in the 1950s sparked a debate over the physical and social viability of New York City across various media cultures.[32]

The *Times* provocation spoke to an ascendant strand of journalistic commentary less sanguine about the prospects of New York's renewal. In July 1960, *Esquire* published a special issue devoted to the spectacle of New York City, including a short vignette by Moses called "Indefinable New York" celebrating the city as Cosmopolis. The rest of the issue seemed attuned to the anxieties of slum clearance, urban renewal, and the pull of suburbia. Harvey Swados's short story "Nights in the Gardens of Brooklyn" considered the psychological trauma of slum clearance on the Lower East Side. John Cheever lamented the shrinking availability of safe residential areas for the white middle class within Manhattan. James Baldwin challenged the structural racism at the heart of Title I implementation, indicting the city's power structure in a view from Harlem. Each article offered a new variation on the narrative attributing the decline of New York City to the master-planning approach. Graphic designer Raymond Loewy lampooned the clean-slate impulse of Moses and his acolytes. Loewy presented "Newyork" [*sic*], a plan for the wholesale clearance of Manhattan renewed with a boxy modern monolith fit for four million inhabitants and situated in the geographical center of the island. The plan caricatured Moses's "authoritarian high modernism," and the phrasing of Loewy's conclusion—"As a matter of fact, give me everything I want, but don't you touch a thing. If I can't have it all my way I want New York to stay as it is"—represented a lighthearted but pertinent send-up of Moses's self-crafted image of benign omniscience.[33]

The most damning critique of Moses came from the liberal *Nation* magazine in 1959, which had paved the way for Loewy's satire. "The Shame of New York" marked the culmination of years of investigative reporting for the *New York Journal-American* on civil and political corruption in the city. In an issue-length article, Fred J. Cook and Gene Gleason linked the mob, organized labor, Madison Avenue advertising agencies, the construction trades, and city agencies including the NYPD with Moses and his authorities in a massive web of municipal corruption. Initiating a refrain that would become commonplace, Cook and Gleason suggested in their findings that *"New York had lost its soul."*[34] In the city wrought by "the man with ten heads," that is, Moses, "the illnesses of New York are many and they run deep." The misdirected aim of slum clearance was a vehicle for large-scale private redevelopment and was "one of many cankers." Crime, too, was a problem "wherever you turn," transforming neighborhoods into "veritable jungles" where "the streets are unsafe at night." On top of physical and social decay, the size of the city's government had surged since 1940. This resulted in an oppressive and seemingly invincible bureaucracy that, in the words of Cook and Gleason, "operate[d] to dwarf the individual and to divorce him from all control of his fate," creating a tremendous cleavage between the establishment and the governed. The case against planning in this period rested on the perceived lack of agency among citizens and communities in shaping the physical spaces they inhabited. This image of the now-powerless republican citizen represented an attack on the otherwise benevolent appearance of the welfare state since the New Deal. Indicative of a changing political culture, Cook and Gleason argued against "big" government in an antiestablishment publication. The *Nation*'s willingness to turn a whole issue over to Cook and Gleason revealed the creeping disillusionment with the state that came to define the urban question.[35]

Throughout the 1950s Moses had been subject to increasing criticism, backlash, and scrutiny—from the families expunged from the Gashouse District by MetLife, parents outraged by plans to remove a beloved Central

Park playground, the displaced residents of the Bronx's East Tremont neighborhood, Greenwich Villagers furious over his plans for their community, and vocal critics from the growing field of urban studies. Moses emerged from these battles with few defeats and an unscathed reputation. He remained a pillar of public trust for a variety of reasons. For one, a number of projects demonstrated his benevolent service to the region. From Jones Beach to the Triborough Bridge, his early works developed comparatively undeveloped landscapes at the time of construction. Transportation improvements on Long Island fostered the commercial and residential development of Queens, Nassau, and Suffolk Counties, and served this ever-growing population for generations to come. Only years later, with Brooklyn and Bronx highway projects, did Moses begin drawing lines through long-established communities. Popular public works operated as a calling card for any opportunities and appointments that augmented his power.[36]

Moses's personality also enhanced his authority, as a different side of the "man with ten heads" held sway off the pages of the *Times* and other sympathetic outlets. When planning his Long Island parkways, Moses blackmailed the likes of William Kingsland Macy, a Suffolk County power broker himself and a significant landowner, by threatening to use his cushy relationship with the press to destroy Macy's reputation. Thus, when Cook and Gleason discovered malfeasance in the "Manhattantown" urban renewal project, they noted that "it was only the most glaring example of what was happening in many projects as Robert Moses, with typical vigor, barked down all opposition and swept ahead on his charted path to remake the face of New York." Moses's power outside of the public sector had scared off a number of potential critics in the fourth estate. Whenever a critique of Moses or his projects appeared in a local newspaper or magazine, there was always room for a personal rebuttal in the "Letters" section of the *Times*, and he continued to enjoy good press in the age of renewal.[37]

Cook and Gleason constituted a minority among local journalists, two of only a few in the late 1950s who were willing to investigate Moses's mismanagement of Title I municipal surgery. They described Moses as vindictive, corrupted, and addicted to power, exposing his benevolence as a façade and demonstrating a distinct lack of compassion in slum clearance. According to their investigation, municipal surgery amounted to a source of Tammany-like graft, feeding the coffers of private enterprise at the expense of the public and displacing slum residents who hoped to matriculate into the modern structures. In this new image of Necropolis, clearance occurred where no slums existed, and renewal programs ignored areas in need of aid and rehabilitation—central arguments in the burgeoning culture war against state planning. The Washington Square Village plan especially irked Cook and Gleason: "You can go almost anywhere in steaming, stinking East and West Harlem and find sweltering humanity crammed into miserable tenements—four, six and sometimes ten persons to a single room," just as Moses observed in 1945. Despite its obvious needs, Cook and Gleason remarked, "Moses turned his back on Harlem and decided to tear apart the business section south of Washington Square." The plan rewrote the slum clearance modus operandi to a point that it stunned federal officials. "This was the first time in the nation that Title I had been applied to wiping out small business." In just over a decade, as the investigators revealed, Moses's Title I practice superseded the sound pragmatism he elucidated in "Slums and City Planning."[38]

In January 1962, Moses responded to the growing indictment of his life's work—"Shame of New York," Jane Jacobs's *Death and Life of Great American Cities*, and Lewis Mumford's *The City in History*—in the pages of the *Atlantic* with an article titled "Are Cities Dead?" His pettiness was still there, expanding to the point where he named names and alluded to specific critics. Economist Robert C. Wood, author of the Harvard University's "New York Metropolitan Region Study" volume on labyrinthine metropolitan management in *1400 Governments* (1961), was dismissed as "an obscure assistant professor with no record of administration, who, enjoying a foundation grant and speaking for a regional civic organization, prophesized imminent chaos and the early disintegration of our metropolis." Moses singled out Mumford as "one of the most-quoted Jeremiahs who inveigh against the condition of our cities," citing the threat *City in History* posed to Cosmopolis. "I object to these Jeremiahs," Moses wrote, "primarily because they attempt to poison a rising generation of ordinarily optimistic young Americans." Indeed, critics of Title I and public works "make municipal administration increasingly unattractive and relegate it finally to the lowest politics and poorest talent." Against the crushing tide of declensionist imagery in *his* New York, the *Atlantic* article constituted Moses's final plea for the pragmatism of his municipal surgeons. Responding to a set of rhetorical inquiries on the practical nature of urban development in the 1960s, he concluded, "Pending responsible answers to these questions, those of us who have work to do and obstacles to overcome, who cannot hide in ivory towers writing encyclopedic theses, whose usefulness is measured by results, must carry on." The article's prologue, while noting his previous experience in public service, only identified him as "president of the New York World's Fair 1964–1965 Corporation."[39]

· · · · · ·

In his 1958 article on the significance of magazine reportage, Norman Podhoretz equated the utility of modern architecture to the magazine article. Each was devoted to functionalism, and the article as a form thrived due to its utility and practicality: "Our sense of beauty today is intimately connected with the sense of usefulness; we consider a building beautiful when it seems to exist not for anyone to enjoy the sight of or to be impressed by, but solely and simply to be used." Podhoretz suggested that writers and readers both had grown "temporarily uncomfortable with the traditional literary forms because they don't *seem* practical, designed for 'use,' whereas a magazine article by its nature satisfies that initial condition." In this milieu, Robert Moses utilized the functional form to condemn Necropolis and envision a renewed city. Urban transformation, urban renewal, and the fate of cities filled the pages of the nation's most popular magazines. How critics utilized these narratives, as the fundamental shift in planning theory from Moses's technocrats demonstrates, transformed the cultural understanding of the city in the age of urban renewal.[40]

Moses once complained that "critics build nothing. They live on mud-throwing and false, garbled statistics." In hindsight, the statement acknowledged the inevitable: in the wake of "Shame of New York," a tidal wave of criticism would soon come crashing down on the house of Moses. He transformed New York City beginning in the 1930s, followed through in the 1940s with more improvements, and dabbled in slum clearance and urban renewal in the 1950s. Confronted by opposition, Moses took to the pages of various magazines to tally the city's problems, present his solution, and attack his adversaries. His writings seemed to assure the public that here was a man of action, a man who could get things done, and a man who builds and therefore knows. Moses had differentiated between the practitioners (planners) and philosophers (critics). For him, only the former were virtuous—the true credible sources on redevelopment.[41]

By the end of the 1950s, however, new voices had turned Moses's rhetoric on its head and built a new Necropolis. They charged that unrelenting optimism, modernist urban design, and top-down planning—the qualities embraced by Moses and his defenders at the *New York Times* and elsewhere— were *idealistic*, not pragmatic, and therefore threatened the viability of the city. Moses's plans were deemed utopian, reserved for the scale models of visionaries like Le Corbusier, but not destined for reality. Moses insisted that critics were holding the city back, allowing the cancer to fester and spread, but the critics in turn argued that slum clearance and urban renewal fostered a problematic city. In response, the goo-goos confronted the master builder with plans and ideas that proved feasible. During the heyday of the magazine article, they constructed a movement against the "rational" planning of Moses through journalistic criticism. This transition in planning theory and ideology rested on perspective. Rather than deeming slums an urban cancer with a broad brush, emergent critics sought to put a human face on slum life. Moses's preferred vantage point was from above, so that the city was a model in miniature replete with movable pieces that made driving an expressway through a neighborhood seem so provocative. In contrast, new critics preferred the vantage of the street, believing that the only way to understand the city was observing how it functioned. In the process, the street offered the requisite perspective for the refashioned image of New York in the 1960s.

4   On Planning Necropolis

. . . .

In 1957 *Fortune* magazine compiled a six-part series on urbanism in America called The Exploding Metropolis. The collection of articles edited by William H. Whyte offered a particularly trenchant analysis of the limitations of planning and urban renewal. Repackaged in paperback form in 1958, *The Exploding Metropolis* fostered an image of crisis by criticizing the planning establishment. Whyte was already a famous critic stemming from *The Organization Man* (1956), his landmark study that shifted the discourse on Cold War conformity, suburbanism, and corporate loyalty. In the pages of *Fortune*, Whyte and fellow contributors saw postwar planners as placating a middle-class hunger for the security of the suburbs. They also asserted that urban renewal worked at cross-purposes with the city by serving the interests of the commuter, the real-estate speculator, and the automobile at the expense of those of the citizen. An image problem resulted, as Whyte suggested in a period-appropriate piece titled "Are Cities Un-American?" Urban renewal, contributors argued, had rendered once-vibrant American cities sterile and lifeless. The collection concluded with "Downtown Is for People" by Jane Jacobs, which critiqued the perspective of planners who saw street life as a symptom of Necropolis, suggesting that Title I redevelopment only functioned to "deaden" places like New York.[1]

The Exploding Metropolis insisted that urban renewal failed as the result of any number of catalysts: crime, congestion, demographic shifts and racial/ethnic difference, public housing, suburbanization, and modern urban design. "Everybody, it would seem, is for the rebuilding of cities," Whyte wrote, "but this is not the same thing as *liking* cities." In fact, "most of the rebuilding under way and in prospect is being designed by people who don't like cities." New development on the outskirts of cities, the model for redevelopment and the preferred residence of planners like Moses, emerged as a target of disdain. Whyte noted that "sub-urbanization," as he pointedly termed it, unleashed an "assault on urbanism," a phrase taken from the paperback's subtitle. For Whyte, the mass suburban exodus threatened the sustainability of cities and rendered them volatile, foreshadowing the urban conflagrations of the following decade. Seymour Freedgood echoed this warning, writing that "the suburbanization of the countryside has plunged American big cities . . . into a time of crisis." The so-called urban crisis would become the frame through which critics viewed New York and other metropolitan areas in the 1960s.[2]

Although *The Exploding Metropolis* explored American urbanism as a whole, New York City—home to the Henry Luce publishing empire and thus *Fortune*—served a critical function within the narrative. Whyte's concern for "the popular image of the city" as "a place of decay, crime, of fouled streets, and of people who are poor or foreign or odd" read like the enduring stereotype of New York rather than a description of the ascendant sun-drenched cities of the South and Southwest. When Francis Bello argued in favor of banning that new urban "monster," the automobile, he was not so concerned with sprawling Houston, but with Manhattan's clogged arteries. Quasi-public authorities, the basis of Robert Moses's power, were critiqued as "a growing external bureaucracy" threatening the democratic city, and Daniel Seligman's "The Enduring Slums" held up Moses's beloved Lincoln Center as a prime example of poorly managed redevelopment. For her part, Jacobs utilized different local neighborhoods to illustrate the successes (in this case Midtown and Rockefeller Center) and failures (Park Avenue and Lincoln Center) of the walkable American city. By situating the city's renewal initiatives within its indictment of planning and redevelopment, *The Exploding Metropolis* directly linked New York with a national crisis.[3]

The inclusion of Jacobs, the only female contributor to the series, proved fortuitous for both herself and New York. In "Downtown Is for People" she rehearsed the ideas that would define *The Death and Life of Great American Cities*, a book that transformed the way civic-minded elites conceptualized the function of cities and challenged prevailing planning theory. Both works recognized that American urbanism was at a critical juncture in the age of Title I. Jacobs argued that downtown redevelopment projects in New York City and elsewhere would "set the character of the center of our cities for generations to come." These projects may be monumental, they may be aesthetically pleasing, Jacobs asserted, but they would also mean the death of the city. As a result of the remarkable sameness in downtown planning and a tendency to ignore public desire in the development of those plans, Jacobs predicted that cities would soon "have all the attributes of a well-kept dignified cemetery."[4]

Employing the narrative of Necropolis, Jacobs challenged the ideology and practice of planning "where buildings come first." She criticized the master planners' "scale models and birds-eye views" for ignoring the pedestrian perspective of the city, and argued that the only way to see how a city functioned was to "get out and walk." Such simple observation, however, became increasingly difficult in the modern landscape. The superblock design favored by Moses and his adherents elsewhere, with their emphasis on order, eliminated the delightful disorder of the street-level city. Jacobs charged that planners were intent on removing the "hustle and bustle of downtown"—in other words, the people—in order to replace it with a sterile colossus. Instead, the citizen played the key role in the future planning of cities, utilizing their unparalleled knowledge of city streets and focal points to enlighten practitioners on neighborhood needs. In contrast to authoritarian high modernism, Jacobs insisted that participant observation and engagement with the public would offer clues to the life of cities.[5]

By 1961 this ascendant narrative was a fully articulated attack on established planning practice. In the age of urban renewal, and fed by master planners, the old narrative saw the city rapidly decaying, a terminally ill patient requiring radical surgery. Slum clearance, master planning, and private redevelopment were the only prescription, and if the patient (New York) refused, then it would soon succumb to death. In her landmark text, Jacobs saw the death of cities in poor design and the security issues that resulted from it. She also attacked the ignorant omniscience of master planners like Moses who assumed expertise in all aspects of urban life. Successfully thwarting his image of the city, Jacobs suggested that a decade of problematic public policy started New York City on the long road of decline, if not onward to its death. Ironically, texts like *Death and Life* and the fates they detailed would provide fodder for conservative and market-oriented critics fully vested in what Jane Jacobs termed "the sacking of cities."[6]

· · · · · ·

In the late 1950s, Whyte's *Fortune* and the investigative reporting of Cook and Gleason constituted the most vocal Title I critiques. Yet the questions they raised commenced a shift in reportage on the limits of "renewal." In an otherwise celebratory issue titled "This Is New York," *Look* magazine pulled back the curtain on Moses, citing Title I's failure to eradicate the problems it sought to solve. The report, "Behind New York's Façade: Slums and Segregation," noted that "the housing projects that replace the old tenements often displace more people than the new buildings can accommodate." *Look* recognized that New York City's high-profile redevelopment plans like Lincoln Square focused on cultural, educational, and middle-class residential construction, and therefore did nothing to abate the problem of low-income tenement housing. Of the city's old tenements, the authors asserted, "If you are rich or lucky (or a tourist), you can spend quite a while in New York without ever seeing any of these scabrous buildings and rubble-strewn lots swarming with dark-skinned children"—an allusion to the demographic changes that coincided with Title I. By obscuring the plight of poor Puerto Ricans and blacks, the glimmering new construction rising across New York indeed functioned as a façade. The indictment of the concealed "ugly streak that runs the length of the island" fed the Necropolis-wrought-by-redevelopment narrative while adding a racial dimension soon fleshed out in subsequent slum ethnographies.[7]

James Baldwin, a native New Yorker and veteran chronicler of his Harlem neighborhood—up to that point in novel (*Go Tell It on the Mountain*, 1953), play (*The Amen Corner*, 1954), and essay ("The Harlem Ghetto" 1948 and "Notes of a Native Son" 1955) form—presented the most serious indictment of the practice of Title I in *Esquire*'s otherwise lily-white ironic and literary critique of New York at the beginning of the 1960s. In "Fifth Avenue, Uptown" (1960), Baldwin noted that "the projects in Harlem are hated. . . . They are hated almost as much as policemen, and this is saying a great deal. . . . The projects are hideous, of course, there being a law, apparently respected throughout the world, that popular housing shall be as cheerless as a prison. They are lumped all over Harlem, colorless, bleak, high, and revolting." Moses's municipal surgeons had failed to alleviate the structural barriers its residents encountered. "The people in the project certainly need [credit]," Baldwin wrote, "far more, indeed, than they ever needed the project." As he observed, Harlemites and black New Yorkers confronted limited choices. They were unwanted in the suburbs where the white victims of slum clearance—the Italians of East Harlem, for example—could begin anew, and the neighborhood only received a private project, Riverton in 1948, because Metropolitan Life's Stuyvesant Town development banned blacks. "The people who have managed to get off this block have only got as far as a more respectable ghetto," he noted with frustration. In Baldwin's estimation, the future of Harlem appeared bleak, an asylum for the political, social, and economic issues that power brokers would prefer to ignore. He prophesied the "exploding metropolises" of the decade—Harlem, Watts, Newark, and Detroit—writing that "the pressure within the ghetto causes the ghetto walls to expand, and this expansion is always violent."[8]

"Fifth Avenue, Uptown" exemplified the turn toward indicting planners and prevailing planning theory for the inequitable social outcomes of spatial transformation. Baldwin had an intimate connection with the area, and his analysis of the discriminatory logic behind Riverton spoke for the citizens of Harlem. As journalists focused on neighborhood demographics, both qualitatively and quantitatively, the story of urban renewal and its impact on communities became more personal and the resistance to it more effective. Articles like "Fifth Avenue, Uptown" built the bridge between the abstractions and statistics of Moses to the observable impact of change on a personal and neighborhood level. Baldwin focused on character development, providing a form and personality to the previously faceless citizen feeling the brunt of large-scale urban renewal. It was fitting, then, that Norman Podhoretz singled out Baldwin as a writer whose nonfiction was proving far more vital than his celebrated fiction. Although his literary musings relegated architecture and urban design to secondary status, personal narratives of decline became the building blocks in this new barricade against sweeping physical change.[9]

These salvos were indicative of the new literary reform movement vis-à-vis the state of cities and "slums," utilizing the tried-and-true pop methodology of earlier muckrakers (Cook and Gleason's "Shame of New York" was a conscious play on Lincoln Steffens's *The Shame of Cities* [1904]). Dan Wakefield ushered in the long-form slum ethnography with *Island in the City* (1959), originating from his volunteer work in East Harlem with the Catholic Worker. The book examined the area's demographic shift toward a Puerto Rican majority but also the neighborhood's structural and social alienation from the rest of New York City, what Wakefield called a "vast separation" and to which the title alluded. In part, this separation manifested itself physically. Tenements in the neighborhood were "dilapidated buildings . . . ghosts of the country's first waves of immigration." The streets were empty save for the dirty and exhaust-stained tenements, and the remarkable sameness stretched for blocks, adding to the neighborhoods' "blemished" character. Tenement interiors offered much of the same story. Wakefield found apartments without heat or hot water, crumbling walls, floors, and ceilings with holes "big enough for the biggest rats," and innumerable cockroaches.[10]

Yet Wakefield went beyond physical descriptions, seeking to dispel the "popular myth" that Puerto Ricans created New York City's slums rather than inherited them. Wakefield profiled dope pushers, reformed drug users, and the neighborhood advocates who helped them kick the habit; documented a vibrant Harlem street life; and explored Puerto Rican youth culture. In the case of East Harlem teenagers, he demonstrated how a local gang known as the Conservatives did its part to counteract neighborhood violence rather than perpetuate it. Challenging concurrent youth culture fears, Wakefield highlighted the Conservatives' work as community organizers and crime patrol, filling in for an apathetic municipal bureaucracy. While he recognized the "abstract good" of modern housing development, Wakefield criticized the administration of the program, citing the transient living of dislocated citizens. His ethnographic research revealed how despite the structural moat the city constructed around the island of East Harlem, Puerto Rican migrants built a community out of what they had on the street.[11]

At a time when historian Richard Hofstadter popularized the successes of an earlier *Age of Reform* (1955), new progressive critiques of American society like Wakefield's emerged from the wilderness of conformity and complacency. *Island in the City* was inspired by George Orwell's *Down and Out in Paris and London* (1933), a memoir/novel that detailed the author's travails in the slums of Europe's refined capitals. Wakefield "was following the same path in New York's premier slum, purposely going to live in the place so [he] could write about it authentically." Other popular investigations from the period included Rachel Carson's *Silent Spring* (1962) and Ralph Nader's *Unsafe at Any Speed* (1965), which spurred the environmental and consumer advocacy movements, respectively, and fostered dramatic political change. Betty Friedan in *The Feminine Mystique* (1963) and John Howard Griffin in *Black Like Me* (1961) used participant observation and privileged positions to reveal the experience of second-class citizenship among women and minorities in the era of second-wave feminism and civil rights. The growing discontent around slum clearance and redevelopment also required a national voice, and in this milieu of consciousness-raising, Jane Jacobs challenged planning's status quo.[12]

According to the consensus among urban and architectural historians, Jacobs shattered the dominant paradigm. In the process, the journalist and activist so transformed urban theory and the narrative of the city that her work became an essential planning text despite its limited guidelines for future development. Enamored with urban design, New York, and especially Greenwich Village after her arrival from Pennsylvania circa 1934, Jacobs traveled swiftly up the ladder of cultural criticism following World War II. Prior to the war, she wrote for popular newspapers and magazines including *Vogue* and the *Herald Tribune* as well as trade publications. *Architectural Forum* hired Jacobs in 1952 even though she had few credentials in architecture. Later, on assignment in urban renewal–era Philadelphia, Jacobs toured the city with Edmund Bacon, the master planner behind that city's transformation. To demonstrate the point of Philadelphia's renewal effort, Bacon showed Jacobs examples of both slums and slum clearance. At the "before" instance, an aged section of downtown with vibrant street life, Bacon noted without irony that this street was next in line for the bulldozer. In contrast, the "after" example consisted of an orderly modern megaproject. Jacobs took note of the area's emptiness and boredom. "Where are the people?" she asked Bacon. That question guided the attack that followed.[13]

At *Architectural Forum* Jacobs developed a reputation as a contrarian, suggesting at every opportunity that urban renewal and the modern aesthetic it prized ravaged cities. Most magazines adored Robert Moses, and *Architectural Forum*, the country's reigning authority on urban design, was no exception. When Jacobs questioned the efficacy of Title I, it stunned coworkers: this was a public program meant to save cities, not to mention one that showcased an innovative and fresh architectural style. In 1956, Jacobs raised more eyebrows, and her profile, with a scathing speech to the Conference on Urban Design at Harvard University's Graduate School of Design. Firmly wedded to the modern aesthetic, the Harvard institution had recently commissioned buildings by Le Corbusier and Minoru Yamasaki, of the late Pruitt-Igoe Houses in St. Louis and the World Trade Center in New York. The Bauhaus's Walter Gropius taught at Harvard as well. To an audience of those architects' admirers, Jacobs excoriated urban renewal and its modernist inclinations. She cited statistics on the displacement of people and small business—particularly in East Harlem, a neighborhood that attracted her attention as well thanks to a consultation with a local minister—as a contingency of urban renewal. Jacobs also emphasized the importance of the street in everyday urban life, an element that Le Corbusier and his adherents often dismissed. Ironically, the speech was well received, and drew the attention of notable urbanists including Whyte and Lewis Mumford. Whyte immediately tapped Jacobs to pen "Downtown Is for People" for *Fortune*.[14]

The article crafted an image of New York as Necropolis in attempt to undermine municipal surgeons and their power. Jacobs indicted planners for municipal malfeasance, and noted how their favored superblock design element emphasized order at the expense of the sidewalk, eliminating the disorderly automobiles, commercial establishments, and crowds that came with it. "They banish the street. They banish their function. They banish its variety," the critic charged. Removing the citizens from the public spaces of the city seemed paramount. Instead, Jacobs called for using the public sphere to guide the planning process, encouraging greater engagement between citizens and municipal surgeons.[15] Her insinuations sent shock waves through the planning and architectural establishment. Jaws dropped at the critique of Moses's Lincoln Center project, much beloved in architectural circles because it adhered to modernist design principles and featured work from international stylists like Eero Saarinen. The critical response to "Downtown Is for People" earned Jacobs a Rockefeller Foundation grant for a broader examination of urban life and redevelopment. With the award in hand, Jacobs commenced work on *The Death and Life of Great American Cities*.[16]

On the streets of New York, as the narrative of postwar New York City history goes, Jacobs supported her words with action. When Robert Moses unveiled plans to bisect Greenwich Village's beloved Washington Square Park with a freeway onramp, Jacobs helped organize the opposition that ultimately sunk the plan. She utilized the pages of downtown's alternative press, the young *Village Voice* in particular, and astutely enlisted local housewives and children in the protest that resulted in a public relations nightmare for Moses. In the "blighted" West Village, Jacobs pioneered urban resettlement, what would later be known as the process of "gentrification," investing in and rehabilitating a home on working-class Hudson Street. When the city drew up renewal plans for the area—a recent biographer suggests that Moses wanted payback for the Washington Square defeat—the Jacobs-led direct-action opposition not only successfully defeated Moses but also developed the alternative community plan the city implemented. Finally, the dramatic fight against Moses's Lower Manhattan Expressway—which would have destroyed the now-opulent SoHo neighborhood (then known as the "cast iron district" and later branded for its location "south of Houston Street")—solidified the image of Jacobs as a superhero waging war against authoritarian redevelopment.[17]

This spirited activism and the hunger for engagement translated into Jacobs's writing. "This book is an attack," she wrote on page one of *Death and Life of Great American Cities*, published in 1961. A specific type of planning, labeled as "modern," was the subject of that assault. Clear from the beginning, the models for "current city plan and rebuilding" were the Robert Moseses and the Le Corbusiers of urban bureaucracy, design, and architecture. It was also clear that in order to attack modern planning, Jacobs would also have to counteract the prevailing narrative of the city. Her experience at *Architectural Forum* and the publicity struggles she faced in the fight over Washington Square demonstrated that despite *The Exploding Metropolis* and Cook and Gleason's exposé, a strong bond still existed between the establishment press and the city's redevelopment regime—the former wedded to the latter's apparent service in the salvation of urban ills. *Death and Life*, then, offered a total rethinking of accepted urban thought, a philosophy "different and even opposite from those now taught in everything from schools of architecture and planning, the Sunday supplements and women's magazines." (The mention of the "Sunday supplements" was no coincidence, given Moses's frequent contributions to the *New York Times Magazine*.) Understanding that descriptions of Cosmopolis were not enough to halt the bulldozer, Jacobs countered the narrative of municipal surgeons with an image of the dying city wrought by their malfeasance.[18]

Much like her activism, the bulk of *Death and Life of Great American Cities* was devoted to the proposition of alternative planning principles: mixed uses as opposed to segregating residential, commercial, and industrial zones; more streets and sidewalks rather than eliminating them in favor of the plaza; infill rather than displacement; and diversity rather than order. Moses claimed that critics built nothing, but Jacobs argued that nothing needed to be built. Here the critic noted that much of what makes cities so attractive is already there—cities just need nurturing. It was certainly a message that subsumed the inherent paternalism of master planners; a message glaringly laissez-faire compared to the massive public funds and corporate welfare invested in urban renewal. Its limited government conservatism resonated in the wake of Cook and Gleason's revelations of municipal corruption.[19]

The accessibility of Jacobs's work also contributed to its reception and influence. The critic chose to examine the reality of everyday urban life, selecting the obvious and mundane and explicating its significance—like showing how something as commonplace as people staring out of windows functioned as a neighborhood policing mechanism, the so-called eyes-on-the-street theory of surveillance and thus safety. This stood in contrast to Moses and others who spoke of the chaos and sickness of city life and who worked to impose order on perceived disorder. Jacobs spelled this out from the start: "In setting forth different principles, I shall mainly be writing about common, ordinary things," which included safe city streets, the creation and regeneration of "slums," and "what, if anything, is a city neighborhood." Street life, parks, and crime were topics with public familiarity. Readers were more likely to comprehend the sidewalk ballet and the culture of the corner store than the logic behind the utopian fantasy of Le Corbusier's Radiant City or Ebenezer Howard's Garden City—visions that Jacobs argued had influenced modern planners. Jacobs's accessible writing style—distinctly lacking the paternal sanctimony of Moses—added to her appeal and fluidity.[20]

Throughout the pages of *Death and Life*, Jacobs examined a number of American metropolitan centers. But she eschewed the emergent cities of the South and Southwest like Houston and Los Angeles except to note their penchant for criminal activity and to argue that decentralization did not ensure security. Instead, the older urban form of the country's northeastern and midwestern metropolises—the "great American cities" of the title—attracted the bulk of Jacobs's attention and analysis. Select neighborhoods emerged as testaments to her philosophy on the workings of urban life. Philadelphia's Rittenhouse Square, Chicago's Back-of-the-Yards, and Boston's North End—a district then receiving the participant observer treatment by sociologist Herbert Gans, for what would become *The Urban Villagers* (1962)—appeared as supporting characters in Jacobs's thesis.[21]

New York City and Greenwich Village and the narratives they portended served as the book's feature players, however. Growing up in Scranton, Pennsylvania, Jacobs, an ambitious and creative woman in an era of sex and gender discrimination, saw New York as Cosmopolis, and its open neighborhood of Greenwich Village in particular as a destination. The Village was Jacobs's home, and the bohemian quarter possessed the elements her spatial theory favored: a diversity of class, race, and ethnicity; mixed uses including low-density residential areas with commercial overlays and the working-class waterfront filled with thirsty stevedores to fill the area's taverns; a well-used park, Washington Square; small blocks and streets that did not adhere to Manhattan's rigid gridiron design; and a dynamic street life. Other New York neighborhoods, like Harlem, served as useful case studies for Jacobs as well, but it was the Village that became the exemplar for how a neighborhood could and should work.[22]

Accordingly, planners engaged in the systematic destruction of these traditional neighborhood attributes. As with the design of suburban developments, postwar planners admired the decentralization that birthed the profession in the first place. Reformers since the turn of the century emphasized the segregation of uses in planning. By midcentury, zoning for residential, commercial, and manufacturing was de rigueur, and only in older cities like New York did the preplanning layout persist, and even there only in neighborhoods like Greenwich Village and the Lower West Side. With Stuyvesant Town in the 1940s, multifamily housing took on a new design, one that enhanced the amount of fresh air and sunlight apartments received. These towers, while rising higher than the four- and five-floor walk-ups they replaced, maintained or even decreased population density because they left a much smaller footprint. Surrounding the footprints—commonly pinwheel, X-shaped, or linear in design—planners placed grass and greenspace in imitation of suburban lawns and parks. Form followed function: residents would recreate on the parkland because there was parkland to recreate on. Blocks of city land were further consolidated into so-called superblocks that interrupted the street grid at various and often inconvenient points. The grand designs of Le Corbusier and other modern visionaries were utopian by definition, and could function as a whole only under the direction of the state. City planners, however, went about injecting these schemes in small doses (relative to Le Corbusier's plans for Paris and the Radiant City but within the context of American cities, master planning was still clean-slate planning), creating chaos in their attempts to establish order through physical improvements.[23]

Jacobs noted this new mode of living based on order and conformity sacrificed the delights of urban life. Tower-in-a-park construction, while indeed offering better light and air than its predecessor, did little more than showcase the conceit of architects and master planners. The buildings shout " 'Look what I made!' Like a great, visible ego it tells of someone's achievement. But as to how the city works, it tells . . . nothing but lies." Designed to make urban living functional, decentralized apartment towers resulted in urban dysfunction and disorder. With commerce zoned out, the empty space provided no reason for pedestrian nonresidents to pass through. Jacobs related an anecdote about the impact of modern design on the East Harlem neighborhood from one tenant's perspective: "Nobody cared what we wanted when they built this place. They threw our houses down and pushed us here and pushed our friends somewhere else. We don't have a place around here to get a cup of coffee or a newspaper even, or borrow fifty cents. Nobody cared what we need. But the big men come and look at that grass and say, 'Isn't it wonderful! Now the poor have everything.'" As Jacobs interpreted it, "There is a quality even meaner than outright ugliness or disorder, and this meaner quality is the dishonest mask of pretended order, achieved by ignoring or suppressing the real order that is struggling to exist and be served." This passage highlighted the disconnect between planners and the indigent they purported to serve—a sign that urban renewal was failing in its mission to combat inequality.[24]

Planning's desire for order resulted from narratives of urban fear and insecurity. Jacobs set forth to correct that image from the first chapter of *Death and Life*. "When people say that a city, or a part of it, is dangerous or is a jungle what they mean primarily is that they do not feel safe on the sidewalks," wrote the critic. She admitted that crime was a part of urban and street life, but the sidewalk's reputation as a site of random criminality was a self-fulfilling prophecy. As Whyte later defined it, "fear proves itself" in public space. Urban anxieties begat security apparatuses which begat more fear. The more people fear the street, the less likely they are to use the sidewalk, which results in less pedestrian traffic and thus, in Jacobs's theory, less safe streets. The push for order and continuity through design removed this crucial lens that preserved sidewalk safety. For Jacobs, it was not the police department that patrolled an area and eradicated urban crime; rather, it was the neighborhood that surveilled itself through pedestrian traffic, watchful eyes taking in the scene from above, and commercial establishments that generated traffic throughout the day and put even more eyes on the street.[25]

In the process of correcting Moses's fear imagery, *Death and Life of Great American Cities* demonstrated the centrality of security concerns to the narrative of the postwar city. As Lewis Mumford argued, Jacobs's obsession with surveillance inferred that the dying "great American cities" were inherently unsafe places. "This reveals an overruling fear of living in the big city she so openly adores, and, as all New Yorkers know, she has considerable reasons to fear," he wrote in a stinging *New Yorker* review. Despite defending New York City against charges of hazard and peril, Jacobs popularized a new image of Necropolis, one whose fatalism was on par with the message she sought to dispel. Its charged title signaled the impending death of New York: if citizens allowed master planners like Robert Moses to fulfill their visions, then all that gave cities life could fall under the blade of the bulldozer. Jacobs understood that order-obsessed planners would not cease their work until the city had all the charm, security, and conformity of placeless suburbia. The book's aggressive sentiment, its forceful argument, its compelling prose, and its insistence that the end was nigh signaled an urgency that current practice must change *now* or the city might cease to exist.[26]

Large-scale construction projects, especially highways, continued in the years following *Death and Life*'s release, but Jacobs's theory commenced an evolutionary shift from municipal surgery to community advocacy. Whereas Moses proceeded quickly from plans to development with most of his projects, the New York City planning process integrated community participation and further checks and balances. The expected expertise of the planner shifted from a mix of architect, engineer, and designer to that of communicator. As Paul Davidoff articulated in "Advocacy and Pluralism in Planning" (1965), "urban politics, in an era of increasing government activity in planning and welfare, must balance the demands for ever-increasing central bureaucratic control against the demands for increased concern for the unique requirements of local specialized interests. The welfare of all and the welfare of minorities are both deserving of support: Planning must be so structured and so practiced as to account for this unavoidable bifurcation of the public interest." While architects and theorists continued to dream of the utopian landscape of harmony and community, advocacy supplanted physical design in the planner's toolbox.[27]

Jacobs's book also altered the dynamic of urban political economy, particularly in New York. As Necropolis became associated with modern design, a premium was placed on the types of architecture and urban form that Jacobs glorified. Beginning in the 1950s, areas of New York City witnessed an influx of neopioneers "settling" neighborhoods otherwise deemed blighted by the local real estate regime. Greenwich Village, as noted, was long home to New York's bohemian milieu. For much of its modern history, from Henry James and Emma Goldman to Irving Howe and James Baldwin, the neighborhood served as the salon of the city's intellectual vanguard and cultural avant-garde. After World War II, demand for real estate and an influx of professionals and white-collar "experts" forced the intellectually rich but financially insecure to search elsewhere for affordable living quarters. The migration rippled outward from the Village in each direction, and even across the East River into Brooklyn. Historian Suleiman Osman has dubbed these outerborough settlers "brownstoners" after their architectural and urban form fetishes. They were the "artists, lawyers, bankers, and other white-collar workers" who staked a claim, first in Brooklyn Heights beginning in the 1940s and then in the surrounding areas victimized by industrial capital migration. Branded with a historical noms de guerre like Cobble Hill and Carroll Gardens, these neighborhoods constituted the archipelago of districts that came to be known as "Brownstone Brooklyn" in the postindustrial era, and its residents brought the same kind of exclusionary verve to regulating local settlement and development as the despised suburbs and their restrictive covenants and homeowners' associations. Inspired by critics and activists engaged in the attack on planning, the brownstoners "championed a new urban ideal" in theory and practice that set the tone for postwar urban gentrification and neoliberal redevelopment.[28]

Jacobs served as a de facto spiritual advisor for the second wave of this back-to-the-city movement. In many ways, *Death and Life of Great American Cities* was the brownstoner's Tao. While Jacobs offered a complicated critique of planning and city design, upper- and upper-middle-class pioneers relied on a crude interpretation of vital neighborhood living. As Osman writes, "it was the simple rather than complex pastoral tropes that more often resonated with her new urban middle-class readers." Securing a home on a pedestrian-friendly, historically authentic mixed-use block, for example, superseded the need to preserve the kind of awkward class diversity Jacobs cloyingly advocated in her narrative. This minimal reading was aided by the remarkable similarity between Jacobs's New York story and that of the second-wave brownstoner. When she arrived in New York, Jacobs settled in Greenwich Village. Later, as her career evolved, the Jacobses moved a short distance from the neighborhood to Hudson Street in the West Village. While "Greenwich Village" and "West Village" have been used interchangeably, the West Village and Greenwich Village at the time of Jacobs's writing featured qualitatively different political economies. Most notably, Jacobs's West Village was a working-class hub, populated by stevedores working the west-side docks in the twilight of New York City's autonomous port industry. Jacobs celebrated the longshoremen and their drinking habits in passages on the White Horse Tavern and the importance of continuous neighborhood use, just as she outlined the importance of residents from seemingly all walks of life. Yet there were few mechanisms in place to preserve working-class jobs, much less residences, in the postwar economic restructuring that occurred in American cities. If plans were put forth to retrofit the west-side docks for containerization, the proposal would have faced considerable community backlash, not unlike the fight over the Westway highway project in the 1970s and 1980s. As such, the docks and warehouses of the West Village, as with Brownstone Brooklyn's industrial concerns, would be shuttered and repurposed within her lifetime.[29]

These phenomena reveal the limits of Jacobs's planning theory for policy and development practice. Much of *Death and Life*'s allure may have stemmed from its allusions to everyday life and accessible prose, but Jacobs's conservative argument appealed to political elites and grassroots citizens frustrated with state planning. As urbanism became associated with progressive politics and values distinct from socially conservative suburban or rural districts, Jacobs evolved into an icon of activism and community planning. Yet when it first appeared, *Death and Life*'s condemnation of the welfare state received a warm embrace from torchbearers of the New Right, most notably William F. Buckley Jr., who placed Jacobs in his canon of conservative thought. In this era of modernist visioning, Moses and master planners were the radicals. They advocated an active state (to fund private development at least) in the hope of transforming American life. In contrast, Jacobs's attitude toward urban development seemed laissez-faire to say the least. Although her work inspired a generation of "new urbanists"—in effect clean-slate utopian planners designing communities from scratch—Jacobs imagined that neighborhoods like Greenwich Village developed, for lack of a better term, organically, or with little to no state intervention and planning. Jacobs proposed no social programs nor presented any grand vision beyond the idealized Greenwich Village community. Outside of her state critique, Jacobs's politics blurred: she embraced urban life, she vocally protested the Vietnam War and was part of a larger antiestablishment struggle in the 1960s, and she took pride in being a writer in an era inhospitable to career women, pausing only to take on the "housewife" moniker when it made good press for her opposition campaigns. At its essence, though, *Death and Life of Great American Cities* played off the inherent resistance to change in American culture.[30]

More importantly, Jacobs shaped a political debate over the role of the state in combating so-called slums and urban poverty that captivated Left and Right alike in the 1960s. At the end of the decade, Buckley wrote, "Jane Jacobs would never classify herself as a conservative . . . [but] she argues a thesis concerning the city which is conservative by general understanding, an oversimplification of which is that there are profound human and aesthetic satisfactions to be had in a city that grows as it is disposed to grow, free of the superimpositions and the great allocations of the planners." Jacobs would not have identified as a conservative, but with a vision at once liberal—celebrating diversity and the commonly understood dreadful city—and at the same time, as Buckley pointed out, conservative, Jacobs established a political and economic fluidity that allowed successors to manipulate her theories however they saw fit, making nearly any kind of urban development, even the kind of projects she fought against, seem "Jacobsesque." The attack on the state further ensured inequitable development in the years to come, and as conservative commentators like Buckley appropriated her language on organic development and neighborhood safety, it opened the door for municipal neoliberal redevelopment policy.[31]

Jacobs's purpose was to frame New York and its dense mixed-use neighborhoods as Cosmopolis. She wished, like White, to draw people into New

York City, but whom it drew had implications for social and economic justice, a question she refused to engage directly. Her economic writings in particular spoke to an ascendant conservative vision of growth. *The Economy of Cities* (1969) furthered Jacobs's project of liberating the city and economic development from the reins of the state. The text creatively rethought economic development in the same way *Death and Life* considered urban redevelopment. Prior to its publication, the accepted narrative of human economic history understood that developments in agriculture begat the clustering of clans and thus cities. According to Jacobs, however, urbanization fostered ancient productive innovation, establishing central hubs for the development of tools and knowledge that allowed systematic agriculture to flourish. The salient development of the Neolithic Age, then, was "sustained, interdependent, creative city economies that made possible many new kinds of work, agriculture among them." This, in turn, was relevant for contemporary cities, for "a city grows by a process of gradual diversification and differentiation of its economy, starting from little or nothing more than its initial export work and the suppliers of that work." In essence, Jacobs put forth the argument that the clustering of population in dense cities like New York, along with competition wrought by free enterprise, spurred creative innovation that contributed to not only the economy at large but the growth and sustainability of the city as well. Jacobs's theory offered a roadmap for the emergent postindustrial economy, finding an audience among leading social scientists in an age when the discourse on creative innovation in the field of information technology reached a fever pitch. First with *Death and Life*, then with *The Economy of Cities* and *Cities and the Wealth of Nations* (1984), Jacobs catalogued the inherent agency of communities and private individuals in shaping cities and local economies in the face of municipal authority and corporate conformity. These principles worked effortlessly in concert with emergent neoclassical economics and libertarian ideology.[32]

· · · · · ·

Over the next few decades, as New York and other American cities cycled through decline and rebirth, Jacobs's legacy underwent a process of narrative embellishment. In the classic depiction, Jacobs the writer and activist was pitted against Robert Moses the builder, the untouchable New York City bureaucrat orchestrating the city's redevelopment regime and stand-in for the planning establishment. In the early historiography Moses wholly transformed New York into a sterile modernist dystopia that favored car-loving commuters and relegated the poor to the barren streetless superblocks where he set his housing "barracks." Indictments of Moses solidified an authoritarian image indubitably responsible for New York's "fall" in the 1960s and 1970s. But as critics of Jacobs's fight against Moses are wont to point out, the writer/activist received no mention in *The Power Broker* (1974) (Caro recognized the power of "The Shame of New York," however). This recent scholarship suggests a more complicated reality. Historians contend that the time has come for a reevaluation of Moses's work, thus validating the power broker's common refrain: the ends justified the means. Historian Samuel Zipp argues that Moses's urban renewal program differentiated New York from its Rust Belt counterparts and ensured that the city remained a global financial and cultural capital. In an important revelation, Zipp writes that street-level opposition to Moses in New York City predated Jacobs's activism and writing. Her place in the annals of urban renewal resistance was more the consequence and not the cause of the Title I struggle. Her eloquent attack on planning via imagery of a dying city was another story.[33]

Popular works have sought to correct this wave of Moses revisionism. Anthony Flint and Roberta Brandes Gratz reify the narrative of postwar New York redevelopment as a great struggle between the powerful and seemingly unstoppable forces of top-down planning embodied by Moses versus the organic bottom-up paradigm embodied by Jacobs. Flint and Gratz cast Jacobs as the hero and effectively attribute the city's recent rebirth to her literal and ideological victory over Moses in the 1960s. The Rockefeller Foundation, which funded her early work, has similarly canonized Jacobs through the annual Jane Jacobs Medal. The prize, honoring "those whose creative uses of the urban environment build a more diverse, dynamic and equitable city," has been awarded to an assorted group of urbanists, from community planners to high-profile actors operating within the public-private partnership model. The range of honorees testifies to Jacobs's broad but confused legacy.[34]

Jacobs's fluidity emerged from the shifting political winds of the 1960s. The attack on welfare-state planning transcended the simple dichotomy of American politics, featuring critiques from the New Left ("The Port Huron Statement" [1962]), the "vital center" of the postwar liberal consensus (*The Exploding Metropolis*), and the libertarian Right (Martin Anderson's *The Federal Bulldozer*). Jacobs's critique incorporated themes from each faction, from the community empowerment aims of the New Left to the antistatist critique of Anderson. Yet Jacobs was solidly part of a broad liberal–New Left coalition reacting against an amorphous establishment that consisted of not only authoritarian planners like Robert Moses but architects of the postwar welfare state, southern segregationists, Cold War imperialists, the military-industrial complex, and corporate CEOs seeking a new liberal—in the classical sense—restructured economy. Jacobs and others channeled this discontent into vocal opposition to the Vietnam War, free speech movements on American campuses, and a nearly global revolutionary moment in 1968. Jacobs, for her part, participated in these protests, and even relocated to Toronto to protect her family from the draft. According to geographer David Harvey, the movements of the 1960s saw an intrusive state in need of reform, "and on that, the neoliberals could easily agree."[35]

This ultimately speaks to the significant limitation of Jacobs's attack on planning: the lack of progressive vision and the absence of a sustainable, replicable model for urban economic development. Jacobs's progressive social and cultural politics masked her most potent economic politics, at least in the elaboration of her theories by Richard Florida and other neoliberal thinkers in the twenty-first century. Florida, like Jacobs, managed to tap into the development zeitgeist, but their innovative theories, though grounded in pragmatism, have failed to translate effortlessly across space and place. Jacobs and Florida specialized in observation, examining how cities work and economies develop, but they failed to provide a coherent and adaptable vision for said development. Their conclusions put the onus on communities rather than on themselves. In the end, the community planning of Jacobs and the "creative-class" development of Florida functioned and continue to function as convenient façades for old-fashioned capitalist creative destruction, ensuring the accommodation of the expanding global neoliberal economy with great social costs.[36]

In the annals of postwar New York, the place of Jacobs belongs squarely in cultural criticism. Her writings warrant credit for highlighting the vibrant and dynamic life of the city in the face of unmitigated sprawl and fears of slum cancer. However, *Death and Life* and *The Exploding Metropolis*, among other redevelopment critiques, constituted a turning point in planning rhetoric, utilizing the impending death of New York to discredit urban renewal and municipal government. Their assessment of civil servants like Moses condemned the seemingly benevolent welfare state—urban renewal originally promised some form of social uplift—and tarnished public policy. The state's once proactive role in subsidized and affordable housing development declined after the 1960s. In addition, the lack of a social program in *Death and Life* allowed the work to serve as a primer on the gentrification that has increasingly priced out the lower and working classes of American cities. As the case of Jacobs indicates, the state of postrenewal New York City played a vital role in the political realignment of the 1960s. Reforming and remaking American cities—appropriating spaces left for dead by the establishment—were central to the New Left movement of the sixties (consider the extensive literature devoted to cities in the Port Huron Statement or the Black Panthers' neighborhood programs in Oakland). Jacobs represented the intellectual arm of these interests invested in the future of American urbanism and the future of New York City, a group that employed narratives of decline to that end.[37] As a decade of consensus concluded and a decade of social consciousness commenced, Jacobs ushered in a brief age of reform around the fate of cities, offsetting the urban crisis if only for a moment, that is, until fully dismantling the welfare state became the primary objective within an emergent political movement.

Part III **The Other New York**

Intellectuals in Necropolis, 1961–1967

. . . .

5 Farewell to the Universal City

By the 1960s, New York City no longer appealed the generation of Old Left intellectuals who had weathered the Great Depression, World War II, and the restrictive political culture of the Cold War. They saw the city as in decline, so much so that it distinguished their urban politics from an emergent New Left. In fact, the themes running through the Old Left's writings on New York City forged an alliance—at least in the discourse on cities—with ascendant conservative trends, both the neo and New varieties. The Left's vanguard, which included Greenwich Village migrants like Jane Jacobs, painted a bleak picture of New York, but did so with purpose: to inform and warn of the city's impending fall at the hands of irresponsible bureaucrats and elites, and to offer pragmatic responses to the urban crisis. They sought to salvage Cosmopolis by confronting the bulldozer. In contrast, the Left's rear guard critics saw the city's death as an inevitable casualty of postwar political change.

The "New York Intellectuals," predominantly native Jews educated at City College and committed to an anti-Stalinist version of international socialism, had played a part in American politics and culture since the 1930s, huddling around journals of opinion and reportage like *Partisan Review* and *Commentary*.[1] In 1954, Irving Howe cofounded a new journal called *Dissent*. Within a few years, the New Left controlled its pages—as well as American campuses—with a style that disillusioned many of Howe's fellow travelers. Michael Harrington and other socialist intellectuals, scholars like C. Wright Mills, and Students for a Democratic Society (SDS) defined this group, and it became the driving force in progressive politics in the 1960s. While they turned on, the frustrated Old Left tuned out or turned right. The New York Intellectuals completed their fracturing by the end of the decade, diverging into the realms of intellectual neoconservatism and the New Right political culture as embodied in the ascendancy of Barry Goldwater and Ronald Reagan. Even though Howe remained committed to the cause of social democracy, he often felt frustrated by the politics and practice of SDS and others.[2]

These political and intellectual factions converged in the Summer 1961 issue of Howe's journal, which presented a comprehensive examination of New York City at the dawn of a transformative decade. Titled simply "New York, N.Y.," it offered a significant contribution to the discourse around the city in this period, for as sociologist Herbert Gans recognized within its pages, the intellectual was in the process of supplanting the municipal surgeon as the key force in urban redevelopment. How the intellectuals in the *Dissent* orbit addressed New York City's problems highlighted the nascent ideological fractures between the rear guard and the vanguard, even if the gulf was not readily apparent at the time.[3] Contributors tied to the ascendant "Movement" of the 1960s demonstrated their desire to reclaim an increasingly decaying city, but Howe, sociologist Daniel Bell, and cultural critic/playwright Lionel Abel infused their contributions with a sentimental nostalgia that celebrated the New York City that shaped their intellectual development in the 1930s and 1940s. In the process, these "New Criticism" stalwarts, who had their fingers on the cultural pulse of New York for nearly three decades, succumbed to Necropolis, turning their backs on their once-beloved hometown.

The break among intellectuals consummated a profound shift in the image of fear and decline. In the 1950s, critics concerned themselves with the physical sustainability of the city. Robert Moses wrote of urban renewal's preparation of New York City for postwar prosperity. Jane Jacobs and facilitators of the attack on planning also feared the physical sustainability of New York in the wake of slum clearance. The physically defined Necropolis was inherently tied to social change and the anxieties that grew out of those changes, but prescriptions altered public policy related to the physical landscape: zoning, urban renewal, preservation, and so on. In the 1960s, anxieties about personal safety and security, tied wholeheartedly to social problems rather than physical decay, came to define New York as Necropolis. Crime, despite a relatively stable murder rate, emerged as the primary concern, as did fears of a "spiritual decay" in New York.[4] Rear-guard intellectuals felt a sense of unease in the changing city, representing a loss of the "universal access" their cultural and political liberalism, in addition to their working-class Jewish upbringing, afforded them in ethnic and racial enclaves.[5] Their safety concerns, coupled with complaints about the municipal welfare system and its bureaucratic failure, fed fears of the city's "ungovernability," a New York-specific term coined by one of their own.[6] High culture appropriated Necropolis, and thus cemented the popular image of New York that would be ubiquitous by decade's end.

In the previous decade, a cadre of predominantly Jewish literary critics governed New York's intellectual community, as they had since emerging from City College during the Great Depression. Between 1960 and 1980, however, a fissure occurred within the group. Prominent New York intellectuals included anti-Stalinist literary critics Lionel Trilling and Irving Howe, sociologists Daniel Bell and Nathan Glazer, journalists and policy wonks Irving Kristol and Norman Podhoretz, and novelist Saul Bellow. In the 1930s and 1940s they operated out of the pages of leftist journals like *Partisan Review*. During the early 1950s when Nixon, McCarthy, and Kennedy sniffed out anything fragrantly left of the consensus "vital center," these critics proudly let their radical flag fly. Irving Howe and Lewis Coser even founded *Dissent: A Quarterly of Socialist Opinion* at the height of McCarthyist hysteria. New York, with an established political and cultural vanguard centered in bohemian Greenwich Village, remained a site of political freedom during the Cold War, and the Village ethos catered to a radical critique of the establishment and suburban society.[7]

A counterculture emerged in the 1960s: a new political Left that took hold in bohemian neighborhoods and college campuses across the country. New York City, with the Village and various universities, was no exception. The Intellectuals suddenly faced fresh competition in the marketplace of ideas, including voices from the New Left and the New Right (William F. Buckley's Young Americans for Freedom party formed in 1960). Historians argue that these emergent cultural and political movements left the Intellectuals disillusioned and frustrated. While the Old Left critiqued American society, it hardly advocated a counterculture, and the appearance of such contributed to the fracturing. Most disdained the Left's vanguard as well as the expanding welfare state under President Johnson's Great Society. These "neoconservatives," as Michael Harrington coined them, retreated to *Public Interest* (founded by Irving Kristol and Daniel Bell) and *Commentary*, under the stewardship of a reformed Norman Podhoretz. A few critics fell in with the new conservatism centered at William F. Buckley's *National Review*.[8] The intellectual community realigned as ascendant critics across the political spectrum competed for the public consciousness, and New York City, with its exceptional assortment of voices and an increasingly troubled image, played a feature role in that shift.

In its premiere issue, editors of *Dissent* described themselves as "independent radicals bound together by common values and ideas." The founders took umbrage with "the bleak atmosphere of conformism that pervades the political and intellectual life of the United States."[9] By 1961, the journal remained committed to this mission. Its masthead featured a balanced mix of old (e.g., Howe, Coser, and Joseph Buttinger) and new (e.g., Michael Harrington and Norman Mailer), and contributors to the Summer issue reflected that balance: Daniel Bell, Howe, and Lionel Abel alongside Mailer, Harrington, Herbert Gans, and Paul Goodman, whose *Growing Up Absurd* was a must-read in New Left circles.[10] Along these lines, the vanguard confronted New York City's problems with pragmatic goals, while the rear guard retreated into nostalgic portraits of a lost Cosmopolis.[11]

The "New York, N.Y." issue acknowledged and affirmed the city's perceived postwar crisis. By the end of the 1950s, a media market existed for New York narratives, and the Summer 1961 issue followed suit. By then it seemed that the public gravitated toward tales of how and when, as contributor Edward T. Chase riffed, "New York Could Die."[12] Tellingly, Howe and the editors sought to increase *Dissent*'s reach and readership, as the Summer 1961 issue's run was the largest—selling 14,000 copies—and costliest in the journal's young history.[13] With topical articles running the gamut from public housing and the automobile scourge to jazz and juvenile delinquency, the Summer 1961 issue proposed "a critical and, often, constructive picture of the city as drawn by people deeply attached to it." Despite divergent points of view, the editors recognized a common layer running through the issue. Each contributor, they wrote, held in common "a strong feeling, even love, for New York and evidence a common sadness over its decline and its difficulties."[14] It was the manifestation of this sadness in the pages that followed that highlighted the intellectual community's conflicted ideologies.

In his review of Paul and Percival Goodman's utopian vision of urban reorganization, *Communitas* (1947), Herbert Gans, an important scholarly figure within the concurrent urban renewal debate, alluded to the differing visions of the city that governed the special issue.[15] When it was published in 1947, *Communitas*, reflecting the Goodman brothers' anarchist leanings, envisioned a radical urban transformation based on a shared common culture and reinforced by active public spaces, community planning, and a reformed meaning of labor. The Goodmans lampooned the looming era of conspicuous consumption and illustrated alternatives grounded in communitarian self-determination, foretelling the narratives of Gans and Jacobs in the 1960s. This vision proved antithetical to the prevailing planning ideology, as represented by Title I. Even so, the book arrived on the scene when it appeared that the total remaking of American cities was a distinct possibility. As the critique of authoritarian redevelopment intensified, *Communitas* earned a reissue and a revised edition in 1960, rendering the Goodmans' proposal even more pertinent.[16]

Gans argued that the publication of *Communitas* was a turning point in planning theory. He suggested that the Goodmans' "goal-based" vision tilted the profession toward the theorist, with the struggle over urban redevelopment pitting the planner against the intellectual. Planners transformed physical space at the expense of the city's social and economic realms, but the intellectual, in contrast, utilized a goal-oriented approach that "determines the public and private goals of the community, ranks them in priority, and finds the best means for their achievement from among all available resources, human as well as physical." Ideological and utopian impulses drove *Communitas*, yet by 1961 the impulses influenced and enlightened city planning at a time when the profession struggled to find a solution for the urban crisis.[17] Gans validated goal-oriented ideology as a practical response to New York's problems, imploring intellectuals to continue to tackle the urban question in the same way that the Goodmans, Whyte, and Jacobs had. And the vanguard at *Dissent* toed that line.

The inclusion of architectural critic Stephen Zoll testified to Jacobs's growing influence in development theory. In "Let There Be Blight" he echoed her depiction of the West Village down to the street ballet and sense of community that transcended race and class. "The streets here are dotted with an amazing display of urban diversity and lively activities," he wrote in praise of the neighborhood. Filled with stores and residences of various design and era, the Village's "separate features, the bad and the worst, the good and the surprising, are mingled inextricably in a community, that is a rare and valuable part of a city." That inimitable quality along with its recent gentrification allowed the area to undergo renewal without the aid of the state. "Because the price of real estate has been low [in the West Village], the area has accommodated both people of means who wanted to remodel and tenants content with space in which they were not overcrowded. . . . It is a process that took a great deal of time and has achieved a solid stability. In the best sense, one can say that *this* is urban renewal."[18] It was Jacobs's vision of rehabilitation via community involvement, through and through.

For the most part, *Dissent*'s vanguard found ailments arising from New York's postwar redevelopment regime and its dramatic transformation of the city. Whereas Moses invoked cancer to characterize the problem of the slums, critics like Edward T. Chase and Paul Goodman saw New York City as a circulatory system of clogged arteries and capillaries—vessels built and fed by Moses's grand design for the metropolitan area. Until the city finally sacked the Lower Manhattan Expressway plans in the late sixties, it seemed possible that New York would be crisscrossed by ever-newer freeway arterials. Chase prescribed a healthy mass-transit system to counteract the allure of the car, arguing that such an innovation would trickle down and create "in its wake better housing, better schools, a more heterogeneous and better balanced urban residential population."[19] He was one of many critics who echoed a common refrain: Moses's failure to address New York's mass-transit needs contributed to the city's "fall."[20]

In "Banning Cars from Manhattan," the Goodmans offered up goal-oriented yet utopian solutions for the automobile scourge.[21] They proposed the removal of "all cars" from the island, "except buses, small taxis, vehicles for essential services (doctor, police, sanitation, vans, etc.), and the trucking used in light industry" in the name of "common sense."[22] Peripheral parking would keep automobiles at city's edge. They planned to retain the island's busiest crosstown streets and half of the existing north–south avenues. Taxis and delivery trucks could access these thoroughfares, but "bridge buildings" would straddle the roadways—a scheme seemingly out of Le Corbusier. The plan sought to transform Manhattan's famous gridiron design, dating from 1811, into 1,200- to 1,600-foot superblocks—the equivalent of ten square city blocks—that would theoretically foster the communitarian spirit at the heart of their planning ideology.[23] The Goodmans and Chase expressed a progressive vision of New York insisting that change could and should happen—indeed, it was imperative to save the city.[24]

New York City's demographic shift, which had ignited a debate about the role of newcomers in perpetuating "problems," also caught the vanguard's attention. E. B. White's image of Cosmopolis and understanding of New York as a site of irreplaceable innovation, ingenuity, and excitement united *Dissent* writers welcoming the city's racial and ethnic migration. As White argued, migrants provided the city's intoxicating allure. Yet for some commentators in the 1950s and 1960s, or at least their sources, these migrants were destroying the city. Newly arrived Puerto Ricans and blacks from the rural South, such jeremiads suggested, exacerbated the growth of slums, drove the white tax base from the city, disproportionally contributed to an emergent narcotics supply and demand, disproportionally participated in violent crime and juvenile gang activity, and bloated welfare rolls.[25] Racialized rhetoric was perhaps more of a national than a New York City phenomenon, but in the local press, blacks and Puerto Ricans became convenient scapegoats for the city's financial woes and perceived social crisis.[26]

Dissent contributors countered this narrative through ethnographies of Central Harlem, El Barrio (East/Spanish Harlem), and local youth culture. For the most part, they argued that white society's pathological discrimination against blacks and Puerto Ricans constituted a structural roadblock in the path of upward mobility. As Dan Wakefield highlighted a few years prior, New York City's Puerto Rican population wallowed in uptown misery. Employing autobiographical experience to counter white critics' connection between Necropolis and postwar demographic change, Eileen Diaz's "A Puerto Rican in New York" argued that migrants longed to merge with the national culture only to find, upon arrival, the road to acceptance "complicated by color." "Economic and social discrimination," along with other barriers, led these migrants down a path of hardship and despair. "In the dope-pusher streets of New York there is no hope of Eden or promise of abundant life, only small, dead hours of escape between hunts, between thefts," Diaz wrote in Beat-like style. "The young girl puts on a starched white blouse and goes out to sell herself. She escapes the slavery of her life in vague dreams and the warm sleep into which she enters with the hypodermic needle." The litany of ailments found in New York's barrios should sicken the progressive observer: young prostitutes, heroin pushers and addicts, "erupting violence," "the dull groaning isolation of death, persistent as the overflowing garbage pails and the glitter of broken glass crushed into the expressionless earth of empty lots." So long as such problems existed, Diaz suggested, "we have no right to call ourselves a just society." Puerto Ricans were not destroying New York; rather, the weight of discrimination crushed the ambitious spirit and hope of a significant segment of the city.[27]

Diaz and the vanguard at *Dissent* rebutted the myths of Necropolis in a push for social reform. The legends were many: Puerto Ricans are impoverished and unwilling to assimilate; blacks dominate the welfare rolls; minority populations perpetuate slum conditions; juvenile delinquents terrorize and disrespect elders; the city is decaying, declining, and near death; and New York has become too dangerous and unlivable. In this milieu, essayist Barbara Probst Solomon noted, "the isolation of the individual caught in the prison of an overcrowded but lonely civilization" emerged as a leading cultural theme.[28] Norman Mailer critiqued the cold, isolated, and bored imagination of urban doomsayers when he observed a gang of so-called juvenile delinquents. Challenging the narrative that saw delinquency as "wasted lives and growing blight," Mailer cited the "courage, loyalty, honor and the urge for adventure" among the "Dealers." "Most of them are rather good pieces of work, bright, sensitive to what is true and what is not true," he wrote. "They suffer from only one disease, the national disease—it is boredom."[29] Written in the wake of Mailer's more famous contrarian hypermasculine tributes—"The White Negro" (*Dissent*, 1957) and "Superman Comes to the Supermarket" (1960)—"'She Thought the Russians Was Coming'" appeared to poke and prod the growing disillusionment among his compatriots within the New York intellectual orbit, whose claims of political decline and social decay were symptomatic of this national disease.[30]

The Summer 1961 issue also featured the first published work of Claude Brown, a reformed delinquent himself who along with Michael Harrington (sharing a chapter on the neighborhood from the forthcoming *The Other America*) examined the problems of black Harlem. In the autobiographical "Harlem, My Harlem," Brown recalled his time as a dealer and a junkie in order to illustrate the impact of heroin on the ghetto. For him, the drug scourge was yet another problem that the city, the state, and/or the federal government failed to curb. Harlem, Brown wrote, "still has a much greater number of the miserable than any place else I know, [but] where else can one find so many people in such pain and so few crying about it?" Highlighting both the structural obstacles Harlemites faced and the neighborhood's persistent fortitude in the face of those barriers earned Brown wide praise.[31] He soon expanded his memories and contemporary analysis into *Manchild in the Promised Land* (1965), a landmark in urban crisis literature and a text whose credentials were widely debated among the New York intellectual community, including his fellow contributors. While Brown offered data on a community that even the most universal intellectuals could view only from privileged positions outside the ghetto, the vanguard came to reject his work for its failure to confront structure and indict capitalism. As historian Carlo Rotella notes, Paul Goodman "identified *Manchild* as part of the problem to which Goodman and his allies were seeking solutions." Nat Hentoff, another *Dissent* contributor, later suggested that "Brown falls far short of a comprehensive assessment of 'today's under-class' in concentrating on the superficial and highly remarkable details of his own story." The Left's fear about Brown's book, and the verisimilitude of stories about the black experience in New York in general, was that it would provide fodder for intellectuals and critics circulating theories on the cultural origins of persistent urban problems. Attaching that publicity to Brown's autobiography, and in the process potentially silencing any similar utilitarian narratives of black life in New York, functioned in part as a self-fulfilling prophecy. Edward Banfield, for instance, the neoconservative scholar behind the national indictment of Necropolis and the urban crisis, *The Unheavenly City*, adored *Manchild*.[32]

The early rumblings of Necropolis as a cultural phenomenon were found in the contributions of Old Left intellectuals at *Dissent*.[33] Articles by Daniel Bell, Irving Howe, and Lionel Abel contained the seeds of discontent, not only with the city but with the shifting political culture as well. Fueled by fond memories of old New York, their neoliberal and neoconservative voices foretold the Right's apathy with and antipathy toward dense American cities in our own time—a political culture where New York City, San Francisco, and others are held up as bastions of ill-conceived radicalism. Despite *Dissent*'s niche readership, the old guard's Necropolis of fiscal irresponsibility, nostalgia, terror, and dread highlighted prevailing cultural currents. The intellectual community's misgivings about the city's ability to adapt to common urban concerns spoke volumes about the range of discontent in this era. In due time, the image these critics crafted would be echoed in middle- and lowbrow media cultures aimed at a wider audience than *Dissent*'s orbit.

Social scientists were one set of observers who saw utility in researching the postwar Petri dish of New York City in the early stages of crisis.[34] Circa 1960, a consortium of researchers from Harvard University published a comprehensive examination of New York City's political economy. Their multivolume "New York Metropolitan Region Study" explored the past and present, and prophesied the future of the city (*Metropolis 1985*) in detailed analyses from a number of interdisciplinary scholars. Of utmost concern was the changing dynamic of the city's industrial and economic output. After the war, manufacturing went into decline and New York shifted wholeheartedly to the so-called FIRE (Finance, Insurance, and Real Estate) sector of the economy. Raymond Vernon, director of the study, examined the impact of this economic upheaval and accurately predicted the city's sustained drift toward service delivery. Robert C. Wood's *1400 Governments* explored the increasingly complex web of metropolitan governance, a problem exacerbated by a decade of suburban growth. In all, the "Metropolitan Region Study" detailed the travails of New York City in tackling the contingencies of decline, deindustrialization, and suburbanization in this period.[35]

As a sociologist himself, Daniel Bell found much to dispute in the Harvard study. An established cultural critic and newly minted Columbia University professor, he had recently published one of his more notable works, *The End of Ideology* (1960).[36] Bell predicted a revolution in American politics whereby pragmatism would replace the orthodox ideology of his youth and of the New Left intelligentsia. Although he later criticized neoconservatism and disdained the label, the insistence on pragmatism transformed Bell into one of the faces of the burgeoning intellectual consortium.[37] His review of the "Metropolitan Region Study," titled "The Three Faces of New York," reflected a growing unease with the redevelopment of New York City and offered a glimpse into his nascent neoconservative, if not neoliberal, ideology. Using the "sociological nuances" of the city's history to clarify its recent evolution into a "headquarters city," Bell criticized the forces of FIRE-brand capitalism by presenting a sentimental reminder of small enterprise, moral economy, and past cosmopolitanism.[38]

According to Bell, the shiny new headquarters along Park and Sixth Avenues concealed an economic reality that threatened the sustainability of New York. Echoing concurrent commentators, Bell argued that these "sleek symbols of the new bazaar" obscured the city's increasing class and racial polarization. Prosperity was an illusion, an iceberg: "The visible portions are the theaters, art galleries, museums, universities, publishing houses, restaurants, night clubs, *espresso* cafés, smart stores—all the activities that give the city its peculiarly glittering place as the metropolis of America." Beneath the visible cultural economy sat a system of labor that, while not as flashy as the gray flannel suit crowd, maintained the city's reputable status. This "fantastic variety of non-rationalized enterprises and services," the light industries and the exporters of homegrown and sewn wares, allowed the local economy to prosper. As Bell put it, "New York is usually thought of primarily as a business and finance center, yet two out of every three jobs in its national-market activities are in manufacturing."[39] Arguing that New York's sustainability rested on the preservation of its immigrant middle- and working-class heritage, "The Three Faces of New York" cautioned against the move toward a wholly corporate economy, a path that the city followed nonetheless.

The evolution of American capitalism in the late twentieth century consumed Bell in the 1960s. In 1973, he published *The Coming of the Post-Industrial Society*, which explored the social and cultural implications of the shift from manufacturing to the production of services in this era.[40] This shift, also characterized by the neoliberal transition to a more global and privatized economy, portended the great restructuring of American life. "Three Faces," for instance, catalogued the city's impending deindustrialization: "port employment will probably decline" and "manufacturing will barely manage to hold pace with the growth of the region."[41] As bureaucrats, planners, and various political and economic actors implemented redevelopment schemes that catered to a strategic vision of New York as a "headquarters city," Bell sought to keep the city productive, particularly in the realm of manufacturing. The decline of this important New York "face" represented a social and spiritual loss for the city.[42]

Bell's prophetic side merged with his pragmatic side, particularly regarding housing. He expressed contempt for Moses's intention to transform the city through transportation and slum clearance improvements. The plans were too shortsighted or misdirected, Bell argued, and it was foolish to believe that more highways could solve the congestion problem. Redevelopment could not fully address physical decay and deindustrialization either. Clearance and subsidized development had no business in Manhattan in the first place, he claimed, because the real estate was too valuable to be wasted on eminent domain. For an intellectual identifying as "a socialist in economics," this represented a stunning ideological turn.[43]

Bell's privatized vision of urban redevelopment extended to New York City public housing as well. In his narrative, Nimbyism ("not in my backyard" sentiment) kept public housing out of outerborough sites like Staten Island, while "Negro politicians" looking to maintain their constituencies and "liberals, who felt it was wrong to penalize public-housing residents by increasing the time travelled to work," fought for its development in the city core. As a result, "high-rising, high-density barracks were built on the most expensive land in the world." Bell suggested that "if housing is to be subsidized, why shouldn't its beneficiaries pay for this, in part, with travel time— particularly when the social gains would have been greater—in larger rooms and more open space."[44] Fellow contributor and sociologist Ernest van den Haag reiterated this sentiment, asking, "Why should a Missouri farmer be asked to house a Puerto Rican as soon as the latter decides to move to New York?"[45] As such, New Right–style racial arguments against uneven social welfare received full play in the pages of Dissent, with Bell and van den Haag advocating for market-driven considerations in Manhattan redevelopment. On the one hand, "Three Faces" was a harbinger of neoconservative policy criticism. On the other hand, it foretold neoliberal development theories that sought limits on the state's role in the redevelopment process.[46]

In this way, Bell was the transitional figure in the Summer 1961 issue. He stressed pragmatism in his vision of New York City redevelopment, and did not paint a portrait of the city in the throes of social chaos. As a cautionary tale, "Three Faces" avoided prescriptive suggestions to tackle the city's economic transformation—with the glaring exception of his criticism of state-sponsored redevelopment and public housing. Yet Bell's nostalgia for a New York where the economy ran on the sweat of immigrant workers and shopkeepers linked him with *Dissent*'s more sentimental contributors. Their remembrances functioned somewhat like Jacobs's *Death and Life*, utilizing nostalgic portraits of the city's past to insinuate a modern Necropolis. But unlike Jacobs and even Bell, Irving Howe and Lionel Abel offered nothing tangible to counteract that impending death. For them, 1930s New York was a vibrant time when radicalism ruled, and neighborhoods from Greenwich Village to the Bronx fostered a dramatic transformation in American politics and culture. This nostalgia suggested that the city's political and cultural renaissance was over, consigning the future New York to whatever despairs followed.

Howe, himself, presented "some fragments of memory" from the 1930s, featuring fond invocations of his adolescence in the East Bronx and Greenwich Village. New York was a mix of neighborhoods defined by deep community bonds. Bronx slums featured "endless talk about Hitler, money worries of my parents migrating to my own psyche, public schools that really were schools and devoted teachers whose faces lived in memory longer than their names, fantasies of heroism drawn from Austria and Spain to excite my imagination." More than anything there was "the Movement," a consortium of Trotskyites, socialists, and anti-Stalinists like the socialist youth, which Howe joined as a teenager. In Howe's telling, courage and political conviction then reigned among the young. Men recognized heroism in the just fight against fascism and Stalinism. They took advantage of the city's unique educational opportunities, and in the Movement, young adults read their Marx and modern literature, which was more than could be said of the comic book–crazed juvenile delinquents of the 1950s.[47]

In Howe's depiction, the political milieu of the 1930s created an exciting backdrop in New York City, a politically transformative period in which the city's Depression-era troubles seemed to fade away. Even with its problems, Howe noted, "if someone had asked me in 1939 what I thought of New York, I would have been puzzled, for that was not the kind of question one worried about in those days." To agonize over the physical or social condition of New York was unheard of, akin to being asked "what I thought about my family: there seemed no choice but to accept the one I had. . . . I no more imagined that I would ever live—or be able to live—anywhere but in New York than that I could find myself a more fashionable set of parents."[48] His recollection suggested that, in years hence, the postwar political economy had rendered these questions much more agonizing for intellectuals and their publics alike.

Howe highlighted a growing disconnect between citizens, especially the city's splintering class and ethnic enclaves. Similar to Bell's portrait of earlier industrial relations, Howe wrote of his neighborhood's survival due to its moral economy—a mutual-aid society of like-minded working-class Jews. "While the East Bronx was a place of poverty, it kept an inner discipline," he recalled. "Jews felt obligated to look after each other, they fought desperately to avoid going on relief."[49] The neighborhood's Jewish culture abated the threat of Depression poverty, signaling an argument that would define the decade's urban debate for neoconservatives. Howe's recollection of the Great Depression as an era free from want and worry stood in contrast to articles on inequality within the same issue by Catholic Worker stalwarts Dorothy Day and Michael Harrington. As practitioners of aid and charity in New York's poorest neighborhoods, Day and Harrington insisted that social capital and the moral economy were hardly enough.[50] Still, Howe's analysis suggested that a cohesive community and collective ambition could dually combat hard times in urban America.

The streets of contemporary New York were a mere allusion in Howe's narrative, a symbol of ruptured social capital and fractured politics. The city played a de facto role, as if Howe sampled the spoiled madeleine of New York and suddenly longed for the days of old. The spirit of the 1930s Movement, he concluded, "is all gone and I do not want it back." Although there was nothing Howe desired "more than a revival of American radicalism," he accepted that "the past is done with, and I have no wish to re-create it nor any belief in the possibility of doing so." While New York's political prospects appeared dim, the old city remained a fond memory: "There are moments now and again when I recall the life of New York in the thirties, and see it through the lens of affection; and then it all seems pure in the light of time, I feel with pleasure the old stirrings of faith and conviction, that love for the unborn future which may redeem the past."[51] Howe's misgivings about Necropolis could only be drawn by inference—deduced from the fragments of memory he jotted down on paper.[52]

What he failed to say was critical. Howe asserted that 1930s radicalism could not be replicated, a concept that ignored the countercultural/New Left assets readily present in the city, including Harrington, the Goodmans, C. Wright Mills, the Beats (who were despised by the literary critics at *Dissent*), the Village folk music scene, and avant-garde artists.[53] Howe charged himself, as the journal's editor, with assembling the "New York, N.Y." issue, but when the opportunity to explore the nascent New Left Cosmopolis presented itself, he submitted a sentimental portrait of an arcadian New York. Howe's unwillingness to embrace the city's emergent political and cultural currents represented a requiem for his hometown, and he erected an ideological barrier between himself and vanguard writers at *Dissent*.

Howe's autobiography validated this assessment through more fragments of memory. Not long after the publication of the "New York, N.Y." issue, he accepted a position at Stanford University, where he spent the next few years teaching. In 1964, equally disgusted with life in California, Howe leapt at the chance to teach at the City University of New York, and returned to his hometown. But he hardly recognized the city: "New York was changing, seldom for the better. The city had lost some of its plebian easiness; there was a new air of menace hanging over the streets." There were concerns about personal safety and implied racial fears of violent behavior limiting the universal access that bohemians like Howe once enjoyed. "It was no longer comfortable to go up to the Apollo Theatre on 125th Street for the Saturday night show. It was dangerous to sit, alone or with a woman, in Central Park on summer nights. Appetites of irrational violence were building up, and not much solace or protection was to be had from either one's old habits of liberal tolerance or Norman Mailer's catchy theories about the iconography of hipsterdom." Howe admitted that he "no longer loved the city, [and] only remained hopelessly attached to it."[54] While nearly two decades of Necropolis colored Howe's recollection, his contribution to the Summer 1961 issue revealed this feeling of hopelessness and disaffection unequivocally. Then, as the image of fear and panic intensified, Howe allied himself with doomsayers like his erstwhile comrade Lionel Abel.

Abel's "New York City: A Remembrance" constituted an ad hominem jeremiad in the otherwise deliberate pages of *Dissent*. Abel came of age with the New York Intellectuals, harboring leftist sympathies without subscribing to the orthodoxy of his contemporaries. While lacking the reputation of his more famous counterparts, Abel made a name for himself as a playwright, an academic, and a literary critic.[55] Friends in the intellectual community characterized him as a polemicist with a penchant for argument and contrarian viewpoints, so much so that his political drift to the far right by the end of his life outflanked his colleagues. Abel's contribution to the issue, an article that functioned as an angry and apathetic elegy for the city, showed hints of this polemical style and nascent conservatism. For him,

New York in 1961 shared few similarities with the center of politics, intellect, and excitement that defined his old Cosmopolis.[56]

Abel pointed to the past to critique the city's deficiencies in the sixties. In the 1930s and 1940s, a "human being could live" in New York. It was "The City" of limited difference, enthusiasm, and passion. "There was a wickedness in it, there were women—maybe there was even one woman; there were people who talked about poetry—and people who actually wrote poetry, or who made paintings, the next best thing. . . . New York contained just about every sort of person." Something in the 1950s altered the universal city that once inspired creativity and intellectual growth. Friends moved away or shifting political views drove them apart, and New York no longer carried that promise of excitement and intellect. Abel insisted that the sentimental nostalgia of a middle-aged intellectual did not color his portrait of the city, but indeed it did.

To Abel, New York City had already destroyed itself. Its wonderful kinetic quality, in a mere three decades, had given way to fear, social decline, or the wrecking ball. Abel wrote of walking the streets, which "were then safe at night," from midnight until dawn—no more. The propriety associated with certain New York City neighborhoods also disappeared. For example, in the thirties one would not attend a Broadway show "without top hat and white tie." Abel's comment that "living in New York was almost a wandering from apartment to apartment" suggested access and mobility, and the freedom to sample the city's spatial delights distinguished the thirties from the static and bored city of the sixties. By contrast, thirties New York was liberating: "Like most of humanity, but much more pleasantly, you were on the march."[57]

The city's cultural, political, and social excitement centered on Greenwich Village, Manhattan's universal neighborhood. Its oblique thoroughfares, a physical allegory of the district's nonconformist ethos, represented the center of Cosmopolis and the intellectual's universe. "There was no other residential section in New York. Those who lived outside this area were just pariahs—or did not even exist." According to the playwright, "in the important part of New York, at that time, there was not a single person who had not once in his life looked exultant, exalted, or at the very least, distinguished. There was not one person who had not at least once in his life said something which could be—and maybe was—repeated." For that moment, the Village harbored lonely dreamers and hard, bright men. In the spirit of vital center intellectuals, Abel noted that people in New York "tended to be hard"; in fact, "they wanted to be hard [and] they were living up to an ideal of hardness."[58] The recent arrival of migrants such as the Beats, James Baldwin, Bob Dylan, and Jane Jacobs challenged Cold War conceptions of gender and sexuality and undoubtedly softened the image of its virility.

In Abel's narrative, as well as Howe's, the Village reached the pinnacle of its political and cultural importance during the Great Depression. As New York embraced the New Deal and fostered Popular Front culture, the city evolved into a hotbed of socialism and functioned as a laboratory of social democracy under fellow traveler Mayor Fiorello LaGuardia.[59] Abel described this moment as New York's "last great act": "In its excitement and depression the city picked itself up and went to Russia. Yes, New York, not just one section of it, but New York City entire. . . . Politically New York City then became the most interesting part of the Soviet Union." This was an honor Abel bestowed since one "enjoyed more freedom in New York City than Russians not in New York City did" and could engage conversations about the merits of Trotsky versus Stalin without retribution.[60] Not unlike the rationale of later neoliberal critics, Abel argued that an increasingly collectivized city stifled creative growth, and thus the city's evolution. New York then drifted toward the abyss.[61]

In the 1940s and 1950s, Abel and friends negotiated the perceived ailments plaguing Necropolis. Residents that Abel admired, his neighbors in the Village—"the most important people in the city"—started to leave. They moved to larger residences on the Upper West Side (e.g., Howe and Irving Kristol) or into Brooklyn and beyond, a phenomenon that only intensified in ensuing years. Then came the war: Stalin signed a pact with Hitler, which swiftly ended the Left's enchantment with the Soviet Union. Then came the crisis, which Abel's reductive narrative simplified in the cultural terms preferred by postwar Jeremiahs: "Came the blackout. Came the first delinquents onto the darkened streets. . . . Came the Puerto Ricans, invisibly, and not to be seen in their full consequence until about fifteen years later [about the time of his writing]. Came the desire to get out of New York once the world fracas was over." World War II and its social shifts, Abel argued, destroyed his Cosmopolis. Apathy and boredom, the diseases inducing New York's slow death, set in: "In the later forties almost everyone I knew in New York got sick of the person nearest to him or her." The city "had become for me little more than the streets over which a taxicab would take me to a boat leaving for Paris."[62]

Abel asked a simple but poignant question, one that critics had asked since the end of the war: "What is New York today?" In truth, the city's new racial and ethnic dynamic sickened him, and he wondered why others were not disgusted as well. New York was now best viewed from the perspective of a runaway or shut-in. It has a certain beauty, he admitted, "at least when seen at night from a speeding car, from a penthouse very high up—or from a deck of a ship taking you away from it," the preferred vantage points of authoritarian high modernists. But one discovers the "dirty details" close up, that is, "the noise and the haste of the streets. . . . Its congestion of cars and men, it is most unlovely; who can like it?"[63] Such passages questioned the sanity of anyone willing to live in New York City, much less invest in the city's future. Advising his son two decades later, he advertised Gotham as such: "Of course New York City is not today [1984] the city I knew when I came to it from a small town. It is not the city of the thirties, the forties, the fifties, or the sixties (*when its disintegration began in earnest*)." Most of the public spaces were unsafe; "the subways *are* dangerous; I avoid the train whenever possible."

In this case, Abel asked, "to what am I asking you to come back?" New York City nurtured the creative mind like no other town. Come for the opportunity, he admitted, "to the city where it is still possible to talk to somebody about something that is not purely practical; to the city where the things that mean most to you are already expressed, at least in part, in the skyline, in the beauty of the bridges, and in the general intelligence of at least a very large number of people in Manhattan, in the wit and cunning of the taxi drivers, in the number of places still available for the pursuit of nonpractical activities or purely social contacts."[64] In many ways, this was Abel's mea culpa. Unfortunately, the damage had been done. By 1984, Necropolis had since given way to a cultural renaissance and white-collar economic growth in New York.[65]

In the intervening years, Abel's anger and disgust governed the sentiment of the Right's urban criticism, much of it centered on narrativizing the connection between race and crime. Saul Bellow, the Chicago writer who traveled in the New York Intellectuals' circle and later followed them to the right, employed this trope in New York–set *Mr. Sammler's Planet* (1970), a book that historian Andrew Hartman calls "the neoconservative novel par excellence."[66] Bellow's protagonist struggles with life on the Upper West Side, where he deals with muggings and random violence at the hands of wilding youths. "A powerful Negro" whose "face showed the effrontery of a big animal" terrorizes the elderly Sammler on West Seventy-Second Street. Bellow describes an unlivable and unruly city, offering Abel-like observations: "Buses were bearable, subways were killing." When Sammler seeks the police, "of course the phone was smashed." In fact, "most outdoor phones were smashed, crippled. They were urinals, also. New York was getting worse than Naples or Salonika. It was like an Asian, an African town, from this standpoint."[67] Bellow's Necropolis was no country for old men, much less a place for the respectable and civilized. Deployed outside the bounds of *Dissent*'s limited orbit, generalized representations of people and place and images of random violence, like Bellow's, unquestionably influenced readers' own sweeping views about race, ethnicity, and the state of cities like New York in this period.[68]

Abel also imagined an out-of-control and increasingly "ungovernable city," a label coined by Nathan Glazer in *Commentary* that same year. The term gained traction in the years leading up to the fiscal crisis, and alluded to various ailments, including a surging technocratic bureaucracy, union unrest, and expanding welfare rolls.[69] Abel suggested a breakdown of the public sector: "The city has become too big, it is overgrown, it now impedes rather than aids those who grow up in it. Its schools have broken down, its administration is unwieldy, inefficient, corrupt. New York cannot clean its streets. It has become afraid of the snow." He implied that crime and delinquency—at least fear and paranoia about disorder—took over. Anxiety about crime waves, particularly random street crime, emerged as New York City's most vital and vicious problem, completing the discursive turn from fears of physical decline to concerns about cultural decay and rampant social disorder. Successive "studies" of New York crime and safety only fed the fire.[70]

Defined by fear and disgust, "New York City: A Remembrance" dismissed the city of the sixties, transferring power from de facto leaders, the intellectuals who ascended to that title in the thirties, forties, and fifties, to the bureaucratic and criminal forces driving the city into the ground. This brand of resignation went beyond Abel and Bellow. John Cheever's concurrent essay "Moving Out" detailed his own escape from New York. Demographic changes in Manhattan placed pressure on whites seeking homogenous, "safe" neighborhoods. Feeling pushed out of Sutton Place, one of the remaining white districts in Manhattan, by elite demand and rising rents, Cheever found solace in the Westchester suburbs.[71] With its privacy, cleanliness, and lack of street hassles and hustles, Cheever realized his decision was sound. As he concluded: "The truth is that I'm crazy about the suburbs and I don't care who knows it"—good riddance New York.[72] Lewis Mumford, a once proud leftist intellectual and the consummate urban advocate, also saw the attraction of the small town and suburb in this era: "those who leave the city wish to escape its snarling violence and its sickening perversions of life, its traffic in narcotics and its gangster-organized lewdness, which break into the lives of even children."[73] New York slouched, as Mumford put it explicitly, toward "Necropolis."[74]

In *The City in History*, published in 1961, Mumford elaborated on the meaning of Necropolis, alluding to New York's various ailments. More than a decade prior, Mickey Spillane likened crime and disorder in his fictional city to Roman spectacle, where only the "quick" and "able" gladiators stave off certain death. As Mumford noted, Rome was history's exemplar for the city's end, offering a "series of classic danger signals" for places on the path to Necropolis. "Whenever crowds gather in suffocating numbers, wherever rents rise steeply and housing conditions deteriorate, wherever a one-side exploitation of distant territories removes the pressure to achieve balance and harmony nearer at hand, there the precedents of Roman building almost automatically revive, as they have come back today: the arena, the tall tenement, the mass contests and exhibitions, the football matches, the international beauty contests, the strip-tease made ubiquitous by advertisement, the constant titillation of the sense by sex, liquor, and violence—all in true Roman style." Social and economic conditions devolving into moral chaos amounted to the aging urban intellectual's trope of choice in the 1960s. "When these signs multiply," Mumford wrote, "Necropolis is near, though not a stone has yet crumbled. For the barbarian has already captured the city from within. Come, hangman! Come, vulture!"[75]

Writing in the pages of *Dissent* Abel saw the vultures circling above New York. "The city may disintegrate, it may die. . . . [It] cannot grow as it once did," he wrote. He presented no plans and no proposals for change, as Moses and emergent critics continued to do. Abel merely asked rhetorically, "Shall we turn from it, despise it, as we watch its former qualities converted into faults? Shall we take a hand in changing it? In making it like other cities, and one, too that will not reflect our own image? Should we not rather lament the passing of something extraordinary, which perhaps will never be seen again?"[76] Abel may have had no answers, but such apocalyptic fears, such ad hominem attacks on New York City, and such antipathy only intensified as the decade dragged on. Few old guard intellectuals would provide the necessary rejoinders on delivering New York from its Necropolis fate.

• • • • • •

"It is often said that New York is a city for only the very rich and the very poor," wrote essayist Joan Didion in "Farewell to the Enchanted City" (1967). "It is less often said that New York is also, at least for those who came there from somewhere else, a city only for the very young." In this essay, more familiarly known as "Goodbye to All That," Didion related the story of her early years as a cosmopolitan migrant from Sacramento. Despite the warnings of weathered, apathetic, and bitter acquaintances that she, too, would outgrow the city, twenty-year-old Didion epitomized White's archetype, falling "in love with New York . . . the way you love the first person who ever touches you and you never love quite that way again." She "still believed in the possibilities then, still had the sense, so peculiar to New York, that something extraordinary would happen any minute, any day, any month." Yet her connection to the city devolved as she aged. A weathered New Yorker by the mid-1960s, Didion "hurt the people [she] cared about, and insulted those [she] did not." She married, and a provisional hiatus in Los Angeles turned permanent. Although some aspects of the city elicited a Proustian response, Didion insisted that New York suited a certain type of person—young, persistent, opportunistic, and ready to grapple with the great questions of the day. Her love was fleeting: "The last time I was in New York was in a cold January, and everyone was ill and tired."[77]

In the summer of 1961, youthful and still young at heart contributors to *Dissent*'s special issue on New York tackled concerns about the city. If, as Daniel Bell's seminal work suggested, the struggle between ideology and pragmatism partially defined intellectual culture in the sixties, *Dissent*'s vanguard synthesized the two on the topic of New York City's growing crisis. Harrington's work, for example, helped inspire Great Society initiatives. Zoll worked with Jacobs on community development projects in the West Village. For the rear guard, ideology reigned in an issue that constituted its collective farewell to the enchanted universal city of the past. Bell somewhat, but Irving Howe and Lionel Abel most glaringly, reverted to "fragments of memory," painting a picture of 1930s New York as its zenith and 1961 as its nadir. They once controlled the field of cultural and political criticism, but during the sixties these intellectuals transferred New York's care to a new breed of thinkers. In part, the predominantly Jewish intellectuals followed a path similar to a significant segment of working-class Jews who, increasingly disillusioned by political defeats (the Ocean Hill/Brownsville School Board test case in self-governance in particular) and growing social disorder in their outerborough enclaves, left the city in this era as well.[78]

In the political upheaval of the 1960s, New York City became a focal point of public contention (e.g., the 1965 mayoral race and the Columbia University lockdown of 1968) and an exemplar of poorly managed public policy. If welfare state critiques dominated the political interest of the neoconservatives and the libertarian faction of the Right—as historians suggest—one could find no better view than on the streets of New York City. In the process, the city emerged as the poster child for overextended bureaucracy, a symbol of liberalism's decline.[79] Few critics or journalists were left to defend programs like urban renewal, public housing, and antipoverty programs. Instead, jeremiads perpetuated the fear of New York as modern-day Sodom—an unsalvageable trash heap that only self-destruction could correct.[80] A disparate coalition of socialist intellectuals, liberal journalists, and conservative academics saw New York's greatness consigned to the past. They willingly left Necropolis to the criminals, delinquents, and deviants of their imagination. While scholarship tends to situate Old Left discontent within conflicts over ideology versus pragmatism, as a product of the welfare state debate, or an intellectual quirk lying dormant since the 1930s, the above demonstrates that the Left's fracture and its connection with ascendant conservatism may be explained by the rear guard's interpretation of what was happening in the streets, particularly the moribund sidewalks of New York at the beginning of the 1960s.

6 Untangling the Pathologies of Ungovernability

....

In "Mother Jacobs' Home Remedies," Lewis Mumford chastised Jane Jacobs for ignoring the genuine reason some urban spaces were underutilized. New Yorkers avoided parks, sidewalks, public places, and the greenspaces between superblock structures due to what he termed "the increasing pathology of the whole mode of life in the great metropolis, a pathology that is directly proportionate to its overgrowth, its purposeless materialism, its congestion, and its insensate disorder—the very conditions [Jacobs] vehemently upholds as marks of urban vitality." Mumford raised questions about the sanity of the citizen, noting the "enormous sums spent on narcotics, sedatives, stimulants, hypnotics, and tranquilizers to keep the population of our 'great' cities from coming to terms with the vacuous desperation of their daily lives." Ultimately, he celebrated those, like himself, who had managed to flee the aforementioned "snarling violence and its sickening perversions of life," because in New York there was no escaping the clutches of pathology that had rendered the city unlivable. Jacobs, Mumford wrote, "forgets that in organisms there is no tissue quite as 'vital' or 'dynamic' as cancer growths."[1]

While commentators had long written of New York's various ailments, including Robert Moses's enduring "cancer" metaphor, anxiety over the city's pathologies crescendoed in the mid-1960s. The diagnosis was twofold, with the mutually dependent ailments of poverty and crime seemingly entangling sensitive New Yorkers in a city otherwise "ungovernable." The world of urban poverty, and of New York's poor in particular, was rendered visible by Michael Harrington's *The Other America*. According to Harrington, urban renewal effectively destroyed urban social capital and any semblance of an earlier moral economy. Real slums, meaning the pockets of helpless poor that Harrington observed, had been concealed behind new modern buildings. Elevated interstates carried elite commuters over the landscape of the other America, leaving the impoverished out of capital's sight and, hence, out of mind. In an age of supposed affluence, those still relegated to New York's slums had fallen into what Harrington labeled— borrowing from sociologist Oscar Lewis—a "culture of poverty" that was increasingly difficult to snap. Uncovering the various faces of urban poor in the 1960s, Harrington called for a more proactive welfare state to counteract the perpetual cycle now quashing the "American Dream" of social mobility. Along with the image of the "tangle of pathology" in African American enclaves like Harlem, a phrase coined by psychologist Kenneth C. Clark and popularized by Daniel Patrick Moynihan, the narrative of a permanent class of poor proved a central turning point in the political debate on the crisis of New York.[2]

As postwar popular culture established an image of mass prosperity, *The Other America* prompted a narrative that saw New York in perpetual economic decline and increasingly segregated by class and race. Urban elites sequestered themselves in exclusive enclaves rising on the sites of old slums, as the white middle and working classes gravitated to single-family homes in homogenous suburbs, ensuring minimal contact with minorities and the poor. Harrington suggested that unless the federal government intervened, the other America could look forward to increasingly uninhabitable housing conditions and few economic opportunities. In essence he established an image of a permanent unemployed and indigent class that without social services and access to the labor market might be driven to extremes. Turn-of-the-century critics like Jacob Riis, who's *How the Other Half Lives* (1890) inspired the title of Harrington's book, feared that extreme wealth polarization and the inequitable conditions that resulted from it would bring about violent consequences for elites. Planning and government regulation emerged to quell this threat. Harrington's Necropolis prophecy implied a similar and timely possibility of class and racial disorder, and his notion of a "culture of poverty" as well as the image of the "underclass" run amok evolved into an effective trope within a variety of New York texts produced in the 1960s.[3]

New York's most respected broadsheets—the *Times* and the *Herald Tribune*—played to public fears of a pathological crime wave wrought by this underclass. Reporting in the *Times* on the random and terrifying rape and murder of Katherine "Kitty" Genovese in middle-class Kew Gardens probed the collective psyche of New York. Overshadowing the questions of why and how Genovese was attacked was the "revelation" about the circumstances surrounding the event. Thirty-eight neighbors were said to have witnessed the attack and heard Genovese's cries for help. One called the police, but only after an hour of deliberation, and by that time Genovese's death was imminent. This, along with the seeming lack of motive and the racial and sexual implications of the crime, spawned a series of works highlighting the tangle of apathy that had befallen New York since its halcyon days. In contrast to the war years and the period prior, as the *Herald Tribune* put it, "the complex problems of today often appear to have no solution at all." As a result, "the citizen becomes bewildered, frustrated, enraged and finally in all too many cases, succumbs to fear and indifference." With a subtitle that signaled the ascendant role of pathology in the narratives of New York ("A Study in Depth of Urban Sickness"), the *Herald Tribune*'s bound collection *New York City in Crisis* (1965) defined the rhetoric of crime, poverty, and "welfare" in the critical election year of 1965. As New Yorkers went to the polls, high-profile *Herald Tribune* columnists Jimmy Breslin and Dick Schaap shoved New York's "lonely crimes," or the everyday inconveniences newspapers otherwise had no column space for, into the spotlight. The nearly pathological coverage of violent attacks, random crimes, and public apathy raised grave questions about what lurked beyond the window frames from the breakfast table, recliner, or train where residents and readers beyond absorbed these tales of Necropolis.[4]

Seizing on the city's growing association with a variety of pathologies, authors of anti–New York jeremiads wrestled the political debate over slum poverty from the likes of Harrington to highlight the failures of the welfare state. Richard Whalen's *A City Destroying Itself* demonstrated the centrality of urban issues in emergent conservative rhetoric in the 1960s. The *Fortune* article, later published as a stand-alone book, was an "angry" ad hominem attack on perceived social disorder and underclass behavior in New York, with arguably no mission beyond fear-mongering and image-craft. By the 1980s, Whalen's fellow travelers in the New Right captured the falling flags of poverty and crime, the two major urban issues of the sixties and seventies. Retooling the rhetoric and representation of Michael Harrington, that is, the culture of poverty and the permanent underclass, the Right controlled the debate on public assistance, policing, and the role of the state in planning and economic development, effectively winning the war on the "War on Poverty" in our own time.[5] For Harrington, a self-described socialist aiming to expand social services in American cities, this proved an unfortunate contingency of his narrative.

· · · · · ·

The context from which Harrington emerged was defined by a flourishing of the social sciences, as a popular audience turned to academics and intellectuals in order to understand the complex issues confronting the nation in the Cold War. Common themes within this canon included economic polarization, middle-class complacency, and the postwar problems of race, ethnicity, and class. David Riesman's *The Lonely Crowd* (1950) set the tone with its study of American character and its fears that cultural conformity would suppress individuality. Joining Riesman were the works of Columbia University sociologist C. Wright Mills, whose *White Collar* (1951) also explored the life of the country's expanding middle class. Mills's follow-up critique of the relationship between capital and the state, *The Power Elite* (1956), was another essential work within the discipline. Against the backdrop of civil rights activism, race emerged as the most important focus of inquiry, particularly in studies of New York City like psychologist Kenneth C. Clark's *Dark Ghetto* (1965). *Beyond the Melting Pot* (1963), a collaboration between sociologists Nathan Glazer (later an influential neoconservative) and Daniel Patrick Moynihan (later labeled a neoconservative by association), proved pertinent for the racial debate among white neoconservatives in the 1960s. Glazer and Moynihan challenged the notion that New York's white ethnics expedited assimilation since their arrival from Europe. While the sociologists noted that recent migrants were not exceptional in that respect, *Beyond the Melting Pot* damned the city's racial minorities by arguing, among other things, that the prevalence of blacks and Puerto Ricans on public assistance threatened the postwar city. The argument crafted an image of postwar migration as antithetical to the European migrations of yesteryear, and highlighted the allure of cultural explanations for poverty in the wake of *The Other America*. Statistical analysis on black female–headed households in particular, while authored by Glazer, foretold the assumptions catalogued by Moynihan, then working within the Johnson administration, in his infamous policy memo, "The Negro Family: A Case for National Action" (1965).[6]

This collection of landmark scholarship converged on the notion that urban and suburban space had repercussions for human behavior, particularly in the development of disparate cultures and subcultures along class, racial, and ethnic lines. Sociological methodology, feeding off the discipline's influential heights in this period, trickled down into the world of journalism and criticism, spawning works linked to spatial transformation and redevelopment like William H. Whyte's *The Organization Man*, John Kenneth Galbraith's *The Affluent Society* (1958), and especially Harrington's *The Other America*.[7] Harrington's was a unique text for the period, not only for its influence on the social programs of Presidents Kennedy and Johnson but for distancing itself from these otherwise generalist, monolithic works through an ethnographic examination of the various "faces" of poverty.

Race and ethnic lines blurred in Harrington's qualitative observations of the elderly, the victims of discrimination, and the perpetual slum dweller, exposing for a general audience firsthand experiences of the poor.[8]

Riis's fin de siècle study of New York City poverty, it has been said, opened elite eyes to the problem of industrial cities. Riis ventured into the ethnic slums of New York to expose the literal hell that constituted life in congested Gilded Age contingencies with the hope of inspiring reform, and his book indeed had an impact on public policy. New York City unleashed a period of unprecedented urban renewal, demolishing some of its worst slums, including the famed Mulberry Bend, an outgrowth of the notorious "Five Points," home to "Bandit's Roost" and "Bottle Alley," and the site that inspired Riis's most righteous indignation.[9] The city cleared the Bend and turned it into a park but, as with later renewal projects, took no role in housing the displaced poor. Other parks were created, too, along with public bathhouses to head off the threat of disease and other hygienic pandemics. New laws regulated the construction of tenements, representing one of the initial state interventions into private enterprise.[10] Harrington's goals were similar: provoke the state into action in order to solve the problems of its own making.

The flip side of *How the Other Half Lives*' intent and legacy was less than sanguine. The bulk of Riis's prose sought control over the suspected liberties of Cosmopolis. He staged his groundbreaking photography in order to serve his mission of highlighting the respective pathologies of New York's lower classes, which he segregated along racial lines. Disrupting that period's narrative of the "melting pot," Riis ascribed general patterns of behavior to the city's blacks and immigrant masses within Lower Manhattan's various enclaves. The Italian (Riis preferred the essentialist singular plural), although "welcomed as a tenant" in the "slums," was disgusting, dumb, and prone to destructive gambling—the only ethnicity willing to endure life in Mulberry Bend. Clinging to stereotypes that would terrorize Jews for decades to come, Riis described the Lower East Side's "Jewtown" as a neighborhood populated by residents for whom "money is their god" and where "thrift is the watchword." The Chinese, due to the author's blatant ignorance, earned the most contempt for their non-Christian religious practice, supposed secretive nature, liberal drug habits, and seductive allure that fueled the era's "white slavery" fears.[11] Despite these gross generalizations, Riis's work filtered into other areas of progressive reform: the settlement house movement emerged in those years with the goal of "Americanizing" newly arrived immigrants and unbinding them from the strictures of Old

World ethnicity and un-American pluralism that Riis so disdained. However, Riis's essentialism sparked a flurry of investigative journalism and state reform that similarly transformed the turn-of-the-century status quo. In an unfortunate irony, *The Other America*'s policy response became overshadowed by contingent distortions of Harrington's argument on poverty's persistence in an affluent age.[12]

Like Progressive Era reformers, Harrington and other observers took to the slums of the 1950s and 1960s to detail the experience of upheaval wrought by slum clearance and urban renewal. Social workers' critiques of East Harlem superblock public housing developments, in addition to the critiques of Jane Jacobs and Dan Wakefield, maligned the modern design paradigm of postwar redevelopment and fostered an unfavorable image of state planning in this vital period. As Samuel Zipp argues, "their findings and programs, while never intended to undermine public housing, did much to guide the terms of the debate that doomed the reputations of public housing and urban renewal." An added contingency was their suggestion that a small minority of "problem families"—single-parent households and/or mentally ill, unemployed, alcoholic, and drug-addicted, criminal residents— were putting added stress on the New York City Housing Authority to function in a world where planners prioritized private redevelopment. As the urban crisis intensified, the problems of the few became the pathology of the many. In the 1960s, as Zipp notes, "the emphasis on 'problem families' would harden into the widespread public, national consensus that the 'pathological' behavior of nonwhite residents, mired in a 'culture of poverty,' was to blame for public housing's woes."[13] It was the kind of exaggerated misreading that Michael Harrington would find familiar.

Harrington entered the world of New York's impoverished neighborhoods through his work for New York City's Catholic Worker movement, an organization created at the height of the Great Depression by Dorothy Day and Peter Maurin. With missions situated in the city's most heartbreaking enclaves, the Catholic Worker followed in the tradition of the settlement house movement, adhering to Riis's notion that charities must do the work of aiding the indigent. It went further by advocating for social justice and greater state intervention in the economy. Day's radicalism, particularly her unabashed pacifism and socialism, never jibed with local mainstream Catholicism under the conservative regime of Cardinal Spellman, and her group was regularly subjected to the McCarthy-era harassment reserved for agitators. Harrington, a socialist from St. Louis and thus a cosmopolitan migrant, volunteered at the Worker's Bowery Mission, doling out meals and rooms to the area's infamous mendicants. As a leveler, he even took a personal vow of poverty.[14]

His participant observation inspired *The Other America*, which chronicled life in two of New York City's iconic postwar "slums:" Harlem and the Bowery.[15] Both neighborhoods had been saddled with lasting narratives that Harrington sought to complicate. Once a suburb for wealthy Jews and Germans, Harlem evolved into a black community early in the twentieth century as redevelopment evicted blacks from enclaves downtown. Within two decades the neighborhood cemented its reputation as the center of African American political and cultural influence in the United States. In the mid-1960s, however, the first comprehensive history of Harlem explored its development into an "enduring" black "ghetto."[16] Likewise, the Bowery, an area named after the major north-south thoroughfare running through the heart of Manhattan's Lower East Side, carried the weight of neglect and a nasty reputation—it inspired the elite sporting practice of "slumming" after all—grounded in its long down-and-out social history.[17] Lined with "stale beer dives" and "flophouses" hidden beneath the blanket of the Third Avenue elevated railroad, the Bowery attracted the extremely poor, and the neighborhood maintained this reputation well into the 1960s, even after the roof came off (the transit platform was removed in the late 1950s).[18]

The Bowery was one of the more miserable and visible sites of poverty in the city. Various alcoholics—mid-century successors of a long line of "bowery bums"—waddled in the shadows of the Third Avenue elevated looking for a drink and shelter. The grim prospects for Bowery residents— "the end of the line for the Bowery is the hospital and potter's field," wrote Harrington—inspired the first in a series of reports published in *Commentary* and *Dissent* that would be assembled as *The Other America*.[19] With the book, Harrington sought to alter the image of so-called slum life by rendering it more visible to the naked elite eye—to lift the veil, so to speak, that concealed the economic realities of the postwar era. He also wanted to disrupt the standard policy diagnoses of neighborhood clearance adhered to by redevelopment regimes like New York's Committee on Slum Clearance.

The narrative of mass affluence in the 1950s failed to correspond to Harrington's experience in the Bowery. Hollywood, television, and advertising defined the moment as one of unprecedented prosperity following the Great Depression's long economic nightmare. After World War II, the white working class could afford to purchase new homes, spurring the growth of the suburb and all the amenities that went along with it. Automobiles, time-saving and food-preserving appliances, and modern home furnishings became the symbol of this prosperity. Americans, the narrative went, slipped the surly bonds of poverty, and rose into a new world of clean and comfortable living, replete with newfound wealth and leisure.[20] Harrington, however, cited elite and middle-class complacency as a reason for their cultural illiteracy when it came to impoverished Americans. "The millions who are poor in the United States tend to become increasingly invisible. Here is a great mass of people, yet it takes an effort of the intellect and will even to see them," he wrote. "The other America, the America of poverty, is hidden today in a way that it never was before."[21] The image of a class-less nation certainly contributed to poverty's obscurity, but Harrington argued that this ignorance also resulted from increased polarization wrought by the new middle class. The economic divide was implicit, but a spatial polarization that emerged with the suburban exodus and urban renewal of the 1950s was equally vital to this new narrative.[22]

According to Harrington, suburbanites no longer confronted the realities of the poor as metropolitan growth and urban redevelopment segregated and shielded the affluent from the helpless. New expressways carried them over or under the residential areas of the city, and deposited them in the central business district—a homogenous outpost of wealth and finance. The Lower Manhattan Expressway, which was still on the table in 1962, was a planned elevated highway over the "slums." It would have offered commuters safe haven from the Bowery by leaping over the thoroughfare to and from the Williamsburg Bridge and the Holland Tunnel and once again capped a section of the street, not unlike the old El, between Broome Street and the Manhattan Bridge. In addition to these barriers, the poor—along with racial and ethnic minorities who were legally banned or excluded de facto through "gentlemen's agreements"—were prohibited from peripheral developments via the lack of public transit options—Robert Moses famously constructed the overpasses of his Long Island parkways to prohibit bus travel. Harrington reminded readers of a time when the middle class "was at least aware" of impoverished city districts. "There were forays into slums at Christmas time; there were charitable organizations that brought contact with the poor. Occasionally, almost everyone passed through the Negro ghetto or the blocks of tenements, if only to get downtown to work or to entertainment."[23] Evoking Jacobs's discussion of trust and sidewalk cross-class contact and Irving Howe's memory of growing up in the East Bronx, Harrington suggested that the proximity of rich and poor within New York once fostered meaningful charitable giving and empathy, which had disappeared in the new landscape.

Postwar creative destruction altered the nature of human interaction in such a way as to allow for the swift and trouble-free transmission of simplified narratives and representations of the lower classes. Despite attempts at renewal, Harrington noted, "the poor still inhabit the miserable housing in the central area, but they are increasingly isolated from contact with, or sight of, anybody else." Planners accommodated the middle class so that "the business or professional man may drive along the fringes of slums in a car or bus, but it is not an important experience to him." Redevelopment had effectively "removed poverty from the living, emotional experience of millions upon millions of middle-class Americans. Living out in the suburbs, it is easy to assume that ours is, indeed, an affluent society."[24] Also contributing to this assumption was, again, the refracted image of 1950s America as a prosperous society in the process of lifting all boats. Popular culture manufactured a consistent narrative that, despite the ubiquitous fear of nuclear annihilation, noted, "Everything is fine."[25]

According to Harrington, postwar prosperity and the ascendant welfare state missed the exit to the Bowery. There he found the lowest of the low: skid row alcoholics hopeless about finding a home or employment. Purveyors of fear had illustrated a thoroughfare dominated by cheap liquor stores and rooms rented by the night, places where, come morning, proprietors swept through the building looking for the dead. Over the street "there hung the smell of urine. The men lived out of doors when they didn't have money for a flop. Sometimes, in the winter, they passed out in the snow or crawled into a doorway." This was the "almost typical face" of skid row, one that Harrington quite often encountered during his tenure with the Catholic Worker. "The men are dirty, and often their faces are caked with blood after a particularly terrible drunk. They wake up without knowing how they were hurt. Their clothes are ragged, ill-fitting, incongruous. Their trousers stink of the streets and of dried urine." It was the kind of nonnormative appearance that rendered the most down-and-out denizen embarrassed and "afraid of direct and full contact with someone else's eyes."[26]

The Bowery's glassy far-away stare symbolized *The Other America*'s primary diagnosis: the urban poor's lack of aspiration in a polarized society. When reformers looked at older ethnic slums, they saw only the façade of aging infrastructure alongside customs out of sync with their own. As Harrington described it, "If a group has an internal vitality, a will—if it has aspiration—it may live in dilapidated housing, it may eat an inadequate diet, and it may suffer poverty, but it is not impoverished. So it was in those ethnic slums of the immigrants that played such a dramatic role in the unfolding of the American dream. The people found themselves in slums, but they were not slum dwellers." In contrast to these strivers in the slums of old, their descendants on the Bowery succumbed to the wake left by the rush to the American Dream in the 1950s. Postwar poverty destroyed their aspiration through what Harrington called both the "cycle of poverty" and the "culture of poverty" that constrained hope and promise. The other America was "populated by the failures, by those driven from the land and bewildered by the city, by old people suddenly confronted with the torments of loneliness and poverty, and by minorities facing a wall of prejudice."[27]

For the minority residents of Harlem, where an influx of new housing failed to solve the problem of poverty in the 1950s and 1960s, urban renewal seemed oxymoronic. There it was "renewal" only in the sense of reinforcing the cycle rather than breaking it and building anew. Large swaths of the area between 110th Street and the Harlem River went under the bulldozer for the standard tower-in-a-park development. Title I and public housing projects, as James Baldwin had noted, were "hideous" and "hated"— "cheerless as a prison."[28] Harrington concurred: Harlem residents did not need redevelopment as much as they needed an escape route. Baldwin wrote of blacks' horizontal mobility, skipping from one decaying Harlem block to another slightly better Harlem block but never able to remove the clutches of poverty and ghetto life. In Harrington's Necropolis, sustained racial segregation ensured it remained so, softening the "impact of all civil-rights legislation" passed in the previous decade. In other words, the integration of schools (the major civil rights legislation at the time of his writing) meant little if school districts remained segregated. Racial discrimination was Harlem's real crisis.[29]

Like emergent critics of urban renewal, including Jacobs and Martin Anderson, Harrington argued that the welfare state, as it functioned, only exacerbated the poor's problems. His narrative critiqued federal urban renewal, suggesting that the modern design paradigm pushed slums into their own cycle of decline. In fact, slum clearance and urban renewal represented "one of the greatest single domestic scandals of postwar America," perpetuating decline and allowing poverty and crime to proliferate. "This is where the nation builds the environment of the culture of poverty," he wrote of low-cost housing proposals, and he cited a manifold of problems to support that claim. "Many of them have become income ghettos"; they foster juvenile delinquency and gangs, are "modern poor farms where social disintegration is institutionalized," and result in displacement and mass evictions with no guarantee of resident relocation. In other words, the state had shaped a landscape fostering what would come to be known as the "under-class." The "old slums" were functioning neighborhoods with strong social bonds and mutual community aid. "Where the slum becomes truly perni-cious is when it becomes the environment of the culture of poverty, a spiritual and personal reality for its inhabitants as well as an area of dilapi-dation. This is when the slum becomes the breeding ground of crime, of vice, the creator of people who are lost to themselves and society." By building "new slums" to replace the "old slums," urban renewal allowed this culture to fester, thus creating a class of citizens isolated from those with economic and political power.[30]

To solve these problems, Harrington prescribed enhanced federal policy. He was a minority voice for stronger state influence among New York intel-lectuals confronting the city. His critique of the welfare state was largely a plea for a stronger and refocused federal program aimed at urban and ru-ral poor. As he put it, "only the Federal Government has the power to abol-ish poverty." The current system failed because it "helped those who are already capable of helping themselves," while "the poor get less out of the welfare state than any group in America." They were especially victimized by urban renewal, a federal project that wiped away their "slums" in favor of private, often high-priced, development.[31] Harrington recommended that "public housing must be conceived of as something more than improved physical shelter with heat and plumbing. It must be seen as an important organism for the creation of community life in the cities. . . . The projects and subsidized homes should be located as parts of neighborhoods, so that income groups, races, and cultures will mingle."[32] By 1962, however, the im-age of the welfare state was already in disrepair, and new public housing construction foundered in the period that followed.[33]

Rather than inspiring state intervention on a grand scale, Harrington's representation of the poverty issue, in the hands of critics on the right, soon emerged as the key argument against public welfare policy. In the words of historian Michael Katz, writers examining poverty in the 1960s, drawing on work by Harrington and others, "formalized long-standing arguments about behavioral pathology into a theory of culture, which, despite shifts in its political connotation, has proved remarkably tenacious." Harrington and the forerunner in the "culture of poverty" cycle, Oscar Lewis, ap-proached the problem from the left. Their understanding of the condition "meshed with developments in social psychology and reflected the assump-tion, widespread among liberal intellectuals, of the helplessness and passivity of dependent peoples, who needed the assistance of outsiders to break the cycles of deprivation and degradation that reproduced it from generation to generation." As a means to an end, they envisioned their writings "as a force energizing activist, interventionist public policy."[34] Scholars like Kenneth B. Clark, who examined the "pathology" of Harlem in *Dark Ghetto* and along with spouse Mamie Clark conducted pathbreaking work on the power of racial imagery in their "doll study" in the 1940s, as well as Gilbert Osofsky, whose history of the neighborhood prophesied "an enduring ghetto," had similar goals, arguing that workplace discrimination and substandard education opportunities contributed to the persistent cycle of Harlem life—a "permanent economic proletariat" or worse.[35]

The most infamous culture of poverty argument emerged from within the Johnson administration, seeking, as *The Other America* had, to influence and inform Great Society policy. In 1965, Daniel Patrick Moynihan published a seventy-eight-page internal report titled "The Negro Family: The Case for National Action," which echoed Harrington's analysis of Harlem.[36] Moynihan, noting the preponderance of female-headed households among blacks, was particularly critical of urban lower-class life. He wrote of black families caught in Clark's "tangle of pathology" with a genealogy that Moynihan traced to American slavery. The purpose of the "Moynihan Report," as it became known in popular culture, was, as scholar James T. Patterson argues, "to start a serious conversation among policymakers and to prod government officials into devising far-reaching socioeconomic reforms."[37] In this sense, "The Negro Family" differed little from Harrington's work, but it sparked a stinging backlash among progressives in ways that *The Other America* did not. The report converged on an important political moment where the New Left, southern Civil Rights groups, and the burgeoning "Black Power" movement possessed increasing leverage and power in liberal politics. Critics from these factions seized on selective passages and choice phrases from the report, particularly Moynihan's emphasis on culture and pathology. As historian Daniel Geary notes, "the report's ambiguity helped it become a crucial text in American political culture," offering a set of abstruse "keywords" that armed rhetoricians across the political spectrum.[38] For declensionist urban critics, Moynihan explicitly linked race with poverty culture and behavioral psychology in ways that keywords like "slums" and "blight" previously only implied. Fused with the narratives of Harrington, Clark, Osofsky, and other scholars, Moynihan's "tangle of pathology" provided a new language for opponents of civil rights, social programs, and the welfare state for years to come.[39]

In New York, imagery denoting a persistent "culture of poverty" or a "tangle of pathology" found a home in the investigative reports of the city's daily newspapers, feeding the backlash against public assistance and the welfare state. In the papers New York was changing, but no longer was the establishment press optimistic about that trend. The *Herald Tribune*'s collection *New York City in Crisis* put it bluntly: "During the past two decades, as problem has piled upon problem and crisis has followed crisis, more and more people have begun to wonder whether New York will continue to survive as a great city, or at least whether they can continue to survive it." These problems, as the narrative went, extended across the sectors of the city. They were "everywhere—in our schools, in our rising crime rate, in our frightening, skyrocketing narcotics problem, in our troubled hospitals, in our poverty and welfare programs—New York City is in trouble."[40]

New York City in Crisis propagated a narrative of a city that had lost its soul. Locating the turning point in 1945, the authors evoked White's Cosmopolis, citing New York's "dynamic character" as "a restless unwillingness to accept the status quo," which "in the past . . . was channeled into a tremendous creative civic energy." In the years since World War II, "the administrative machinery of the city has become so complicated and bureaucratic that few people know how their government functions, and—this is the tragedy—*even fewer have the slightest interest in finding out*." As the municipality separated itself from public oversight, the overseers—the press and the public—eventually retreated into fear and apathy. The report cataloged the complaints of the city's disparate critics since the war: New York was in the midst of a middle-class exodus; it was controlled by a Democratic machine that limited progress and was rarely held accountable; it was ravaged by urban renewal schemes and failed programs; and its young revolted in the streets.

Chapters on the "the disease of the slums" in Spanish and Central (black) Harlem reiterated the findings of concurrent observers of the "tangle of pathology." Testimony from Puerto Rican leader Dr. Francisco Trilla echoed Harrington's assessment of the Bowery poor and Harlem's blacks for his own community: "The Puerto Rican New Yorker is today caught in a poverty trap" that limited social mobility and resigned migrants and their children to perpetual "low occupational status." Similarly, the *Herald Tribune* noted the lack of attention Harlem received from the planners and developers orchestrating urban renewal. Unsatisfied with those causal interpretations, however, the series's authors turned to an emergent trope in the poverty debate: "welfare" dependency. They quoted the personal analysis of an unemployed Spanish Harlem resident in patronizing phonetics: "I need a job to feed some keeds. . . . I need money to leef" [sic]. Yet the reporter concluded, "As he grows more and more discouraged, he becomes increasingly resigned to living on welfare." In place of the lack of opportunity and support that Harrington associated with the cycle of poverty, *New York City in Crisis* argued that public assistance perpetuated poverty in the "cancerous" slums. "Of the more than 13,000 applications received by the Department of Welfare each month, more than 72 per cent come from Negroes and Puerto Ricans. . . . For many families on welfare, there is little incentive and less encouragement to break the chain."[41] Welfare "abuse" and "dependency" affixed additional keywords to the vocabulary of ghetto pathology.

In addition, *New York in Crisis* linked slum pathology with rising crime rates and public fears in an explicit manner. Whereas theorists like Jacobs saw community disintegration as the source of social disorder in New York City, the *Herald Tribune* reached another conclusion: moral decay wrought by the nature of slum life. "It is not the lack of a sense of community that drives people to rob, steal, murder, and take drugs," they wrote. "It is a sickness, a sickness of the mind and the body, often brought on by the deprivations that poverty and prejudice impose. *This is what has created terror in the streets.*" As a result of this pathology, New York's sidewalks were no longer safe for residents and visitors. Police Commissioner Michael Patrick Murphy admitted that the NYPD was engaged in "a war that seemingly has no end" in a city where daily averages were "nearly two murders, just under three forcible rapes, twenty-two robberies, and forty-one assaults." As if the shock value of those statistics were not enough, the *Herald Tribune* added that "these are complaints actually received; *no one knows how many crimes go unreported for one reason or another.*" At a loss for how to win back the streets, the authors noted that citizen vigilante groups in Crown Heights, Brooklyn, Clay Avenue in the Bronx, and a housing development in Manhattan had found some success, if anything, "in making the police, as well as themselves, feel safer in the areas they patrol."[42] Where state security apparatuses failed, the report implied, Mike Hammer's school of policing prevailed.

In October 1965, *Herald Tribune* columnists Jimmy Breslin and Dick Schaap intensified the image of Necropolis with tales of pathological crime perpetrators "you don't read about." Shortly before the mayoral election, they delivered a weeklong series on "the lonely crimes." In their words, "crime in New York City in the fall of 1965 is a compilation of little things. Lonely things that happen to people where they live, and where they are most frightened; all of it not big enough to reach newspaper readers." Dear reader, these were "*the crimes that can happen to you*."[43] Consisting of random criminal acts, less violent than rape and murder but no less terrorizing, "the lonely crimes" illustrated the nuisance of residing in New York City. The new bêtes noires were the mugger, the burglar, and the batterer, among others. Reporting a subway mugging, Schaap described the attacker as "one of hundreds, perhaps thousands, of criminals who perpetrate crimes of violence upon the people of New York, who have turned the city's streets and subways into lonely battle grounds, who have driven the city's residents into a frightening situation, trapped between terror and apathy, afraid of becoming a victim, almost equally afraid of helping a victim." One such victim voiced the anxiety of many New Yorkers in the 1960s: "I am always scared."[44]

That palpable sense of fear was a product of the racial and ethnic make-up, explicitly outlined by Schaap and Breslin, of the pathological criminal invasion. In their words, "No one disputes the fact that a large percentage of the crimes of violence in New York City are committed by Negroes and Puerto Ricans. . . . They are at the bottom economic level, and they are striking back and have no sense of what is right." A delicatessen owner and robbery victim noted that if "anybody comes in here with his hands in his pockets, I'm frightened." A thirty-six-year resident of New York, he insisted, "It was never like this. I never used to worry." Schaap and Breslin pointed to drugs as an ascendant problem with a trickle-down effect on crime. "There are thousands of addicts roaming the city streets and subways, almost all of them desperate to find some money for a fix." Wilding youths reemerged from their post-fifties funk to terrorize older adults. A sixty-one-year-old man was assaulted by teenagers in Brownsville, an increasingly impoverished Brooklyn neighborhood, who allegedly shouted, "Kill him, he's white"—a quote that undoubtedly confirmed white New York's worst fears about the era's demographic changes. The victim—foreshadowing vigilante revenge films—wished aloud that the neighborhood's infamous crime syndicate "Murder, Incorporated" "were back already instead of what we got going on here now." One victim "has never been so frightened—not even when he left Europe, fleeing from the Nazis a quarter of a century ago."[45]

Schaap and Breslin concluded with a resonant image of 1965 New York City, one eerily reminiscent of a Mickey Spillane fantasy: "Women carry tear-gas pens in their pocketbooks. Cab drivers rest iron bars on the front seat next to them. Store owners keep billy sticks next to the cash register. And people enter parks and the subways and the side streets of New York, the most important city in the world, only in fear." The worry and the weapons, according to the reporters, were justified. Like the victims living in constant fear, New Yorkers were to remain vigilant, steadily aware that crime was just around the corner. As they wrote, "These crimes of violence, these senseless spontaneous crimes against people, can happen to anyone, in any place at any time, on Park Avenue or on Broadway, at home or at work, and . . . they are everyone's responsibility."[46] In the mid-sixties, then, the *Herald Tribune*'s staffers defined the crime-ridden Necropolis. They set the city on edge through their allusions to impoverished slums caught up in a spiral of decline and turning out a pathological underclass of criminals—muggers, rapists, and general misfits—that emerged at night from the projects and shadows to terrorize an innocent public. Heavy on the sensational acts and light on potential remedies, series like "The Lonely Crimes" fed elite concerns about citizen apathy and an ever-more-"ungovernable" New York.

Acquiring the knowledge of crimes that "were not big enough to reach the newspapers" intensified the sense of fear, if only because the acts worthy of headlines were so horrid and seemingly random. High-profile cases like the rape and slaying of Katherine "Kitty" Genovese in March 1964 added to the anxiety in the city. Not since the infamous "Capeman" murder underscored ethnic tensions between Puerto Ricans and white West Siders in 1957 had a crime so confused and disturbed New Yorkers.[47] In the darkness of Kew Gardens, Queens, Winston Moseley stabbed Genovese as she tried to enter her house after a long night of work. Nearly an hour passed before a bleeding Genovese was loaded into an ambulance and taken to a hospital; she died en route. The events in the interim proved most troubling to the readers of the *Times* and other dailies. Ten minutes after the initial attack, Moseley had returned to find Genovese struggling inside the rear foyer of her apartment building. He proceeded to rape her multiple times as she cried out in horror. Neighbors had heard her pleas for help, but most failed to act. Their inaction complicated Jacobs's "eyes [and ears] on the street" theory of neighborhood safety, which on that night in Kew Gardens seemed largely deaf and blind to the carnage.[48]

Subsequent coverage of the Genovese murder in the *Times* spun a literal narrative of the incident, indicting another pathological urban ailment in the 1960s: public apathy. At a lunch meeting with *Times* metropolitan editor A. M. Rosenthal, Commissioner Murphy noted the high number of witnesses who failed to come to Genovese's rescue, much less call the police. Rosenthal sent reporter Martin Gansberg to investigate, and the resulting article, "37 People Who Saw Murder Didn't Call the Police," alarmed citizens and warranted further consideration. Gansberg reported that despite the fact that nearby voices had twice scared off Moseley, "not one person telephoned the police during the assault; one witness called after the woman was dead." That witness "explained that he had called the police after much deliberation," which included phoning a friend for advice and then crossing the roof to another apartment. Witness testimony fed the narrative: "We thought it was a lovers' quarrel"; "I didn't want my husband to get involved"; "Frankly, we were afraid"; "I was tired . . . I went back to bed." The resident who finally called admitted that he too didn't want to get involved. In both the act and its aftermath, the Kitty Genovese murder validated critics and citizens' worst fears about urban safety.[49]

Rosenthal's swiftly published book, a thin volume ruminating on the murder, inefficient policing, and fear entitled *Thirty-Eight Witnesses* (1964), further sensationalized the event and fueled the potent narrative of neighborhood apathy. While Rosenthal and the *Times* shunned the tabloid embellishment of Moseley's race and Genovese's homosexuality—Rosenthal revealed that in the aftermath of the murder he "received a few nasty letters demanding to know why we 'concealed' the fact that Moseley was a Negro," indicating the importance among white readers to underscore the connection between race and crime—*Thirty-Eight Witnesses* broadly considered what the author termed "the disease of apathy." According to Rosenthal's reading, New York had been afflicted with a pathology that left critics and scholars mystified. Rosenthal cited the varied diagnoses of local social scientists, heightening concerns about the mental health of the city and its citizens. The behavior of the witnesses "goes to the heart of whether this is a community or a jungle," noted one. One psychiatrist, echoing Harrington, indicted the middle class, who have "a nice life" but disassociate themselves from matters of the street. "It's the air of all New York, the air of injustice," the psychiatrist said. "The feeling that you might get hurt if you act and that whatever you do, you will be the one to suffer."[50] As these passages suggest, Gansberg's reportage and Rosenthal's book—in addition to the public outrage surrounding the case—focused on the behavior of the witnesses at the expense of the crime itself. The image emphasized the crumbling of the social realm, the disintegration of community bonds, and the fear of public space—apathy as urban pathology. It was a diagnosis that has been perpetually linked to 1960s New York, despite the fact that the circumstances of that Kew Gardens night have long been disputed.[51]

Necropolis imagery of the reciprocal pathologies of slum poverty, crime, and middle-class apathy migrated into influential jeremiads on New York and the urban crisis. Richard Whalen's *A City Destroying Itself*, a sullied version of "Here Is New York," was emblematic of the trend. Whalen, a Queens native and columnist in the Luce empire, became a major figure in the Republican Party, working on Richard Nixon's presidential campaign in 1968 and later with Ronald Reagan and George H. W. Bush. In between Whalen published an influential Republican call-to-arms, *Catch the Falling Flag* (1972), and served as a vital New Right strategist.[52] Published in 1965, Whalen's unapologetic "angry view of New York" was so harsh even the managing editor found it "a bit extreme."[53] Combining the themes of sustainability with safety concerns, *A City Destroying Itself* featured detailed analysis of Whalen's interest in architecture and urban space. From the American Institute of Architects report of 1964, he presented a compendium of political and economic ailments facing the city. Class was a concern, as white flight left a polarized Manhattan in its wake. Commuters expended their civic energy where they lived rather than worked—Whalen, himself, was writing from suburban Sands Point. For Whalen this demographic shift posed a significant risk to the city's fiscal durability as tax revenue left and the poor became increasingly dependent on the state, thus playing on the trope of the "ungovernable city" and its unsustainable public sector. Business interests too were at fault. Large corporations and their leaders, he noted, gravitated to New York City because its size and oversaturation of capital allowed institutions to shirk responsibility. In smaller cities, locally based corporations had a de facto civic duty because of pure visibility, but "vast and diverse New York offers the opportunity to hide, and corporations generally, to their discredit and New York's disadvantage, have taken it."[54] In this sense, Whalen's practical appeal for reform and renewed capital investment echoed Harrington's assessment of civic responsibility and class segregation. Much of his text featured a pragmatic approach to the city's political, economic, and environmental problems, arguably absent of any strict ideology. In this section of the book there was little that lived up to Whalen's promise of an "angry view of New York."

But in the first twenty pages, the reader encountered abundant grievances concerning crime and cultural decay. Like other critics of apathetic New York, Whalen perceived a social breakdown—a pathological rot—as the city's greatest threat going forward. The first few chapters fabricated an image of the city in chaos—it was a picture utterly incongruous to his troubled, but manageable, image of New York's political economy. As he put it, "it is not the economic disorder of New York that throws a shadow across an urban civilization. The truly terrible costs of New York are social and spiritual. These accrue in endless human discomfort, inconvenience, harassment, and fear, which become part of the pervasive background, like the noise and filth, but are much deadlier."[55] Whalen suggested that somewhere in the 1950s and early 1960s the city's personality underwent a radical shift that spelled destruction for the city's "heritage."

Decay manifested itself on the street—in New York's diverse public sphere. Violence and crime, according to Whalen, were now a part of every-day life in New York City—a "crime flood" by 1964.[56] For the "most prudent citizen," an encounter with random crime, he argued, was a distinct possibility; "indeed, the distinctive characteristic of crime in New York may be its random, unprovoked savagery." The criminal element constituted the city's most terminal ailment: "Anyone searching for the causes of New York's decline encounters problems of awesome complexity, but a fundamental cause is starkly apparent and simply expressed: *the city is not safe.*" Thus, Whalen echoed the trope of ubiquitous random crime going back to Spillane. It was now a city "best enjoyed from a comfortable seat" rather than on the street.[57]

Whalen's narrative of New York's decline pointed to crime and pathology in the guise of spiritual loss—a cause célèbre among urban critics on the right who saw an increasingly acquiescent public idly watch while the city crumbled. Whalen wrote that "New York shows alarming signs of spiritual malnutrition and death-by-inches." It was the kind of sick city "that cries 'Jump' to a would-be suicide perched on a window ledge."[58] Edward C. Banfield, one of the first academic chroniclers of the urban crisis, reiterated this idea of spiritual loss. In *The Unheavenly City*, Banfield disputed the existence of the crisis, calling it a product of heightened expectations. Instead he argued that slum pathology had taken hold in American cities and its unholy nature spelled doom. In Banfield's Necropolis, slums were plagued by pathological "present-oriented" denizens whose search for sexual satisfaction and quick and easy ecstasy contributed to a spike in violent crime and an overall moral decline.[59]

As Robert Beauregard observes, Banfield's book shifted the paradigm on the urban crisis. New Left critics pilloried his research and methodology, ridiculing his less-than-rigorous scholarship and laissez-faire urban economics. Figures on the right, including fellow academic James Q. Wilson and Irving Kristol, praised *The Unheavenly City* as "the only serious intellectual book that has been written about urban problems" and "easily the most enlightening book that has been written about the 'urban crisis' in the U.S.," respectively.[60] Whalen and Banfield suggested that New York and similar cities required "benign neglect," a phrase popularized by Moynihan then working under Nixon, to purge their blasphemous elements and bloated welfare systems. These critics literally or figuratively left the city behind, and were not above fear-mongering and sensationalizing when making their case in the 1960s. Citations of New York's pathologies played a formative role in the political shake-up of the decade, and fortified an ever-stronger critique of state intervention on behalf of the city.

· · · · · ·

By the end of the 1960s, consumers of a diverse media understood that New York City was in a full-blown economic, social, and cultural crisis, riddled with a pathological underclass, and, from the perspective of cultural elites, "ungovernable." Michael Harrington believed that only a more proactive state could address the problems of poverty and government inefficiency. Yet, as poverty historian Michael Katz has argued, political leaders seeking to overhaul the welfare system, including Kennedy and Johnson, were hamstrung by the design of the welfare system going back to the New Deal. Its original policy architects "bifurcated" the American system "into social insurance and public assistance"—what Katz calls a "unique, unsatisfactory, semiwelfare state." When Harrington brought the problem of poverty to the nation's attention in 1962, the "semiwelfare" state's design constrained policymakers and all but eliminated the possibility of any major overhauls to the already-in-decline welfare capitalism of the era—despite later proposals for a negative income tax to ensure a guaranteed income for all Americans or even universal health care.[61] Moreover, consistent critiques of the state's signature programs, including Harrington's indictment of urban renewal, questioned the efficacy of planning and other government social programs.

Neoconservatives and critics within the emerging New Right like Whalen and Banfield, nonetheless, seized on Harrington and Moynihan's cultural and psychological explanations for urban poverty and "turned the concept's original politics on its head." According to Katz, "the culture of poverty became a euphemism for the pathology of the undeserving poor, an explanation for their condition, an excuse as in the writing of Edward Banfield, for both inaction and harsh, punitive public policy."[62] Despite Moynihan's otherwise liberal credentials, his critics labeled him neoconservative, and his open companionship with members of that movement's vanguard, including Nathan Glazer, James Q. Wilson, and Irving Kristol, damaged his reputation as a pro-welfare advocate.[63] Instead of inciting a proactive state—beyond the limited programs initiated by Congress and the Johnson administration in the "War on Poverty"—the narratives of Harrington and Moynihan inspired an ensuing "underclass debate" around crime and race, in the guise of urban economics, that consumed antiwelfare state discourse into the Reagan era.

Beginning with journalist Ken Auletta, critics of the new underclass, a simplified category of poverty that lumped together the interests of long-term welfare recipients and citizens with a mental illness with criminals, drug addicts, hustlers, drifters, and "shoppingbag ladies," defined poverty by behavior. Echoing Jacob Riis's earlier essentialist characterizations of the lower orders, this catchall designation of class—a category long associated with political economy now employed culturally—allowed impoverished citizens like East Harlem public housing's "problem families" to become poster children of physical decline and government waste. Later the underclass's "welfare queen" would be added to the arsenal of coded racial rhetoric employed in the New Right's monolithic attack on state antipoverty programs. Also out of the underclass debate emerged James Q. Wilson and George L. Kelling's influential "broken windows" theory in 1982. Wilson and Kelling explicitly linked underclass behavior to urban decay, suggesting that social disorder was the overwhelming contributing factor to the decline of cities like New York. The only way to reverse said decline was to attack the root of the problem and wipe out disorder and underclass activities. Hence, the state's primary role in "combating" the problem of poverty became policing deviants, graffiti artists, addicts, and drifters—a "zero tolerance" policy on nonnormative behavior in public spaces. The "broken windows" theory had profound implications for New York City as officials ushered in neoliberal economic development beginning under Ed Koch and bolstered police powers, most notably under the regime of Rudolph Giuliani. If anything, the success of the underclass debate in limiting the state's redevelopment powers highlights the vital role of Necropolis's pathologies in shaping political culture during and after the "urban crisis."[64] For this considerable sea change, politicians like Koch and Giuliani received assistance from Hollywood filmmakers who offered the city's underclass a starring role in the crime films of the 1970s.

Part IV **Detour to Fun City**

Cultural Responses to the Death of New York,
1967–1985

· ·

Fear City on Film

....

In 1966, very early in his first term, Mayor John Lindsay asserted that New York was "still a fun city." From the day he took office, Lindsay faced a variety of challenges, including a crippling transit strike that left commuters stranded in the cold. Fearing disorder in such situations, he took to the streets and the airwaves preaching calm, civility, and patience. In reaction to Lindsay's narrative of "Fun City," however, *Herald Tribune* columnist Dick Schaap mocked the mayor for his "wonderful sense of humor," while at the same time suggesting that the transit strike might provide relief from the lonely crimes on the city's subways and buses. Although it disturbed the purveyors of Necropolis like Schaap, portraying New York as Fun City was a conscious project for Lindsay.[1] During his first year in office, he established the Mayor's Office of Film, Theater, and Broadcasting to encourage film production on the streets of New York, creating jobs and revenue for the city, with the added intent of informally advertising Lindsay's fun cosmopolitan vision.[2]

The most successful of the over three hundred productions filmed in New York City during Lindsay's tenure, however, failed to portray Fun City. Postwar films set in New York prior to 1966 imagined the kind of white-collar glamour Lindsay represented, but these images mostly emanated from Hollywood soundstages.[3] As biographer Vincent Cannato points out, "the tone of New York movies changed by the late 1960s and early 1970s. It became darker. . . . The city was a near-immovable obstacle to the happiness of men and women determined to live there . . . [and] crime—a seedy kind of crime—became the center of many New York movies of the time." In fact, the message of these films seemed to validate the fears propagated by concurrent commentators. In the words of Cannato, "with these portrayals, the image of New York City as a place of danger, decay, and division became solidified in the nation's mind."[4]

The image was so powerful that the Council for Public Safety, in its struggle with Lindsay, distributed leaflets declaring "Welcome to Fear City" and detailing the perils of New York to tourists and visitors at the city's transportation hubs. The film industry projected a similar greeting. In Hollywood, a new ratings system classified feature films by age-appropriate

FIGURE 5 Mayor John Lindsay's creation of the Mayor's Office of Film, Theater, and Broadcasting allowed for more authentic, sometimes improvised, representations of New York City life. For instance, the famous "I'm walking here!" scene from *Midnight Cowboy*, pictured above, was allegedly the product of driver error, as the unscripted and unsolicited taxi driver arrived unannounced and nearly hit actors Jon Voight and Dustin Hoffman.

categories, which allowed for greater verisimilitude in depictions of violence, sex, and speech. Structural changes within the industry ushered in a new wave of filmmaking that transferred the means of production from the old studio system to young, bold filmmakers who grew up within the confines of Cold War conformity, digested film theory and the European new wave, attended film school, and sought to utterly transform American cinema. This group centered itself in Los Angeles, but many, including native Martin Scorsese, used New York as a backdrop for their groundbreaking works.[5] With Lindsay's incentives for location shooting, filmmakers could now represent cities like New York with added realism. Recognizing the power of popular culture to shape public perception during a crisis, Lindsay wished to restore Cosmopolis—New York City as a great place to live, work, play, and invest. Yet liberated from the strictures of old Hollywood, emergent filmmakers working on the streets of New York destroyed Fun City.

New Hollywood, then, brought narratives of New York's pathologies to the national stage. With a special emphasis on crime (*Mean Streets, Serpico, Dog Day Afternoon, Shaft*), disorder (*Death Wish, Taxi Driver, Panic in Needle Park*), illegal narcotics (*Panic in Needle Park, Super Fly*), sexual danger (*Klute, Looking for Mr. Goodbar*), and the general inconvenience of living in the city (*Midnight Cowboy, The Out of Towners*), New York productions portrayed a place where "fun" and economic opportunity came with great risk, if not a heavy price. These films seemed to say, as *Times* critic Vincent Canby noted, "New York City is a mess. . . . It's run by fools. Its citizens are at the mercy of its criminals who, as often as not, are protected by an unholy alliance of civil libertarians and crooked cops. The air is foul. The traffic is impossible. Services are diminishing and the morale is such that ordering a cup of coffee in a diner can turn into a request for a fat lip."[6] This cycle of stories consummated the postwar narrative of Necropolis at arguably New York City's lowest point: the "drop dead" moment of the seventies' political, economic, and social crisis. If anything, the films of this era established an enduring image of New York and its citizens, one that still resonates in the popular culture of today—dirty, gritty, gruff, and often violent.

Criminal activity and its causes, effects, and potential remedies were central to the filmic narrative, as many films examined Schaap and Breslin's "lonely crimes." From *Midnight Cowboy*, one of the earlier New York productions, films portrayed an inconvenient city defined by swindles, muggings, and other annoyances. As new production rules opened the door for vivid depictions of violence, the authoritarian vigilante reemerged in films like *Death Wish*, feeding the reactionary backlash politics that defined the era and transforming the likes of Charles Bronson into an American hero.[7] Most films, however, offered a more passive and less risky response: escape—and many New Yorkers took this lesson to heart. The filmic Necropolis would have other historical consequences as well. When the city needed a bailout in the mid-1970s, Gerald Ford's spiteful response was rendered all the more amenable because of the vicious image of New York that the nation digested. The lack of empathy for New York's plight resulted from an antiurban milieu that advocated individualistic reactionary politics, the gutting of the municipal welfare state, and neoliberal economics—a political culture molded by the image of Necropolis in both intellectual critique and popular amusements.[8]

· · · · · ·

Almost twenty years earlier, E. B. White, in less ominous tones, celebrated the intrepid migrants who came to New York City to fulfill their dreams.

The transplanted New Yorker gave the city its verve and excitement and ultimately its power as an economic and cultural innovator. Two decades later, American films portrayed a city where migrants and visitors were only welcomed as targets for an enterprising native underclass. The late 1960s city required a relative knowledge base, because, as these films suggested, urban social life had morphed into an elaborate confidence game. The narrative went as such: small-town dreamers, coming from the trustworthy communities of Nixon's "Middle America," find themselves in a city distinctly lacking in trust. Disembarking into the crowded streets of Manhattan via Grand Central Station or Port Authority Bus Terminal, characters such as Joe Buck in *Midnight Cowboy* and George and Gwen Kellerman in *The Out of Towners* (1970) behaved like any lost tourist, seeking help from strangers on how to navigate the confusing vertical and horizontal geography of the metropolis.[9] Uncorrupted by fear, antisocial behavior, and the lonely crimes of deception, natural community instincts took over even when New Yorkers appeared all too eager to offer guidance. The swindles that followed left visitors distraught and penniless, trapped in a city that literally crumbles before them. Repudiating Jane Jacobs's claim that the trust of the city materialized out of informal contact on the streets, these films suggested that such contact only led to disaster, whether through crime, heartache, or an overstressed bureaucracy. In the case of Joe Buck, only his deep formal relationship with Enrico Rizzo provides any semblance of comfort and hope.[10]

In John Schlesinger's *Midnight Cowboy*, Joe Buck escapes the containment, confinement, and violence of Texas for the perceived liberty of New York.[11] Brutalized by a past of sexual abuse and a dead-end diner gig, Buck dreams of fulfilling the sexual fantasies of bored housewives up and down Park Avenue. His violent past certainly warped his odd ambition, but Buck's belief in the feasibility of such an occupation symbolized the long-standing image of New York as a site of freedom and liberation, a destination for outsiders like himself leaving restrictive loose-talking small towns.[12] This was not the city Buck encounters upon his arrival in New York; rather, his distinctive cowboy garb makes him an easy mark, and natives swiftly fleece him out of his marginal nest egg. The hotel porter silently takes him for a twenty-dollar tip. Just when Buck thinks he has found his first hustle, she takes him for cab fare. One afternoon in New York City, and Buck is forty short in the wallet. Plot points like this led critic Rex Reed to call *Midnight Cowboy* "perhaps the worst indictment of the city of New York ever captured on film."[13]

FIGURE 6 In *Midnight Cowboy*, Joe Buck's (Jon Voight) arrival in New York begins with him stumbling upon a body lying on the sidewalk, which his fellow citizens ignore, outside the famous Fifth Avenue address of Tiffany & Co.

Flung out onto the street, Buck makes the acquaintance that will eventually transform him into a citizen, but not before learning valuable lessons on the nature of New York street life. Enrico Rizzo, learning of Buck's ambition, feigns knowledge of New York's sexual underworld. "Society dames" are not going down to Forty-Second Street to pick up "street trade," he notes. For a modest finder's fee, Rizzo sets Buck up with his "friend" O'Daniel, who, as it turns out, is a hustler of the spiritual variety. In one day, Joe Buck, who came to New York to hustle, has been hustled up and down the island. Buck seeks vengeance on the native, chasing Rizzo's apparition through the city only to find he is always one step ahead. Rizzo represents the city personified, willing to kick a man when he is down and rob him blind. Lonely and dejected in the heartless city, Buck watches television. As he stares onto Times Square below, the show's host asks of a fad product, "Isn't this a case of conning a lot of lonely people?"[14] In *Midnight Cowboy*'s Necropolis, he might as well have been talking about the so-called crossroads of the world.

Following a series of travails that rob Joe Buck of his savings, he discovers that the source of the city's misery may in turn be his salvation. To survive he becomes skilled in the lonely crimes and accepts Rizzo's companionship and instruction on New York City's confidence game. Thus commences a series of long and short cons, Rizzo's tutorial on urban survival for the down and out. At the laundry, Rizzo demonstrates how an offer of help turns into a free wash. At the hatter, where Buck's Stetson gets a much-needed steam, they skip out on the check and steal another customer's chapeau. Rizzo breaks into a subway shine box to clean Buck's boots. Now properly groomed for success and educated by Rizzo, Buck is transformed into a New Yorker prepared to perpetrate crime for their mutual fiscal benefit.[15]

Joe Buck's transformation also marked a shift from his deferent, polite chivalrous manners to a more confrontational, if not vulgar, attitude that came to symbolize New Yorkers in this period. In 1970, the *Times* pointed to an air of rudeness and incivility that had descended upon residents. It could not be measured—"unlike violent crimes"—"but almost any trip to the public [is] evidence that traditional patterns of civil behavior are breaking down." It was particularly apparent to the "out-of-towners who are in the city on business or for pleasure, and New Yorkers who have moved away and have returned for a visit—all seem to sense the current climate of rudeness." Regarding the city's sudden penchant for anger and hostility, one psychologist noted that "uncivil behavior stems from feelings of anonymity," what he called "deindividuation." Feelings of instability, uncertainty, and alienation drove citizens away from social interaction and thus destroyed communities.[16]

Arthur Hiller's *The Out of Towners* fused these recognized themes of incivility, rudeness, and a declining business climate to paint an ugly portrait of the city. The film starred Jack Lemmon and Sandy Dennis as George and Gwen Kellerman, an Ohio couple that travels to New York for George's potential promotion and transfer. At home, the Kellermans live a rather charmed life replete with two children, a dog, and a large, but relatively modest, suburban home. While Gwen remains hesitant about the move, George's excitement can hardly be contained. For him, New York is still Cosmopolis, a city defined by mobility, wealth, and status, and a site of liberation from staid suburban and midwestern conformity. Once their trip commences, however, Gwen's fears are confirmed. *The Out of Towners* is Murphy's Law manifested, with the lonely crimes in a starring role.[17]

As the protagonists encounter an amalgamation of urban ills, the film showcases New York City's ungovernability in Technicolor. An overtaxed JFK Airport first delays, then reroutes the Kellermans' flight to Boston, which, as the flight attendant informs them, occurs "almost every night." Upon arrival in New York, preceded by a long and harrowing railway journey along the Northeast corridor, they find the city crippled by labor grievances beyond their imagination. A transit strike—"How can a big city like this have a transit strike?" George asks rhetorically—grinds the city to a halt, clogging Grand Central Terminal with immobile citizens much like the futuristic transients in another dystopic vision of New York, *Soylent Green* (1973).[18] Parodying actual events, like the 1966 transit strike, a sanitation strike like the one Lindsay confronted in 1968 inundates the city with mountains of trash, even on Park Avenue, "one of the cleanest streets in the world."[19] In this sense, the film suggested that a bloated public sector paralyzed New York, limiting its progress as more modern cities, less reliant on public transportation and municipal unions, moved forward and embraced the neoliberal economy.[20]

By demonstrating the exhausting inconvenience of urban life, *The Out of Towners* echoed Necropolis's trope of apathy. Like Joe Buck's passage through the gates of the Port Authority, the Kellermans' New York arrival carries an initiation into the local hustle. The Waldorf-Astoria Hotel cancels their reservation, turning their room over to one of the many stranded transients taking up lodging in the lobby. An unsuspecting stranger offers unsolicited guidance to the helpless visitors. In a city of no vacancies, the Samaritan tells of a friend who owns a "small hotel" a few blocks away and offers to help them in exchange for $10. George, fearful of being conned, questions the existence of said hotel. "No one trusts anyone anymore," the stranger replies; "you don't trust me, I'll take you there then." He even offers to return the money to ease their lack of trust, yet once it has been restored, the stranger mugs the visitors at gunpoint on the dark street outside the hotel.[21]

Images like these animated the supposed ubiquity of the lonely crimes. The Kellermans are robbed on Park Avenue, a remaining bastion of white New York wealth in the late sixties. Later, they are dropped off at Central Park, where, against their best wishes, they pass out in a meadow. As they drift asleep, George notes the dramatic changes of New York City in recent years, citing the halcyon days of World War II, when "people were safer. . . . With bombs dropping they were safer in the war!" As they grab a few hours of rest before George's interview, a man wearing a black cape walks off with George's expensive watch, and a stray dog steals their only hope for breakfast. When George refuses to get help for a Spanish-speaking child they find on a bench, Gwen reveals her true feelings about New York: "Go on, become like everybody else in this city, don't worry about anyone but yourself." Ultimately, the muggings, the deception, and the lonely crimes threaten to destroy their marriage—as symbolized by Gwen's missing wedding ring. She is ready to "surrender" to New York City, while George remains defiant: "You're just a city. . . . Persons are stronger than cities!" Necropolis suggested otherwise.[22]

The Out of Towners functioned as poor marketing for a city in crisis—the kind of image the later "I Love NY" campaign sought to counteract.[23] Its arguments against the city range from short—a police officer tells them "You're lucky [that they live elsewhere]"—to dissertation length. In the end, Gwen finds no joy in George's successful pursuit of the promotion. Instead, she synthesizes feelings she had bottled up: "I was hoping you would say no. I was hoping you would say that you and your wife don't really belong in New York. You wanted to live the rest of your life in Ohio. That you never want to see a big city again as long as you live. That you didn't want to live here or in, uh, Chicago or San Francisco or New Orleans or Paris or any other place where people have to live on top of each other, and they don't have enough room to walk or to breathe or to smile at each other. You don't want to step on garbage in the street or be attacked by dogs or have to give away watches in the middle of your sleep to men in black capes. . . . That you wish you never came here." Gwen's soliloquy constitutes her actual surrender to New York, the city that defeated and crushed her family. The white postwar American Dream, Gwen suggests, has no place in Necropolis. To live "on top of one another," navigating garbage and burdened by labor disputes, was hardly the virtue of civilization. With Cosmopolis in flux, admitting defeat and escaping the city's clutches were far more attractive options.[24]

As a dark farce, *The Out of Towners* showcased ubiquitous crime, but the film eschewed graphic representation of violence. Most New York films in this period, however, took advantage of the industry's new license to imagine murder and mayhem beyond the melodramatic last-gasp death scene of classical Hollywood. Films like *Mean Streets* (1973), *Shaft* (1971), *Super Fly* (1972), and *The Godfather* (1972) spilled blood in new provocative ways.[25] Before the ratings system was put in place, killings often featured bloodless or off-screen murders. Now, viewers watched as Michael Corleone, in cold blood, blasted Sollozzo's and McCluskey's brains across a Bronx restaurant. *Klute* (1971) and *Looking for Mr. Goodbar* (1977) portrayed the travails of female sexuality and sexual assault unlike ever before, when limitations on representations of sex similarly limited depictions of sexual violence.[26] Relaxed restrictions on violence and sex pushed filmmakers toward sensational depictions of those acts. Just as the lonely crimes inspired the trope of inconvenience in *Midnight Cowboy* and *The Out of Towners*, high-profile violence provided fodder for exploitive productions that pushed the boundaries of taste and intensified Necropolis's connection with random criminality.[27]

Michael Winner's *Death Wish* was the most extreme example of the ex-ploitive, sadistic New York crisis film. Running the gamut of violent urban fears in astonishingly unapologetic form, it told the story of Paul Kersey (Charles Bronson), a man poised "to clean up the most violent town in the world." In *Death Wish* a Genovese-like home invasion leads to a mother and daughter's brutal murder and rape, characterizing what the film's trailer called a "typical afternoon in New York City."[28] In many respects, *Death Wish* functioned as a Mickey Spillane novel on celluloid—much more so than the film version of *Kiss Me Deadly*. *Death Wish* was a blatant response to ascendant "southern strategy" backlash politics in both dialogue and action, and the city's film critics were nonplussed. *The Today Show*'s Gene Shalit said it was "the thriller that the 'fed-up' generation has been waiting for." Canby called it "despicable," "a bird brained movie to cheer the hearts of the far-right wing . . . one that raises complex questions in order to offer bigoted, frivolous, oversimplified answers." He argued that *Death Wish* "exploit[ed] fear irresponsibly," confirming the era's anxiety that cultural texts validated ideologies bent on damaging New York's reputation. As he noted, this movie, "produced by tourists, exploits very real fears and social problems and suggests simple-minded remedies." Noted psychiatrist Fred-eric Wertham, critic of crime representations in popular culture since the comic book scare he fostered in the 1950s, argued that *Death Wish* was "con-tinuing to create a whole atmosphere of brutality," a film "based not on freedom but on fear."[29]

New Yorkers polled by reporter Judy Klemesrud affirmed the assessment. Most were entertained by the film and cheered Paul Kersey's impressive body count, but many insisted that the movie portrayed a fantastic New York, and they were left disturbed by its "vigilante philosophy." While a sixty-two-year-old woman called it a "lovely [film], a very *comfortable* pic-ture," male respondents were more critical. One called *Death Wish* "the worst picture I've ever seen in my life" and insisted that racism was central to its theme: "A white man [like Kersey] can get away with anything in America." Another noted, "It's untrue of the New York I know. . . . I never come across those situations." Still, *Death Wish* found success across the country, with millions in ticket receipts, and sparked four sequels also starring Charles Bronson between 1982 and 1994. Despite local distaste for the film, its representation of violence and vigilantism shaped the national perception of New York City. One viewer said that "everyone should see 'Death Wish' in order to have his consciousness raised."[30] Wertham researched *Death Wish* viewers as well and concluded that "if one probes a little beneath the immediate reaction to the film one finds not a longing for violence but a pervasive fear of what in these times might happen to oneself and one's loved ones, and a deepening feeling of pessimism about being protected."[31]

According to the film, ubiquitous crime—including lonely crimes tinged with violence—merged with an ineffective police force and an apathetic citizenry to render the city uninhabitable. After a romantic vacation in Hawaii, Paul Kersey returns to his office only to be greeted with harrowing crime statistics from Sam, his neofascist coworker. "How does it feel to be back in the war zone?" Sam asks, and then delivers the alarming number of murders Kersey missed. Seeing the city as a battlefield, Sam suggests housing "underprivileged" criminals in concentration camps and establishing a 1:1 ratio of police officers to citizens. Dino De Laurentiis, the film's producer, argued that the film was "an open invitation to the authorities to come up with remedies to the problem of urban violence, and fast." In this sense, Sam's reactionary obsession with order provides one of two voices of reason in the film.[32]

According to the geography of *Death Wish*, no part of New York City is secure from random violence. Although the Kerseys reside on the white, middle-class outpost of Riverside Drive, their block is a hotbed of criminality and disorder. When Paul fashions a weapon out of a roll of quarters and a sock, he merely steps outside his door to find target practice, as omnipresent street crime is the natural order. Finding three black men terrorizing a white male in an alley is depicted as normal, as are "thugs" surveying the subway for potential victims. Even the supermarket functions as a site of terror. Three young delinquents eyeball Paul's wife and daughter and acquire their address off a delivery slip. Moments later, posing as the supermarket's delivery clerk, the three gain entry into the Kersey home and proceed to burglarize, rape, and murder with abandon. In all areas of the city, including the supermarket and the "good neighborhoods," the filmmakers suggested that violent crime could happen anywhere to anyone.[33]

Against the backdrop of the Knapp Commission's revelations of police corruption, crime victims in filmic Necropolis could expect little assistance from the NYPD.[34] After the Kellermans' mugging in *The Out of Towners*,

FIGURE 7 Charles Bronson as Paul Kersey (center of each frame) hunts muggers in New York City. As Vincent Canby wrote, *Death Wish* "exploited fears irresponsibly." The film was the consummate vehicle for New York City's alleged pathologies, which did not render street, subway, or home safe from wanton (mostly black as seen here) criminality.

the NYPD demonstrates little interest in pursuing the matter. In *Death Wish*, bureaucratic red tape, incompetent and corrupt superiors, and a time-consuming focus on victimless crime prevented the police from containing the violent criminals threatening civilization. Hence the film entered into the conversation on effective policing that ruled political discourse after the urban rebellions of the 1960s. As historian Michael Flamm has shown, the "law and order" issue, exploited by Richard Nixon and George Wallace on the national stage, resulted from both an actual rise in public fear and the manipulation of the public by the New Right. The film functioned as part of the latter, exploiting fears in order to trumpet the Right's critique of liberal social and economic policy in the Nixon era, and thus operating as agitprop for law-and-order proponents. *Death Wish* was a filmic all-points bulletin about the contingencies of police work overseen by liberal mayoral administrations like John Lindsay's.[35]

Portraying the NYPD as overextended and ineffective proved central to the law-and-order propaganda to which *Death Wish* subscribed. After the home invasion, Kersey inquires about the probability of capturing his wife's killers. As the detective responds, "There's a chance—sure . . . [but] I'd be

FIGURE 8 In *Death Wish*, as Paul Kersey's body count rises and crime declines, sensational media coverage of his exploits, as well as commentary on the effectiveness of vigilantism in combating urban crime, becomes a key subplot of the film.

less than honest if I gave you more hope, Mr. Kersey. *In the city, that's the way it is.*" Pursuing random violent crimes proves a futile endeavor. Detective Ochoa, the clumsy buffoon investigating Kersey's own crimes as "the vigilante," presses officers to feed reporters lies about progress in the case, not to lie to protect police information on suspects, but rather to put forth the narrative that the investigation has progressed and suspects are under surveillance. Despite this fabrication, the hunt for the vigilante proceeds slowly when competent police intelligence would have pinpointed Kersey in a matter of hours. In a most interesting turn of events, the district attorney, in order to prevent public uproar and copycat crimes, pushes Ochoa to chase Kersey out of town rather than arrest him. Kersey's frontier justice decreases crime, but, as the district attorney and police commissioner explain, that is bad for police business. In Necropolis, random violent crime equals job security for corrupt public servants.[36]

Apathetic politicos and rampant violent crime also found a home in Martin Scorsese's *Taxi Driver* (1976), a film that shared as many similarities as differences with *Death Wish*.[37] Whereas *Death Wish* was a blatant exploitation film featuring B-level acting, hyperbolic plot points, and tired stereotypes about liberals and the West, *Taxi Driver* was A-grade "New Hollywood" by way of New York City. Written in the film noir tradition by acclaimed highbrow critic Paul Schrader—who made his name with an essay on the hopeless tone of the original noir cycle—and directed by Scorsese, the film meditated on the political and cultural milieu of New York in the 1970s.[38] In *Taxi Driver*, based on the journals of George Wallace's would-be assassin Arthur Bremer (whose attack occurred in Milwaukee), "protagonist" Travis Bickle (Robert De Niro) is a hack and a veteran of the Vietnam War so psychologically disturbed that he has trouble sleeping and maintaining stable relationships. "As nutty as they come," Vincent Canby noted, "[Travis] is a projection of all our nightmares of urban alienation."[39]

Travis's "universal access"—signified by his willingness to work "anytime, anywhere," a practice mocked by his fellow hacks—offered insight into a seedy underbelly of New York City where illicit sexuality and violence seemingly held sway. On a date he drags his love interest, Betsy (Cybill Shepherd), to the pornographic theaters on Forty-Second Street.[40] In his mind, warped by the experience of Vietnam and life in New York City, this is what modern couples do: squeeze into small theaters and watch snuff films. He complains about the morning ritual of cleaning blood and semen off of the backseat of his taxicab. One fare, Scorsese in a memorable cameo, offers unsolicited racist and sexist discourse, intending to murder his wife for infidelities involving an African American sexual partner. Travis develops violent intentions himself, plotting to assassinate Betsy's employer Charles Palantine, a major presidential candidate and silk-stocking liberal modeled on John Lindsay, in an attempt to garner the attention of Betsy once again. He stalks both her and the candidate, drawing the attention of fellow employees and the secret service with his suspicious appearance and mental state.[41]

In the *Taxi Driver* narrative, the city's decline and the madness that results from it mark the pathology of ubiquitous violence. Crime, the film suggested, served as the cause and effect of New York's self-perpetuating cycle—or tangle—of insanity. Alone in a small tenement apartment, replete with peeling paint and an obstructed view, Travis chronicles his own decline. Along with Betsy, New York City's ills are his unhealthy obsession, and "he comes to loathe the inhabitants of the city to which he has been drawn."[42] Travis regurgitates the hallmarks of Necropolis, writing, "Thank God for the rain, which has helped to wash the trash and the garbage off the sidewalks." The city of darkness haunts him, as it is when "all the animals come out. . . . Whores, skunk pussies, buggers, queens, fairies, dopers, junkies. Sick. Venal." He dreams that "someday a real rain will come and wash all this scum off the streets." When a nervous Charles Palantine—as part of a leveling campaign stunt—hops a ride with Travis rather than a limousine, it provides the hack an opportunity to opine on the place of the city within the national context. The next president, he says, "should clean up this city here because this city is like an open sewer, it's full of filth and scum. Sometimes I can hardly take it. Whoever becomes the president should just really clean it up. You know what I mean? Sometimes I go out and I smell it. I get headaches, it's so bad. It's like they never go away, you know? It's like the president should clean up this whole mess here. He should just flush it down the fucking toilet."[43] Following the argument of *Death Wish*, Travis's soliloquy suggests that the city needs a clean slate, a man who can get things done à la Robert Moses or Mike Hammer.

Filmic narratives solidified not only the fears of Schaap and Jimmy Breslin but the violent fear-mongering of soothsayers like Lionel Abel and Richard Whalen as well. As Scorsese conveyed, violence "is always erupting when you don't expect it, particularly in a city like New York. You're sitting in a restaurant, eating, and suddenly a car crashes through the window and you're dead." E. B. White noted this risk as well, but he believed that the size and scope of the city insulated citizens from such random events. To Scorsese it was the rule rather than the exception. While he was scouting locations for *Taxi Driver* near Lincoln Center, "a big guy walked over to a very old lady and punched her in the mouth, and a young lady began screaming and crying. The guy just turned around and walked away. Senseless violence. Yet if you got into that guy's head—into his character—who knows?"[44] *Taxi Driver* and *Death Wish* tried to analyze that mind, showcasing the deranged individual driven to madness and violence by Necropolis. In the process, these films portrayed the shifting dynamic of the city in the late sixties and seventies, and proposed a series of problematic remedies for violent crime. Like a certain "private detective" shooting down commies, mobsters, and transgender women in the 1950s, the vigilante offered a logical solution to an increasingly fearful and apathetic citizenry, a bloated bureaucracy, and an ineffective police department.

The vigilante awoke from a postnoir slumber most famously in the guise of Harry Callahan, the rebel cop searching the streets of San Francisco for a crazed hippie serial killer in *Dirty Harry* (1971).[45] Vigilante films responded raucously to the anxieties of the era, and provided a space where the violent fantasies of the white working and middle classes, as imagined by elite cultural producers, could be acted out. As historian Jefferson Cowie notes, "urban crime—even occupational life itself—was similar, where the system allegedly created an unwinnable scenario because of victims' rights and clay-footed liberals afraid of doing the wrong thing."[46] The purveyors of New York vigilante fantasies reflected the conservative politics bubbling under the surface of Nixonian "silent majority" machismo and the pandering of George Wallace. In John Avildsen's *Joe* (1970) and *Death Wish*, the protagonists were backlash warriors confronting a liberal state responsible for moral and economic decline. Echoing calls for law and order, these films provided a model of violent individual action against the inefficiencies of social justice.[47]

The title character of *Joe* (Peter Boyle), an outerborough factory worker and embodiment of the working-class silent majority, served as a young prototype for Archie Bunker. Joe sits in a bar decidedly unsilent, spewing underclass vile to no one in particular, and citing simplified grievances of the urban crisis. He complains ad hominem, "The niggers are getting all the money. Why work, you tell me? Why the fuck work when you can screw, have babies, and get paid for it? Welfare. They got all that welfare money. . . . All you got to do is act black and you get paid for it. Set fire to the cities, burn a few buildings, you get paid for it. Throw a few bombs, you get money and jobs." Joe's hatred extends to whites whose "kids are worse than the niggers." Racial quotas kept his son out of college, for which he is thankful because the educated and sexually liberated are "all the same 'screw America' way." Disheartened by the status anxiety of urban and industrial decline, Joe fantasizes about killing "hippies," but is too cowardly to act.[48]

As filmic fate and the backlash narrative would have it, the man atop the neighboring barstool has just fulfilled such a fantasy. Enter William Compton, a Manhattan business executive, fresh from murdering his daughter's "junkie" boyfriend. Certain he has found a kindred spirit, Compton comes clean about the murder, creating a lasting bond between the two. Thus commences an awkward but mutually beneficial cross-class relationship bound by white conservative masculinity, a shared hatred of youth culture, and Joe's blackmailing that later culminates in violent revenge. After dinner parties on the Upper East Side and in working-class Queens and a hypnotic, hypocritical journey into the East Village narcotic and sexual underworld, thus linking drugs and open sexuality to urban decline, Joe and Compton team up to annihilate a group of young hippies, including the latter's own daughter.[49]

Joe was meant as a cautionary tale, a film highlighting the contingencies of hatred and difference in the 1960s, but instead it reimagined *Easy Rider* (1969) from the perspective of the southern neo-Klansmen that abruptly concluded Dennis Hopper's New Hollywood film. Both nodded to sixties youth culture and depended on the young adult audience for success. According to historian Rick Perelstein, "the filmmakers' thesis . . . argued that people loathed and feared the hippies because deep down they knew the hippies, whose freedom they envied, were right."[50] In *Joe*, the protagonists revel in hallucinatory drugs and partake in the free love offered during some East Village slumming—testifying to that notion of envy and the native New Yorker's jealousy of youth culture's enthusiasm. Yet, not unlike those of Archie Bunker a few years later, *Joe*'s words and actions found many sympathizers in the audience. At Peter Boyle's local butcher shop in Manhattan, an elderly white woman told him, "I agree with *everything* you said, young man. Someone should have said it a long time ago."[51] Despite holding political beliefs that contrasted with his character, Boyle feared for his safety after learning of audience reactions to the film, and had nightmares of being shot down on the streets of New York. "I get scared when I meet people like Joe. And I get scared when I hear that kids are standing up at the end of the movie and yelling, 'I'm going to shoot back, Joe.'" Such spirited reaction spoke to the power of film in this era: fictional characters resonating with the populace; aberrations of violent confrontations between disgruntled urbanites and a rebellious youth; and fears of vigilantism and assassination in response to illusory narrative.[52]

The filmmakers even took advantage of actual New York City disorder in order to enhance *Joe*'s box office appeal. Tensions between the white working class and young antiwar protestors in New York came to a head in early May 1970. Hundreds of college and high school students staged a rally downtown in response to the U.S. invasion of Cambodia and the shootings at Kent State University. Construction workers, laboring in the vicinity, converged on the crowd at lunchtime and began fulfilling *Joe*'s fantasy, "hitting the students with fists, hardhats, and tools and chasing them through the narrow streets of the financial district." The so-called Hardhat Riot inspired a number of subsequent prowar rallies in New York City, and delighted the likes of Nixon. As historian Joshua Freeman notes, "the New York demonstrations made construction workers—'hardhats,' as they came to be called—prime symbols of 'Middle America,' [and] the 'silent majority.'"[53] In the riot's aftermath, the film had its release date pushed up, was retitled to emphasize the centrality of Boyle's character, and was edited to appeal to a silent majority audience.[54]

Joe's expedited release and its "hardhat" pandering disturbed and confused the film's star, but solidified the film's place in the annals of Necropolis. Boyle insisted Joe was hardly a sympathetic protagonist, and that the film was a comment on his ideology. "The message of the movie is very plain. It says that we'd just better stop that war in Vietnam now; that we'd just better stop killing our children there or we're going to be killing our children in the streets here."[55] Boyle's encounter with fans and tales of teenagers threatening to shoot back suggested this message failed. Even the *Times* was dumbfounded by the narrative leaps and the characters' motivation, noting that "well before [the climactic scene], realism, conviction and even common sense have disappeared." Still, the studio and filmmakers' willingness to placate this burgeoning political impulse exemplified the popular hunger for representations justifying urban fears as well as vigilante vengeance heaped upon them. *Joe* opened the door for the reactionary agents of violence that followed.[56]

In *Death Wish*, Kersey's vigilante transformation requires the stewardship of a Joe-like figure, someone who dreams of frontier justice and defending white heritage against sixties liberalism. Following his wife's murder, Kersey relocates to Tucson, Arizona. His new project, designing homes for gun-toting developer Ames Jainchill, turns into the platonic relationship that eventually reforms the grieving Kersey. Ames reintroduces the architect to gunplay—taking in a few rounds at the local indoor firing range—and frontier justice on a trip to the amusing carnival town "Old Tucson." When Kersey leaves, Ames presents a gift, a glistening .32 pistol, which symbolizes the last phase of Kersey's resurrection. Back in New York, Kersey and his pistol produce a staggering body count that stands in contrast to the helpless and ineffective NYPD.[57]

As the film imagines, frontier justice, and thus vigilantism, is portrayed as an integral part of American heritage and history. Old Tucson is a phony movie set where "the wild west lives again." While there, Kersey receives a primer on western justice and acquires his modus operandi of self-defense and preemptive strikes. The nostalgic production renders this argument in voiceover narration: "The outlaw life seemed a short-cut to easy money, which could buy liquor, women, and a turn at the gambling table, but there were honest men with dreams who would fight to protect their way of life and would plant the roots that would grow into a nation." The decline of

FIGURE 9 Paul Kersey takes aim at subway muggers. Ten years after *Death Wish* appeared in theaters, Bernhard Goetz would makes headlines as the "Subway Vigilante" after shooting four young black men who allegedly tried to mug him on a train.

this tradition in American culture, the film suggests, is partially to blame for the decline of cities in the 1970s. Not long after the lesson, Kersey and Ames visit a "gun-club" where the developer delivers the National Rifle Association's party line for the architect, offering platitudes about guns, gun control advocates, liberals, and New York City.[58]

Despite its use of western history, *Death Wish* offered a new radical and reactionary vision of effective law and order. Back in New York, the NYPD's apathetic response to violent crime is matched only by the success of Kersey's tactics. Despite protestations to the contrary from the film's star—Bronson believed the film's message to be "that violence is senseless because it only begets more violence" (but then why was Kersey so successful and immune from justice?)—vigilante frontier justice and an armed and mobilized citizenry were portrayed as the final solution to urban crime and therefore the urban crisis.[59] Armed with his gift, Kersey has a quick and indiscriminate trigger finger. His victims are both white and black, and a simple demand for money or the drawing of a blade is worthy of Kersey's death sentence. In the tradition of Mike Hammer, Kersey defies due process and crowns himself authority—judge, jury, and executioner.[60] Wertham called the Kersey

FIGURE 10 Not long after purchasing a cache of weapons from a black market gun and drug dealer, Travis Bickle (right) plays out the fantasy of the "good guy with a gun" (and judge, jury, and executioner) at a bodega robbery in the film *Taxi Driver*.

character "the apotheosis of try-it-you'll-like-it violence," or as Canby described the film's message, "KILL. TRY IT. YOU'LL LIKE IT."[61]

Travis Bickle's vigilantism, which accomplishes what the NYPD cannot, is similarly lauded as heroic by a press corps hungry for triumph-over-crisis narratives. Like Paul Kersey with his sock full of quarters, Travis forges his vigilante identity in the solitary confinement of his modest New York apartment. He masters his weaponry and strengthens his body through calisthenics. His journal chronicles his conscious transformation into a "man who would not take it anymore . . . someone who stood up." The language foreshadows the creepy correspondence of the so-called Son of Sam, David Berkowitz, who terrorized the city through words and action in 1977. À la *Death Wish*, once Travis is ready, he need not travel far for target practice. At the corner store he shoots a would-be robber, killing him instantly. The gracious shopkeeper notes—signifying an uncontrollable crimescape—"this is the fifth motherfucker this year" before releasing his frustration on the corpse with a tire-iron.[62]

Travis, like Kersey, subscribes to a frontier version of justice. In the filmic narrative, New York is a western-style ghost town, welcoming to the hustler and yearning for the loner-turned-marshal willing to tame the violent city. The corrupt hotel manager, who turns a blind eye to Sport's (Harvey Keitel) child prostitution ring, sees this in Travis, calling him "cowboy." Travis, in fact, embraces both "traditions" of the West, showing up at a Palantine rally in Columbus Circle sporting a "Mohawk" hairstyle. With the transformation complete, he realizes that his "life has pointed in one direction. I see it now. There has never been another choice for me." On the quiet yet crime-ridden East Village street, Travis unleashes his frontier justice, shooting Sport, Iris's (Jodie Foster) pimp, in the stomach before heading into the neighboring hot-sheet hotel to liberate her. An OK Corral–style bloodbath ensues, and after eliminating the hotel manager and Iris's john, Travis turns the gun on himself—only to be foiled by his lack of ammunition. In the end, there are a few less hustlers bringing New York down, and a child prostitute and victim of the city's pathologies is liberated by the vigilante.[63]

Showcasing Travis's just reward in a brief coda, Scorsese and Schrader at once critiqued sensational journalism and highlighted the remedial quality of vigilantism. The camera pans across various headlines pinned to the wall of Travis's apartment. One reads, "Taxi Driver Battles Gangsters"; another, the headline of a *Times* article, states, "Refuted New York Mafioso Killed in Bizarre Shooting." The headlines reek of hyperbole, a comment on crime coverage in the city—Sport was clearly small-time and most likely working on his own—suggesting that perception rarely, if ever, mirrors reality. Travis echoes this sentiment when he serendipitously picks up Betsy outside a stately apartment building. Fighting crime, getting the scum off the streets, and battling New York's worst demons finally earns his obsession's respect. He hides his modesty under a façade of humility: "Papers always blow these things up," he says. Alongside the press's superficial accolades, a letter from Iris's father brings Travis's act into focus. Iris is now back home in Pittsburgh, where she is *"safe"* (itself remarkable given the city's history of industrial decline in this period) from the ills and madness of New York. In this sense, the father's voice validates the assassination. Fed up with Necropolis, Travis Bickle finds redemption as a vigilante and beloved hero far and wide.[64]

Joe, Death Wish, and *Taxi Driver*, along with *Dirty Harry*, glorified the vigilante in the 1970s. Vengeance against the worn-out New Deal order along with reforming police tactics motivated Joe and Paul Kersey.[65] Kersey, despite his pacifist past, unapologetically went beyond his family's crimes to take on the whole city. He becomes a New York hero, and the embarrassed yet grateful NYPD drives him out of town, not unlike the effective named and nameless men of mythic western film narratives. *Taxi Driver* is a film about the wandering mass of disillusioned and defeated Vietnam veterans who returned home to little opportunity in the increasingly neoliberal economic environment. *First Blood* (1982) is perhaps the most infamous and violent example, but *Coming Home* (1978) examined similar themes without the off-the-deep-end bloodbaths.[66] Travis carries his war demons, but the citizens of New York City drive his madness rather than the memories of the Far East jungle. Instead of the anti-Asian racial discourse that dominated Vietnam War narratives, his roll call features the guerilla warriors of the street: "whores, skunk pussies, buggers, queens, fairies, dopers, junkies." It is not the battlefield of Khe Sanh that ravages Travis's mind, it is the warzone of New York City. As he asks Iris, *"Don't you wanna get outta here?"*[67]

While vigilantism served as a proactive remedy to the urban crisis, the New York film cycle offered a more passive response: escape from the city. As *Midnight Cowboy* and *The Out of Towners* highlighted a city inhospitable to visitors and migrants, the nation's industrial capital began drifting from the Northeast and the Midwest to the sunnier climes of the South and the West. The year 1970 was a critical turning point for New York's economic stability, as during the preceding decade dozens of firms left because of perceived social and cultural problems.[68] According to the *Times*, atomic fear was the motivation for significant capital moves in the 1950s. Twenty years later a "fear of crime was a major factor in the exodus." Congressman Edward Koch's polling of Midtown businesses found that 90 percent of respondents cited that fear as "adversely affecting their operations by forcing them into expensive security arrangements and by inhibiting night work of employees." As one quoted "real estate leader" hinted, "many of the firms don't want to admit that they are really 'running away from the blacks.'" Cosmopolis's promise of economic opportunity appeared to be fading, and films like *The Out of Towners* played on the perceived diminishing returns of doing business in New York City. In fact, a comment from Koch seemed lifted from the fictional experience of George Kellerman: "It used to be that when a company tapped an employe [sic] in Minneapolis and asked him to come to New York, he considered it an honor. Now he wonders, 'Why are they picking on me? What have I done wrong?'"[69]

Midnight Cowboy was one of the first productions to engage in the political and cultural debate over regional economic differences. It portrayed the city as lacking in employment prospects, especially for a handicapped man and an unskilled migrant. Leaving New York for Florida is a recurring theme, and Miami becomes Buck and Rizzo's city of destination. Rizzo plasters advertisements for orange juice on the walls of his tenement squat,

FIGURE 11 For Joe Buck and Enrico Rizzo, Florida and the Sunbelt replace New York City as the land of economic opportunity, which is denoted in filmic dreamscapes and advertisements. Here a billboard for a regional airline promises "Steak for everybody every lunch and dinner" on its flights from New York to Florida.

and speaks often of relocating to the Sunshine State. A lifelong New Yorker, he knows the city's days are numbered and survival lies south. As the abandoned tenement's demolition approaches, Buck and Rizzo rummage for their existence by day, while at night they warm themselves by dancing to Florida orange juice commercials on Buck's transistor radio, until he is forced to hock it—their last bit of capital. When the two make an outerborough pilgrimage to the Rizzo family grave, they pass an airline's billboard that advertises "steak for everybody every lunch and dinner" on its Florida routes. Despite Rizzo's declining health—seemingly paralleling the city's—not even renewed economic opportunity for Buck, in the form of a regular clientele, discourages the move. Instead, Buck applies his learned knowledge of New York and brutally assaults and mugs a queer businessman he cruises on Forty-Second Street—linking nonnormative sexuality with urban decline once again. The former Texas outsider, so gullible and ignorant as to relinquish his humble nest egg in mere hours, has transformed into a violent criminal. In the following scene, Buck and Rizzo are on a bus heading through the Lincoln Tunnel.[70]

Escape allows Buck to shed the ills of New York City and reinvent himself. Rizzo, too, hopes to cast off the derogatory "Ratso" nickname that plagued his New York existence. Buck relinquishes his cowboy image in favor of a new conservative wardrobe. There must be a better way of living than hustling, he wonders aloud, meaning there is work preferable to selling one's body but also there are alternatives to urban life. Buck wants a real job, "something outdoors" like gardening or landscaping—occupations not readily available in New York's asphalt jungle. As they enter Miami, its clean modern architecture, reflecting off the bus window, is a symbol of hope running across his face. Rizzo does not survive the trip, but Joe Buck emerges from the rubble of New York City to be born anew. Florida represents economic and social paradise, its limitless opportunity contrasting with New York City's increasingly dark and deadly milieu.[71]

Death Wish offered a lesson on battling this milieu, but it also contributed to the debate over regional spatial transformation in more literal ways. As in various mythic narratives of territorial expansion, the West in *Death Wish* symbolized salvation from the dying city, a site of liberation and liberty that stood in stark contrast to the burden of Necropolis. In this sense it reified Frederick Jackson Turner's "frontier thesis" of eighty years prior. Like Turner, *Death Wish* suggested that the frontier functioned as a "safety valve," a space of hope that beckoned people out of crowded cities like New York. It promoted "American Exceptionalism" and a belief that westward movement transformed settlers and pioneers into italicized *Americans*. Also invoking Turner's thesis, *Death Wish* linked geography with a distinct American character associated with individualism, democratic values, and an effective form of justice.[72] Tucson, according to Ames, is "gun country" where "unlike [New York] we can walk through our streets and through our parks at night and feel safe." Such scenes endorsed the trope of urban difference perpetuated by the Right in the sixties and seventies, a narrative that suggested the frontier West and urban East featured dissimilar values and brands of law and order that worked at cross-purposes.[73]

In addition to the West-versus-East dichotomy, *Death Wish* used suburban expansion as a counterpoint to the violent urbanism of the era. Kersey designs modern skyscrapers in downtown Manhattan, but heads west to build safe and secure homes in a new development in Tucson's suburban foothills. As Ames and Kersey survey the rolling hills of cacti and sagebrush where homes will rise, Kersey points out how the plan wastes valuable space.

FIGURE 12 Ames Jainchill (r.), Paul Kersey (c.), and a passing cowboy (l.) survey the rugged undeveloped landscape outside of Tucson where their new planned subdivision will rise.

Taken aback, Ames retorts: "Wasting space, those are some words you developers have to change—space for life, space for people," adding, "I don't build a thing that will turn into a slum in 20 years," a comment on the state of Title I projects in the 1970s. In *Death Wish*, Sunbelt suburbs appropriated the mantle of civilization from the increasingly uncivilized urban East. "Muggers get their asses blown off" in Tucson, and one has to be insane to live in a city like New York. With its allusion to Sunbelt growth and western opportunity, the film seemed to express a wish for Necropolis. Instead it imagined a sprawling western utopia of space, individual dominion, and do-it-yourself law and order.[74]

Employing familiar American tropes to comment on timely issues of law and order, regionalism, and metropolitanism, *Death Wish* offered a clear critique of urban political economy at the height of crisis. It emerged from a conservative political perspective that fetishized the Sunbelt suburbs and Goldwater gun country featured in the film. Despite its comic and oversimplified narrative, its straightforward yet sensational plot, and its poor writing and acting, *Death Wish* was incredibly popular and its themes resonated with audiences. Most importantly, the film situated New York City at the heart of the urban crisis. It was at the nexus of crime, municipal blundering and corruption, and economic decline, the attributes ascribed to cities during the era's near-death fiscal emergencies, of which New York became the national poster child in 1975.[75]

As such the film industry typecast New York City as unlivable and unenviable in this period. The cycle included studies of its crime problems in gritty features like *The French Connection* (1971) and *The Seven-Ups* (1973). The "Blaxploitation" cycle examined urban crime from an African American perspective in locally produced independent films like *Shaft* (1971) and *Super Fly* (1972). There were films about urban madness similar to *Taxi Driver*: *Network* (1976), the overcrowded dystopic fantasy of *Soylent Green*, and even another Neil Simon/Jack Lemmon comedy about the hell of living in New York, *The Prisoner of Second Avenue* (1975). Escape, however, was the dominant theme of feature films set in New York City in the 1970s. In Sidney Lumet's *Dog Day Afternoon* (1975), loosely based on an actual event, bank robbers-turned-heroes nearly escape with their dignity and booty before being gunned down on the tarmac at JFK Airport. The marginalized protagonist of Lumet's *Serpico* (1973), the preeminent realist indictment of NYPD corruption, leaves the crucible of New York for the solace of France. Even *The Godfather* narrative arc alluded to the migration of opportunistic capital to new frontiers south and west. The theme finally burned out with John Carpenter's futuristic comic book fantasy, *Escape from New York* (1981). Only *Saturday Night Fever* (1977) featured characters looking to escape a homogenous bedroom community for the liberty of universal Manhattan—a theme that would become more prevalent in the 1980s.[76]

· · · · · ·

As the New York film cycle broadcast Necropolis across the country, over a million persons escaped the city. Incidents of violent and lonely crimes rose steadily throughout the seventies.[77] An overtaxed public sector crawled along, barely surviving on dwindling revenues and increasing debt. In 1973, Lindsay left the mayor's post, turning it over to city comptroller Abraham Beame. In terms of image, the transfer of power from the tall, handsome, congenial, and wealthy Lindsay to the short, gruff, awkward, and machine-worn Beame seemed to parallel the era's filmic narrative of the city—as if Enrico Rizzo succeeded Charles Palantine in City Hall. Beame's toughest challenge came in autumn 1975 when New York City sat on the verge of bankruptcy. When Beame solicited Washington and Albany for help, President Gerald Ford relented. On October 30, 1975, the *Daily News* ran its infamous headline: "FORD TO CITY: DROP DEAD." Although not an exact quote, the *News* had a point. Ford preached to the choir, a nation that had digested years of Necropolis in popular culture. Why should hardworking Americans foot the bill for a welfare case like New York? Ford and Governor Hugh Carey, along with investment banker Felix Rohatyn, eventually stepped in to salvage the city, and put it on a course toward privatization and neoliberal economic development.[78] But the damage was done: New York was near death. A year earlier Robert Caro published the first in a series of home-grown tomes detailing "the fall of New York."[79]

As journalist Jonathan Mahler details in his thrilling history of the tumultuous year, the bottom dropped out in 1977. With Beame out, the mayor's race pitted New York's political saviors of the 1980s: Mario Cuomo and Edward Koch. In sports, the New York Yankees returned to relevance under the ownership of George Steinbrenner and the bat of superstar Reggie Jackson. At the same time, baseball fans from across the country watched in horror as Bronx tenements burned within eyesight of the World Series. In crime, a serial killer terrorized the city, preying on unsuspecting blonde women and their male partners, and corresponding with Jimmy Breslin (then at the *Daily News*) as the "Son of Sam." In Spike Lee's *Summer of Sam* (1998), New Yorkers form vigilante patrols and neighborhood watch groups that ultimately suspect a figure of cosmopolitan difference—a queer punk music enthusiast with a Brit fetish—still residing in their conservative Italian-American enclave. Yet it was the ineffective and corrupt NYPD detectives—as they were portrayed in Necropolis—that captured the white killer, mail carrier David Berkowitz, thanks to an unpaid parking ticket.[80] In the realm of disorder, a July blackout led to New York City's worst rioting and looting since the Civil War. In the heat, whole neighborhoods were destroyed, and the images of the violence and chaos were broadcast across the country on television. It looked like the last gasp of a dying city.[81]

As bad as it got for New York in the 1970s, a film like *Death Wish* never mirrored reality. In the "culture of fear" tradition, the mainstream New York film cycle obscured the creative and democratic changes happening downtown and underground. For years, as historian Max Page has shown, cultural producers imagined the end of New York City.[82] Films sensationalized a dysfunctional city that audiences across the country devoured. While New Yorkers wrestled with real political, economic, and social crises, apoplectic viewers across the country celebrated the dangerous bastion of liberalism getting its comeuppance. In October 1977, President Jimmy Carter walked down Charlotte Street in the South Bronx, an area brutally ravaged by arson and decay. In the wire photos and television coverage, the Bronx looked like London's East End after the blitz. The images said that New York, in order to survive, would have to rebuild. The apathetic and lonely New York would continue to be exploited in the late night monologues of hosts Johnny Carson and David Letterman, sitcoms, and satires like *Ghostbusters* (1984).[83] As Necropolis began to lose its luster, the hearty New Yorkers who weathered crisis or gravitated to the decay found that the rubble was fertile.

8 The Lure of Decay

· ·

Vigilante fantasies, random violence, and the hunger for escape remained consistent tropes for New York exploitation films in the 1980s. Necropolis earned top billing in productions like *Fort Apache, The Bronx* (1981), Abel Ferrara's *Fear City* (1984), and *Death Wish 3* (1985), in which Paul Kersey commandeers Brooklyn's blighted East New York neighborhood.[1] For a brief window in the 1980s, however, a new visual and aural narrative highlighting the lure of Necropolis reigned. Just as the discourses of the 1950s and 1960s entered the films of the 1970s, the pop culture narratives of the 1980s were made possible by the structural changes of the previous decade. Despite its aura of decline and despair, New York City remained an attractive destination to certain groups and subcultures through the crisis era. The powerful Necropolis narrative and the vacuum left by population and capital migration created affordable space for migrants and native New Yorkers alike seeking Cosmopolis and opened up appropriate space for new forms of native cultural expression. For housing, the city offered cheap rents, abandoned lofts, squatter cooperatives, and urban homesteading programs. Out of these places there was an explosion of culture: the formation of the downtown art scene in the shells of industrial decline, the emergence of city-centric new wave music on the Bowery, and the rise of graffiti and hip-hop in the Bronx and Brooklyn, along with the local manifestations of feminist, black, and queer liberation and the growth of community-based development organizations working to salvage neighborhoods in between. The lure of decay and the appropriation of blight constituted an exercise in what Henri Lefebvre termed "the right to the city," a more radical interpretation of Cosmopolis defined by claims of autonomy within and a collective reshaping of urban space. In the open city, a spontaneous, collective, and democratic New York seemed a real possibility.[2]

The successes and failures of those asserting their "right" to New York had a direct and lasting influence on the culture of cities. The appropriators found fertile ground for exploration, adventure, and creative production. As a result a renaissance occurred in the tarnished old "slums" of Downtown Manhattan and its outerboroughs as musicians, artists, queers, punks, and lower-class strivers established vibrant communities out of the perceived ruins of areas labeled "unsafe" by the prevailing narrative of New York City. Observing the South Bronx, author Grace Paley evoked this sensibility: "The block is burning down on one side of the street, and the kids are trying to build something on the other." This was at a time when the borough was the province of national political figures searching through the ruins and paying lip service to the pathologies of the urban crisis. As the stenciled graffiti BROKEN PROMISES hovered in the background, President Carter and soon-to-be President Reagan offered little in policy response to the multitude of poor and newly homeless. Therein was the paradox of the lure of decay in New York. While "right to the city" seekers confronted the coded language of domestic doomsayers, they in turn brought forth homegrown solutions to the problem of decline that, like the theories of Jane Jacobs, proved useful and malleable to the city's power brokers in due time.[3]

The ascendance of New York's new narrative resigned much of city's nadir image to the distant past. Despite an increase in violent crime and the emergence of new civic emergencies like the crack cocaine and AIDS epidemics, the New York City pathologies of old took a backseat to a cultural renaissance in the hollowed-out shells of capital flight and the resettlement of rehabilitated districts by the postindustrial cluster of like-minded seekers of authentic urban experience. Such experiential authenticity included elite modes of consumption, most notably the purchase and renovation of the city's pre–World War II, and thus premodern, housing stock and a stake in the downtown art world. In the elite social milieu of neoliberal New York, to confront the ills of city life or to be victimized by lonely criminals proved a mere contingency of urban authenticity, a rite of passage for a migrant or bridge-and-tunnel status-seeker looking for the all-important *real* New Yorker badge of honor. In a few short years, the image of New York City shifted from the dread of *Death Wish* and "Drop Dead" to the child-safe spectacle of *Big*, which projected the fantastic possibility of a twelve-year-old man-child living alone in a massive SoHo romper room. As media culture in the 1980s refashioned Cosmopolis as a neoliberal Fun City, it brought with it uneven returns for the populations that asserted their "right to the city" in the decade prior.

· · · · · ·

While the history of New York resettlement and the city's "renaissance" is largely the tale of postindustrial gentrification, it is also a history of spatial appropriation from below. Neighborhoods where the "right to the city" ethos proved fertile were areas deemed in decline by the chroniclers of the city in the 1960s. Some were "slums" slated for clearance the decade prior. In Greenwich Village, the neighborhood's gay population took on a greater public presence in the late 1960s and 1970s, powered in part by the district's increasing allure as a cosmopolitan open space for migrants marginalized in less tolerant places. While the Village's bohemian and queer reputation was nothing new—its history stretched back into the nineteenth century and was open enough for xenophobic Mickey Spillane to line it in lavender in the 1940s—gay men asserted their stake in the public sphere in the 1960s. They demanded access to and service in the neighborhood's public places, and experimented with and later cultivated original cultural forms and performances in spaces of their own. The June 27, 1969, police raid on the Stonewall Inn, a mob-controlled gay bar located on Christopher Street in the heart of the Village, and the uprising that followed have long been seen as the turning point for gay liberation within popular history. The back-lash to the raid, however, was indicative of a longer push for respectability in the city. In the years leading up to Stonewall, the New York Mattachine Society, the city's most powerful homophile organization, staged "sip-ins" at Village bars seeking the abolition of state laws forbidding the service to groups of suspected homosexuals. Downtown bathhouses, those products of Old World immigrant culture if not earlier Necropolis-laden public health scares, were appropriated as sites of gay sociability and sexual encounters safe from public scrutiny for a population excluded from the hetero "sexual revolution" occurring outside. Continental Baths in particular became a ma-jor queer hub and a performance space for gay-friendly musicians, most notably launching the career of "Bathhouse" Bette Midler.[4]

Collective experiences structured around music and dance constituted the "cry and demand"—to use Lefebvre's terms—of empowered gay men in the Village. After the sip-ins and Stonewall, gay liberation groups from the radical Gay Liberation Front to the moderate Gay Activist Alliance (GAA) began organizing dances in Manhattan in an attempt to move away from a bar culture that seemed to signify commercial capitalism's exploitation of their subordination. These dances represented the origins of the era's disco revolution, which has since been remembered for its crass, indulgent, com-modified culture of Donna Summer, the Bee Gees, *Saturday Night Fever*, and the exclusive Studio 54. Between 1970 and 1974, however, gay discos Down-town and the disk jockeys (DJs) who experimented with a combination of soul, rhythm and blues, and bathhouse beats in many respects laid down the soundtrack for liberation, remaking both gay nightlife and the image of queer masculinity, from effeminate to the "macho man." As historian Alice Echols notes, "GAA dances suggest the intimate and synergistic connection between gay liberation and gay disco. . . . Sometimes the dance floor became the launching pad for political action." One gay activist argued that his "newfound sense of freedom" after Stonewall was channeled in the city's dance clubs.[5]

Yet there were social and spatial limits artificially placed on this "right to the city" movement. The appropriated clubs proved transitory after disco's increasing popularity attracted heterosexual public figures and eventually the bridge-and-tunnel crowd. According to Echols, "this process whereby below the radar gay clubs were discovered by celebrities, set upon by those judged unhip, and then abandoned by the original gay partygoers occurred time and again."[6] Outside of the clubs, the prevailing culture pushed back against the appropriation of emergent gay neighborhoods like the Village and Chelsea to the north, most notably in William Friedkin's problematic and homophobic *Cruising* (1980), which marked public queer culture as a symptom of Necropolis.[7] Nevertheless, this political and cultural movement would not have been possible without earlier narratives of decline linking the Village with queerness, thus drawing homosexual men and women to the cosmopolitan open neighborhood and contributing to the demand for space in the increasingly animated Downtown Manhattan.

The "cast iron district," just south of the Village, was another case of a deindustrialized and designated blighted area that emerged as a hotbed of culture. Robert Moses's planned Lower Manhattan Expressway (Lomex) would have elevated Broome Street, the area's primary east–west thoroughfare, as its right-of-way. In the 1960s, nearby neighborhood groups led by local working-class Italian-Americans and Village liberals like Jacobs saw value in the area's exceptional and unique cast-iron design, and mobilized around the issues of community and architectural preservation. The expressway struggle proved a major front of resistance in the fight against modern city planning and bureaucratic narratives of decline. In the midst of the fight, the cast iron district earned its nom de guerre, SoHo, a lasting label that is now synonymous with elite urban vitality. Yet the evolution of SoHo departed from the "pioneering" resettlement of Brownstone Brooklyn, for example, because it sprung from the adoption of former industrial space by cultural producers, at least initially. The old warehouse lofts seemed ideal for the burgeoning art scene, offering ample light and space for oversized canvases and sculptures, not to mention the oversized lifestyles, of the art world's new wave. By the end of the 1970s, SoHo and place-based creative industry were synonymous.[8]

A housing shortage wrought in part by slum clearance and deindustrialization contributed to the settlement of SoHo. Urban renewal in New York City meant devastation for a sizable portion of potential artist housing after the war. The city lost over seven million square feet of loft warehouse space including the old Radio Row neighborhood that was cleared for the World Trade Center, Brooklyn Bridge–area lofts replaced by the Pace University physical plant, and various demolitions in once-industrial Chelsea. To the south, the Lower Manhattan Expressway plans quelled long-term demand for real estate in the cast iron district, rendering the neighborhood as a liminal space. Some small manufacturing concerns remained, but for the most part the loft warehouses and their vaulted ceilings and open floor areas drew the attention of emergent large-form artists priced out of other bohemian districts. Due to the idiosyncratic architecture and the relative unmatched affordability, select members of New York's art world began settling in the combined flats and studios of the cast iron district, and by the mid-1960s their numbers measured in the several hundreds. A homegrown coalition, Artists Against the Expressway, even played a part in the fight against Lomex.[9]

The organic success of SoHo's artist appropriation received early support from sympathetic city and state governments, thus establishing a vital public-private partnership in creative redevelopment. This innovative collaboration sprung from the legal reality of loft living. Long a manufacturing area codified in zoning, residences in the cast iron district were hardly a permitted use. As such, illicit renters were subjected to the whims of crooked landlords, which included threats of eviction, rent gouging, and limited city services, all without the standard legal base reserved for residential lessees. Many of the structures also failed to meet local fire codes. Responding to tenant mobilization in the area, Mayor Robert Wagner agreed in late 1961 to allow artists to reside in commercial lofts if buildings met required standards. When the city threatened warehouses with rezoning again in 1963, New York State stepped in to ensure artists could reside in manufacturing and commercial structures.[10]

Later artists found an important ally in Doris C. Freedman, commissioner of New York City's Department of Cultural Affairs (DCA), an agency formed in 1968 during John Lindsay's reign and another symbol of culture's ascendant role in his imagined postindustrial Fun City. The DCA certified artists-in-residence, and Freedman lobbied for loft rent control and the coexistence of mixed uses within buildings. After years of spatial appropriation, the City Planning Commission, in 1971, finally legalized residential use in former manufacturing buildings within the "SoHo artists' district," a move celebrated by Lindsay for solidifying New York's reputation as "one of the great creative centers of the world." After the failure of slum clearance and urban renewal, SoHo offered a viable example of effective state support for neighborhood rehabilitation without the politically challenging social welfare considerations that came with Title I. Combined with an influx of national arts funding, limited and indirect local, state, and federal investment in the cast iron district allowed for piecemeal renewal that altered the nature of the former industrial area.[11]

Through the 1970s, SoHo developed significant creative cachet, heralding the crucial links between artistic production, conspicuous consumption, and postindustrial urban living. In the 1980s, this image was broadcast around the globe. After filming the "mean streets" east of SoHo and seedy Times Square in the 1970s, Martin Scorsese turned his lens to the cast iron district in *After Hours* (1985). While the film took place in the 1980s, the mise-en-scène reflected the nascent state of SoHo in the prior decade. The narrow cobblestone streets were decidedly dark, the amenities limited, the bars dives, and the clubs obscure and exclusive. Access to artist lofts required keys dropped from windows above. Moreover, there was still the profound threat of lurking danger in the streets, including murder, burglary, and narcotics. The film's plot revolved around an everyday organization man (Paul) who meets an aloof visitor (Marcy) staying in the loft of an artist (Kiki). An invitation to evaluate and purchase Kiki's homemade work—plaster-of-Paris bagels-with-cream-cheese—leads to an odyssey of sex, drugs, death, art, and empty wallets. Wrongly accused of burglary and Marcy's murder and "persecuted by a vigilante mob," Paul eventually escapes the otherworldliness of the cast iron district and returns to the normalcy of pencil-pushing by daybreak. *After Hours* depicted SoHo as New York City's funhouse, a hip neighborhood where an uptown professional could get lost for a night and still find his way back to the desk by morning.[12]

Despite the sexual liberation of the 1960s, sexuality suffered in the New York City films of the 1970s where heterosexuality tended to be depicted as depraved (*Taxi Driver*), violent (*Death Wish*), professional (*Midnight Cowboy*), or puritanical (*The Out of Towners*). The emergence of SoHo as an alluring neighborhood, however, transformed the representation of heterosexual adventure in the city. In *Hannah and Her Sisters* (1986), Woody Allen eschewed his typical Uptown and Greenwich Village locales to frame his tale of lust and betrayal amid the grimy, graffiti-laden converted ware-houses of the neighborhood. Adrian Lyne's *9 ½ Weeks* (1986), pairing a wealthy stockbroker and a SoHo gallery manager, was most indicative of the trend. Lyne filmed Downtown as a site of sexual exploration and personal escape—albeit shrouded in misogynistic overtones of white male wealth and power as impetus for female sexual liberation. Brought together through chance meetings at a Chinatown grocer and a downtown flea market, previously prime locales for the "Welcome to Fear City" hustle, the characters in *9 ½ Weeks* cognitively mapped a New York City now open to the white professional classes post–fiscal crisis. SoHo could also serve as a site of PG-variety male sexual awakening. In Penny Marshall's *Big* (1988), the main character, a suburban twelve-year-old in the body of a twenty-something, takes up residence in a spacious SoHo loft, now devoid of the industrial sheen of earlier years, and in due course "sleeps" with a female character in his bunk-bed. Glaringly, Tom Hanks's Josh was not an artist, but rather, a toy company executive working in Midtown, thus marking SoHo's shift from conscious artist colony to gentrified wonderland. On film at least, SoHo epitomized open sexuality and postmodern amusements—a Coney Island for the revitalized Cosmopolis in the 1970s and 1980s.[13]

Like Coney Island at the turn of the century, SoHo's development as a neighborhood stemmed largely from its ability to attract visitors. The district's foundation was laid by the sweat equity of migrant artists, who not only transformed former industrial lofts into residential and studio space but poured their time and skill, in addition to financial capital, into gallery construction as well. Given the scale of loft-produced works, adjacent exhibition space, which simplified transportation issues, seemed a natural fit, and by 1968 mainstream outlets like the *Times* reported SoHo gallery openings and crafted articles detailing the new "Downtown Scene." As historian Aaron Shkuda notes, local galleries were not bazaars frequented by New York City art consumers. Rather, large-scale artworks were more likely sold to collectors inquiring from a distance. The fact that the art was exhibited close to the point of production drew the curious and the art-conscious from around the region, country, and world. These "floaters," as Shkuda terms them, inspired entrepreneurs in the service industry looking to cash in on the surge of bourgeois visitors. By the early 1970s, the neighborhood was recognized by local publications as a "frontier" of boutiques, and national magazines described the SoHo "look" as the height of vanguard fashion. As a result, SoHo "was a site where culture production helped create an exportable model of urban development that provided a way for cities to develop retail districts that appealed to visitors and residents." The once-blighted cast iron district demonstrated how nonconsumptive places with a certain cultural cachet might spawn consumptive amenities necessary for neighborhood revitalization (or gentrification), and legitimized a postindustrial development modus around services and tourism. It was a remarkable shift: in the 1960s and early 1970s fear culture rendered many sections of the city impassable, but cultural production in SoHo and the publicity thereof made a formerly "dead" neighborhood thrilling and alluring, not to mention a sound market investment.[14]

The appropriation of SoHo thus foretold its gentrification. There was limited policy to temper development in the neighborhood once elites had a taste of the new wave Downtown. While the city and the state implemented policy strategies intended to secure SoHo's unique cultural industry and architecture, the failure of those policies to become entrenched ensured its hypergentrification. Homegrown narrative creation helped as well. With a dearth of upper-middle-class and middle-class options for central city housing following a period of white flight, racial and class segregation, and declining infrastructure, celebratory articles in *Life* and the *Times* shaped the public image of SoHo and heightened demand for its real estate. The city's countercultural publications like *New York*, a hub of new journalism in the 1960s and 1970s, also contributed to the publicity. *SoHo Weekly News* served as the neighborhood's *Village Voice*, publishing articles and advertising downtown amusements. New York's media culture and political culture combined to forge high-market redevelopment in Lower Manhattan, renewal grounded in the Jacobean ideal of neighborhood authenticity but driven by the underregulated market structure that defined neoliberal gentrification. In the end, SoHo was twice appropriated, and residents with means won out.[15]

As those hooked on the downtown ethos were priced out of SoHo and Greenwich Village, alternative frontiers of spatial appropriation emerged nearby. Unlike the cast iron district, the Lower East Side had a storied history as an area defined by its tenements and flophouses. Since the late nineteenth century, the neighborhood served as the entry point for countless immigrants, primarily European Jews escaping persecution and unrest in their native lands. In the age of Title I, significant swaths of the Lower East Side had been transformed into public housing developments and assorted renewal projects. From there the neighborhood underwent a series of demographic changes as the Jewish population largely left for the Bronx and Brooklyn. Puerto Rican migrants arrived in their wake, but the shake-up wrought by redevelopment and the hollowing out of the city linked the Lower East Side with Necropolis. It also kept the neighborhood's remaining tenements and cold-water flats some of the most affordable in Manhattan. Beginning in the 1960s and in keeping with the social history of the area, the section of the neighborhood north of Houston Street became a repository for migrants, bohemians, and Beats—most notably poets and partners Allen Ginsberg and Peter Orlovsky in 1975—unable to afford adjacent neighborhoods and/or disillusioned by their declining authenticity. This phenomenon and, as with SoHo, the real-estate industry's desire to capitalize on it earned the northern half of the Lower East Side a new moniker: the "East Village."[16]

As old-law tenements housed an emergent population of artists and strivers, the Lower East Side's Bowery district became the nucleus of a more egalitarian and underground downtown appropriation. Long home to the city's cheapest beds and liquor, the Bowery by the 1970s was the kind of place even slumming tourists avoided. Surveying the area's nightlife, then a hub of off-off-Broadway theater companies and music clubs, David McReynolds described an avenue that "seemed to continue its slow death" since the old elevated tracks came down and social workers like Michael Harrington at the Bowery Mission tried to stem the tide of alcoholism and chronic poverty that plagued the artery.[17] That changed when new drinking and music venues opened, catering to a clientele of neighborhood migrants and visitors. In 1974 Hilly Kristal opened "CBGB and OMFUG," an acronym for the type of music Kristal sought for his new establishment: Country, Blue Grass, Blues and Other Music For Uplifting Gourmandizers. When the market for the old folkways proved dim, local Tom Verlaine convinced Kristal to allow his band Television to take the stage at CBGB, and a movement was born. CBGB became the salon of a New York sound, which was given the misleading label "punk" and more aptly described at the time as "new wave." This new sound included stylings as diverse as the music of the Talking Heads, the Ramones, the New York Dolls, Patti Smith, and Blondie. With songs and fashion that highlighted the city's daring side, its wide-open sexuality, and its emergent sounds, the Bowery scene ironically critiqued the hypermasculine corporate rock, saccharine AM radio pop, and overindulgent commercial disco then controlling the airwaves. This new wave seemed grounded in space and place, and that made Downtown a destination for outsiders.[18]

Similar to its hip neighbor to the southwest, the appropriation of skid row swiftly drew the attention of the city's major media outlets. Downtown may have birthed the folk scene in the 1950s and fostered the New York jazz sound earlier in the century, but by the 1970s those genres and the clubs that stuck with them tended to serve tourists. With the exception of the Velvet Underground and Max's Kansas City, vanguard rock-and-roll largely bypassed New York. As the *Times* put it in the mid-seventies, there were "few public places for aspiring young bands to play. Every third door in Greenwich Village seems to offer an earnestly strumming folkie, but rock poses problems of image and amplitude that seem to daunt all but the most intrepid of clubowners." Kristal's club altered the dynamic. Television played their first show at CBGB in 1974, and the following year they would share the stage with Blondie and Patti Smith. The Ramones first came to CBGB in May 1975, and within a month they were featured in a twin bill with the Talking Heads. By July, the "otherwise unprepossessing bar at 315 Bowery" was hosting a twelve-day festival that featured forty New York City bands, including Television, the Ramones, and other "Velvet Undergroundish ensembles." For the *Times*'s music critic, the aptly named John Rockwell, the festival and an invigorated downtown scene demonstrated that in the midst of crisis the city's cultural experience transcended decay. It reaffirmed "that New York, which has sometimes been accused of being more a marketplace than a producer of homegrown talent, is full of musically active young people." According to Rockwell, "in these days of municipal self-doubt, it's cause for consolation."[19]

The Lower East Side was in transition, and the "right to the city" ethos extended beyond the province of the artist and musician. Many residents worked to rehabilitate whole buildings where banks and landlords failed. Puerto Rican migrants, in particular, participated in large-scale housing redevelopment, creating more livable spaces and offering opportunities for economic mobility if not homeownership. As with the redevelopment of SoHo, this "homesteading" movement earned support from the city, which allowed the rehabilitators to establish cooperatives constructed in their own hand. In addition, a significant squatters movement, itself a radical critique of the postindustrial real estate regime, occupied abandoned structures, transforming otherwise "blighted" buildings into functional living and working spaces. Alongside the heightened publicity around what brokers now refer to as "gayborhoods" in Chelsea and the West Village, it appeared that within the hollow of the urban crisis a new kind of social democratic city was in the making. The neighborhood where Harrington once found "the bitterest, most physical and obvious poverty" was no exception. By 1977, the *Times* had found a new Lower East Side, where only "a few Bowery derelicts" could still be found, "but they were hardly noticeable in the throng of entertainment seekers."[20]

The newspaper cited the "long, dark esophagus" of CBGB as the driving force behind the area's resurgence as an entertainment district (New York City's original theater district was in nearby Astor Place). The *Times* also singled out young people as the agents of this changing Bowery face; snatching up cheap apartments, fostering a "phenomenal spurt in building and renovation," and in general making the neighborhood "one of the liveliest entertainment districts in Manhattan." But the Bowery had become more than just a music venue. Rather, the sound emanating from CBGB synced itself with ascendant forms of downtown cultural production including the visual arts, which were priced out of fashionable SoHo, and the return of theater in off-Broadway form. As the *Times* profile put it, "to younger people, the Bowery is more synonymous with NoHo, SoHo, loft living and theatrical artistic expression." The only thing "containing [the Bowery's] growth," or preventing it from becoming SoHo redux, was "the area's unsavory reputation."[21]

Similar to SoHo, the new Lower East Side was an area where postcrisis fantasies could play out on film. *Desperately Seeking Susan* (1985) marked the new fun city flipside of the *Death Wish* narrative. Mike Hammer once stood on the George Washington Bridge daydreaming about a tranquil life with his secretary Velda and their brood in the New Jersey suburbs, but three decades later Susan Seidelman depicted the metropolitan hinterland as boring and dull, particularly for a housewife like Roberta Glass (Rosanna Arquette) yearning for meaning beyond the cul-de-sac. Madonna, then emerging from the downtown disco scene and in her first major film role, plays Susan, a transient Lower East Sider with a Dean Moriarty–like existence carrying on an on-again-off-again relationship with a local artist through personal ads in alternative newspapers. When Roberta catches on to the crafty liaison between Susan and her suitor, she becomes a New York voyeur, spying on their proposed meeting and shadowing Susan back to her Lower East Side apartment. Within the confines of Manhattan, Roberta falls victim to a case of mistaken identity and amnesia, and she appropriates the role of Susan in the downtown milieu. Ultimately, the downtown escape proves liberating for Roberta, allowing both a release from the confines of suburbia and an opportunity to interact with a cluster of Lower East Siders more attuned to her interests. As with *After Hours*, which went to theaters the same year and also starred Arquette, *Desperately Seeking Susan* represented Downtown as an alternate reality; the inverse of conformist upper-class sanctuaries Uptown and out of town—a moveable feast of art, intellect, sexuality, and adventure.[22]

Fun City was best represented in the musicians who called Downtown their home and in the music they created. The Talking Heads—David Byrne, Chris Frantz, and Tina Weymouth—were a natural link between the established art scene in SoHo and the Bowery new wave. The white cosmopolitan trio migrated to the Lower East Side from the Rhode Island School of Design, and their sound reflected the experimentalism, diligence, and precision of the visual artists they admired. Because of this they were seen as the "superior band on the New York underground" whose "claim to distinctiveness is better founded than most." Local coverage of the city's CBGB "circuit" made customary note of Byrne, Frantz, and Weymouth's scholastic credentials, which legitimized their music and their appropriation of the East Village and the Bowery. The Talking Heads were, after all, "people who thought of themselves as artists and who, through a series of accidents and historical circumstances (the particularly fruitful nexus between the 1970s SoHo artistic community and underground rock-and-roll), found themselves working in rock."[23] Although their reputations as visual artists floundered, the Talking Heads developed an aural accompaniment to the new downtown art scene. Their connection with CBGB represented the 1970s analogue to the 1960s connection between Velvet Underground and Andy Warhol's Factory scene—the height of avant-garde respectability. Even when the band was in its infancy, prestigious publications recognized that "insofar as there is an underground hierarchy," the Talking Heads were "right at the top."[24]

While the Talking Heads were the establishment's new wave leader, the loose, unrefined quality of CBGB's other mainstays reflected the Lower East Side's renaissance. In the early 1970s, it was the "unquestionably brilliant" yet "spare" New York Dolls that assumed the underground mantle from the Velvets.[25] Patti Smith's popular rise coincided with the transformation of Kristal's club. The *Times* described Smith on the cusp of "stardom" as an "alien muse who has come down and captured the essence of the stylized punk defiance that is at the heart of rock music."[26] Verlaine wrote a number of Smith's songs, and Television often shared the bill when Smith performed on the Bowery. Television's style, defined by "Verlaine's raw, spat-out singing, by the twanging solidity of the massed guitars and their sweet solo flights and odd, even psychotically opaque yet telling and evocative lyrics," epitomized New York's new wave. Their success exemplified the cosmopolitan ethos, as well. Verlaine arrived in the city from Wilmington, Delaware, as a young adult, taking odd entry-level jobs and bumming around in a few lesser-known bands. Despite his lack of success, he hung around New York because he "really [didn't] like it much anywhere else," finding a niche within the "poets and artists" of the downtown renaissance.[27]

No high-profile CBGB regulars exuded the Lower East Side antiestablishment sensibility more than the Ramones. Raised on the semisuburban streets of Forest Hills, Queens, the four bandmates—Joey, Johnny, Dee Dee, and Tommy—adopted a common surname and migrated to the affordable confines of lower Manhattan. In the early 1970s, they advertised themselves in the *Village Voice* music section. Soon they were sharing the stage with fellow new wave artists Blondie at places like Performance Studios "uptown" near Union Square and, not long after, headlining at CBGB.[28] Similar to the Sex Pistols and the British new wave, the Ramones crafted an aesthetic that eventually came to represent the American "punk." Tight denim and leather outerwear, basic sneakers, disheveled greasy hair in short spikes or long lengths, leather accessories, and ripped everything defined the look—the style of the underemployed migrant and the Lower East Side homesteader. The sound, too, became a signifier. The Ramones' music stripped rock and roll down to the bare minimum. Songs were short—two to three minutes at the most, which contrasted sharply with the self-indulgent ballads, rock operas, and concept albums of the sixties and seventies—consisting of a few chords on driving guitars, pounding drums, and vocal shouts. The lyrics were often ironic twists on past pop hits—for example, "Blitzkrieg Bop," "The KKK Took My Baby Away," "You're Gonna Kill That Girl"—or evocative of New York adolescence, as was the case with "Rockaway Beach," an homage to their native borough's oceanfront peninsula. "53rd and 3rd," a murder ballad about the masculine sex trade Uptown, served as a corollary to the Velvet Underground's "I'm Waiting for the Man," mapping a transgressive geography of New York that taunted purveyors of pathology and fear. That kind of reappropriation of the city in decline defined the sensibility of the CBGB scene. As the *Times* pointed out in 1975, the Ramones were "a lot of fun" with their "black leather jackets, a parodistic macho-camp swagger, and furious, blasting rock 'n' roll." Their presence Downtown transformed the Bowery into a long middle finger running uptown into the faces of New York's political and economic establishment, and personified the possibilities of a truly fun city.[29]

This sensibility played out in Allan Moyle's *Times Square* (1980), a film that despite the uptown title had a distinct downtown, antiestablishment feel. Set against the backdrop of Times Square redevelopment and campaigns to sanitize the "X rated city," it features two young women—escapees from the Bellevue psych ward—who take a punk rock adventure through the city while subverting the neoliberal order along the way. The film's antagonist, David Pearl, heads the "Times Square Renaissance," a public-private partnership guided by a mission to "Reclaim the Heart of the City" and stand-in for the actual institutions working to clear the "Deuce" of the stench left by *Midnight Cowboy, Taxi Driver*, and other business-unfriendly representations in the 1970s. From whom Times Square must be reclaimed was clear: the hustlers, queers, cons, and sex shop operators who appropriated the space in the neighborhood's postwar abandonment. As Pearl works to impose order on the unruly district, his domestic life spins out of control. His daughter, Pamela, is on the verge of estrangement from her overworked father, invoking the typical eighties trope of the New York hyperstriver, and suffers from a series of mysterious seizures and outbursts. Pamela's turning point comes at Bellevue Hospital, where Nicky, a poor and parentless kindred spirit, connects with her and plots their escape from the confines of the ward.[30]

Despite their maladies, Pamela and Nicky represent the only sane minds in a borough duped by narratives of Necropolis and the redevelopment imperative of postcrisis New York. Freed from the bonds of parents, doctors, and their surrogates, the two women delight in the urban experience neoliberal municipal surgeons like David Pearl seek to eradicate. In Pamela's words, they are "having our own renaissance" cut to the sounds of a downtown-heavy new wave soundtrack. On a West Side waterfront gutted by industrialization, they have no difficulty finding space to squat. In Midtown they assume the life of "squeegee" women, the "quality of life" scourge of Rudolph Giuliani and others, who clean the car windows of suburban commuters in hope of acquiring pocket change. When that fails, they deal three-card monte to unsuspecting tourists and visitors, seeking a modern-day Ratso Rizzo–like take. As the straits become dire, Pamela and Nicky resort to mugging and theft, not unlike the protagonists of *Midnight Cowboy* before them. In due time, Pamela willingly takes a job as a burlesque dancer on "X rated" Forty-Second Street.[31]

Beyond the struggle of everyday existence, Pamela and Nicky cultivate their artistic side, mastering a punk sound and earning the admiration of one of the city's premier disc jockeys. The Sleaze Sisters—a name that invokes the city's uncleanliness, its lack of luster, and the lure thereof—produce a hit titled "Sleaze Sister Voodoo," a track that mocks the establishment's blatant and coded slurs for the underclass, signifying their marginalized identities as the city's "problem." Pamela's vocals, in particular, scold the

FIGURE 13 At the finale of *Times Square*, the Sleaze Sisters (on top of the marquee at right) put on a public show near the offices of the Times Square Renaissance, a public-private partnership seeking to "Reclaim, Rebuild, [and] Restore" the neighborhood.

attempts of her father and the redevelopment regime to turn Times Square "as cold as [David Pearl's] stare." The film's showcase of youthful adventure and cultural production as well as its new wave soundtrack connected the downtown scene with the dual critique of emergent neoliberal redevelopment politics and the establishment's collective misunderstanding of artistic and creative autonomy in the "decaying" sections of New York City.[32]

Amid the city's neoliberal transformation in SoHo and Times Square, a collective movement emerged on the fringes of Manhattan and the outerboroughs. While migrants were largely responsible for the downtown phenomenon, native New Yorkers sparked a wave of cultural production with the goal of shaping a new city out of the rubble of the urban crisis. Artists in Uptown Manhattan, the Bronx, and Brooklyn appropriated the decaying and dull physical plant as grand canvases, draping the city in an explosion of color and commentary. Since the 1960s, the trend of inking and painting public spaces had been a thorn in the side of the city's boosters. Coinciding with the consolidation of the Metropolitan Transit Authority (MTA), graffiti "writers" began marking subway trains and other infrastructure with "tags" identifying the author of the work. The movement started with felt markers, and the graffiti itself tended toward a monochromatic and two-dimensional perspective. As the form evolved from tags to the "throw-up" (a slightly more elaborate painted version of the tag) to the "masterpiece" or "piece" (the colorful three-dimensional narrative murals that decorated many a train car in the seventies), so too did the fear around the practice.

In the echo of urban "law and order" discourse, graffiti writing was immediately recognized as a problem among city power brokers. As early as 1972, the *Times* transportation reporter highlighted the strain that paint and marker put on MTA maintenance officials. Soon local elites saw graffiti, in the words of historian Joe Austin, as a "dangerous and even subversive threat to local authority." Tags, throw-ups, and pieces within the mobile and static landscape became low-hanging fruit for fear narratives and politicians unwilling to investigate New York's deep social and economic problems in the 1970s. As such, the representation of the graffiti "problem" in the local media "narrowed and closed off the possibility for understanding writing on the trains as an important grassroots urban mural movement, a movement that could have complemented the already-significant cultural tourism that supports the city's economy." Instead, the movement developed into an analogue of the fiscal crisis, as newspapers, magazines, and television reports shaped the "subway crisis" and neoconservatives elucidated the city's cultural decline at the hands of disorderly vandals.[33]

Within the context of the city's larger shift in political economy, intellectuals recognized the graffiti form as an integral part of New York's complicated "rebirth." Norman Mailer, a persistent contrarian amid postwar narratives of decline and John Lindsay's opponent in the 1969 mayoral election, published *The Faith of Graffiti* in 1974. The large-format book, which featured an essay by Mailer and photographs of various "pieces" by Jon Naar, illustrated the importance of unsolicited public painting on the landscape of crisis. Mailer had no reservations about the works' value as art and political criticism. He noted that during the Lindsay administration, "the ugliest architecture in the history of New York had also gone up," leaving the city's skyline "as undistinguished in much of its appearance as Cleveland or Dallas." In contrast, writing offered much-needed foliage in an otherwise austere and homogenous environment. According to Mailer, the movement began "as the expression of tropical peoples living in a monotonous iron-gray and dull brown brick environment, surrounded by asphalt, concrete, and clangor . . . [in the] halls of every high-rise low-rent housing project which looked like a prison (and all did)" and ended when the city cracked down on the writers. "If it had gone on, this entire city of bland architectural high-rise horrors would have been covered with paint." And to the postwar contrarian that would have been aesthetically and politically pleasing.[34]

The Faith of Graffiti continued Mailer's new journalist examination of the city's maligned and marginalized by engaging a variety of well-known local graffiti writers.[35] A-1, Mailer's self-applied street name, spent the bulk of his essay attacking Lindsay for his narrow treatment of the city's new artistic trend and for decrying writers as "insecure cowards" and "a dirty shame." In a telling passage, Jon Naar commented on a sign imploring "DON'T POLLUTE—KEEP THE CITY CLEAN." As Naar noted, "they don't see . . . that sign is a form of pollution itself," thus suggesting that graffiti enforcement and warnings silenced the grassroots appropriation of city infrastructure. State-sanctioned signage in this sense only validated the writers' critique of power and decay in the urban crisis. Mailer fantasized about his handling of the situation had he been elected mayor, spreading the gospel of graffiti as modern art. He then laughed it off: "nobody like himself would ever be elected Mayor until the people agreed bad architecture was as poisonous as bad food." Mailer, who elsewhere decried the "barracks" design of public housing, recognized that aesthetics was not the establishment's strong suit.[36]

Contemporary intellectuals, however, lacked Mailer's enlightenment on this new wave of visual art and its chosen canvas. Citing it as the bête noire du jour in their backlash against urbanism, neoconservatives offered a powerful critique of graffiti. They evaluated writing not for its aesthetics, but rather for the problematic image that it signified. The "graffiti problem" was a minor penal offense, as Nathan Glazer noted in *Public Interest*, yet it had a significant cultural implication for the status of urban governments in an inhospitable political milieu. The widespread presence of graffiti, as Austin interprets Glazer's argument, "told the citizens of New York that the city authorities were unable to deal with even minor misdeeds." It sent the message "that if the city government could not control these petty crimes, then it could certainly not solve the more severe crimes committed on the subways, nor was it likely to solve the host of even more serious problems facing the city." This rationale evolved into the influential "broken windows" theory explicated by neocon scholars in the 1980s. The theory relied on a distinctly cultural interpretation of the city. As misdemeanors and their visual evidence climb in a neighborhood, so too will crime in increasing severity. Perceived signs of disorder like graffiti were "texts" read in a very specific way: "toleration of visible disruptions in the normative aesthetic order of urban space could lead to a general collapse into lawlessness." In the eyes of neoconservatives and policy makers, they symbolized the most potent trope of Necropolis—that crime could pop up anytime and anywhere. This ideology shaped policing strategy going forward.[37]

In part, the neoconservatives were correct: writing signified urban issues, but in a more sophisticated manner than suggested by Glazer and the like. On the one hand, the art of graffiti writing was an individual appropriation of neglected neighborhoods and declining infrastructure. As Austin argues, the artists " 'made a place' for themselves in the city's public network, claiming a 'right to the city' as a valuable and necessary part of its social and cultural life." They established a new City Beautiful movement from below, serving as subversive boosters for those who fought through the urban crisis on the bottom and were still left behind. On the other hand, writers offered a collective critique of the new austere state, creating in the process an indelible image of urbanism. For some—elites in particular—graffiti represented a crisis and justified many fears, but for those underrepresented in the political and economic arena, writing symbolized risk, adventure, and fun—the qualities that defined Cosmopolis. Even the opening scene of *West Side Story*, filmed in early 1960s Lincoln Square, featured the primitive brush-painted tags of the Jets and Sharks alongside other markings. When the producers of the mid-1970s high-school-set situation comedy *Welcome Back, Kotter* chose the mise-en-scène for the show's credit sequence, they decided on throw-up-laden trains, an image of working-class Brooklyn as enduring as tenement block clotheslines, small-scale ethnic commercial streets, and the shadows of elevated rail. The titles' font, too, echoed at once chalk on a blackboard and paintbrush script. The playful relationship between writing and popular culture suggested that perhaps the masses outside New York were less antagonized by the graffiti act. For those living on the city's margins, it symbolized home.[38]

Graffiti art was part of a larger phenomenon that has been cataloged since as "hip-hop," a cultural movement within communities of color that united elements of writing with music and dancing, and discoursed on the "pleasure and problems" of "life on the margins in postindustrial urban America."[39] The South Bronx served as the epicenter of mid-1970s hip-hop, and by the end of the decade the form's influence had already extended Downtown and beyond. The problems of the South Bronx were notorious in this period. In early 1977 Bill Moyers introduced the world to the Bronx in CBS Reports' *The Fire Next Door*. "This is the Bronx, New York," he began. "One and a half million people live in this borough, equal to the population of

FIGURE 14 Graffiti as commentary—in this shot from *Wild Style*, tags and a
throw-up mingle alongside the remnants of a poster indicting "the Reagan Program
of cutbacks, racism & war."

Houston or Washington or San Diego. It's the home of the New York Yankees,
the Bronx Zoo, and the Grand Concourse. It has also become the arson
capital of the world. Once that smoke on the horizon meant industry, progress, jobs. Now it means someone is burning down a building: a landlord
for profit, a tenant for revenge, junkies, vandals. It happens thirty times a
day and the flames are the signal of a national disaster."[40] In private, Daniel Patrick Moynihan, the Bronx's elected representative to the U.S. Senate, allegedly remarked, "People in the South Bronx don't want housing or
they wouldn't burn it down."[41] Following Moyers's report, President Carter
visited the borough to survey the damage, and Ronald Reagan made a similar stop in the South Bronx to highlight Carter's failure to stem the urban
crisis. Viewers of the 1977 World Series, featuring the hometown Yankees
against the team that escaped New York (the Los Angeles Dodgers), caught
a glimpse of the furnace and abandonment when television cameras seized
on a tenement fire mere blocks from Yankee Stadium. Over aerial footage
of the flames, announcer Howard Cosell intoned, "that's the very area
where President Carter trod just a few days ago." (His comments have

been incorrectly memorialized as "there it is, ladies and gentlemen, the Bronx is burning.")[42] As the political economy of the city shifted toward service delivery, the Bronx was hit particularly hard. The borough lost 600,000 manufacturing jobs in the 1970s, and per capita income was about half of the New York City average. Declining income, increasing energy costs, poor public policy, and blatant insurance corruption fed the fires of abandonment as disgruntled landlords in mostly minority neighborhoods burned whole blocks of apartment buildings to the ground. The South Bronx alone lost 43,000 housing units in this period.[43] For the political establishment, the Bronx symbolized the scourge of the welfare state and its overdependent underclass.[44]

The Bronx was more than a wasteland of fire and rot, however. As journalist and critic Nelson George remembers it, "behind the decay and neglect the place was a cauldron of vibrant, unnoticed, and quite visionary creativity born of it racial mix and its relative isolation."[45] In the 1970s, black disc jockeys, drawing from a mélange of influences, began experimenting with a new kind of sound montage composed of classic rhythm-and-blues strains and the thumping beats of funk. It has been said that hip-hop was born in the Bronx—1520 Sedgwick Avenue, to be specific—when DJ Kool Herc appropriated the recreation space of his parents' apartment building for weekend music parties. Herc's ability to isolate the heavily percussive "breaks" on soul records and to combine loops of breaks with abrupt switchbacks to other loops proved fortuitous. Emcees (MCs) layered the sounds with phrases, slang, callouts, and freestyle rhymes, that is, "rapping." On the dance floor, "b-boys" and "b-girls" provided the corporeal manifestation of hip-hop. Not unlike the popular representations of disco dancing, which ultimately mixed group performance with individual conceits, break-dancers or breakers—hence "b"—thrived on physically and mentally demanding, sometimes contortionist, routines. Along with graffiti, which offered a visual manifestation of the ethos, hip-hop represented the cultural expression of the "right to the city" in abandoned and burned-out minority neighborhoods segregated from the rebirth of New York.[46]

First-generation hip-hop music was driven by the work of DJs like Kool Herc, who developed star-like quality in New York and the Bronx in particular. Alongside Herc in the West Bronx, Afrika Bambaataa ruled the East Bronx and Grandmaster Flash held sway in the South Bronx, territory that fell in line with the disintegrating street gangs that once controlled those areas. In contrast to the problematic turf negotiations of gang life, hip-hop emerged as a cultural community organizer, bringing people from around the borough and the city proper into public space to celebrate the spectacle of urban life in the midst of elite doomsaying. The gatherings were not without the occasional dustup or even eruptions of violence, but early hip-hop was the consummate expression of Fun City, as New Yorkers living on the margins appropriated what remained of the increasingly burned-out Bronx. The record industry coopted and commodified hip-hop soon enough. The genre's first breakout hit, "Rapper's Delight" (1979) by the Sugar Hill Gang, was to hip-hop what the Monkees were to rock-and-roll, purely fabricated for profit, but the hip-hop movement's origins were democratic and anti-capitalist, less concerned with material gain than with fostering community and mutual aid. As with graffiti, the hip-hop purveyor's worst sin was envy and status-seeking, which she or he tempered with mutual appreciation for the form. "The idea of parties in parks and community centers, which is celebrated nostalgically as the true essence of hip-hop, means that money was not a goal," Nelson George writes. "None of the three original DJs—Herc, Flash, Bambaataa—expected anything from the music but local fame, respect in the neighborhood, and the modest fees from the parties given at uptown clubs or the odd midtown ballroom. . . . Like the graffiti writers and the break dancers, the old-school DJs, and those that quickly followed their lead did it because it felt good and because they could."[47]

Despite the challenging political economy of the Bronx and its residents, early hip-hop featured a decidedly egalitarian character, and if anything, the movement united the homegrown appropriation of New York with the happenings Downtown. A worldview that transcended the Bronx and Uptown emerged in the early recordings of artists like Bambaataa. "Planet Rock" (1982), his foundational record, was a product of transnational connections, highlighting at once Bambaataa's spiritual solidarity with the South African Zulu people and the influence of West German electronica innovators Kraftwerk (particularly *Trans Europa Express* [1977]). Prior to the record's release, Bambaataa had found a home Downtown, playing regular shows at the club Negril on the Lower East Side. In 1981 the connection between the Bowery scene and hip-hop was immortalized in Blondie's "Rapture," a track that features Debbie Harry rapping about a transformative meeting with Grandmaster Flash. (The unpredictable Blondie also had a disco hit with "Heart of Glass.") By that time, new wave and hip-hop were each a part of the city's cultural mainstream. The genres shifted the center of gravity of New York's music scene from the elite decadence of disco's playground, Studio 54, to the democratic mixed culture of the Roxy in the burgeoning warehouse district of Chelsea. Organized by Ruza Blue, also known as Kool Lady Blue, the Roxy hosted shows open to all regardless of age and color that featured Bambaataa, Flash, and ascendant talents like Grand Wizard Theodore (inventor of the scratch technique) on the turntables.[48]

When the size and brilliance of elaborate "masterpieces" evoked the large forms preferred by the pioneers of the cast iron district, graffiti merged hip-hop with the downtown visual art scene centered in SoHo. Fred Brathwaite, also known as Fab Five Freddy, was the fluid New York figure who bridged the art worlds of SoHo and the railyards in the 1970s and the 1980s. While elites pushed policing and "the buff" to eradicate the graffiti scourge, Brathwaite organized graffiti artists, including renowned writer Lee Quinones, and brought them and their work Downtown. As the man about the underground, Fab Five Freddy "hung out at *Interview* magazine editor Glen O'Brien's cable access show, a central hub of the New Wave/No Wave movement. He partied at the Mudd Club with Deborah Harry and Blondie, Jean-Michel Basquiat, Keith Haring and Andy Warhol." Graffiti artists like Quinones now moved in the same circles as Downtowners Haring and Basquiat—painters who increasingly drew on street aesthetics. Brathwaite also integrated the Lower East Side, bringing tapes of uptown DJs and MCs to musicians and venue owners Downtown. Like the movement, he was young and fresh, a teenager "moving through two very different worlds, and he had both the charisma and the desire to bring them together."[49] As George notes, "[Brathwaite's] point was that this living, aggressive art was the perfect fit with the same antiestablishment attitudes that ruled at punk landmarks like CBGBs. If punk was rebel music, this was just as truly rebel art."[50] This melding of scenes culminated in the "now-mythic" *Times Square Show* put on by Colab (Collaborative Projects, Inc.) in the summer of 1980, which showcased the work of over one hundred artists from around the city in "an empty massage parlor" at the heart of the crossroads.[51]

Beyond the *Times Square Show*, Charlie Ahearn's film *Wild Style* (1983) cataloged the right-to-the-city ethos of hip-hop and its place in New York at large. Shot in a documentary cinema verité style, the unscripted fictional film examined the life of artist Zoro, played by Quinones. Zoro is a star on the make, but in typical Hollywood fashion, his lover—played by Quinones's real-life partner Lady Pink, a celebrated writer herself—is unaware of his talent. She does not know that he rappels down walls to put up a piece, or that he ventures over and under barbed-wire fences surrounding the city's subway yards to paint cars before the police arrive. His girlfriend ignores him and his brother chastises his hobby. Yet Zoro is the talk of the

FIGURE 15 In a scene from *Wild Style*, Zoro (Lee Quinones) walks among the rubble and burned-out buildings of the South Bronx in the early 1980s.

neighborhood, and his work catches the eye of a downtown reporter who drags him to elite art parties in SoHo, sparking a series of verbal contracts for commissioned projects. Zoro's identity is eventually revealed, and he earns the respect of his once beloved when he orchestrates the artwork for a hip-hop appropriation of the abandoned and decayed East River Park bandshell on the margins of the Lower East Side. Combining controversial subject matter with film industry tropes regarding humility and love, the film put a human face on the mysterious graffiti culture: Zoro lives in the Bronx, comes from a lower- or working-class family, and is an otherwise law-abiding citizen—not the terror depicted by culture warriors. Coproduced by the omnipresent Fab Five Freddy, *Wild Style* surveyed hip-hop at large, functioning as a long-form music video for the DJs, MCs, and breakdancers of the Bronx. Brathwaite also scored the film, which featured an extended playground freestyling session between the Cold Crush Brothers and the Fantastic Five. Even Grandmaster Flash cameos, DJ-ing the uptown party that Zoro visits with the downtown reporter in tow. With its sprawling cast, broad subject matter, and loose verisimilitude, *Wild Style* was the film equivalent of the throw-up come masterpiece.[52]

While Fun City was a significant element of hip-hop, the movement, as Mailer's graffiti analysis suggested, also reserved space for politics within its various forms of expression. *Wild Style* reflected this duality, offering comment on the political economy of New York in the early 1980s: post–fiscal crisis but still smoldering in the poorer districts. Ahearn filmed the colorful trains of Quinones, Lady Pink, and others amid the backdrop of the burned-out and abandoned Bronx, frames that supported Mailer's aesthetic argument. The soundtrack also fostered a narrative of life in a struggling New York City. In the film's penultimate scene, Zoro rides the elevated train to the tune of Grandmaster Caz's "South Bronx Subway Rap": "South Bronx New York is where I dwell / To a lot of people it's a living hell / Full of frustration and poverty / But that's not how it looks it to me / But it's a challenge and opportunity." As this verse suggests, *Wild Style* and hip-hop offered counterarguments to the naysayers of the urban crisis. The message paralleled Paley's observation: from the ruins, innovative and unique cultural production and community development might spring.[53]

Grandmaster Flash and the Furious Five's hit "The Message" (1983) worked in this vein by exploring the paradox of homegrown Necropolis narratives. The song was mostly a fabricated commercial opus à la "Rapper's Delight"—manufactured by the same production team at Sugar Hill Records—but it showcased a valid sentiment about the struggle in postindustrial New York City.[54] The lyrics detailed a laundry list of ghetto tropes and profound images of the new underclass, enough to delight the hearts of neoconservatives. According to Melle Mel, representing the ascendant MC stardom in hip-hop (as opposed to the DJs of old), New York was the site of ubiquitous misery. "Broken glass everywhere," he sings, playing off the concurrent writings of James Q. Wilson and George Kelling. So too are pimps and prostitutes, the insane, and the apathetic who urinate in the streets, make noise, and ignore the plight of fellow citizens. The schools are failing, and the hustle remains the only viable option for the impoverished slum dweller. It may offer instant gratification, but in the end the "cool" are found in prison, hanging from a rope in their cell. Unlike those casting aspersions on the underclass from afar, however, this voice was coming straight out of the ravaged boroughs and neighborhoods themselves. It attacked the suggestion that "people in the South Bronx don't want housing." The city was certainly "like a jungle sometimes," as the narrator notes in the chorus, so much so that it makes one "wonder how I keep from going under." Yet "The Message" seemed to say that yes, the neighborhood is in shambles, and citizens could respond with apathy, despair, and, if fortunate enough, flight. But they were still there confronting the problem.[55]

. . . . . .

Felix Rohatyn, chairman of the Municipal Assistance Corporation, Mayor Ed Koch, and other power brokers may receive credit for salvaging New York, but citizens like Grandmaster Flash and Melle Mel kept the city from going under in the wake of the fiscal crisis. The vast and diverse geography of cultural expression sent the message that New York was still a destination for the weary dreamer—a site of adventure and discovery. In places like Harlem and the Bronx, blocks could burn, but someone would be there to pick up the pieces and upcycle the neighborhood. The late 1970s to early 1980s was the age of appropriation in the city, as intrepid citizens exercised their right to it. As critic and scene participant Carlo McCormick recalls, "like mongrel mutts marking territory in daily streams of urination, the creative community thrived off its isolation from the larger culture, inhabiting abandoned spaces, protected (if perilously) by the majority's fear of subjecting themselves to its inherent indignities of crime and squalor." The cast iron district and the Lower East Side were "abandoned space[s], left bereft of its original function by the 'white flight' of the first- and second-generation European immigrants moving family and business to the suburbs, and a sanctified space where, due to the larger woes of the city, whatever transgressions a bunch of artist-types might be up to in its neglected nether-zones were granted unprecedented free rein."[56] Downtown, a theme of subversion ran through the works of artists and musicians, signifying their disregard for the postindustrial status quo.[57]

Uptown, citizens of color and cultural producers subverted the narratives that wrote them off in the 1960s and 1970s. From the well of poverty and neglect, as well as arson and abandonment, sprung a font of original artistic expression that symbolized the possibilities of the open and fun city. Graffiti writers' civil disobedience exposed the hypocrisy of the state as it transitioned from a "War on Poverty" to a war on disruptions to elite quality of life. DJ's and MCs and the public gatherings they orchestrated served as aural analogues to the famous Parisian graffiti from May 1968: "*Sous les pavés, la plage!*" (Under the cobblestones, the beach!). B-boys and b-girls brought electricity to the streets, showcasing the latent talent, wisdom, and sophistication among the so-called underclass. The map of appropriation from Downtown to Brooklyn to the South Bronx seemed to consume the whole of the city as the spaces of ethnic whiteness left vacant in the "death" of New York filled with a cosmopolitan crowd and an explosion of authentic creativity. "The mass of cultural production that took effect in New York City . . . was nothing if not extremely prolific and polymorphous," writes McCormick.[58] Citizens were molding a new democratic New York in their image—so what happened?

The success of the "right to the city" strivers in the 1970s had a through-the-looking-glass effect on Reagan-era New York. In the case of SoHo, for instance, elites understood that the former industrial neighborhood became more fashionable without the working class and their places of employ. Thus, the city, too, might be more fashionable sans the lower orders, provided the physical plant—that is, the façades—that once sustained them remained intact and proved habitable through rehabilitation. As a result, the transformation of culture and space became commodified in the form of loft-living gentrification and neighborhood branding. Any undesirables who hindered the quality of professional-class lifestyles confronted a revitalized post–Knapp Commission police state. Recent scholarship on planning and economic development that hails New York City's enduring "creative economy," born in this expressive moment in the 1970s and 1980s, tends to highlight the successful commodification of this cultural production. It celebrates outlets of conspicuous consumption like fashion designer John Varvatos's appropriation of CBGB, which shuttered in the early 2000s following a rent dispute. Varvatos swiftly transformed the space into a boutique where the venue's downtown aesthetic endures amid his denim selling for outsized prices. Neoliberal scholars of creativity seem to fetishize capital's seizure of unique cultural expression spawned by the lure of decay, obscuring its genesis in a distinctly anticapitalist milieu. Instead, using New York City as a model, they repackage cultural production and its service components as a struggling community's key to postindustrial economic growth.

New York's economic turnaround did not occur without its own costs, often inflicted on the subcultures responsible for the pluralistic explosion of culture in the revitalized universal city. While the 1980s media culture highlighted the creative growth of the 1970s, the postindustrial fixes that were put in place in the wake of the fiscal crisis altered the city's political economy. Wall Street was renewed, and the city retooled the public sector, instituting severe austerity measures within its sizable bureaucracy. Power brokers molded a city attractive to the FIRE economy dominated by financial, insurance, and real estate services, a departure from the diversified and productive economy of the past. Such a dramatic transformation necessitated a redefined Cosmopolis, and *The Secret of My Success* (1987), among other cultural expressions, signaled the new trend. The film starred Michael J. Fox as a Kansan farmboy and recent college graduate who moves to New York on a whim. He is not the rural migrant with the cultural or small-business ambitions of White's imagination; rather, he arrives with neoliberal aspirations of streamlining and merging the city's FIRE sector companies. He willingly works pro bono for rear-guard corporate drones driving his uncle's institution into the ground, that is, until his secret is revealed and he assumes a chief upper management position in the reorganized and efficient company. By and large, similar productions such as *Wall Street* (1987), *Big,* and *Working Girl* (1988) and novels like *Bright Lights, Big City* (1984) and *The Bonfire of the Vanities* (1987), while often cautionary moralistic tales, showcased a glamorous and wealthy party city brokered by white corporate "masters of the universe," a precursor to the image of the city proffered by the growth machines of Michael Bloomberg and recent mayoral administrations. Development regimes since the 1980s, insulated by private sector growth and broken-windows policing, have managed to erase not only the image of Necropolis but that of the more fair and equitable city as well.[59]

Epilogue

. . . .

Assessing the landscape since the 1960s in the pages of *Dissent*, Marshall Berman noted that "things that happen in New York are beamed instantly all over America, indeed, the world, thanks to all the mass media that are located here. Facts become symbols instantly—often long before they are understood." During the urban crisis, "New York came to symbolize 'urban violence.'" These words appeared in the Fall 1987 issue, "In Search of New York," after ten years of postcrisis restructuring under Mayor Edward Koch. Berman's "Ruins and Reforms" offered a rose-colored remembrance of the journal's "splendid issue on New York" in 1961, "almost every [article] of which still stands up today." The journal's look at New York was driven by "passion" and bound to this distinct "place," with the contributors "happy to identify themselves as New Yorkers, rather than trying to sound like universal beings." While Berman admitted that "those writers were often bitter or sad" and that "they saw New York deteriorating in all sorts of ways," he did not connect their bitter tales to the "facts" that became the "symbols" beamed across the land during the ascendant urban crisis. Indictments of poverty and racial inequality by the New Left were recognized, as were Daniel Bell's perceptive analysis of the city's changing political economy and Irving Howe's "memoir." Berman suggested that collection of intellectuals "saw themselves as part of a large, growing, increasingly self-confident reforming public, a public that cared passionately about the city and had the energy to make real changes, if it could just understand what was going on." Lionel Abel was one of the few contributors Berman did not cite by name.[1]

This time around Howe, still the editor of the journal, reserved a section for recollections of old New York, echoing his earlier nostalgia for the 1930s Movement. Michael Harrington, critic Alfred Kazin, scholar Morris Dickstein, and novelist Paula Fox, among others, offered "Memories and Impressions" of the city gone by. Harrington, for example, recalled his own Movement of the 1960s and the way that Koch, then a liberal reform congressman from the Village, responded to the political impulses emerging from the bohemian district.[2] Just as the Summer 1961 issue of *Dissent* examined the city's changing

cultural landscape in the period—the Beats, new jazz, off-Broadway theater, the loner in New York literature—*Dissent*'s Fall 1987 issue took note of
the downtown and uptown scenes that arose from the lure of decay. Juan
Flores celebrated the intersection of black and Puerto Rican cultures on the
sidewalks of New York and the rich hip-hop ethos that resulted, including
writing, rap, and break dancing. Paul Berman, writer for the *Village Voice*,
recognized the "face of Downtown" as a "prisoner of culture," who "gazes
in the direction of real life, and it is movies, plays, books, and pop music
that gaze back." The Downtowner "resents this situation" caused by "modern culture—especially popular culture" because, as the "great original
radical thinkers of the 1960s" theorized, "culture is a tool of manipulation."[3]
According to the intellectuals at *Dissent*, popular representations of New
York had manipulated an anxious populace into accepting problematic responses to the fiscal crisis.

The issue appeared amid a violent white backlash to the steady diet of
narratives tying race to criminal pathology, in particular two high-profile
events seemingly ripped from the plot of *Death Wish*. In December 1984,
Bernhard Goetz shot four young black men on the subway, alleging that the
victims were armed and threatened to mug him. In five shots, Goetz hit all
four, with one victim suffering paralysis and brain damage as a result. Labeled the "Subway Vigilante" by the tabloid press and portrayed as the real-
life equivalent of Paul Kersey (who shoots a would-be subway mugger
through his newspaper), Goetz became a symbol for those disillusioned by
rising violence and the coded link between race and crime—a white man, in
the immortal words of Travis Bickle, "who would not take it anymore." Two
years later, in the white ethnic outpost of Howard Beach, Queens, teenage
vigilantes decided to take a preemptive strike on three black men whose
car broke down in the neighborhood and committed the cultural crime of
decompressing in a local pizzeria. The carload of white youths, prompted
by an exchange of insults along the neighborhood's main drag, chased Michael Griffith, Cedric Sandiford, and Timothy Grimes from the pizzeria.
Grimes escaped, Sandiford fell victim to the mob's assault and lived, and
Griffith made the fatal mistake of running onto the nearby Belt Parkway,
where he was hit by an oncoming car. Highlighting simmering racial and
class tensions in the postindustrial city, these events sparked a series of
literal and figurative conflagrations that New York navigated long after
Dissent went to press.[4]

For the contributors scanning the city from the street, such events signaled the declining promise of Cosmopolis. Reactionary violence exempli-

fied seething white and black rage in the neoliberal city, the former of which Koch pandered to in his campaigning. Turf negotiations that resulted from fear and anxiety, which played out previously in the former white ethnic Brooklyn enclaves of Canarsie and Brownsville, demonstrated that New York City was "a social experiment that has failed," as noted by an uncle of Jennifer Levin, the eighteen-year-old victim of the "Preppie Killer" (Robert Chambers) in 1986. According to Jim Sleeper, "the decay of white ethnic political culture" stemming from reform politics and the impact of deindustrialization on employment opportunities prompted racial vengeance. White rage constituted the wish fulfillment of Dick Schaap's Brownsville mugging victim nostalgic for Murder Incorporated's swift law-and-order policies. In contrast, black rage was legitimate. While the white working class internalized the racial narratives of Necropolis, the city's power brokers exploited impending demographic change for gain. In the words of Sleeper, "when the full history of the agony of the South Bronx and central Brooklyn in the 1970s is written, the pathologies of 'multi-problem' speculators and other, mostly white, schemers will assume great prominence alongside the pathologies of the larger welfare families who were the ultimate victims of bank redlining, blockbusting, and mortgage insurance scams." That Sleeper deemed this corrective necessary among *Dissent*'s audience speaks to the fog of pathological decline even into the 1980s.[5]

It was also clear that Goetz and the Howard Beach terrorists had absorbed the narratives of Necropolis. Since the 1960s, columnists, critics, and reporters had detailed the seeming randomness of New York's crime problem. The impulses of the underclass, they said, sprung from a set of ghetto pathologies, a culture that did not discriminate among chosen victims. According to their reading, a mugging, robbery, rape, or murder could happen at any time and at any place. Just look at the qualitative (Katherine Genovese and the lonely crimes) and quantitative ("Up, Up, Up") evidence![6] In the hands of conservative scholars and commentators, jeremiads citing those data shaped an influential discourse on the welfare state and policing in a period of economic and social uncertainty. As their fears were transferred onto celluloid and video, consumers of popular culture in the 1970s absorbed the verisimilitude of New York's mean streets broadcast near and far. In Necropolis, as Paul Kersey and Travis Bickle had shown, it was every man for himself. When confronted with a situation echoing the sensational world of violent headlines and taglines, Goetz reached for the authoritarian template offered by Spillane and Mike Hammer: Shoot first; ask questions later. Stand your ground. Crown yourself the judge, jury, and executioner. John

Avildsen's *Joe* might have suggested that youth culture and the "hippies" were at fault for moral and economic decline in the 1960s, but in the 1980s, as a result of narratives of dependence and "welfare queens," blacks represented that scourge. As such, when confronted with seemingly aimless outsiders enjoying a slice of pizza in an outerborough enclave, the Howard Beach crew took a page from *Joe's* Curran and Compton: hurling epithets first before going on a preemptive strike to preserve the status quo.

Of course, the impact of Necropolis extended beyond the orbit of New York City psychopaths. Prior to becoming mayor, Koch understood that large corporations left New York in the 1960s and 1970s because of the racial image of crime and the cost of public services in the city. When he was in office, Koch instituted a variety of policy reforms to ensure corporate stability. *Dissent* contributors cited the mayor's recent $42 million giveaway, in the form of property tax abatements, to AT&T in response to the company's threat to relocate to Basking Ridge, New Jersey, where land was cheap and taxes were low. Gambits like this symbolized Koch's neoliberal reorganization of New York's public sector.[7] Under the three-term mayor, a "rightward shift in social policy" effectively destroyed the island fantasy of welfare democracy.[8] In the land vacuum created by abandonment and population decline, real estate developers subsidized by Koch reaped the benefits. The ascendance of the FIRE sector under his regime transformed New York, as Gus Tyler put it, into the polarized city of three faces: an "upper" and "lower" economy with the "under" (i.e., underground and perhaps underclass) economy mixed in and increasingly alluring to the marginalized and service-starved lower orders.[9] In the midst of an incredible building boom, affordable and public housing starts proved wanting. Public-private partnerships became the name of the game as Koch offered abandoned blocks in minority communities free of charge to charities, churches, and other community organizations to build affordable housing under the Nehemiah program beginning in 1982. The bombed-out blocks of Charlotte Street, the rubble of which Carter and Reagan once trod, became a simulacrum of a suburban subdivision surrounded by tenements, elevated trains, and enduring poverty. Howe, who seemed to view contemporary New York through the lens of previous radical eras, noted how Koch seized on the "sullen" sense of fear: "The mood of the city now revealed a weariness with the language of idealism, a coarsening of social sentiments, a resignation before inequities that had once troubled consciences."[10] Koch believed that New York must act in its own self-interest, which meant linking gratified, revitalized corporate capital to the preservation of Cosmopolis.

In this sense, his policies expanded the polarized "dual city" that pitted FIRE's administrators against an increasingly isolated, displaced, and servile lower class. According to historian Jonathan Soffer, Koch "pioneered the Democratic Party version of neoliberalism, which allowed for government intervention to shape and subsidize private enterprise . . . [pouring] hundreds of millions of dollars into tax abatements to subsidize construction of office buildings and luxury housing and to keep corporate headquarters in the city."[11] Firms like AT&T threatened to relocate to tax-friendly municipalities within the metro area unless the city conceded certain financial conditions. As David Harvey notes, in seeking to "create a good business climate" in the competitive neoliberal era, "the state assumes much of the risk while the private sector takes most of the profits."[12] The successive administrations of David Dinkins, Rudolph Giuliani, and Michael Bloomberg followed through on Koch's public-private partnership model. Gone were the days of direct state intervention in redevelopment, much less new investment in public housing—which in New York's case has been historically and comparatively successful.[13]

The city's public-private priorities had significant implications for planning and design, which also ate away at White's Cosmopolis. In "Stumbling toward Tomorrow," critic Ada Louise Huxtable derided the decline of "vision" in New York. In the 1930s, the Regional Plan Association and the Regional Plan Association of America imagined a futuristic, grand, and efficient "city of tomorrow." In the age of renewal, Robert Moses shaped the dramatic bird's eye view with a similar vision in mind. The city spent years assembling the massive 1969 *Plan for New York*, but for Huxtable it was about "thirty years late." By then the nature of planning had changed. "The comprehensive struggle to eradicate urban blight had failed to alleviate the pressures of poverty and deprivation or the growing cataclysm of drugs and despair." As the fiscal crisis belied large-scale planning, the work of the city's planning regime transitioned from design to evaluation, a judge of individual and corporate visions rather than a visionary itself. "Even with the return of the good times, the position, prestige and strength of the Planning Commission were never regained." In the world of community planning, the city turned to "street-corner surgery, and sometimes to cosmetic surgery at that," failing to cure the new urban cancers. The attack on planning had succeeded in many ways, but not without some limitations. For one, developer-driven design exacerbated the polarization within the city. Like urban renewal of old, the city's redevelopment regime excised any social component of planning and development, segregating and subjugating the un- and underemployed—"a record 25% of the city's population" in 1987—while the real estate industry flourished. Tied to that was a failure of spirit and the decline of the idealism of the Regional Planning Association of America in the 1920s, an organization of intellectuals turned developers that saw the New York metropolitan area as the testing ground for modern visioning and comprehensive planning. "For developers and investors, this shimmering mirage is a money machine," wrote Huxtable. "For the rest of the world New York's skyscrapers are still poetry and fantasy. They continue to intimidate and exhilarate in a perennial sky show. But they have ceased to be beacons of hope."[14]

Nowhere was this sea change more apparent than in the redevelopment plans for Times Square, as hinted at in the eponymous film from a few years prior. The transgressive haunt of Joe Buck and Travis Bickle served as laboratory for public-private partnerships in the 1980s and 1990s. The city would seize the porn theaters and peep shows in return for private investment by some of the country's major corporations. In collaboration with the Walt Disney Company and fulfilling the dream of David Pearl's "Times Square Renaissance," Forty-Second Street became a testing ground for eliminating crime and disorder through development—in effect, neoliberal slum clearance and city building.[15] Following Koch, crime rates decreased as Dinkins and Giuliani, under the guidance of innovative NYPD commissioner William Bratton, targeted the scourge of so-called quality of life incidents and enacted new City Beautiful–style civic improvements to counteract any lingering Necropolis imagery, particularly in Times Square. Giuliani touted the disappearance of the iconic "squeegee man," an enduring symbol of decline whose elimination became the fact of the changing environment under his reign. Altering the quality of life in New York City also required removing chronic symbols of disorder and decline like graffiti and the broken and boarded-up windows of seventies and eighties abandonment. Public-private partnerships under Dinkins and Giuliani transformed whole areas of New York City, rendering space more amenable to tourists, visitors, and elite migrants. At the end of the century, Forty-Second Street and the Broadway–Seventh Avenue bowtie were a chaste suburban theme park. Historian and novelist Samuel Delany observes that Times Square was "designed to look safe . . . [but] promotes precisely the sort of isolation, inhumanity, and violence that everyone abhors."[16] Under Bloomberg, Broadway portions of the area became a pedestrian plaza free of automobile traffic—yielding the dream of Paul and Percival Goodman to tourists rather than to residents.

Over *Dissent*'s search for New York hung E. B. White's great fear: the decline of the city's exceptional, cosmopolitan allure. Contributors, including Huxtable, saw the city, as Mailer feared in *The Faith of Graffiti*, emulating every other standardized outpost of postindustrial economic growth. Historian Thomas Bender suggested that New York's exceptional qualities—its cosmopolitan ethos, the way it functioned as a "center of difference" in a sea of homogenous Puritan and Jeffersonian mythology—withered away under the Koch regime. Times Square was ground zero for this contestation: "Is it to remain and be renewed as a New Yorkish public space, or is it to be transformed, with vastly overscaled corporate towers designed by Phillip Johnson, into a mere episode in crass government-sponsored but private real estate development that could occur anywhere in America?" Since the city was well into the process of selecting the latter, Bender presented another vital question: "What is the source of the loss of confidence that is eroding our cosmopolitanism?" A substantial source of that decline was the lingering effects of Necropolis, as evident in Bender's follow-up. "From whence the idea that in New York it is necessary—or even possible— to remove completely all sources of tension, or even struggles in a public space?" A sense of safety is necessary for the physical public sphere to function, "but one must have the confidence to weigh, with some delicacy, the legitimate claims of security against the dynamic, even messy elements that make a space public and that impel the process of making public culture."[17] Despite the incredible masses that fill its canyons, twenty-first-century Times Square today ceases to be a public space, at least for New Yorkers, since most citizens avoid it unless compelled by employment, necessary services, or guiding tourists.

Although Irving Howe cited cultural disintegration for the city's decline in the 1960s, he saw the 1980s through a Marxian lens. "Television, of course," may be "responsible for the changes in political life," but neoliberal economics took its toll on the city in particular. "New York becomes harder and harder to live in," not because of Howe's age, but rather because of the city's obsession with Wall Street. Greed and corporate redevelopment obstructed the cultural and social cosmopolitanism that once drew intrepid migrants to New York. It was "its diversities, its unconventionalities" that made the city alluring and the "place one loved" upon arrival. Now that was "being swept away by the forces of money, the developers and foreign investors, the corporations with their sleek facades." According to Howe, the result was political sterility and cultural boredom. "What has been lacking now for some years is a fresh surge of energy, a new direction or a new idea, a shared and irresistible impulse that could give writers that feeling that they are part of a 'movement' or 'trend' that might, if only slightly, reinvigorate American culture."[18] In the realm of FIRE economics and its hold over New York development, Sleeper echoed this fate. "New York will remain the capital of cultural certification, marketing, and consumption, but its indigenous young white middle-class culture could approach the sterility" attributed to ascendant Sunbelt giants like Dallas.[19] Bender, Howe, and Sleeper appeared to be in search of a modern-day E. B. White, someone who could extol the cultural virtues of the once-enchanting metropolis.

While he ignored the old guard's reckoning with Necropolis in 1961, Marshall Berman found New York's intellectual community culpable in Koch's "spectacular giveaways" and "attacks on the poor." Since the fiscal crisis, New York had transformed "into a place where capital from anywhere in the world is instantly at home, while everybody without capital is increasingly out of place." This trend had bleak returns for the city's once-dynamic "civic culture." Echoing Howe's 1961 assessment of the fertile Movement of his youth, Berman complained that "the generosity of spirit, the reforming vision and energy of the 1960s seem to be gone with the wind. The dominant modes of civic consciousness today help to keep New Yorkers unconscious of the gigantic development deals that will blow them all away tomorrow." It was up to New York's learned and progressive minds, those conscious of the ways in which the city's universal cosmopolitanism fostered their intellectual and cultural development, to correct this trend. From the origin of democracy, "intellectuals took their stand in public spaces, and took it on themselves to act as the consciousness and conscience of their cities." Since the fiscal crisis, however, "New York's intellectuals haven't done much lately to live up to this legacy. We've stayed indoors, upstairs, while more and more of our city has been sold and bulldozed out from under us." The time had come for intellectuals to once again shape the public image and control the narrative of the city. Koch's machinations in particular required a renewal of White's message of liberty, equity, and diversity. "We still have plenty of brains and energy, and we still love New York. If we expose some of our inner wounds to the air, we can not only discover their sources, but we see how widely they are shared. . . . We need first to mourn. . . . Then we will be able to let go of our pain, and to build over the ruins a city we can share." It was an inspiring sermon on the power of culture in shaping the political economy of the city, if not the right to the city, from one of the city's most robust intellectual advocates.[20]

In neoliberal New York, however, real power rested with the FIRE sector and its advocates at City Hall then remaking the city and recasting Cosmopolis. The sterilized city that Koch and then Dinkins left in their wake witnessed a decrease in crime and an increase in population. Yet the vestiges of Necropolis revealed themselves in police violence against New Yorkers of color. Giuliani increased the size of the NYPD to an army of over 25,000 in order to secure New York, and its crackdown on quality of life issues provided fodder for critics who saw the mayor establishing a quasi-police state. The February 1999 murder of Amadou Diallo, a Guinean immigrant, by plainclothed officers in the contentious Giuliani-endorsed "Street Crimes Unit," the brutal precinct beating and rape of Haitian Abner Louima in 1997, and the 2000 murder of Patrick Dorismond by an undercover NYPD officer, along with his posthumous public shaming by none other than Giuliani (intending to show that Dorismond "was no altar boy"), as well as the mayor's failure to claim any responsibility for these events, heightened tensions between New Yorkers at large and the mayor in the waning days of his administration.[21] (This was before his response to the attacks on September 11, 2001, which altered the narrative of "America's Mayor.") High-profile NYPD brutality served as Kitty Genovese–like revelations for the era, but that did not stop the ex-mayor from lauding his accomplishments on the campaign trail. Indicative of the lasting mark Necropolis made on the national consciousness, Giuliani the presidential candidate described New York as "the city he has tamed and the place where he stared down—as he tells appreciative Republicans to hearty applause—liberals, criminals, welfare recipients, big-spending City Council members and the editorial writers of *The New York Times*."[22]

September 11, 2001, should have, for all intents and purposes, been New York City's downfall, sparking at a minimum a revival of Necropolis prophecies with "terrorists" as the new bête noire—if not a mass exodus from the dense, targeted city. Remarkably, New York witnessed considerable population growth. New housing development, as in the rest of the United States, sprouted up throughout the city in a rash of speculation. "Pioneers" and gentrification took over disparate neighborhoods that the most ardent municipal surgeons would have certainly remade if narratives had never limited urban renewal. Rents rose exponentially in former working-class districts of Queens and Brooklyn, not to mention old enclaves of Harlem and Washington Heights.[23] The administration of Bloomberg—a Boston-bred entrepreneur who came out of nowhere to win the mayoralty in 2001 after the local Democratic coalition collapsed in the wake of the World Trade Center attacks—became an icon of the neoliberal, culturally centered, creative-class planning sold by Richard Florida and a ceaseless advocate for an energized, elite Cosmopolis. Florida saw Bloomberg as a leadership model for ailing municipalities to follow, lauding the mayor for bringing "modern management techniques to government," and introducing neoliberal approaches to education, crime, and public health.[24] Despite the rise of progressive Bill de Blasio in 2013 and the growing discontent among the other New York (i.e., those citizens marginalized or displaced under the previous regimes) his campaign represented, Bloomberg's initiatives still dominate the playbook on municipal governance.

In popular culture, New York is at once exceptional and emblematic of the nation as a whole. Novels by local authors—Brooklyn is the city's Bloomsbury—showcase the anxieties of the gentry, not unlike Woody Allen's crisis-era masterpieces. But these bourgeois problems are no longer confined to the Upper East Side or Greenwich Village; rather, they are the province of all of Manhattan and the outerboroughs.[25] Television shows since *Seinfeld*, *Friends*, *Will and Grace*, and *Sex and the City* have showcased a fun and liberating New York for the single set. Men and women, gay and straight, stroll through the dark streets of SoHo, the Lower East Side, the "Meatpacking District"—former skeletons of deindustrialization, now the most fashionable and expensive wards—with nary a worry of a mugging or random violent crime. Thousands of tourists come to New York City each year to retrace the steps of *Sex and the City* character Carrie Bradshaw and her compatriots. Romantic comedies represent the defining New York films of the new millennium. Creative-class, predominantly white, migrants navigate the travails of dating and adapting to city life after a suburban childhood—providing their means of mobility—that they could not help but escape. New York City, once the crucible of all urban crisis ailments, is now a romantic wonderland of wealth, adventure, sex, and, of course, love that contrasts sharply with the boring flyover country between New York and California—and without a single member of the "underclass" in sight.[26] Even a counterexample like *Sweet Home Alabama* (2002) may argue that one cannot find happiness in the Big Apple, but at least the city will not eat you alive.[27] Of course New York is still a popular location for crime serials of the *Law and Order* vein, but not even an update of *Death Wish* starring Jodie Foster—*The Brave One* (2007)—can detract from the fact that New York is the safest large city in the country.[28] Conservative fantasies of order, justice, and police benevolence play out every Friday night on the streets of

New York in CBS's *Blue Bloods*, shot on location with the assistance of the NYPD. By contrast, inner-ring suburbs, small towns, and monoindustrial Rust Belt cities with massive foreclosures and lingering economic depressions are the new victims of persistent declension narratives. Vigilante copycat crimes and *Death Wish*–style preemptive gun violence occur all too often in the United States, but mostly outside New York, in places such as suburban Colorado, suburban Florida, suburban Connecticut, and Charleston.[29]

In the postwar era, critics of various stripes asked rhetorically, "What is New York today?" It is one of the safest cities in the country, and thanks to its new reputation, accessible public transportation, massive service industry, cultural cachet, and unmatched culture industry, New York City still lures national and international migrants of appropriate means or skills. That said, the city remains polarized by wealth. Only in the recent debate over what pseudonymous Jeremiah Moss, chronicler of "Vanishing New York," has termed "hypergentrification" has the question of inequality and uneven development been raised. The glittering glass façade of contemporary architecture conceals a certain ugly streak throughout the five boroughs, especially in neighborhoods where the narratives of decline and decay remain (i.e., districts untouched by gentrification). Occasionally, when a rash of violent crime hits the city or when infrastructure falls into disrepair, reporters and talking heads will prophesy the return of the "bad old days," by which they mean the state of affairs that ravaged New York in the sixties and the seventies. Such concern demonstrates the resonant power of the postwar Necropolis narrative in the city's history.[30] The power of culture is also magnified during high-profile events that seem to harken back to those days, such as the videotaped murder of Eric Garner on a Staten Island sidewalk by an NYPD officer in 2014. The situation echoed the climax of Spike Lee's masterpiece *Do the Right Thing* (1989), a rare nuanced examination of race, class, and the history of turf negotiation in New York City, which climaxed in the murder of black Bedford-Stuyvesant resident Radio Raheem by a police officer's chokehold—itself an allusion to Michael Stewart, a graffiti artist who died in police custody a few years prior.[31] Perhaps the two cities of Cosmopolis and Necropolis, signifying New York's hopes and fears, function like the waters of the East River, a tidal strait where the currents rush north and south at the whim of the moon's gravity yet the contents never leave.

Astonishingly, New York City, despite the incredible cost of living there, remains an entry point for creative people and capital, and that gives the city a certain vitality. Gone are the days, however, of Jacobs's West Village universal community, having since been replaced by fears that chain stores and restaurants have transformed the city into Anytown, U.S.A, thus fulfilling the prophecies of *Dissent*'s search for New York. Academics now walk the streets detailing the decline of "authenticity," a term that alludes in part to the grit of yore.[32] Such walking cures suggest that the rough, on-the-brink-of-death image of Necropolis—the place both dangerous and alluring—has remained New York's most enduring signifier. If so, what purpose did that image serve, or does it serve now? To borrow from Jacobs's cynical indictment of master planner sanctimony, it provides city officials and their private partners a site of reference, something to point to and say, "Hey, look at what I made! We brought New York back from the brink!" But one wonders, like Marshall Berman back in 1987, whether the city's intellectuals and other messengers can stem the tide of concentrated wealth and power, to fulfill the vision of E. B. White and restore the laboratory of social democracy and internationalism—that universal, equitable New York (the island fantasy)—that fear and its wielders largely reduced to rubble after World War II.

Notes

Introduction

1. Shenker, "18 Urban Experts."

2. Historians have debated New York's political economy preceding the "fiscal crisis." Vincent Cannato argues that the rise of the New Left, the dismantling of New Deal liberalism that coalesced during the administration of Mayor John Lindsay, and Lindsay's inability to control these dual forces exacerbated New York's decline in the 1960s. Cannato, *Ungovernable City*. Others have emphasized more structural constraints. Joshua Freeman argues that the diminishing influence of the city's working class in the 1960s and 1970s created a "less civilized, more alienated community." J. Freeman, *Working-Class New York*. Robert Fitch offers a compelling study of Nelson and David Rockefeller's "assassination of New York" in the sixties and seventies, when the brothers controlled the state government and the city's financial sector, respectively. Fitch, *Assassination of New York*.

3. Zevin, "New York City Crisis," 11. See also Epstein, "Last Days of New York." Selections from Shenker's *Times* article were published as the first chapter of Alcaly and Mermelstein, *Fiscal Crisis of American Cities*.

4. Shenker, "18 Urban Experts." On the debates over these bills, see Cowie, *Stayin' Alive*, 270–88.

5. Soffer, *Ed Koch and the Rebuilding of New York*, 6.

6. Shenker, "18 Urban Experts"

7. Ibid.

8. Ibid.

9. J. Jacobs, *Death and Life of Great American Cites*; Banfield, *Unheavenly City*; Glazer and Moynihan, *Beyond the Melting Pot*; Harrington, *Other America*.

10. Mumford, "Sky Line." Mumford examines ancient Rome as the original Necropolis in *City in History*.

11. Kenneth Jackson and Arnold Hirsch established foundational paradigms on the political economy of suburban growth and urban crisis. See Hirsch, *Making the Second Ghetto*; Jackson, *Crabgrass Frontier*. For more recent interpretations of the political economy of suburbanization and the urban crisis, see Sugrue, *Origins of the Urban Crisis*. See also Beauregard, *When America Became Suburban*; Kruse and Sugrue, *New Suburban History*; Weise, *Places of Their Own*; Sides, *L.A. City Limits*; Self, *American Babylon*; Katznelson, *When Affirmative Action Was White*.

12. Sugrue, *Origins of the Urban Crisis*; Neumann, *Remaking the Rust Belt*; Schulman, *From Cotton Belt to Sunbelt*; High, *Industrial Sunset*; Cowie, *Stayin' Alive*;

Manuel, *Taconite Dreams*; Nickerson, Dochuk, and Clements, *Sunbelt Rising*; Teaford, *Cities of the Heartland*; Linkon and Russo, *Steeltown U.S.A.*; Safford, *Why the Garden Club Couldn't Save Youngstown*; Gordon, *Mapping Decline*.

13. In addition to previously cited scholarship on postwar metropolitan political economy, see Ballon, "Robert Moses and Urban Renewal"; Ballon and Jackson, *Robert Moses and the Modern City*; Bender, *Unfinished City*; M. Berman, *On the Town*; N. D. Bloom, *Public Housing That Worked*; Chronopoulos, *Spatial Regulation*; Corkin, *Starring New York*; Fishman, "Revolt of the Urbs"; Flowers, *Skyscraper*; Gutfreund, "Rebuilding New York in the Auto Age"; Schneider, *Vampires, Dragons, and Egyptian Kings*; Schneider, *Smack*; Schwartz, *New York Approach*; Schwartz, "Robert Moses and City Planning"; Osman, *Invention of Brownstone Brooklyn*; Klemek, *Transatlantic Collapse of Urban Renewal*.

14. Source of data is Integrated Public Use Microdata Series courtesy of the Minnesota Population Center at the University of Minnesota.

15. Snyder, "Crime"; Monkkonen, *Murder in New York City*.

16. M. Stern, "Rep. Koch Finds 27 Major Companies." As Kenneth Jackson notes, between 1955 and 1980 no fewer than fifty major corporations left New York City, including IBM, "Gulf Oil, Texaco, Union Carbide, General Telephone, American Cyanamid, Xerox, PepsiCo, U.S. Tobacco, Chesebrough-Ponds, Nestlé, American Can, Singer, Champion International, and Olin." Jackson, *Crabgrass Frontier*, 268.

17. See, for example, the declensionist histories of New York that emerged in the 1970s: Auletta, *Streets Were Paved with Gold*; Alcaly and Mermelstein, *Fiscal Crisis of American Cities*; Newfield and Du Brul, *Abuse of Power*; Caro, *Power Broker*.

18. Quote from a 1969 speech Agnew delivered attacking the culture industry. For full text, see http://www.americanrhetoric.com/speeches/spiroagnewtv newscoverage.htm (accessed August 11, 2016).

19. Fishman, *Bourgeois Utopias*; E. May, *Homeward Bound*; Cohen, *Consumers' Republic*.

20. Beauregard, *Voices of Decline*; Conn, *Americans against the City*; Avila, *Popular Culture in the Age of White Flight*; M. Davis, *City of Quartz*; Page, *City's End*.

21. Rome, *Bulldozer in the Countryside*; Lassiter, *Silent Majority*; Kruse, *White Flight*; McGirr, *Suburban Warriors*; Shermer, *Barry Goldwater*; Shermer, *Sunbelt Capitalism*; Dochuk, *From Bible Belt to Sunbelt*; Kruse and Sugrue, *New Suburban History*.

22. As highlighted in the work of Carlo Rotella, intellectuals, authors, and critics experimented with form and language to adequately convey the ongoing transformation of American cities in the postwar era to a national audience ill- or uninformed of the processes at work. Fused, narratives and the physical space they described functioned in a feedback loop, first advocating for investment and urban policy through narratives about the declining city, then criticizing the transformed spaces and places wrought by those actions through similar tropes. See Rotella, *October Cities*.

23. New York City has often been represented dialectically. When Bill de Blasio was a mayoral candidate, his rhetoric revolved around "a tale of two cities" divided

by class and race. Twenty years earlier, political scientists examining economic inequality labeled it the "dual city." In his history of graffiti writing, Joe Austin illustrated the tensions between competing visions of New York as "Naked City" versus "New Rome." See Austin, *Taking the Train*; Mollenkopf and Castells, *Dual City*; Hernandez, "New York's Next Mayor."

24. On the meaning of "cosmopolis" in planning theory, see Sandercock, *Towards Cosmopolis*; Sandercock and Lyssiotis, *Cosmopolis II*. As for its application to New York City in the past, see Episode Five of Burns and Ades, *New York*. It is also the title of a 2003 Don DeLillo novel that was later adapted into a film set in New York.

25. White, *Here Is New York*.

26. Council for Public Safety, "Welcome to Fear City."

27. M. Berman, "Introduction," 20.

28. See scholarship on the machinations of right-wing organizations like the Mount Pelerin Society: Phillips-Fein, *Invisible Hands*; Stahl, *Right Moves*.

29. See the expanding literature on the historical geography of the New Right: Shermer, *Barry Goldwater*; Dochuk, *From Bible Belt to Sunbelt*; Lassiter, *Silent Majority*; Kruse, *White Flight*. The intellectual and cultural history of recent conservative trends is also useful for this study. See Rodgers, *Age of Fracture*; Self, *All in the Family*; Robin, *Reactionary Mind*; Perelstein, *Nixonland*; Kruse, *One Nation under God*; Hartman, *War for the Soul of America*.

30. On Agnew's antiurban rhetoric, see Perelstein, *Nixonland*. For Giuliani's use of New York imagery on the national stage, see Nagourney, "Giuliani Sells New York."

31. Chase, "New York Could Die." On nativism in nineteenth-century New York, see Burrows and Wallace, *Gotham*, 631–38, 828–40. See also Riis, *How the Other Half Lives*.

32. Goldsmith and Lynne, *What We See*; Flint, *Wrestling with Moses*; Gratz, *Battle for Gotham*. Marshall Berman also created an aura around the Jacobs and Moses struggle in the "Modernism in New York" section of M. Berman, *All That Is Solid Melts into Air*, 287–348.

33. Abel, "New York City"; Whalen, *City Destroying Itself*.

34. Spillane, *Kiss Me, Deadly*.

35. "Judge Halts 'Fear City' Campaign."

36. Cannato, *Ungovernable City*.

37. Soffer, *Ed Koch and the Rebuilding of New York*, 4.

38. Harvey, *Brief History of Neoliberalism*, 77. "Space of Flows" borrowed from Castells, *Rise of the Network Society*.

39. Kelling and Wilson, "Police and Neighborhood Safety."

40. On these policies, see Katznelson, *When Affirmative Action Was White*; Zipp, *Manhattan Projects*; Katz, *In the Shadow of the Poorhouse*. On the intellectual history of fear in the United States, see Robin, *Fear*.

41. On culture as a driver of economic development, see Florida, *Rise of the Creative Class*; Florida, *Who's Your City?* On cultural tourism, see Hoffman, Fainstein, and Judd, *Cities and Visitors*.

42. Miriam Greenberg argues that in the late 1970s, political and economic elites came together to establish an image of New York as business- and tourist-friendly. Greenberg, *Branding New York*. Earlier in the twentieth century, as Angela Blake shows, reformers, cultural purveyors, boosters, officials, and others worked in harmony to "brand" New York as appealing and American in hopes of attracting capital investment and tourists. Blake, *How New York Became American*. "Spaces of hope" references David Harvey's work on the "right to the city." See Harvey, *Spaces of Hope*; Harvey, "Right to the City."

43. On neoliberal redevelopment and gentrification, see Harvey, *Brief History of Neoliberalism*; Greenberg, *Branding New York*; Squires, "Partnership"; N. Smith, *New Urban Frontier*; Tochterman, "Theorizing Neoliberal Urban Development." On the rural crisis, see Flora, Flora, and Gasteyer, *Rural Communities*; Carr and Kefalas, *Hollowing out the Middle*; Manuel, *Taconite Dreams*.

44. Lefebvre, *Writings on Cities*; Harvey, "Right to the City."

45. Jonnes, *South Bronx Rising*; M. Berman, "Introduction"; Berman and Berger, *New York Calling*; Delany, *Times Square Red*; Currid, *Warhol Economy*.

46. Glassner, *Culture of Fear*. Glassner's text applies "cultivation theory" which equates media consumption with behavior. See Gerbner, "Cultivation Analysis."

47. For example, the shift from working-class nickelodeons to motion picture palaces or the normalizing of jazz, rock-and-roll, and hip-hop culture over the course of the twentieth century. On the former, see Peiss, *Cheap Amusements*; May, *Screening out the Past*.

48. On the issue of gentrification, see Taylor, *Harlem*; L. Freeman, *There Goes the Hood*; Maurrasse, *Listening to Harlem*; Osman, *Invention of Brownstone Brooklyn*.

Chapter One

1. M. Berman, *On the Town*, 45–50. Civic boosters and capitalists had spent the better part of a century molding New York City into a symbol of American industrial and financial might. See Page, *Creative Destruction of Manhattan*; Beckert, *Monied Metropolis*; Scobey, *Empire City*; Blake, *How New York Became American*. Regarding the photograph itself, since the sailor and nurse were reunited in August 2012, the details surrounding the event have commenced a discussion of the lack of consent on the nurse's part. See "The Kissing Sailor, or 'The Selective Blindness of Rape Culture'" *Crates and Ribbons* (blog), September 30, 2012, http://cratesandribbons .com/2012/09/30/the-kissing-sailor-or-the-selective-blindness-of-rape-culture-vj -day-times-square/; and "The Kissing Sailor, Part 2—Debunking Misconceptions" *Crates and Ribbons* (blog), October 5, 2012, http://cratesandribbons.com/2012/10 /05/the-kissing-sailor-part-2-debunking-misconceptions/.

2. Bender, *New York Intellect*, xiii.

3. White, *Here Is New York*, 50–51. Useful primary sources on New York City civil defense planning in the 1960s include Moses, "Civil Defense Fiasco"; Moses and

Wallander, *New York City Civil Defense*; Wakefield, "Good-by New York." On the history of civil defense, see McEnaney, *Civil Defense Begins at Home*; Boyer, *By the Bomb's Early Light*.

4. White, *Here Is New York*. On the development of Levittown and early postwar suburbs, see Jackson, *Crabgrass Frontier*, 143–62; Beauregard, *When America Became Suburban*, 122–43; Cohen, *Consumers' Republic*, 194–256; Katznelson, *When Affirmative Action Was White*, 133–41.

5. White, *Essays of E. B. White*; Elledge, *E. B. White*.

6. Asbury, *Gangs of New York*; Beckert, *Monied Metropolis*; Bernstein, *New York City Draft Riots*; Blake, *How New York Became American*; Chauncey, *Gay New York*; J. Freeman, *Working-Class New York*; Peiss, *Cheap Amusements*.

7. Elledge, *E. B. White*.

8. White, *The Lady Is Cold*.

9. Elledge, *E. B. White*; Root, *E. B. White*; White and Guth, *Letters of E. B. White*; Thurber and E. B. White, *Is Sex Necessary?*

10. Root, *E. B. White*, 15.

11. "World of Tomorrow" in White, *One Man's Meat*; Root, *E. B. White*; White, *Essays of E. B. White*. For GM's vision of 1960s urbanism, see General Motors Corporation, "To New Horizons."

12. White and Guth, *Letters of E. B. White*, 148.

13. Root, *E. B. White*, 117. On the United Nations development project, see Zipp, *Manhattan Projects*, 33–72; Caro, *Power Broker*, 771–75.

14. White and Guth, *Letters of E. B. White*, 219; Root, *E. B. White*, 117–27.

15. White and Guth, *Letters of E. B. White*, 285–86.

16. Ibid., 290, 298, 300–301.

17. White, *Here Is New York*. On the role of turn-of-the-century immigrants in forging a new culture in New York City, see Enstad, *Ladies of Labor*; Peiss, *Cheap Amusements*. On the evolution of Greenwich Village and other areas of New York City into a hub of bohemian modernism, see Stansell, *American Moderns*; M. Berman, *On the Town*. On the emergence of New York as an "international capital of culture" in the first half of the twentieth century, see Bender, *New York Intellect*, 321–43. On developments in cultural production, particularly in Harlem, see D. L. Lewis, *When Harlem Was in Vogue*; Douglas, *Terrible Honesty*.

18. White, *Here Is New York*, 9, 16.

19. Ibid., 10–13, 16.

20. Ibid., 17–21.

21. Ibid., 18.

22. Thomas Bender cites New York City as the "international capital of culture" in the first half of the twentieth century. Bender, *New York Intellect*, 321–43. The lure of New York City in this period is perhaps best encapsulated in the film *On the Town* (1944) in which a group of sailors delight in the attractions New York has to offer at midcentury. See Marshall Berman's analysis of the film and its context: Berman, *On the Town*, 43–102.

23. Sante, *Low Life*; Asbury, *Gangs of New York*. On New York City and turn-of-the-century immigration and immigrant culture, see among others Bailey, "Adjustment of Italian Immigrants"; Chauncey, *Gay New York*; Gilfoyle, *Pickpocket's Tale*; Gilfoyle, *City of Eros*; Enstad, *Ladies of Labor*; Peiss, *Cheap Amusements*; Blake, *How New York Became American*; Burrows and Wallace, *Gotham*; Stansell, *American Moderns*.

24. White, *Here Is New York*, 31–32.

25. Ibid., 44–45.

26. Ibid., 41–42. Quotes on Bourne and New York versus America from Bender, *New York Intellect*; Bender, "New York as a Center of 'Difference.'" Marshall Berman's work is also instructive on New York's cosmopolitanism: M. Berman, *On the Town*; Berman and Berger, *New York Calling*.

27. White, *Here Is New York*, 38–39, 50–53.

28. Ibid., 53–54.

29. Ibid.; White, *Poems and Sketches*, 11–12.

30. On the discussion regarding film and television versions of "Here Is New York," see White and Guth, *Letters of E. B. White*.

31. Edwards, *Breakfast at Tiffany's*; Copyright Collection, *That Girl*.

32. Allen, *Annie Hall*.

33. Ibid.

34. Allen, *Manhattan*.

35. Ellison, *Invisible Man*.

36. Salinger, *Catcher in the Rye*.

37. White and Guth, *Letters of E. B. White*, 556–57, 593.

38. Ibid., 645.

Chapter Two

1. Spillane, *Big Kill*, 225.

2. Spillane, *Vengeance Is Mine*, 453–55.

3. Spillane, *One Lonely Night*, 75.

4. Spillane, *I, the Jury*; Spillane, *My Gun Is Quick*; Spillane, *Vengeance Is Mine*; Spillane, *One Lonely Night*; Spillane, *Big Kill*; Spillane, *Kiss Me, Deadly*.

5. Severo, "Mickey Spillane."

6. Block, "Introduction."

7. Geherin, *American Private Eye*, 125.

8. Spillane carved out a working-class identity, to wit: "I live kind of a plain life. I have a modest house and drive a Ford pickup truck. My needs are pretty simple." Silet, "Mickey Spillane," 117.

9. Collins, "Introduction," 1; Silet, "Mickey Spillane," 114.

10. Severo, "Mickey Spillane."

11. Geherin, *American Private Eye*.

12. Katz, *In the Shadow of the Poorhouse*, 257.

13. Aldrich, *Kiss Me Deadly*; Victor and White, *My Gun Is Quick*.

14. Severo, "Mickey Spillane."

15. Quoted in Southern, "Investigation of the Mid-Century Literary Phenomenon," and Geherin, *American Private Eye*, 129.

16. Letter to Mickey Spillane dated October 2, 1961 in Berliner, *Letters of Ayn Rand*.

17. Robin, *Reactionary Mind*, 76–96.

18. Letter from Mickey Spillane to Hy Gardner dated November 8, 1953. In author's possession.

19. J. Kenneth Van Dover writes, "The film of *The Girl Hunters* symbolizes [Spillane's] ethical solipsism: self is all." Van Dover, *Murder in the Millions*, 152.

20. Southern, "Investigation of the Mid-Century Literary Phenomenon." Quote taken from a British press release during the filming of *The Girl Hunters*.

21. Collins, "Mickey Spillane," x.

22. Jameson's conception of "universal access" comes from his writings on Raymond Chandler. See Jameson, "On Raymond Chandler." Also see E. Smith, *Hard-Boiled*, 104.

23. K. Davis, *Two-Bit Culture*, 182.

24. Cuordileone, *Manhood*, viii–xiv. See also E. May, *Homeward Bound*; A. Schlesinger, *Vital Center*.

25. McCann, *Gumshoe America*; Chandler, "Simple Art of Murder."

26. Collins, "Mickey Spillane."

27. Chandler quoted in Geherin, *American Private Eye*, 121.

28. Grella, "Hard-Boiled Detective Novel," 117.

29. K. Davis, *Two-Bit Culture*, 181.

30. Geherin, *American Private Eye*, 125; Collins, "Introduction."

31. McCann, *Gumshoe America*, 40.

32. K. Davis, *Two-Bit Culture*, 184.

33. Susman and Griffin, "Did Success Spoil the United States?," 19, 24, 30.

34. Dimendberg, *Film Noir*, 121. On walking in the city, see Benjamin, *Arcades Project*; de Certeau, *Practice of Everyday Life*, 91–110; Berman, *All That Is Solid Melts*, 131–72.

35. Spillane, *My Gun Is Quick*, 283; Spillane, *One Lonely Night*, 5; Spillane, *I, the Jury*, 36.

36. Spillane, *Vengeance Is Mine*, 387.

37. Ibid., 387, 504.

38. Spillane, *Kiss Me, Deadly*, 481.

39. Spillane, *My Gun Is Quick*, 260–62. On the Lavender Scare, see Friedman, "Smearing of Joe McCarthy"; D. Johnson, *Lavender Scare*.

40. Spillane, *Big Kill*, 221. On bohemianism in New York, see Stansell, *American Moderns*. On the development of queer neighborhoods in New York in the 1950s and earlier, see Kaiser, *Gay Metropolis 1940–1996*, 63–132. On Greenwich Village as a queer neighborhood in the first half of the twentieth century, see Chauncey, *Gay*

New York, 227–69; Heise, *Urban Underworlds*, 77–126; Carter, *Stonewall*, 5–29; Heap, *Slumming*, 154–76; K. Mumford, *Interzones*, 73–92. On the sexual and gender politics of the era, see Corber, *In the Name of National Security*; Cuordileone, *Manhood*; D. Johnson, *Lavender Scare*.

41. Jackson, *Crabgrass Frontier*, 195–217. For more on redlining, racism, and discrimination in housing lending following the war, see Cohen, *Consumers' Republic*; Sugrue, *Origins of the Urban Crisis*, 33–56. Self, *American Babylon*, 96–132; Hirsch, "'Containment'"; Weise, *Places of Their Own*, 94–109.

42. Spillane, *One Lonely Night*, 49, 159–60.

43. Spillane, *Kiss Me, Deadly*, 453. On Hell's Kitchen and demographic change, see Schneider, *Vampires, Dragons, and Egyptian Kings*.

44. Spillane, *Big Kill*, 196–97. On slum clearance and urban renewal at the United Nations site, see Zipp, *Manhattan Projects*, 33–72.

45. Spillane, *Big Kill*, 340.

46. Spillane, *Body Lovers*, 44, 49, 70–71.

47. Spillane, *Survival Zero*, 14. On the transformative Seagram's building and the move to modern architecture more generally in postwar New York City, see Flowers, *Skyscraper*, 87–144; Stern, Mellins, and Fishman, *New York 1960*, 342–53.

48. Spillane, *One Lonely Night*, 133.

49. Spillane, *Kiss Me, Deadly*, 418. On postwar New York's racial and ethnic demographic change wrought by white ethnic suburbanization, African American northern migration, and the United States' "Operation Bootstrap" in Puerto Rico, see Pritchett, *Brownsville, Brooklyn*, 105–74; Schneider, *Vampires, Dragons, and Egyptian Kings*, 27–50; J. Freeman, *Working-Class New York*, 25–34; Rieder, *Canarsie*, 13–56.

50. Quotes from Spillane, *Kiss Me, Deadly*, 381, 396.

51. Spillane, *I, the Jury*, 84.

52. Spillane, *Vengeance Is Mine*, 418, 365.

53. Cameron, "Soft Side of a Hard Egg." On fears of juvenile delinquency wrought by mass media in this period, see Gilbert, *Cycle of Outrage*, 143–61.

54. Spillane, *Kiss Me, Deadly*, 433. Johnny Carson uttered something very similar on the *Tonight Show* in the 1970s: "New York is an exciting town where something is happening all the time, most unsolved."

55. Spillane, *One Lonely Night*, 114; Spillane, *Big Kill*, 181.

56. Spillane, *Vengeance Is Mine*, 446.

57. Spillane, *One Lonely Night*, 51.

58. See, for example, Weegee's classic collection of photographs from the 1940s: Weegee, *Naked City*. The book inspired a classic New York film noir of the same name, one of the few films in the 1940s filmed on location in New York City. Dimendberg, *Film Noir*, 21–85.

59. Spillane, *One Lonely Night*, 5–13.

60. Spillane, *I, the Jury*, 14.

61. Spillane, *Big Kill*, 186.

62. On the "do-it-yourself" culture of the 1950s, see Susman and Griffin, "Did Success Spoil the United States?," 22–25.

63. Spillane, *I, the Jury*, 6.

64. Spillane, *One Lonely Night*, 132.

65. Michael Flamm has written the most comprehensive investigation into the "law and order" discourse that emerged out of the urban conflagrations of the 1960s. See Flamm, *Law and Order*. On Richard Nixon's effective use of the discourse, see Perelstein, *Nixonland*, 328–71; Schulman, *The Seventies*, 23–52.

66. All quotes since the previous footnote from Spillane, *My Gun Is Quick*, 154. Incidentally, this was the message of the NYPD's "Welcome to Fear City" pamphlet in the 1970s. Council for Public Safety, "Welcome to Fear City."

67. Spillane, *Girl Hunters*.

68. Rowland, *Girl Hunters*; Aldrich, *Kiss Me Deadly*. On the place of *Kiss Me Deadly* in film noir history, see Lang, "Looking for the 'Great Whatzit.' " On Spillane's lackluster success in the sixties and beyond, see Severo, "Mickey Spillane"; Van Dover, *Murder in the Millions*.

69. Spillane, *Girl Hunters*, 42.

70. Spillane, *Body Lovers*. 7.

71. Ibid., 12; Spillane, *Girl Hunters*, 160, 49.

72. Grella, "Hard-Boiled Detective Novel," 118; Chandler, "Simple Art of Murder."

Chapter Three

1. Caro, *Power Broker*; Jackson, "Robert Moses"; Ballon and Jackson, *Robert Moses and the Modern City*; Schwartz, "Robert Moses and City Planning"; Zipp, *Manhattan Projects*.

2. Beauregard, *Voices of Decline*, 103–5. On early opposition to Moses's projects, see Samuel Zipp's chapters on the Stuyvesant Town development: Zipp, *Manhattan Projects*, 72–113. See also James C. Scott on Moses's "Authoritarian High Modernism" in Scott, *Seeing like a State*.

3. Podhoretz, "Article as Art." For "Age of Criticism," see Jarrell, *Poetry and the Age*, 73.

4. On redevelopment in New York during this period, see Jackson, *Crabgrass Frontier*; Ballon, "Robert Moses and Urban Renewal"; Zipp, *Manhattan Projects*; Flowers, *Skyscraper*.

5. Cook, "Robert Moses, Glutton for Power"; Cook and Gleason, "Shame of New York"; Baldwin, "Fifth Avenue, Uptown"; Fortune, *Exploding Metropolis*.

6. Scott, *Seeing Like a State*, 87–102.

7. Caro, *Power Broker*; Ballon, "Robert Moses and Urban Renewal"; Berman, *All That Is Solid*, 290–311; Zipp, *Manhattan Projects*, 73–156.

8. Burns and Ades, *New York*; Mennel, "Everything Must Go." On the Robert Moses musical, see Pogrebin, "Sing of the Master Builder." Caro devoted one paragraph to Moses's tremendous writing output in the 1950s. See Caro, *Power Broker*, 811.

9. Samuel Zipp has written extensively on the Gashouse District and the Stuyvesant Town, United Nations, and Lincoln Square renewal projects. See Zipp, *Manhattan Projects*.

10. Fainstein and Fainstein, "Governing Regimes," 185.

11. Ballon, "Robert Moses and Urban Renewal."

12. Ibid. On Moses's Title I projects, see Fainstein and Fainstein, "Governing Regimes"; Zipp, *Manhattan Projects*, 154–252; Ballon, "Robert Moses and Urban Renewal"; Caro, *Power Broker*, 1013–16. On opposition to Moses's work, see Fishman, "Revolt of the Urbs." Regarding NYCHA, Moses did influence design of their developments. N. D. Bloom, *Public Housing That Worked*, 62–72.

13. Chronopoulos, "Robert Moses." Moses's quote is taken from there as well.

14. On the modern paradigm, see Scott, *Seeing Like a State*; J. Jacobs, *Death and Life of Great American Cites*; Hall, *Cities of Tomorrow*.

15. Moses, "Slums and City Planning"; Riis, *How the Other Half Lives*.

16. Moses, "Slums and City Planning."

17. Ibid. On the utopians, see Fishman, *Urban Utopias in the Twentieth Century*; Howard, *Garden Cities of To-Morrow*; Le Corbusier, *City of To-Morrow and Its Planning*; Wright, "Broadacre City."

18. Moses, "Problems."

19. Ibid. On Cold War era discourse and manhood, see Cuordileone, *Manhood*; D. Johnson, *Lavender Scare*; Friedman, "Smearing of Joe McCarthy." Moses's gendered name-calling is reminiscent of Progressive Era political culture, the period of reform with which his power overlaps, where "red bloods" were men of action à la Moses and mollycoddles were inner-directed à la the goo-goos. See Murphy, *Political Manhood*, 11–37.

20. Quotes from Moses, "Problems"; Moses, "Mr. Moses Discusses Planning." Vis-à-vis "authoritarian high modernism," the phrase "you cannot make an omelet without breaking eggs" was a favorite of the fascist antagonist in Sinclair Lewis, *It Can't Happen Here*.

21. Mennel, *Everything Must Go*; Caro, *Power Broker*, 811. Moses finished a "sex-filled" pulp novel called *From Palms to Pines*, but failed to sell it, sending it off to publishing houses under a pseudonym.

22. Moses, "Mr. Moses Discusses Planning"; Moses, "New York Has a Future"; Moses, "Problems."

23. Moses, *Working for the People*, 112.

24. Moses, "Traffic Menace"; Moses, "Civil Defense Fiasco."

25. Moses, "Mr. Moses Discusses Planning."

26. Moses, "Significance"; Moses, "Mr. Moses Discusses Planning." On Dickens's impression of New York City in the mid-nineteenth century, see Dickens, *American Notes*, 81–108.

27. Ballon and Jackson, "Introduction"; Moses, "Significance." On Moses's affection for New York City and its future, see also Moses, "Indefinable New York."

28. Kessel and Grehan, "Newer New York."

29. Quotes from Porter, "Along Manhattan's West Side"; Berger, "Our Changing City." "Our Changing City" writers had hoped that urban renewal projects would aid Harlem, Southeastern Brooklyn, and Staten Island. See Schumach, "Southeastern Brooklyn Area"; Horne, "Staten Island Awaits Bridge"; Robinson, "Harlem Now on the Upswing." Other selections from the series included Amper, "Conflicts in the Upper Bronx"; E. Asbury, "Nassau-Suffolk Area of Long Island"; Grunson, "New Faces in the Lower Bronx"; Gruntzner, "Downtown Brooklyn Glistens"; Ingraham, "Old Lower Manhattan Area"; Kihss, "Upper and Middle East Side"; Salisbury, "Manhattan Midtown Area."

30. McEvoy, "How to Get Things Done."

31. Moses, "New York Has a Future."

32. Ballon, "Robert Moses and Urban Renewal"; Jackson, "Robert Moses and the Rise of New York"; Zipp, *Manhattan Projects*.

33. Loewy, "How I Would Rebuild New York City." See also Baldwin, "Fifth Avenue, Uptown"; Cheever, "Moving Out"; Moses, "Indefinable New York"; Swados, "Nights in the Gardens of Brooklyn."

34. Cook and Gleason, "Shame of New York."

35. Ibid., 261–62.

36. Caro, *Power Broker*; Zipp, *Manhattan Projects*; Flint, *Wrestling with Moses*.

37. Cook and Gleason, "Shame of New York," 292.

38. Ibid., 295–96.

39. Moses, "Are Cities Dead?." See also Mumford, *City in History*; Wood, *1400 Governments*.

40. Podhoretz, "Article as Art." Emphasis in original.

41. Moses, *Working for the People*, 112.

Chapter Four

1. Whyte, "Introduction"; Whyte, "Are Cities Un-American?"; J. Jacobs, "Downtown Is for People," 141.

2. Whyte, "Urban Sprawl"; Whyte, "Are Cities Un-American?"; Whyte, "Introduction"; Freedgood, "New Strength in City Hall," 63.

3. See Seligman, "Enduring Slums"; J. Jacobs, "Downtown Is for People"; Freedgood, "New Strength in City Hall"; Bello, "City and the Car"; Whyte, "Are Cities Un-American?." On Henry Luce, famed publisher of *Time*, *Life*, and *Fortune*, see Brinkley, *Publisher*.

4. J. Jacobs, "Downtown Is for People"; J. Jacobs, *Death and Life of Great American Cites*.

5. J. Jacobs, "Downtown Is for People."

6. Ibid.; J. Jacobs, *Death and Life of Great American Cites*.

7. "Behind New York's Facade."

8. Baldwin, "Fifth Avenue, Uptown." On Baldwin's experience in Harlem, see the chapters "Autobiographical Notes" and "Notes of a Native Son" in his seminal

nonfiction collection, *Notes of a Native Son*, 3–12, 85–116. Baldwin's essays on race relations in the early 1960s in some part foretold these conflagrations; see his *The Fire Next Time*. On Metropolitan Life's Riverton development in Harlem, see Zipp, *Manhattan Projects*, 120–21. On urban uprisings in the 1960s, see the previously cited scholarship on riots and rebellions: Beauregard, *Voices of Decline*, 130–46; J. Freeman, *Working-Class New York*, 192–93; Flamm, *Law and Order*, 37–45; Mumford, *Newark*, 98–148; Sugrue, *Origins of the Urban Crisis*, 259–64; M. Davis, *City of Quartz*, 67–70; Avila, *Popular Culture*, 5–6.

9. Baldwin, "Fifth Avenue, Uptown"; Podhoretz, "Article as Art."

10. Wakefield, *Island in the City*, 226–27.

11. Ibid., 240–41. On New York street gangs, see Schneider, *Vampires, Dragons, and Egyptian Kings*.

12. Quote from Wakefield, *New York in the Fifties*; Orwell, *Down and out in Paris and London*; Carson, *Silent Spring*; Nader, *Unsafe at Any Speed*; Friedan, *Feminine Mystique*; Griffin, *Black Like Me*. On the influence of Carson, Nader, and the like in 1960s culture, see "Systems and the Distrust of Order" in Brick, *Age of Contradiction*, 124–45. On the impact, for example, of Carson and the environmental movement on postwar urban and suburban development trends, see Rome, *Bulldozer in the Countryside*, 5–13. On the influence of Betty Friedan's work in the 1960s, see "End of Containment" in E. May, *Homeward Bound*, 186–203.

13. Stern, Mellins, and Fishman, *New York 1960*, 33–46; Flint, *Wrestling with Moses*, 3–31. On the work of Edmund Bacon, see Knowles, *Imagining Philadelphia*.

14. *Architectural Forum* and its admiration for Moses, as well as the circumstances around the Harvard Speech, are detailed in Flint, *Wrestling with Moses*, 24–27; Alexiou, *Jane Jacobs*, 57–60. On urban renewal in East Harlem, see Zipp, *Manhattan Projects*, 253–350. On the influence of Le Corbusier and the International Style, as well as Yamasaki's Pruitt-Igoe development, see "City of Towers" in Hall, *Cities of Tomorrow*, 218–61.

15. J. Jacobs, "Downtown Is for People."

16. Flint, *Wrestling with Moses*, 90–95.

17. For works in this vein, see Alexiou, *Jane Jacobs*; Zukin, *Naked City*; Sorkin, *Twenty Minutes in Manhattan*; Gratz, *Battle for Gotham*; Goldsmith and Lynne, *What We See*; Flint, *Wrestling with Moses*. On Jacobs and "gentrification," see Osman, *Invention of Brownstone Brooklyn*.

18. J. Jacobs, *Death and Life of Great American Cites*, 3.

19. Ibid.

20. Ibid., 29–54.

21. Ibid., 32. On the North End in the age of urban renewal, see Gans, *Urban Villagers*.

22. Hudson Street, where Jacobs and her family owned a house, played a significant role in the section of the book "The Conditions for City Diversity." J. Jacobs, *Death and Life of Great American Cites*, 143–239.

23. See, for example, Le Corbusier's comprehensive "Voisin" plan for Paris as well as his thoughts in "A Contemporary City" in Le Corbusier, *City of To-Morrow and Its Planning*, 163–289.

24. J. Jacobs, *Death and Life of Great American Cites*, 15, 23. Economist Martin Anderson also noticed the message of modernist design: "These buildings symbolize the progress of the urban renewal program, and in most cases they are the main justification for it. The city planners, the mayors, the urban renewal officials, and other connected with urban renewal can all point their fingers toward the material masses rising skyward and say, '*Look, I helped destroy the slum and built that*'" [emphasis added]. Anderson, *Federal Bulldozer*, 91.

25. See Jacobs's three chapters on the "uses of sidewalks": J. Jacobs, *Death and Life of Great American Cites*, 29–88.

26. L. Mumford, "Sky Line." Retitled as "Home Remedies for Urban Cancer" for the collection *Urban Prospect*, 182–207; J. Jacobs, *Death and Life of Great American Cites*, 3–25. Whyte quoted in M. Davis, *City of Quartz*.

27. Davidoff, "Advocacy and Pluralism in Planning." See also Fainstein, "New Directions in Planning Theory."

28. Osman, *Invention of Brownstone Brooklyn*, 5–10.

29. Ibid., 164–88.

30. Buckley, "Contemporary Challenges and the Social Order"; J. Jacobs, "City"; Flint, *Wrestling with Moses*, 127–29; Fishman, *Urban Utopias*, 268–76. Jacobs utilized her "housewife" image to gain support in the Washington Square Park struggle. See Alexiou, *Jane Jacobs*, 57–67; Flint, *Wrestling with Moses*, 83–85. For more recent studies of the political divide between cities and suburbs, see T. Frank, *What's the Matter with Kansas?*. On New Urbanism, see the original manifesto: Duany, Plater-Zyberk, and Speck, *Suburban Nation*.

31. Buckley, "Contemporary Challenges and the Social Order." Indicative of how conservatives embrace Jacobs even today, see Bramwell, "Cobblestone Conservative"; "Death and Life of Great American Cities at 50."

32. J. Jacobs, *Economy of Cities*, 36, 129; J. Jacobs, *Cities and the Wealth of Nations*.

33. Caro, *Power Broker*; Zipp, *Manhattan Projects*.

34. Alexiou, *Jane Jacobs*; Goldsmith and Lynne, *What We See*; Gratz, *Battle for Gotham*; "Jane Jacobs Medal."

35. Harvey, *Brief History of Neoliberalism*, 42. See also Gitlin, *The Sixties*; Phillips-Fein, *Invisible Hands*.

36. See Richard Florida's comprehensive study of the "creative class" in Florida, *Rise of the Creative Class*; Florida, *Flight of the Creative Class*; Florida, *Who's Your City?*; Florida, *Great Reset*; Florida, "Great Creative Class Debate."

37. Self, *American Babylon*; Gitlin, *The Sixties*; Hartman, *War for the Soul of America*.

Chapter Five

1. The New York Intellectuals are linked by their ties to New York City from the 1930s to the 1960s, its premier universities (City College, NYU, and Columbia), and a certain brand of anti-Stalinist Marxism, which they advocated until the 1950s (although there is room for interpretation for the personal politics of each). While they huddled around certain literary and political journals like *Partisan Review* and *Commentary*, members held various professional positions. The Intellectuals included fiction authors like Saul Bellow, Harvey Swados, and Lionel Abel; cultural critics like Norman Podhoretz and Irving Kristol; literary critics like Irving Howe, Alfred Kazin, Diana Trilling, and Lionel Trilling; and academics like Daniel Bell, Hannah Arendt, Richard Hofstadter, and Nathan Glazer. A number of these intellectuals would reject leftist ideology in the 1960s and become key figures in the neoconservative and the New Right political movements (Bell, Glazer, Kristol, Podhoretz, and Bellow, among others). On the New York Intellectuals' politics and influence, as well as their fracturing in the 1960s, see Pells, *Liberal Mind in a Conservative Age*; Wald, *New York Intellectuals*; Vaïsse, *Neoconservatism*; Cooney, *Rise of the New York Intellectuals*; A. Bloom, *Prodigal Sons*; Hartman, *War for the Soul of America*. Joseph Dorman has produced an insightful oral history of the New York Intellectuals, featuring remembrances from Daniel Bell and Irving Howe, among others: Dorman, *Arguing the World*.

2. Chroniclers of the period recall a fateful meeting between Howe and Tom Hayden in which Howe excoriated the new wave for its unwavering commitment to pacifism and its accommodation of communism in Cuba and Vietnam. This would strain relations for years to come, although *Dissent* was fond of publishing New Left tracts. See Gitlin, *The Sixties*, 171–77; Howe, *Margin of Hope*, 291–93; Dorman, *Arguing the World*, 132–56. Howe would write the introduction to later editions of Harrington's *The Other America*. See Howe, "Introduction."

3. This is especially the case for the New Left. Paul Goodman's *Growing Up Absurd* had recently been released, and the Port Huron Statement, the foundational document of SDS and the New Left, was written in 1962. There was certainly disillusionment regarding the Beats, but they brought more of a cultural disillusionment than political. As for the New York Intellectuals themselves, Jumonville argues that their later political differences were evident even in the 1930s. See Jumonville, *Critical Crossings*. When interviewed later on, Howe, Irving Kristol, and Lionel Abel agreed that in the late 1940s, and especially in the 1950s, the New York Intellectuals were drifting apart politically. See Howe, *Margin of Hope*; Dorman, *Arguing the World*; Abel, *Intellectual Follies*.

4. Erik Monkkonen offers quantitative data on New York's murder rates in the 1950s and 1960s. See Monkkonen, *Murder in New York City*, 8–10. See tables in Snyder, "Crime."

5. As with the private detective, Jameson's "universal access" is a useful descriptive for the relationship between the New York Intellectuals and their city in the 1930s. See Jameson, "On Raymond Chandler."

6. Glazer, "Is New York City Ungovernable?." On the discourse around New York City's "ungovernability" in the 1960s, see Vincent Cannato's biography of Mayor John Lindsay (1966–1973): Cannato, *Ungovernable City*.

7. On the Intellectuals' struggle to navigate the conservative Cold War era as committed leftists, see Pells, *Liberal Mind in a Conservative Age*, 117–345. On the circumstances surrounding the founding of *Dissent*, see Howe, *Margin of Hope*. 234–46. On the development of Greenwich Village's reputation as a site of bohemianism and modernity in the early-twentieth century, see Stansell, *American Moderns*.

8. Pells, *Liberal Mind in a Conservative Age*; Hartman, *War for the Soul of America*, 390–406; Wald, *New York Intellectuals*, 321–34; Vaïsse, *Neoconservatism*. On Howe's tenuous relationship with the New Left, see Howe, *Margin of Hope*, 294–327.

9. Both quotes from "A Word to Our Readers."

10. Paul Goodman, *Growing up Absurd*. On the influence of Goodman's book in the 1960s, see Howe, *Margin of Hope*, 239–45; Gitlin, *The Sixties*, 102–4.

11. In some respects this phenomenon parallels Andrew Hartman's argument about the dividing line between participants in the later cultural wars: "the gulf that separated those who embraced the new America from those who viewed it ominously." Hartman, *War for the Soul of America*, 2.

12. Chase, "New York Could Die."

13. Irving Howe affirmed this in Howe, *Margin of Hope*, 240.

14. "Note from the Editors."

15. Gans's influential work on urban and suburban space includes Gans, *People, Plans, and Policies*; Gans, *Levittowners*; Gans, *Urban Villagers*.

16. Goodman and Goodman, *Communitas*.

17. Gans, " 'Communitas.' "

18. Zoll, "West Village."

19. Chase, "New York Could Die."

20. Robert Caro blames Moses for neglecting mass transit and causing its decline by the mid-1970s. See Caro, *Power Broker*, 898–940; Gratz, *Battle for Gotham*, 141–42; Zukin, *Naked City*, 12–14.

21. Percival Goodman also wrote a separate critique of Lincoln Center that outlined public apathy to the private boondoggle of urban renewal as it functioned in New York City. Percival Goodman, "Lincoln Center, Emporium of the Arts."

22. Goodman and Goodman, "Banning Cars from Manhattan."

23. Ibid.

24. That said, their devotion to superblocks—essentially a group of consolidated blocks that eliminated both streets and street life—seemed out of touch with mainstream planning critique. By the end of 1961 the superblock design scheme favored by master planners since the 1940s had been discredited for destroying the sort of community they sought to cultivate in works like J. Jacobs, *Death and Life of Great American Cities*; Gans, *Urban Villagers*.

25. As Robert Beauregard has argued, the term "urban crisis" was mere code for an urban race problem in the 1960s. See Beauregard, *Voices of Decline*; Schneider, *Vampires, Dragons, and Egyptian Kings*; Sugrue, *Origins of the Urban Crisis*.

26. This point of view is found in works of journalism like *New York Herald Tribune* Staff, *New York City in Crisis*; W. Phillips, "Walk in the Dark"; Robinson, "Harlem Now on the Upswing." Tensions between white ethnics and the city's African American population were the subject of Jonathan Rieder's ethnography of the late 1960s and early 1970s. See Rieder, *Canarsie*. See also Pritchett, *Brownsville, Brooklyn*. For a personal view of both worlds, see Thomas, *Down These Mean Streets*.

27. Diaz, "Puerto Rican in New York"; Wakefield, *Island in the City*. On East Harlem renewal projects, see Zipp, *Manhattan Projects*, 253–350.

28. Solomon, "Person Alone."

29. Mailer, " 'She Thought the Russians Was Coming.' " On tensions between white elites and youth culture in this period, see Schneider, *Vampires, Dragons, and Egyptian Kings*; Gilbert, *Cycle of Outrage*.

30. Mailer, "White Negro"; Mailer, "Superman Comes to the Supermarket." On the relationship between these two Mailer articles and conceptions of masculinity and manhood in the early 1960s, see Cuordileone, *Manhood*, 163–94.

31. Harrington, "Harlem Today"; Brown, "Harlem, My Harlem."

32. Rotella, *October Cities*, 300–301.

33. It is important to note that neoconservatives were not necessarily allied with new conservatives. Bell edited one of the more influential studies of sixties conservatism, Daniel Bell, *Radical Right*. On Bell's intellectual evolution, see Brick, *Daniel Bell*.

34. Whyte, *Organization Man*; Riesman, Glazer, and Denney, *Lonely Crowd*; Glazer and Moynihan, *Beyond the Melting Pot*.

35. Hoover and Vernon, *Anatomy of a Metropolis*; Vernon, *Metropolis 1985*; Wood, *1400 Governments*.

36. Bell, *End of Ideology*.

37. Bell would leave his editorial perch at *The Public Interest* in the early 1970s because of its hard right turn (only to be replaced by Nathan Glazer). See Brick, *Age of Contradiction*, 4–21; Vaïsse, *Neoconservatism*.

38. Bell, "Three Faces of New York." Bell's portrayal of the moral economy was likely fueled by the memory of his family's strife during his own impoverished childhood. See Dorman, *Arguing the World*, 25–29.

39. Bell, "Three Faces of New York."

40. Bell, *Coming of the Post-Industrial Society*.

41. Bell, *End of Ideology*.

42. On the decline of manufacturing, and the transition to an economy dominated by finance, insurance, and real estate (FIRE), see J. Freeman, *Working-Class New York*, 291–333; Fitch, *Assassination of New York*, 130–234; Moody, *From Welfare State to Real Estate*; Soffer, *Koch and the Rebuilding of New York City*, 1–11, 145–203; Zipp, *Manhattan Projects*, 351–72.

43. Bell, "Three Faces of New York." As of Alan Wald's publication of *New York Intellectuals*, Bell still considered himself a socialist, while Wald places him firmly in the neoconservative camp. See Wald, *New York Intellectuals*, 353.

44. Bell, "Three Faces of New York."

45. Van den Haag, "Notes on New York Housing." It is worth noting that van den Haag would soon find a home at the conservative *National Review*. Pells, *Liberal Mind in a Conservative Age*, 220–29.

46. See the historiography on the relationship between emergent conservative thought and urban/suburban politics: McGirr, *Suburban Warriors*; Kruse, *White Flight*; Self, "Prelude to the Tax Revolt"; Lassiter, *Silent Majority*; Cowie, *Stayin' Alive*; Formisano, *Boston against Busing*.

47. Howe, "New York in the Thirties." As historians have shown, there were significant fears around the scourge of youth culture in the 1950s and 1960s. On the 1954 Senate hearings on juvenile delinquency, which were indicative of this anxiety about teenagers, see Gilbert, *Cycle of Outrage*. On middle-class fears of youth culture and delinquency in New York City in this period, see Schneider, *Vampires, Dragons, and Egyptian Kings*. David Hajdu, a journalist, has also written a history of comic books and youth culture in the 1950s. Hajdu, *Ten-Cent Plague*.

48. Howe, "New York in the Thirties."

49. Ibid.

50. Day, "Poverty and Destitution"; Harrington, "Harlem Today." On the Catholic Worker movement in this period, as previously cited, see Wakefield, *New York in the Fifties*, 73–90.

51. Howe, "New York in the Thirties."

52. Howe would use the "fragments" literary device in his autobiography as well to discuss the dizzying 1970s. See Irving Howe, "Fragments of a Decade," in Howe, *Margin of Hope*, 328–53.

53. For *Dissent*'s dismissive response to the Beats, see Polsky, "Village Beat Scene." New York City's New Left credentials would be on display by 1968, with the occupation of Columbia University. See Gitlin, *The Sixties*, 306–9; Cannato, *Ungovernable City*, 229–65. On Columbia's "war on blight," which sparked a student and community backlash that culminated in occupation, see Carriere, "Fight the War against Blight." New York City, of course, would also witness and inspire liberation movements tied to leftist politics. See, for example, Carter, *Stonewall*, 129–208.

54. Howe, *Margin of Hope*, 291.

55. Alan Wald cites Abel as a former leftist turned neoconservative. Wald, *New York Intellectuals*, 7.

56. Dorman, *Arguing the World*; Abel, *Intellectual Follies*, 60–69.

57. Abel, "New York City."

58. Ibid. On hardness in this period, see Cuordileone, *Manhood*. On the "Vital Center" legacy in neoconservative thought, see Vaïsse, *Neoconservatism*.

59. J. Freeman, *Working-Class New York*, 55–71.

60. Some years later, Howe fondly recalled Abel's characterization of New York City as the "most interesting part of the Soviet Union." See Howe, *Margin of Hope*, 25–26. Abel, too, later recalled his contribution to the *Dissent* Summer 1961 issue primarily for this comment (although he did not remember the correct date of his article—1963 rather than 1961). See Abel, *Intellectual Follies*, 55.

61. Abel, "New York City."

62. Ibid. On fears of delinquents and Puerto Ricans, see Schneider, *Vampires, Dragons, and Egyptian Kings*; Gilbert, *Cycle of Outrage*; Hajdu, *Ten-Cent Plague*.

63. Abel, "New York City."

64. Abel, *Intellectual Follies*, 281–89.

65. See previously cited scholarship on New York City's post–fiscal crisis economy: Soffer, *Koch and the Rebuilding of New York City*; Moody, *From Welfare State to Real Estate*; Fitch, *Assassination of New York*.

66. Hartman, *War for the Soul of America*.

67. Bellow, *Mr. Sammler's Planet*, 8–11. Louis Menand, reviewing a recent Bellow biography, notes autobiographical influences in Bellow, with the author himself the as the real-life counterpart to most of his protagonists. Menand, "Young Saul."

68. Joseph Dorman notes the New York Intellectuals' penchant for generalized judgment, and in many ways this characterized the early intellectual lives of this group. They sought to understand a broad range of topics and disciplines, and doing so did not allow them to conduct narrow research with academic rigor. He quotes Glazer: "The old New York intellectual style of pronouncing judgments on a less than adequate knowledge in politics and literature could not survive: it was specialize or die." William Phillips, coeditor of the *Partisan Review*, defined an intellectual as possessing "an independent mind, a generalizing mind, and an original mind." See Dorman, *Arguing the World*, 8–9, 98.

69. Cannato, *Ungovernable City*.

70. *New York Herald Tribune* Staff, *New York City in Crisis*.

71. As Daniel Friedenberg noted in the *Dissent* Summer 1961 issue: "The East Side [site of Sutton Place] is the only place where white people live today—the price must go up." Friedenberg, "Real Estate Confidential."

72. Cheever, "Moving Out."

73. L. Mumford, "Sky Line." Also found in L. Mumford, *Urban Prospect*, under the less patronizing chapter title "Home Remedies for Urban Cancer."

74. L. Mumford, *Urban Prospect*, 234.

75. L. Mumford, *City in History*, 242.

76. Abel, "New York City."

77. Didion, "Farewell to the Enchanted City." See also "Goodbye to All That" in Didion, *Slouching towards Bethlehem*.

78. On the impact of the Ocean Hill/Brownsville school board experiment on racial and ethnic relations, see J. Freeman, *Working-Class New York*, 219–27; Rieder, *Canarsie*, 213–14; Pritchett, *Brownsville, Brooklyn*, 229–36. On the role the ex-

periment played in the political realignment of the New York Intellectuals, see Vaïsse, *Neoconservatism*, 62–64.

79. Cannato, *Ungovernable City*, ix–xv.

80. Whalen, *City Destroying Itself*; Banfield, *Unheavenly City*.

Chapter Six

1. L. Mumford, "Sky Line."

2. Harrington, *Other America*; Clark, *Dark Ghetto*; U.S. Office of Policy Planning and Research, *Negro Family*. On Harrington and social welfare policy, see O'Connor, *Poverty Knowledge*. On the Moynihan Report, see Geary, *Beyond Civil Rights*; Patterson, *Freedom Is Not Enough*. On the historical and concurrent use of cancer as a metaphor, see Sontag, *Illness as Metaphor*.

3. Auletta, *Underclass*, would alter the dynamic of mainstream poverty studies, defining the underclass by a set of disparate behavioral issues rather than social status.

4. Gansberg, "37 Who Saw Murder"; Rosenthal, *Thirty-Eight*; *New York Herald Tribune* Staff, *New York City in Crisis*; Schaap and Breslin, "Lonely Crimes."

5. Katz, *In the Shadow of the Poorhouse*; Katz, *"Underclass" Debate*; Katz, *Improving Poor People*; Chronopoulos, *Spatial Regulation in New York City*.

6. Clark, *Dark Ghetto*; Glazer and Moynihan, *Beyond the Melting Pot*; C. W. Mills, *Power Elite*; C. W. Mills, *White Collar*; Riesman, Glazer, and Denny, *Lonely Crowd*. See also Patterson, *Freedom Is Not Enough*, 9; Geary, *Beyond Civil Rights*.

7. Galbraith, *Affluent Society*; Whyte, *Organization Man*; Harrington, *Other America*. For a primer on the intellectual intersections of these figures, see "Contradictions of the Affluent Society" in Brick, *Age of Contradiction*, 1–22.

8. Katz, *In the Shadow of the Poorhouse*, 251–73; Patterson, *Freedom Is Not Enough*, 19.

9. See the chapter "The Bend" in Riis, *How the Other Half Lives*, 46–57.

10. Keith Gandal situates Riis alongside Stephen Crane as "new ethnographers" of the slum. Gandal, *Virtues of the Vicious*, 27–38; Stange, "Jacob Riis and Urban Visual Culture"; Chronopoulos, *Spatial Regulation*, 5.

11. Riis, *How the Other Half Lives*, 41–45, 73–102.

12. On Riis's place in reform and renewal efforts in Progressive Era New York, see Murphy, *Political Manhood*, 73–90; Page, *Creative Destruction of Manhattan*, 73–104; Sante, *Low Life*, 31–42; Fried, *Makers of the City*. On Riis's biography, see Alland, *Jacob A. Riis*; Meyer, *Not Charity but Justice*.

13. Zipp, *Manhattan Projects*, 300–17. For concurrent East Harlem ethnographic work, see Wakefield, *Island in the City*, 15–16; Thomas, *Down These Mean Streets*.

14. The discussion of the Catholic Worker experience in 1950s New York, as well as Harrington's early days there, comes from Dan Wakefield's account of his own volunteer efforts with the organization. See Wakefield, *New York in the Fifties*, 73–90.

15. It is important to note that *The Other America* did not look only at urban poverty. While many of Harrington's observations were primarily confined to New York, he also examined rural poverty and the plight of the elderly.

16. Osofsky, *Harlem*. Osofsky initiated the ghetto historiography that continued through the mid-1980s. He drew a connection between family stability and the development of black enclaves like Harlem in the early twentieth century. For more on this ghetto historiography and its relationship to poverty studies in the 1960s, see Patterson, *Freedom Is Not Enough*, 129–44. Published around the same time as Osofsky's history, Schoener, *Harlem on My Mind*, provided a counterweight to the ghetto pathology narrative, as did Claude Brown's autobiographical novel on Harlem slum life: Brown, *Manchild in the Promised Land*. On redevelopment in Harlem in the 1960s, see Zipp, *Manhattan Projects*, 253–350; Bradley, *Harlem vs. Columbia University*, 20–62; Carriere, "Fight the War against Blight"; Stern, Mellins, and Fishman, *New York 1960*, 857–91. On Harlem and recent trends in "gentrification," see Monique Taylor, *Harlem between Heaven and Hell*; L. Freeman, *There Goes the Hood*; Maurrasse, *Listening to Harlem*.

17. Harrington found Bowery slumming alive, well, and attracting suburban tourists. "For sheer callousness and cynicism, I have never seen anything to rival the attitudes of the tourists and the police. Just below Houston on the Bowery was a place called Sammy's Bowery Follies. . . . It has been written up in magazines, and it is designed for tourists. . . . Of an evening, well-dressed tourists would arrive there, walking through a couple of rows of human misery, sometimes responding to a panhandler's plea with *noblesse oblige*. They were within a few feet of desperation and degradation, yet they seemed to find it 'interesting' and 'quaint.' This is a small, if radical, case of the invisibility of the poor." Harrington, *Other America*, 94.

18. There was significant elite optimism after the elevated tracks were removed. Meyer Berger, for one, saw this change as an opportunity for regeneration. He wondered what the area would be like in five or ten years when "The Bowery becomes a broad tree-lined street witth [*sic*] decent apartment houses and nicer store fronts." It would take more than five or ten years as the Bowery remained a center of New York lowlife for years to come. Berger, however, might recognize his vision in the transformed Bowery of today. Berger, "Bowery Blinks in the Sunlight."

19. Harrington, *Other America*, 90.

20. The landscape of postwar prosperity and consumption, particularly its gender and class politics, has been explored and critiqued in Cohen, *Consumers' Republic*, 193–290; E. May, *Homeward Bound*, 143–62; Deutsch, *Building a Housewife's Paradise*; 183–218; M. Jacobs, *Pocketbook Politics*.

21. Harrington, *Other America*, 3.

22. Kenneth Jackson first historicized this "polarization of the metropolis" in Jackson, *Crabgrass Frontier*, 274–76. Robert Fishman's chapter on "Technoburbs" is also instructive. See Fishman, *Bourgeois Utopias*, 182–207. By the end of the century, this polarization would have historians like Jackson and social scientists like

Robert Putnam decrying the loss of community and the decline of social capital. Putnam, *Bowling Alone*.

23. Harrington, *Other America*, 4.

24. Ibid.

25. Ibid., 1–18. See the first chapter, which Harrington titled "The Invisible Land."

26. Harrington, *Other America*, 88–89. Luc Sante's narrative history of New York City's lower orders devotes significant attention to the Bowery, including the nature of the street life on the thoroughfare. As he writes, "the Bowery acquired a reputation as the last stop on the way down," as early as the mid-nineteenth century. Sante, *Low Life*, 14. On the Bowery as a "haven and spectacle," see Chauncey, *Gay New York*, 33–46.

27. Harrington, *Other America*, 10.

28. Baldwin, "Fifth Avenue, Uptown."

29. Harrington, *Other America*, 62–79. On systematic racial discrimination in New York City education, see J. Freeman, *Working-Class New York*, 219–27; Rieder, *Canarsie*, 213–14; Pritchett, *Brownsville, Brooklyn*, 229–36. On racial discrimination and the failure of school reform in the 1960s, see, for example, Formisano, *Boston against Busing*; Hirsch, "Less than Plessy"; Baum, *Brown in Baltimore*; Lassiter, *Silent Majority*; Derrick Bell, *Silent Covenants*, 94–137.

30. All quotes from Harrington, *Other America*, 139–40.

31. Ibid., 161–71.

32. Ibid., 155.

33. On the decline of public housing, see, for example, Hunt, *Blueprint for Disaster*.

34. Katz, *Improving Poor People*, 69.

35. Clark, *Dark Ghetto*; Osofsky, *Harlem*; Osofsky, "Enduring Ghetto."

36. U.S. Office of Policy Planning and Research, U.S. Department of Labor, *Negro Family*.

37. Patterson, *Freedom Is Not Enough*, xii.

38. Geary, *Beyond Civil Rights*, 6. Geary is citing Raymond Williams, *Keywords*.

39. Portions of the "underclass" historiography share the argument that the Moynihan report was largely misinterpreted by critics, and Moynihan himself saw the controversy over his report as a "moment lost." Patterson, *Freedom Is Not Enough*, 65–86. See also Geary, *Beyond Civil Rights*. For Moynihan's interpretation of the controversy, see Moynihan, "The President and the Negro." On the "underclass" debate, see Katz, *In the Shadow of the Poorhouse*, 274–92; Katz, *Improving Poor People*, 60–98. And see the edited collections: Katz, *"Underclass" Debate*; Jencks and Peterson, *Urban Underclass*.

40. *New York Herald Tribune* Staff, *New York City in Crisis*.

41. Ibid., 12–30.

42. Ibid., v–vii, 160–69.

43. Schaap and Breslin, "Lonely Crimes."

44. Schaap, "In the Courts"; Schaap and Breslin, "Lonely Crimes."

45. Schaap, "In the Courts"; Breslin, "In the Streets"; Schaap, "In the Streets"; Schaap, "In the Courts."

46. Schaap and Breslin, "Lonely Crimes."

47. On the 1957 murder in Hell's Kitchen, see "The Capeman and the Vampires" in Schneider, *Vampires, Dragons, and Egyptian Kings*, 3–26.

48. Gallo, *No One Helped*; M. Johnson, "Career Girl Murders"; Seyfried, "Kew Gardens"; Snyder, "Kitty Genovese Murder."

49. Gansberg, "37 Who Saw Murder." This was not lost on the writers of *New York in Crisis*: "A recent incident, in which a woman was raped and murdered while more than a score of people ignored her shouts for help, is an extreme example (but not entirely a unique one) of the sort of public apathy that has made the job of the police all the harder." *New York Herald Tribune* Staff, *New York City in Crisis*, 166. On sexual violence in New York City and the cultural response around it in this period, particularly the "career girl murders" that occurred a year before Katherine Genovese's murder, see M. Johnson, "Career Girl Murders." On women and crime fears, see Gordon and Riger, *Female Fear*; Madriz, *Nothing Bad Happens to Good Girls*.

50. Rosenthal, *Thirty-Eight Witnesses*, 18–19, 49–52.

51. L. Kaufman, "Timeless Book May Require Fact Checking." As Kaufman notes, in the years since *Thirty-Eight Witnesses* was published, "as court records have been examined and witnesses reinterviewed, some facts of both the coverage and the book have been challenged on many fronts, including the element at the center of the indictment: 38 silent witnesses." Subsequent analysis revealed that five or six witnesses were in any position to see the crime or hear calls for help. See also Gallo, *No One Helped*.

52. Richard J. Whalen, *Catch the Falling Flag*. On the rise of the New Right in this period, see, among others, Wilentz, *Age of Reagan*; Cowie, *Stayin' Alive*; Perelstein, *Nixonland*; McGirr, *Suburban Warriors*; Phillips-Fein, *Invisible Hands*; Self, *All in the Family*; Kruse, *One Nation under God*; Hartman, *War for the Soul of America*.

53. While the *Fortune* version touched on the same themes as the book, it is abridged and features fewer tales of despair on the street. Whalen, "City Destroying Itself." The letter writers in the following issue were taken aback by Whalen's critique and were decidedly defensive, including a brief message from Robert Moses: "You ask me why should *Fortune* do such a story? Search me. I don't know. It is full of errors and misinformation." "Letters to Fortune."

54. Whalen, *City Destroying Itself*, 112–17.

55. Ibid., 16–17.

56. The statistics say otherwise: Snyder, "Crime."

57. Whalen, *City Destroying Itself*, 12.

58. Ibid., 18.

59. Banfield, *Unheavenly City*. Banfield was one of the critics who pushed the "culture of poverty" argument toward the "underclass" narrative. See Katz, *Improving Poor People*, 70.

60. Quoted in Beauregard, *Voices of Decline*, 171.

61. Katz, *In the Shadow of the Poorhouse*, 246–57. In recent works Katz has been arguing for a stronger and more focused welfare state to deal with contemporary urban poverty issues. See Katz, *Why Don't American Cities Burn?* On the decline of welfare capitalism and the social policy of the Nixon administration, see Self, *All in the Family*; Perelstein, *Nixonland*; Cowie, *Stayin' Alive*.

62. Katz, *Improving Poor People*, 70.

63. Patterson, *Freedom Is Not Enough*, 101–2.

64. Auletta, *Underclass*; Kelling and Wilson, "Police and Neighborhood Safety." On the influence of neoconservatives and the implications of the "broken windows" theory for New York, see Chronopoulos, *Spatial Regulation*. On the "welfare queen" in political context, see Self, *All in the Family*.

Chapter Seven

1. Schaap, "Fun City."

2. Cannato, *Ungovernable City*, 561.

3. Films shot on location tended to be crime capers like Dassin, *Naked City* (1948). Dimendberg, *Film Noir*, 23. On trends in film prior to "New Hollywood," see "Hollywood's Collapse" in Sklar, *Movie Made America*, 286–304.

4. Cannato, *Ungovernable City*, 561–62.

5. On "New Hollywood," see Biskind, *Easy Riders, Raging Bulls*. See also Sklar, *Movie Made America*, 286–338.

6. Canby, "New York Woes." Also quoted in Cannato, *Ungovernable City*, 562.

7. The historiography of the New Right and metropolitan development is instructive on the "backlash" politics of the period. See, for example, Lassiter, *Silent Majority*; Flamm, *Law and Order*; McGirr, *Suburban Warriors*; Kruse, *White Flight*; Schulman, *The Seventies*; Cowie, *Stayin' Alive*; Perelstein, *Nixonland*.

8. On neoliberalism and New York City since the 1970s, see Fitch, *Assassination of New York*; Moody, *From Welfare State to Real Estate*; Soffer, *Ed Koch*.

9. J. Schlesinger, *Midnight Cowboy*; Hiller, *Out of Towners*. All quoted dialogue is taken from repeated viewings of each film and more often than not transcribed from the English subtitles provided on the DVD version of these films.

10. The relationship between Joe and Enrico was subject to much debate and speculation in reviews. See, for example, "Improbable Love Story"; "Joe and Ratso"; S. Kaufmann, "Midnight Cowboy." Gene Phillips, biographer of director John Schlesinger, suggests that the film "marks a milestone in the mature and responsible treatment of sexuality, particularly the self-contained world of the homosexual, in the American commercial cinema." G. Phillips, *John Schlesinger*, 128.

11. I refer to the character of Joe Buck by his last name, so as not to confuse him with the title character of *Joe*, another film discussed in this chapter.

12. For an ethnographic look at male prostitution in Times Square post-*Midnight Cowboy*, see McNamara, *Times Square Hustler*.

13. Reed, "'Cowboy' Walks on the Wild Side."

14. Schlesinger, *Midnight Cowboy*.

15. On Joe Buck's metamorphosis into a New Yorker, see Corkin, "Sex and the City in Decline."

16. All quotes from M. Kaufman, "In Street, Store and Subway."

17. Hiller, *Out of Towners*.

18. Fleischer, *Soylent Green*.

19. Hiller, *Out of Towners*.

20. Greenberg, *Branding New York*. Protesting comparably low public sector wages and benefits, New York City's transit workers went on strike on January 1, 1966, the same day that Mayor Lindsay assumed office. While the strike lasted only a few days, it essentially brought the city to a standstill in the middle of winter. It was a momentary victory, however, for municipal unionism in New York City. Likewise, the city's sanitation workers went on strike in 1968, resulting in the massive mountains of garbage throughout New York City, which *The Out of Towners* represents. For more on these strikes and municipal unionism in this period, see the chapter "Municipal Unionism" in Freeman, *Working-Class New York*, 201–14. Sullivan, *Rats*. Photos of Lindsay visiting poor neighborhoods during the transit strike and walking among the garbage piles of the sanitation strike are forever tied to the image of the "ungovernability" of New York City in this period, and the rhetoric around the strikes demonstrates a disconnect between Lindsay and the city's declining working class in this period. On Lindsay's handling of the strikes, see Cannato, *Ungovernable City*, 78–93, 196–204.

21. Hiller, *Out of Towners*.

22. Ibid.

23. On the State's "I Love NY" marketing campaign in the 1970s, see Greenberg, *Branding New York*, 202–6.

24. Hiller, *Out of Towners*.

25. Coppola, *Godfather*; Parks Jr., *Super Fly*; Scorsese, *Mean Streets*; Parks, *Shaft*. On the emergence of sex and violence on film, see Biskind, *Easy Riders, Raging Bulls*.

26. Brooks, *Looking for Mr. Goodbar*; Pakula, *Klute*.

27. On New York films that examine the relationship between sex and the sex trade and the declining city in the 1970s, see Corkin, "Sex and the City in Decline." The issues of prostitution and pornography, which were tied to a number of New York films in this period, including *Midnight Cowboy* and *Taxi Driver*, and concerns about sexual violence related to both galvanized the feminist movement in the 1970s. See, for example, Whisnant and Stark, *Not for Sale*. Although his work has become discredited by his own indictment on rape charges, Peter Braunstein once argued that New York emerged as "Erotic City" in the 1970s, which elicited a bifurcated response of sexual liberation on the one hand and condemnation on the other. The same might be said of the sexual nature of NYC films in this period. See Braunstein, "Adults Only."

28. The trailer is available on the most recent DVD release of *Death Wish*. https://www.amazon.com/Death-Wish-Various/dp/B00AEFXRG0/ref=ser.

29. Canby, "Screen"; Canby, "'Death Wish' Exploits Fear Irresponsibly," Wertham, July 12, 1975. Shalit quote transcribed by Wertham in his collected file on *Death Wish*,

30. Klemestrud, "What Do They See in 'Death Wish'?." According to the Internet Movie Database (IMDb), *Death Wish* grossed $22,000,000 in its theater run. Adjusted for inflation using http://www.usinflationcalculator.com/ the film's 1974 gross is equivalent to $106 million in 2015 receipts.

31. Wertham, July 12, 1975.

32. Winner, *Death Wish*.

33. Ibid.

34. During his time as mayor, Lindsay fought for the Civilian Complaint Review Board, which would oversee police activity by investigating complaints against the department. The Knapp Commission (1970), which publicly investigated police corruption, created an even wider gulf between Lindsay and the NYPD. At the same time, the very public revelations of Frank Serpico, subject of a popular book and an even more popular film in the 1970s, helped establish an enduring image of the NYPD as corrupt, inept, apathetic, and above the law in this period. On the relationship between Lindsay and the NYPD, see Cannato, *Ungovernable City*, 466–91. On "Fear City" pamphlets and the NYPD in the sixties, see Schneider, *Smack*, 184. On Frank Serpico, see Mass, *Serpico*; Lumet, *Serpico*. See also Knapp Commission, *Knapp Commission Report*.

35. Flamm, *Law and Order*.

36. Winner, *Death Wish*. As previously noted, revelations about police corruption, the Knapp Commission, and the NYPD's backlash against the Civilian Review Board established an image of the NYPD as apathetic and inept. See Cannato, *Ungovernable City*, 466–91; Flamm, *Law and Order*, 76–80.

37. Scorsese, *Taxi Driver*. Scorsese's previous film is also a useful examination of 1970s New York, but it was filmed in Los Angeles: Scorsese, *Mean Streets*. Flatley, "Martin Scorsese's Gamble."

38. Schrader, "Notes on Film Noir."

39. Quote from Canby, "Flamboyant 'Taxi Driver.'" On the production of *Taxi Driver*, see Biskind, *Easy Riders, Raging Bulls*; 299–315. On the film and its relationship to 1970s political culture, see Cowie, *Stayin' Alive*, 331–34; Schulman, *The Seventies*, 148–50.

40. On Forty-Second Street and its association with pornography and sexuality, see Berman and Berger, *On the Town*, 151–92. Also see "Times Square Blue," Samuel Delany's memoir of Forty-Second Street before the Disney Company's redevelopment of the area. Delany, *Times Square Red*, 1–108.

41. Scorsese, *Taxi Driver*.

42. Canby, "Scorsese's Disturbing 'Taxi Driver.'"

43. Scorsese, *Taxi Driver.*

44. Flatley, "Martin Scorsese's Gamble."

45. Siegel, *Dirty Harry.*

46. Cowie, *Stayin' Alive*, 198.

47. Avildsen, *Joe*; Winner, *Death Wish*. On Nixon's backlash politics, see Flamm, *Law and Order*, 163–81; Cowie, *Stayin' Alive*, 125–66; Perelstein, *Nixonland*, 277–28; Lassiter, *Silent Majority*, 253–74; Schulman, *The Seventies*, 35–42.

48. Avildsen, *Joe.*

49. Ibid.

50. Perelstein, *Nixonland*, 519.

51. Quoted ibid., 520.

52. Klemestrud, "His Happiness."

53. Freeman, *Working-Class New York*, 237–39.

54. Cowie, *Stayin' Alive*, 190.

55. Klemestrud, "His Happiness."

56. Thompson, "'Joe,' an East Village Tale"; Klemestrud, "His Happiness."

57. Winner, *Death Wish*. See, for example, this celebratory profile of Bronson in the wake of *Death Wish*: Davidson, "America Discovers a 'Sacred Monster.'"

58. Winner, *Death Wish.*

59. Davidson, "America Discovers a 'Sacred Monster.'"

60. Winner, *Death Wish.*

61. Wertham; Canby, "'Death Wish' Exploits Fear Irresponsibly."

62. Scorsese, *Taxi Driver*. On David Berkowitz and the "Son of Sam" murders, see select sections of Mahler, *Ladies and Gentlemen.*

63. Scorsese, *Taxi Driver.*

64. Ibid.

65. There is a growing historiography that examines the political culture and popular culture of the 1970s to argue that the decade represented the final collapse of the Democratic Party's so-called New Deal Coalition of labor, blacks, intellectuals, and longtime southern Democrats. See Schulman, *The Seventies*; Cowie, *Stayin' Alive*; Rodgers, *Age of Fracture.*

66. Kotcheff, *First Blood*; Ashby, *Coming Home.*

67. Scorsese, *Taxi Driver.*

68. On deindustrialization and the movement of population and capital from the North and the Northeast to the South and the Southwest or from the Rust Belt to the Sunbelt, in this period, see Sugrue, *Origins of the Urban Crisis*; Schulman, *From Cotton Belt to Sunbelt*; Lassiter, *Silent Majority*; McGirr, *Suburban Warriors*; High, *Industrial Sunset*; Schulman, *The Seventies*, 102–20; Rotella, *Good with Their Hands*; Shermer, *Sunbelt Capitalism.*

69. Mandell, "'Wouldn't Want to Work Here'"; Stern, "Rep. Koch." On corporations that actually left Manhattan in this period, see Jackson, *Crabgrass Frontier*, 266–69.

70. Schlesinger, *Midnight Cowboy.*

71. Ibid.

72. Turner, *Frontier in American History*.

73. Winner, *Death Wish*. On the antiurban ethic of conservatism, see McGirr, *Suburban Warriors*; Lassiter, *Silent Majority*.

74. Winner, *Death Wish*. On street crime and calls for law and order, see Flamm, *Law and Order*.

75. Winner, *Death Wish*. On warrior films, see Gibson, *Warrior Dreams*. On the relationship between Sunbelt suburbs and the emergence of the New Right, see McGirr, *Suburban Warriors*; Lassiter, *Silent Majority*; Shermer, *Barry Goldwater*.

76. Friedkin, *French Connection*; Lumet, *Network*; M. Frank, *Prisoner of Second Avenue*; Lumet, *Dog Day Afternoon*; Lumet, *Serpico*; Coppola, *The Godfather*; Carpenter, *Escape from New York*; Badham, *Saturday Night Fever*. On the narrative of *Saturday Night Fever*, see Cowie, *Stayin' Alive*, 313–19.

77. Crime would rise steadily until 1990. Snyder, "Crime."

78. Epstein, "Last Days of New York"; Alcaly and Mermelstein, *Fiscal Crisis of American Cities*; Moody, *From Welfare State to Real Estate*; Soffer, *Ed Koch*, 113–20.

79. Fitch, *Assassination of New York*; Starr, *Rise and Fall of New York City*; Newfield and Du Brul, *Abuse of Power*; Caro, *Power Broker*.

80. Lee, *Summer of Sam*.

81. Mahler, *Ladies and Gentlemen*.

82. Page, *City's End*.

83. Reitman, *Ghostbusters*.

Chapter Eight

1. Ferrara, *Fear City*; Petrie, *Fort Apache, the Bronx*; Winner, *Death Wish 3*; Carpenter, *Escape from New York*.

2. Lefebvre, *Writings on Cities*; Harvey, "Right to the City."

3. Paley, "Somewhere Else." Marshall Berman was fond of Paley's line and cited it in many of his works. See Berman, "Ruins and Reform"; Berman, *All That Is Solid Melts into Air*; Berman, "Introduction"; Burns, *New York*.

4. Echols, *Hot Stuff*. Also see previously cited scholarship on the Village as a queer neighborhood in the first half of the twentieth century: Chauncey, *Gay New York*, 227–69; Heise, *Urban Underworlds*, 77–126; Carter, *Stonewall*, 5–29; Heap, *Slumming*, 154–76; K. Mumford, *Interzones*, 73–92.

5. Echols, *Hot Stuff*, 48–53.

6. Ibid., 61.

7. Friedkin, *Cruising*.

8. Flint, *Wrestling with Moses*; Gratz, *Battle for Gotham*; Zukin, *Loft Living*.

9. Petrus, "From Gritty to Chic"; Shkuda, "Art Market"; M. J. Taylor, "Playing the Field."

10. Petrus, "From Gritty to Chic."

11. Ibid., 73.

12. Scorsese, *After Hours*.

13. Allen, *Hannah and Her Sisters*; Lyne, *Nine 1/2 Weeks*; Marshall, *Big*. On turn-of-the-century Coney Island amusements, see Peiss, *Cheap Amusements*.

14. Shkuda, "Art Market."

15. Ibid.; Petrus, "From Gritty to Chic." *New York* magazine started off as the *Herald Tribune*'s Sunday magazine, before its independence in the 1968.

16. Von Hassell, *Homesteading*; Taylor et al., *Downtown Book*.

17. McReynolds, "New Booze on the Bowery."

18. Bowman, *This Must Be the Place*; Kozak, *This Ain't No Disco*; Brazis, Kristal, and Byrne, *Cbgb & Omfug*. According to Bernard Gendron, "the 'punk' label was foisted on this scene not long after the appearance, in early 1976, of a highly imaginative and humorous Downtown fanzine *Punk*, whose editors, however, used the term generically to designate any hard-rock sound." Gendron, "Downtown Music Scene," 53.

19. Rockwell, "Bowery Is 'Home.'"

20. Palmer, "New Life." On homesteading in the Lower East Side, see von Hassell, *Homesteading*.

21. Palmer, "New Life."

22. Seidelman, *Desperately Seeking Susan*. On Madonna's place in the downtown scene by a local Lower East Side resident, see Sante, "Unlike a Virgin."

23. Rockwell, "Artistic Success."

24. Rockwell, "Cbgb Club." On the history of the Talking Heads, see Bowman, *This Must Be the Place*.

25. Nelson, "Valley of the N.Y. Dolls."

26. Rockwell, "Patti Smith."

27. Rockwell, "Where to Plug into Television."

28. These ads ran in the *Village Voice* between October 1974 and April 1975.

29. Rockwell, "Speculations." On the history of the Ramones, see Beeber, *Heebie Jeebies at Cbgb's*, 103–22. Albums from that period include Ramones, *Ramones*; Ramones, *End of the Century*; Ramones, *Road to Ruin*.

30. Moyle, *Times Square*.

31. Ibid.; Schlesinger, *Midnight Cowboy*.

32. Moyle, *Times Square*.

33. Austin, *Taking the Train*, 3–14.

34. Mailer, *Faith of Graffiti*, 22, 13.

35. Mailer's most famous social commentaries of the sixties and seventies challenged the conservative social politics of consensus, often in the pages of critical journals like *Dissent* and *Esquire*. In "The White Negro" (1957), a problematic analysis of conformist white inhibition versus black beatitude, Mailer sanctified the so-called Beats by ascribing them essentialist and almost retrograde black traits: a thirst for instant, presumably sexual, gratification; bouts of petty larceny; and a tendency toward occasional violence, among others. "Superman Comes to the Supermarket" (1960) highlighted the youthful vigor of John F. Kennedy in a pool of otherwise antiquated clubhouse Democrats. His contribution to *Dissent* in the sum-

mer of 1961, "'She Thought the Russians was Coming,'" in what may be read as a mea culpa for "The White Negro," spins the narrative of juvenile delinquency and youth gangs by suggesting members were "rather good pieces of work . . . bright, sensitive, [and] loyal," victimized by boredom wrought by "middle-aged desperadoes of the corporation." In the Necropolis milieu, Mailer advertised himself as savior of the cash-strapped, crime-ridden city, securing the Democratic nomination for mayor and suggesting the secession of New York City from the State. See Mailer, "Why Are We in New York?"; Mailer, "'She Thought the Russians Was Coming'"; Mailer, "White Negro"; Mailer, "Superman Comes to the Supermarket."

36. Mailer, *Faith of Graffiti*, 14, 25.

37. Austin, *Taking the Train*, 145–46; Wilson, *Thinking about Crime*. See also Chronopoulos, *Spatial Regulation*, 86–109; Klemek, *Transatlantic Collapse*, 52–59.

38. Austin, *Taking the Train*, 4–6; Robbins and Wise, *West Side Story*; Sacks et al., *Welcome Back, Kotter*.

39. Rose, *Black Noise*, 2.

40. Moyers, *CBS Reports*.

41. Chang, *Can't Stop, Won't Stop*, 14.

42. For video coverage of the comments, see "Howard Cosell's 'The Bronx is Burning' Comments During 1977 World Series" YouTube video, posted by "compazine," June 11, 2016, https://www.youtube.com/watch?v=bnVH-BE9CUo. Mahler, *Ladies and Gentlemen*.

43. Chang, *Can't Stop, Won't Stop*, 14–16.

44. Ibid.

45. George, *Hip Hop America*, 10.

46. Ibid.; Chang, *Can't Stop, Won't Stop*; Rose, *Black Noise*; Fricke, Ahearn, and Experience Music Project, *Yes Yes Y'all*.

47. George, *Hip Hop America*, 20. On the geography of hip-hop in the Bronx and the success of "Rapper's Delight," see also Chang, *Can't Stop, Won't Stop*; Fricke, Ahearn, and Experience Music Project, *Yes Yes Y'all*; Rose, *Black Noise*.

48. Rose, *Black Noise*; Chang, *Can't Stop, Won't Stop*; Fricke, Ahearn, and Experience Music Project, *Yes Yes Y'all*; George, *Hip Hop America*; Gendron, "Downtown Music Scene."

49. Chang, *Can't Stop, Won't Stop*, 148.

50. George, *Hip Hop America*, 12.

51. Gumpert, "Foreword," 11.

52. Ahearn, *Wild Style*. On the production of the film, see also George, *Hip Hop America*; Chang, *Can't Stop, Won't Stop*; Fricke, Ahearn, and Experience Music Project, *Yes Yes Y'all*.

53. Ahearn, *Wild Style*; Caz, *South Bronx Subway Rap*.

54. Grandmaster Flash did not want anything to do with the song, deeming it too depressing for a genre centered on the upbeat. See Chang, *Can't Stop, Won't Stop*, 178–79.

55. Grandmaster Flash and Furious Five, *The Message*.

56. McCormick, "Crack in Time," 68–70.

57. M. J. Taylor, "Playing the Field," 25.

58. McCormick, "Crack in Time," 69.

59. Soffer, *Ed Koch*; Moody, *From Welfare State to Real Estate*; Fitch, *Assassination of New York*; Mollenkopf, "Postindustrial Transformation"; Stone, *Wall Street*; Marshall, *Big*; Nichols, *Working Girl*; McInerney, *Bright Lights, Big City*; Wolfe, *Bonfire of the Vanities*; Ross, *Secret of My Success*.

Epilogue

1. Berman and Berger, "Ruins and Reform."

2. Kazin, "They Made It!"; Dickstein, "Neighborhoods"; Fox, "Civil Society"; Harrington, "When Ed Koch Was Still a Liberal."

3. P. Berman, "Face of Downtown." See also Flores, "Rappin', Writin', and Breakin'"; Morton, "Banker's Red Suspenders"; Levy, "Individuals and Autonomists."

4. Sleeper, "Boodling, Bigotry, and Cosmopolitanism"; N. Mills, "Howard Beach."

5. Sleeper, "Boodling, Bigotry, and Cosmopolitanism."

6. "Up, Up, Up" taken from the chapter on crime in New York Herald Tribune Staff, *New York City in Crisis*.

7. Sleeper, "Boom & Bust."

8. Howe, "Social Retreat and the Tumler."

9. Tyler, "Tale of Three Cities."

10. Howe, "Social Retreat and the Tumler."

11. Soffer, *Ed Koch*, 4.

12. Harvey, *Brief History of Neoliberalism*, 77.

13. N. D. Bloom, *Public Housing That Worked*.

14. Huxtable, "Stumbling toward Tomorrow."

15. Fainstein, *City Builders*.

16. Delany, *Times Square Red*, 155.

17. Bender, "New York as a Center of 'Difference.'"

18. Howe, "Social Retreat and the Tumler."

19. Sleeper, "Boom & Bust."

20. Berman, "Ruins and Reform."

21. See the chapter "Louima, Diallo, and Dorismond" in Newfield, *Full Rudy*, 89–120.

22. Nagourney, "Giuliani Sells New York."

23. The most recent phenomenon is to rebrand neighborhoods and/or utterly redefine New York City geography. See, for example, Park, "Borders under Siege."

24. Creative Class Group, "Articles," www.creativeclass.com/rfcgdb/articles/Richard%20Florida.pdf, May 2008 (accessed March 30, 2011). [Emphasis added.]

25. *New York Magazine*, for example, published "Is This Book Worth Getting?: A Roundup of New Brooklyn-Centered Novels" on April 30, 2009: http://nymag.com/arts/books/features/56399/.

26. Examples just from the first decade of the new millenium included *Sex and the City* (2008); *Sex and the City 2* (2010); *Date Night* (2010); *The Switch* (2010); *The Devil Wears Prada* (2008); *The Proposal* (2010); *Going the Distance* (2010); *The Back-up Plan* (2010); *Definitely, Maybe* (2008); *Hitch* (2005); *New York I Love You* (2009); *Nick and Norah's Infinite Playlist* (2008); *27 Dresses* (2008); *How to Lose A Guy in 10 Days* (2003); *Bride Wars* (2009); *Maid in Manhattan* (2002); *Serendipity* (2001), and *Someone Like You . . .* (2001).

27. Tennant, *Sweet Home Alabama*.

28. "Mayor Bloomberg and Police Commissioner Kelly"; Jordan, *Brave One*.

29. Lucy and Phillips, "Suburban Decline."

30. The popular blog *Gothamist* is fond of asking if the "bad old days" are returning to certain neighborhoods. See Johnston, "Is Union Square Slipping Back to the Bad Old Days" and "Is the West Village Slipping Back to the Bad Old Days."

31. Lee, *Do the Right Thing*. Andrew Hartman offers an excellent discussion of the reality and reception of Lee's film. See Hartman, *War for the Soul of America*, 122–24.

32. Goldsmith and Lynne, *What We See*; Sorkin, *Twenty Minutes in Manhattan*; Zukin, *Naked City*.

Bibliography

Abel, Lionel. *The Intellectual Follies: A Memoir of the Literary Venture in New York and Paris*. New York: W. W. Norton, 1984.

——. "New York City: A Remembrance." *Dissent* (Summer 1961), 251–59.

Ahearn, Charlie. *Wild Style*. United States, 1983.

Alcaly, Roger E., and David Mermelstein. *The Fiscal Crisis of American Cities: Essays on the Political Economy of Urban America with Special Reference to New York*. 1st ed. New York: Vintage Books, 1977.

Aldrich, Robert. *Kiss Me Deadly*. United States: Parklane Pictures, 1955.

Alexiou, Alice Sparberg. *Jane Jacobs: Urban Visionary*. Piscataway, NJ: Rutgers University Press, 2006.

Alland, Alexander. *Jacob A. Riis: Photographer and Citizen*. New York: Aperture, 1973.

Allen, Woody. *Annie Hall*. United States: United Artists, 1977.

——. *Hannah and Her Sisters*. United States: Orion Pictures, 1986.

——. *Manhattan*. United States: United Artists, 1979.

Amper, Richard. "Conflicts in the Upper Bronx." *New York Times*, July 15, 1955. Article in a 20-part series, "Our Changing City," begun in the summer of 1955.

Anderson, Martin. *The Federal Bulldozer: Critical Analysis of Urban Renewal, 1949–1962*. Cambridge, MA: M.I.T. Press, 1964.

Asbury, Edith Evans. "Nassau-Suffolk Area of Long Island." *New York Times*, August 19, 1955. Article in a 20-part series, "Our Changing City," begun in the summer of 1955.

Asbury, Herbert. *The Gangs of New York: An Informal History of the Underworld*. New York: Thunder's Mouth Press, 1998.

Ashby, Hal. *Coming Home*. United States: United Artists, 1978.

Auletta, Ken. *The Streets Were Paved with Gold*. New York: Random House, 1979.

——. *The Underclass*. Updated and Revised ed. Woodstock, NY: Overlook 1999.

Austin, Joe. *Taking the Train: How Graffiti Art Became an Urban Crisis in New York*. New York: Columbia University Press, 2001.

Avila, Eric. *Popular Culture in the Age of White Flight: Fear and Fantasy in Suburban Los Angeles*. Berkeley: University of California Press, 2004.

Avildsen, John. *Joe*. United States: Cannon Group, 1970.

Badham, John. *Saturday Night Fever*. United States: Paramount Pictures, 1977.

Bailey, Samuel. "The Adjustment of Italian Immigrants in Buenos Aires and New York." *American Historical Review* 88 (1983): 280–305.

Baldwin, James. "Fifth Avenue, Uptown." *Esquire*, July 1960, 70–76.

——. *The Fire Next Time*. New York: Vintage, 1963, 1993.

——. *Notes of a Native Son*. Boston: Beacon, 1955, 1984.

Ballon, Hilary. "Robert Moses and Urban Renewal: The Title I Program." In *Robert Moses and the Modern City: The Transformation of New York*, edited by Hilary Ballon and Kenneth T. Jackson, 94–115. New York: W. W. Norton, 2007.

Ballon, Hilary, and Kenneth T. Jackson. "Introduction." In *Robert Moses and the Modern City: The Transformation of New York*, edited by Hilary Ballon and Kenneth T. Jackson, 65–66. New York: W. W. Norton, 2007.

Ballon, Hilary, and Kenneth T. Jackson., eds. *Robert Moses and the Modern City: The Transformation of New York*. New York: W. W. Norton, 2007.

Banfield, Edward C. *The Unheavenly City: The Nature and the Future of Our Urban Crisis*. Boston: Little, Brown, 1968.

Baum, Howell S. *Brown in Baltimore: School Segregation and the Limits of Liberalism*. Ithaca, NY: Cornell University Press, 2010.

Beauregard, Robert A. *Voices of Decline: The Postwar Fate of U.S. Cities*. 2nd ed. New York: Routledge, 2003.

——. *When America Became Suburban*. Minneapolis: University of Minnesota Press, 2006.

Beckert, Sven. *The Monied Metropolis: New York City and the Consolidation of the American Bourgeoisie*. New York: Cambridge University Press, 2001.

Beeber, Steven Lee. *The Heebie Jeebies at Cbgb's: A Secret History of Jewish Punk*. Chicago: Chicago Review Press, 2006.

"Behind New York's Facade: Slums and Segregation." *Look*, February 19 1958.

Bell, Daniel. *The Coming of the Post-Industrial Society: A Venture in Social Forecasting*. New York: Basic Books, 1973.

——. *The End of Ideology: On the Exhaustion of Political Ideas in the Fifties*. New York: Free Press, 1960.

——, ed. *The Radical Right*. New York: Doubleday Anchor, 1964.

——. "The Three Faces of New York." *Dissent*, (Summer 1961), 222–32.

Bell, Derrick. *Silent Covenants:* Brown v. Board of Education *and the Unfulfilled Hopes for Racial Reform*. New York: Oxford University Press, 2004.

Bello, Francis. "The City and the Car." In *The Exploding Metropolis: A Study of the Assault on Urbanism and How Our Cities Can Resist It*, edited by *Fortune Magazine*, 32–61. Garden City, NY: Doubleday, 1958.

Bellow, Saul. *Mr. Sammler's Planet*. New York: Viking, 1970.

Bender, Thomas. "New York as a Center of 'Difference': How America's Metropolis Counters American Myth." *Dissent* (Fall 1987): 429–35.

——. *New York Intellect: A History of Intellectual Life in New York City, from 1750 to the Beginnings of Our Own Time*. New York: Knopf, 1987.

——. *The Unfinished City: New York and the Metropolitan Idea*. New York: New Press, 2002.

Benjamin, Walter. *The Arcades Project.* Translated by Howard Eiland and Kevin McLaughlin. Cambridge, MA: The Belknap Press of Harvard University Press, 1999.

Berger, Meyer. "The Bowery Blinks in the Sunlight." *New York Times,* May 20, 1956.

———. "Our Changing City." *New York Times,* June 20, 1955. Article in a 20-part series, "Our Changing City," begun in the summer of 1955.

Berliner, Michael, ed. *Letters of Ayn Rand.* New York: Dutton, 2005.

Berman, Marshall. *All That Is Solid Melts into Air: The Experience of Modernity.* New York: Penguin Books, 1988.

———. "Introduction." In *New York Calling: From Blackout to Bloomberg,* edited by Marshall Berman and Brian Berger, 9–38. London: Reaktion Books, 2007.

———. *On the Town: One Hundred Years of Spectacle in Times Square.* New York: Random House, 2006.

———. "Ruins and Reform: New York Yesterday and Today." *Dissent* (Fall 1987): 421–28.

Berman, Marshall, and Brian Berger, ed. *New York Calling: From Blackout to Bloomberg.* London: Reaktion Books, 2007.

Berman, Paul. "The Face of Downtown: Strokes for a Portrait." *Dissent* (Fall 1987): 569–74.

Bernstein, Iver. *The New York City Draft Riots: Their Significance for American Society and Politics in the Age of the Civil War.* Cambridge: Oxford University Press, 1990.

Biskind, Peter. *Easy Riders, Raging Bulls: How the Sex-Drugs-and-Rock-'N'-Roll Generation Saved Hollywood.* New York: Simon & Schuster, 1998.

Blake, Angela M. *How New York Became American, 1890–1924.* Baltimore: Johns Hopkins University Press, 2006.

Block, Lawrence. "Introduction." In *The Mike Hammer Collection.* Vol. 2. New York: New American Library, 2001.

Bloom, Alexander. *Prodigal Sons: The New York Intellectuals and Their World.* New York: Oxford University Press, 1986.

Bloom, Nicholas Dagen. *Public Housing That Worked: New York in the Twentieth Century.* Philadelphia: University of Pennsylvania Press, 2008.

Bowman, David. *This Must Be the Place: The Adventures of the Talking Heads in the 20th Century.* New York: HarperEntertainment, 2001.

Boyer, Paul. *By the Bomb's Early Light: American Thought and Culture at the Dawn of the Atomic Age.* New York: Pantheon Books, 1985.

Bradley, Stefan M. *Harlem vs. Columbia University.* Champaign: University of Illinois Press, 2009.

Bramwell, Austin. "Cobblestone Conservative." *The American Conservative,* October 2011.

Braunstein, Peter. "Adults Only: The Construction of an Erotic City in New York During the 1970s." In *America in the 70s,* edited by Beth Bailey and David Farber, 129–56. Lawrence: University Press of Kansas, 2004.

Brazis, Tamar, Hilly Kristal, and David Byrne. *Cbgb & Omfug: Thirty Years from the Home of Underground Rock*. 1 volume. New York: Harry N. Abrams, 2005.

Breslin, Jimmy. "In the Streets." *New York Herald Tribune*, October 27, 1965. Article in a 5-day series, "The Lonely Crimes."

Brick, Howard. *Age of Contradiction: American Thought & Culture in the 1960s*. Ithaca, NY: Cornell University Press, 2000.

———. *Daniel Bell and the Decline of Intellectual Radicalism: Social Theory and Political Reconciliation in the 1940s*. Madison: University of Wisconsin Press, 1986.

Brinkley, Alan. *The Publisher: Henry Luce and His American Century*. New York: Vintage, 2011.

Brooks, Richard. *Looking for Mr. Goodbar*. United States: Paramount Pictures, 1977.

Brown, Claude. "Harlem, My Harlem." *Dissent* (Summer 1961), 378–82.

———. *Manchild in the Promised Land*. New York: Signet, 1965.

Buckley, William F., Jr. "Contemporary Challenges and the Social Order." In *Did You Ever See a Dream Walking?: American Conservative Thought in the Twentieth Century*, edited by William F. Buckley, 213–20. Indianapolis, IN: Bobbs-Merrill, 1970.

Burns, Ric, and Lisa Ades. *New York: A Documentary Film*. United States, 1999.

Burrows, Edwin G., and Mike Wallace. *Gotham: A History of New York City to 1898*. New York: Oxford University Press, 1999.

Cameron, Gail. "The Soft Side of a Hard Egg." *Life*, September 8, 1961, 127–30.

Canby, Vincent. " 'Death Wish' Exploits Fear Irresponsibly." *New York Times*, August 4, 1974.

———. "Flamboyant 'Taxi Driver' by Scorsese." *New York Times*, February 9, 1976.

———. "New York Woes Are Good Box Office." *New York Times*, November 10, 1974.

———. "Scorsese's Disturbing 'Taxi Driver.' " *New York Times*, February 15, 1976, D1.

———. "Screen: 'Death Wish' Hunts Muggers." *New York Times*, July 25 1974, 27.

Cannato, Vincent J. *The Ungovernable City: John Lindsay and His Struggle to Save New York*. New York: Basic Books, 2001.

Caro, Robert. *The Power Broker: Robert Moses and the Fall of New York*. New York: Vintage Books, 1975.

Carpenter, John. *Escape from New York*. United States: AVCO Embassy Pictures, 1981.

Carr, Patrick J., and Maria Kefalas. *Hollowing out the Middle: The Rural Brain Drain and What It Means for America*. Boston, MA: Beacon, 2009.

Carriere, Michael. "Fight the War against Blight: Columbia University, Morningside Heights, Inc., and Counterinsurgent Urban Renewal." *Journal of Planning History* 10, no. 1 (2011): 5–29.

Carson, Rachel. *Silent Spring*. New York: Mariner Books, 2002.

Carter, David. *Stonewall: The Riots That Sparked the Gay Revolution*. New York: St. Martin's, 2004.

Castells, Manuel. *The Rise of the Network Society*. Vol. 1. The Information Age: Economy, Society, and Culture Oxford: Blackwell, 2000.

Caz, Grandmaster. *South Bronx Subway Rap*. 1983. Sound Recording.

Chandler, Raymond. *The Maltese Falcon*. Directed by John Huston, 1941.

——. "The Simple Art of Murder." In *The Simple Art of Murder*, 1–18. New York: Vintage Crime, 1988.

Chang, Jeff. *Can't Stop, Won't Stop: A History of the Hip-Hop Generation*. New York: St. Martin's, 2005.

Chase, Edward T. "New York Could Die." *Dissent* (Summer 1961): 297–303.

Chauncey, George. *Gay New York: Gender, Urban Culture, and the Makings of the Gay Male World, 1890–1940*. New York: Basic Books, 1994.

Cheever, John. "Moving Out." *Esquire*, July 1960, 66–68.

Chronopoulos, Themis. "Robert Moses and the Visual Dimension of Physical Disorder: Efforts to Demonstrate Urban Blight in the Age of Slum Clearance." *Journal of Planning History* 13, no. 3 (August 2014): 207–33.

——. *Spatial Regulation in New York City: From Urban Renewal to Zero Tolerance*. New York: Routledge, 2011.

Clark, Kenneth C. *Dark Ghetto: Dilemmas of Social Power*. New York: HarperCollins, 1965.

Cohen, Lizabeth. *A Consumers' Republic: The Politics of Mass Consumption in Postwar America*. New York: Alfred A. Knopf, 2003.

Collins, Max Allan. "Introduction." In *A Century of Noir: Thirty-Two Classic Crime Stories*, edited by Mickey Spillane and Max Allan Collins, 1–3. New York: New American Library, 2002.

——. "Mickey Spillane: This Time It's Personal." In *The Mike Hammer Collection*. Vol. 1, vii–xii. New York: New American Library, 2001.

Conn, Steven. *Americans against the City: Anti-Urbanism in the Twentieth Century*. Oxford: Oxford University Press, 2014.

Cook, Fred J. "Robert Moses, Glutton for Power." *Dissent* (Summer 1961), 312–20.

Cook, Fred J., and Gene Gleason. "The Shame of New York." *The Nation*, October 31, 1959.

Cooney, Terry A. *The Rise of the New York Intellectuals: Partisan Review and Its Circle*. Madison: University of Wisconsin Press, 1986.

Coppola, Francis Ford. *The Godfather*. United States: Paramount Pictures, 1972.

Copyright Collection (Library of Congress). *That Girl. Season One. Vol. 1*. United States: Shout Factory, 2008. 1 videodisc of 1 (DVD) (ca. 170 min.): sd., col.; 4 3/4 in.

Corber, Robert J. *In the Name of National Security: Hitchcock, Homophobia, and the Political Construction of Gender in Postwar America*. Durham, NC: Duke University Press, 1993.

Corkin, Stanley. "Sex and the City in Decline: *Midnight Cowboy* (1969) and *Klute* (1971)." *Journal of Urban History* 36, no. 5 (September 2010): 617–33.
———. *Starring New York: Filming the Grime and the Glamour of the Long 1970s.* New York: Oxford University Press, 2011.
Council for Public Safety. "Welcome to Fear City: A Survival Guide for Visitors to the City of New York." New York: Council for Public Safety, 1975.
Cowie, Jefferson. *Capital Moves: RCA's Seventy-Year Quest for Cheap Labor.* Ithaca, NY: Cornell University Press, 1999.
———. *Stayin' Alive: The 1970s and the Last Days of the Working Class.* New York: New Press, 2010.
Creative Class Group, "Articles," www.creativeclass.com/rfcgdb/articles /Richard%20Florida.pdf, May 2008 (accessed March 30, 2011).
Cuordileone, K. A. *Manhood and American Political Culture in the Cold War.* New York: Routledge, 2005.
Currid, Elizabeth. *The Warhol Economy: How Fashion, Art, and Music Drive New York City.* Princeton, NJ: Princeton University Press, 2007.
Dassin, Jules. *Naked City.* Universal Studios, 1948.
Davidoff, Paul. "Advocacy and Pluralism in Planning." *Journal of the American Institute of Planners* 31, no. 4 (1965): 331–38.
Davidson, Bill. "America Discovers a 'Sacred Monster.'" *New York Times,* September 22, 1974.
Davis, Kenneth C. *Two-Bit Culture: The Paperbacking of America.* Boston: Houghton Mifflin, 1984.
Davis, Mike. *City of Quartz: Excavating the Future in Los Angeles.* New York: Vintage, 1991.
Day, Dorothy. "Poverty and Destitution." *Dissent* (Summer 1961), 233–40.
De Certeau, Michel. *The Practice of Everyday Life.* Berkeley: University of California Press, 1984.
"The Death and Life of Great American Cities at 50: A Tac Symposium." *The American Conservative* (2011). www.theamericanconservative.com/blog /janejacobs/.
Delany, Samuel R. *Times Square Red, Times Square Blue.* New York: New York University Press, 1999.
Deutsch, Tracey. *Building a Housewife's Paradise: Gender, Politics, and American Grocery Stores in the Twentieth Century.* Chapel Hill: University of North Carolina Press, 2010.
Diaz, Eileen. "A Puerto Rican in New York." *Dissent* (Summer 1961), 383–85.
Dickens, Charles. *American Notes: For General Circulation.* New York: Penguin, 1842, 2000.
Dickstein, Morris. "Neighborhoods." *Dissent* (Fall 1987): 602–6.
Didion, Joan. "Farewell to the Enchanted City." *Saturday Evening Post,* January 14, 1967.

———. *Slouching Towards Bethlehem*. New York: Farrar, Straus and Giroux, 1990.

Dimendberg, Edward. *Film Noir and the Spaces of Modernity*. Cambridge, MA: Harvard University Press, 2004.

Dochuk, Darren. *From Bible Belt to Sunbelt: Plain-Folk Religion, Grassroots Politics, and the Rise of Evangelical Conservatism*. 1st ed. New York: W. W. Norton, 2011.

Dorman, Joseph. *Arguing the World: The New York Intellectuals in Their Own Words*. New York: Free Press, 2000.

Douglas, Ann. *Terrible Honesty: Mongrel Manhattan in the 1920s*. New York: Noonday Press, 1995.

Duany, Andres, Elizabeth Plater-Zyberk, and Jeff Speck. *Suburban Nation: The Rise of Sprawl and the Decline of the American Dream*. New York: North Point, 2000.

Echols, Alice. *Hot Stuff: Disco and the Remaking of American Culture*. 1st ed. New York: W. W. Norton, 2010.

Edwards, Blake. *Breakfast at Tiffany's*. United States: Paramount Pictures, 1961.

Elledge, Scott. *E. B. White: A Biography*. New York: W. W. Norton, 1984.

Ellison, Ralph. *Invisible Man*. New York: Vintage, 1952.

Enstad, Nan. *Ladies of Labor, Girls of Adventure*. New York: Columbia University Press, 1999.

Epstein, Jason. "The Last Days of New York." In *The Fiscal Crisis of American Cities: Essays on the Political Economy of Urban America with Special Reference to New York*, edited by Roger E. Alcaly and David Mermelstein, 59–77. New York: Vintage, 1977.

Fainstein, Susan S. *The City Builders: Property Development in New York and London, 1980–2000*. 2nd ed. Lawrence: University Press of Kansas, 1994, 2001.

———. "New Directions in Planning Theory." *Urban Affairs Quarterly* 35, no. 4 (2000): 451–78.

Fainstein, Susan S., and Norman I. Fainstein. "Governing Regimes and the Political Economy of Development in New York City, 1946–1984." In *Power, Culture, and Place: Essays on New York City*, edited by John Hull Mollenkopf, 161–200. New York: Russell Sage Foundation, 1988.

Ferrara, Abel. *Fear City*. United States: Aquarius Releasing, 1984.

Fishman, Robert. *Bourgeois Utopias*. New York: Basic Books, 1987.

———. "Revolt of the Urbs: Robert Moses and His Critics." In *Robert Moses and the Modern City: The Transformation of New York*, edited by Hilary Ballon and Kenneth T. Jackson, 122–29. New York: W. W. Norton, 2007.

———. *Urban Utopias in the Twentieth Century: Ebenezer Howard, Frank Lloyd Wright, Le Corbusier*. Cambridge, MA: MIT Press, 1982.

Fitch, Robert. *The Assassination of New York*. New York: Verso, 1993.

Flamm, Michael. *Law and Order: Street Crime, Civil Unrest, and the Crisis of Liberalism in the 1960s*. New York: Columbia University Press, 2005.

Flatley, Guy. "Martin Scorsese's Gamble." *New York Times*, February 8, 1976.

Fleischer, Richard. *Soylent Green*. United States: Metro-Goldwyn-Mayer, 1973.

Flint, Anthony. *Wrestling with Moses: How Jane Jacobs Took on New York's Master Builder and Transformed the American City*. New York: Random House, 2009.

Flora, Cornelia Butler, Jan L. Flora, and Stephen P. Gasteyer. *Rural Communities: Legacy and Change*. 5th ed. Boulder, CO: Westview, 2015.

Flores, Juan. "Rappin', Writin', and Breakin': Black and Puerto Rican Street Culture in New York." *Dissent* (Fall 1987): 580–84.

Florida, Richard. *The Flight of the Creative Class: The New Global Competition for Talent*. New York: HarperCollins, 2005.

———. "The Great Creative Class Debate: Revenge of the Squelchers." *Next American City*, July 2004.

———. *The Great Reset: How New Ways of Living and Working Drive Post-Crash Prosperity*. New York: HarperCollins, 2010.

———. *The Rise of the Creative Class . . . And How It's Transforming Work, Leisure, Community, and Everyday Life*. New York: Basic Books, 2002.

———. *Who's Your City?: How the Creative Economy Is Making Where to Live the Most Important Decision of Your Life*. New York: Basic Books, 2008.

Flowers, Benjamin. *Skyscraper: The Politics of Power of Building New York City in the Twentieth Century*. Philadelphia: University of Pennsylvania Press, 2009.

Formisano, Ronald P. *Boston against Busing: Race, Class, and Ethnicity in the 1960s and 1970s*. 2nd ed. Chapel Hill: University of North Carolina Press, 2003.

Fortune Magazine, editors of. *The Exploding Metropolis: A Study of the Assault on Urbanism and How Our Cities Can Resist It*. Garden City, NY: Doubleday, 1958.

Fox, Paula. "Civil Society: Moments of Vividness and Promise." *Dissent* (Fall 1987): 593–94.

Frank, Melvin. *The Prisoner of Second Avenue*. United States: Warner Bros., 1975.

Frank, Thomas. *What's the Matter with Kansas? How Conservatives Won the Heart of America*. New York: Metropolitan Books, 2004.

Freedgood, Seymour. "New Strength in City Hall." In *The Exploding Metropolis: A Study of the Assault on Urbanism and How Our Cities Can Resist It*, edited by *Fortune Magazine*, 62–91. Garden City, NY: Doubleday, 1958.

Freeman, Joshua B. *Working-Class New York: Life and Labor since World War II*. New York: New Press, 2000.

Freeman, Lance. *There Goes the Hood: Views of Gentrification from the Ground Up*. Philadelphia: Temple University Press, 2006.

Fricke, Jim, Charlie Ahearn, and Experience Music Project. *Yes Yes Y'all: The Experience Music Project Oral History of Hip-Hop's First Decade*. Cambridge, MA: Da Capo, 2002.

Fried, Lewis. *Makers of the City: Jacob Riis, Lewis Mumford, James T. Farrell, and Paul Goodman*. Amherst: University of Massachusetts Press, 1990.

Friedan, Betty. *The Feminine Mystique*. New York: W. W. Norton, 2001.

Friedenberg, Daniel. "Real Estate Confidential." *Dissent* (Summer 1961), 260–76.

Friedkin, William. *Cruising*. United States, 1980.

——. *The French Connection.* United States, 1971.

Friedman, Andrea. "The Smearing of Joe McCarthy: The Lavender Scare, Gossip, and Cold War Politics." *American Quarterly* 57, no. 4 (December 2005): 1105–29.

Galbraith, John Kenneth. *The Affluent Society.* 40th anniversary ed. New York: Houghton Mifflin, 1998.

Gallo, Marcia M. *No One Helped: Kitty Genovese, New York City, and the Myth of Urban Apathy.* Ithaca, NY: Cornell University Press, 2015.

Gandal, Keith. *The Virtues of the Vicious: Jacob Riis, Stephen Crane, and the Spectacle of the Slum.* New York: Oxford University Press, 1997.

Gans, Herbert J. " 'Communitas'—Its Impact on City Planning." *Dissent* (Summer 1961), 326–32.

——. *The Levittowners.* Reprint ed. New York: Columbia University Press, 1982.

——. *People, Plans, and Policies: Essays on Poverty, Racism, and Other National Urban Problems.* Columbia History of Urban Life. New York: Columbia University Press; Russell Sage Foundation, 1991.

——. *The Urban Villagers: Group and Class in the Life of Italian-Americans.* 1962. New York: Free Press. Updated and expanded ed. New York: Free Press, 1982.

Gansberg, Martin. "37 Who Saw Murder Didn't Call the Police." *New York Times,* March 27, 1964.

Geary, Daniel. *Beyond Civil Rights: The Moynihan Report and Its Legacy.* Politics and Culture in Modern America. Philadelphia: University of Pennsylvania Press, 2015.

Geherin, David. *The American Private Eye: The Image in Fiction.* New York: Frederick Ungar, 1985.

Gendron, Bernard. "The Downtown Music Scene." In *The Downtown Book: The New York Art Scene 1974–1984,* edited by Marvin J. Taylor, 41–65. Princeton, NJ: Princeton University Press, 2006.

General Motors Corporation. "To New Horizons." New York, 1939.

George, Nelson. *Hip Hop America.* New York: Viking, 1998.

Gerbner, George. "Cultivation Analysis: An Overview." *Mass Communication and Society* 1, no. 3–4 (1998): 175–94.

Gibson, James William. *Warrior Dreams: Paramilitary Culture in Post-Vietnam America.* New York: Hill and Wang, 1994.

Gilbert, James Burkhart. *A Cycle of Outrage: America's Reaction to the Juvenile Delinquent in the 1950s.* New York: Oxford University Press, 1986.

Gilfoyle, Timothy J. *City of Eros: New York City, Prostitution, and the Commercialization of Sex, 1790–1920.* New York: W.W. Norton, 1994.

——. *A Pickpocket's Tale: The Underworld of Nineteenth-Century New York.* New York: W. W. Norton, 2006.

Gitlin, Todd. *The Sixties: Years of Hope, Days of Rage.* Revised ed. New York: Bantam, 1993.

Glassner, Barry. *The Culture of Fear: Why Americans Are Afraid of the Wrong Things*. New York: Basic Books, 1999.

Glazer, Nathan. "Is New York City Ungovernable?" *Commentary*, September 1961.

Glazer, Nathan, and Daniel Patrick Moynihan. *Beyond the Melting Pot: The Negroes, Puerto Ricans, Jews, Italians, and Irish of New York City*. 2nd ed. Cambridge, MA: MIT Press, 1970.

Goldsmith, Stephen A., and Elizabeth Lynne, eds. *What We See: Advancing the Observations of Jane Jacobs*. Oakland, CA: New Village, 2010.

Goodman, Paul. *Growing up Absurd: Problems in Youth in the Organized Society*. New York: Vintage, 1960.

Goodman, Percival. "Lincoln Center, Emporium of the Arts." *Dissent* (Summer 1961), 333–38.

Goodman, Percival, and Paul Goodman. "Banning Cars from Manhattan." *Dissent* (Summer 1961), 304–11.

——. *Communitas: Ways of Livelihood and Means of Life*. New York: Columbia University Press, 1960.

Gordon, Colin. *Mapping Decline: St. Louis and the Fate of the American City*. Philadelphia: University of Pennsylvania Press, 2008.

Gordon, Margaret T., and Stephanie Riger. *The Female Fear: The Social Cost of Rape*. New York: Free Press, 1989.

Grandmaster Flash, and Furious Five (musical group). *The Message*. Englewood, NJ: Sugar Hill Records, 1982. Sound recording, 1 sound disc: analog, 33 1/3 rpm; 12 in.

Gratz, Roberta Brandes. *The Battle for Gotham: New York in the Shadow of Robert Moses and Jane Jacobs*. New York: Nation Books, 2010.

Greenberg, Miriam. *Branding New York: How a City in Crisis Was Sold to the World*. New York: Routledge, 2008.

Grella, George. "The Hard-Boiled Detective Novel." In *Detective Fiction: A Collection of Critical Essays*, edited by Robin W. Winks, 103–20. Woodstock, VT: A Foul Play Press, 1988.

Griffin, John Howard. *Black Like Me*. New York: New American Library, 2003.

Grunson, Sydney. "New Faces in the Lower Bronx." *New York Times*, July 11, 1955. Article in a 20-part series, "Our Changing City," begun in the summer of 1955.

Gruntzner, Charles. "Downtown Brooklyn Glistens." *New York Times*, July 18, 1955. Article in a 20-part series, "Our Changing City," begun in the summer of 1955.

Gumpert, Lynn. "Foreword." In *The Downtown Book: The New York Art Scene 1974–1984*, edited by Marvin J. Taylor, 9–15. Princeton, NJ: Princeton University Press, 2006.

Gutfreund, Owen D. "Rebuilding New York in the Auto Age: Robert Moses and His Highways." In *Robert Moses and the Modern City: The Transformation of New York*, edited by Hilary Ballon and Kenneth T. Jackson, 86–93. New York: W. W. Norton, 2007.

Hajdu, David. *The Ten-Cent Plague: The Great Comic-Book Scare and How It Changed America*. New York: Farrar, Straus and Giroux, 2008.

Hall, Peter. *Cities of Tomorrow: An Intellectual History of Urban Planning and Design in the Twentieth Century*. Malden, MA: Blackwell, 2002.

Hammett, Dashiell. *The Maltese Falcon*. New York: Vintage Crime, 1992.

Harrington, Michael. "Harlem Today." *Dissent* (Summer 1961), 371–77.

———. *The Other America: Poverty in the United States*. New York: Simon and Schuster, 1997.

———. "When Ed Koch Was Still a Liberal." *Dissent* (Fall 1987): 595–601.

Harris, Dianne Suzette. *Second Suburb: Levittown, Pennsylvania*. Culture, Politics, and the Built Environment. Pittsburgh, PA: University of Pittsburgh Press, 2010.

Hartman, Andrew. *A War for the Soul of America: A History of the Culture Wars*. Chicago: University of Chicago Press, 2015.

Harvey, David. *A Brief History of Neoliberalism*. Oxford: Oxford University Press, 2005.

———. "The Right to the City." *New Left Review*, no. 53 (2008).

———. *Spaces of Hope*. California Studies in Critical Human Geography. Berkeley: University of California Press, 2000.

Heap, Chad. *Slumming: Sexual and Racial Encounters in American Nightlife, 1885–1940*. Chicago: University of Chicago Press, 2009.

Heise, Thomas. *Urban Underworlds: A Geography of Twentieth-Century American Literature and Culture*. New Brunswick, NJ: Rutgers University Press, 2011.

Hernandez, Javier C. "New York's Next Mayor, an Audacious Liberal." *New York Times*, November 5, 2013.

High, Steven. *Industrial Sunset: The Making of North America's Rust Belt, 1969–1984*. Toronto: University of Toronto Press, 2003.

Hiller, Arthur. *The Out of Towners*. United States, 1970.

Hirsch, Arnold R. " 'Containment' on the Home Front: Race and Federal Housing Policy from the New Deal to the Cold War." *Journal of Urban History* 26, no. 2 (January 2000): 158–89.

———. "Less than Plessy: The Inner City, Suburbs, and State-Sanctioned Residential Segregation in the Age of Brown." In *The New Suburban History*, edited by Kevin M. Kruse and Thomas J. Sugrue, 33–56. Chicago: University of Chicago Press, 2006.

———. *Making the Second Ghetto: Race and Housing in Chicago, 1940–1960*. Cambridge: Cambridge University Press, 1983.

Hoffman, Lily M., Susan S. Fainstein, and Dennis R. Judd, eds. *Cities and Visitors: Regulating People, Markets, and City Space*. Oxford: Blackwell, 2003.

Hoover, Edgar M., and Raymond Vernon. *Anatomy of a Metropolis: The Changing Distribution of People and Jobs within the New York Metropolitan Region*. Garden City, NY: Anchor Books, 1959.

Horne, George. "Staten Island Awaits Bridge." *New York Times*, August 12, 1955. Article in a 20-part series, "Our Changing City," begun in the summer of 1955.

Howard, Ebenezer. *Garden Cities of To-Morrow*. Cambridge, MA: MIT Press, 1902, 1965.

Howe, Irving. "Introduction." In *The Other America: Poverty in the United States*, ix–xvii. New York: Simon and Schuster, 1993.

———. *A Margin of Hope: An Intellectual Autobiography*. New York: Harcourt Brace Jovanovich, 1982.

———. "New York in the Thirties: Some Fragments of Memory." *Dissent* (Summer 1961), 241–50.

———. "Social Retreat and the Tumler." *Dissent* (Fall 1987): 407–12.

Hunt, D. Bradford. *Blueprint for Disaster: The Unraveling of Chicago Public Housing*. Chicago: University of Chicago Press, 2009.

Huxtable, Ada Louise. "Stumbling toward Tomorrow: The Decline and Fall of the New York Vision." *Dissent* (Fall 1987): 453–62.

"Improbable Love Story." *Time*, May 30, 1969, 89.

Ingraham, Joseph C. "Old Lower Manhattan Area." *New York Times*, June 24, 1955. Article in a 20-part series, "Our Changing City," begun in the summer of 1955.

"Is This Book Worth Getting?" (See epilogue note 25).

Jackson, Kenneth T. *Crabgrass Frontier: The Suburbanization of the United States*. New York: Oxford University Press, 1985.

———. "Robert Moses and the Rise of New York: The Power Broker in Perspective." In *Robert Moses and the Modern City: The Transformation of New York*, edited by Hilary Ballon and Kenneth T. Jackson, 67–71. New York: W. W. Norton, 2007.

Jacobs, Jane. *Cities and the Wealth of Nations: Principles of Economic Life*. 1st Vintage Books ed. New York: Vintage Books, 1985.

———. "The City: Some Myths About Diversity." In *Did You Ever See a Dream Walking?: American Conservative Thought in the Twentieth Century*, edited by William F. Buckley, 338–54. New York: Bobbs-Merrill, 1970.

———. *The Death and Life of Great American Cites*. New York: Vintage Books, 1961.

———. "Downtown Is for People." In *The Exploding Metropolis: A Study of the Assault on Urbanism and How Our Cities Can Resist It*, edited by *Fortune Magazine*, 140–68. Garden City, NY: Doubleday, 1957, 1958.

———. *The Economy of Cities*. New York: Random House, 1969.

Jacobs, Meg. *Pocketbook Politics: Economic Citizenship in Twentieth-Century America*. Princeton, NJ: Princeton University Press, 2005.

Jameson, Fredric. "On Raymond Chandler." *Southern Review* 6 (1970): 624–50.

"Jane Jacobs Medal: The Rockefeller Foundation." http://www.rockefellerfoundation.org/what-we-do/where-we-work/new-york-city/jane-jacobs-medal.

Jarrell, Randall. *Poetry and the Age*. New York: Alfred A. Knopf, 1953.

Jencks, Christopher, and Paul E. Peterson, ed. *The Urban Underclass*. Washington, DC: Brookings Institution, 1991.

"Joe and Ratso." *Newsweek*, June 2, 1969, 90.

Johnson, David K. *The Lavender Scare: The Cold War Persecution of Gays and Lesbians in the Federal Government*. Chicago: University of Chicago Press, 2006.

Johnson, Marilynn S. "The Career Girl Murders: Gender, Race, and Crime in 1960s New York." *Women's Studies Quarterly* 39, no. 1 & 2 (Spring–Summer 2011): 244–61.

Johnston, Garth. "Is Union Square Slipping Back to the Bad Old Days" *Gothamist* (blog). May 15, 2011. gothamist.com/2011/05/16/is_union_square_slipping_back _to_th.php.

———. "Is the West Village Slipping Back to the Bad Old Days" *Gothamist* (blog). May 3, 2011. gothamist.com/2011/05/03/is_the_west_village_slipping_back_t.php.

Jonnes, Jill. *South Bronx Rising: The Rise, Fall, and Resurrection of an American City*. New York: Fordham University Press, 2002.

Jordan, Neil. *The Brave One*. United States: Warner Bros., 2007.

"Judge Halts 'Fear City' Campaign as Threat to New York's Economy." *Eugene Register-Guard*, June 13, 1975, 4A.

Jumonville, Neil. *Critical Crossings: The New York Intellectuals in Postwar America*. Berkeley: University of California Press, 1991.

Kaiser, Charles. *The Gay Metropolis 1940–1996*. New York: Houghton Mifflin, 1997.

Katz, Michael B. *Improving Poor People: The Welfare State, the "Underclass," and Urban Schools as History*. Princeton, NJ: Princeton University Press, 1995.

———. *In the Shadow of the Poorhouse: A Social History of Welfare in America*. New York: Basic Books, 1986.

———, ed. *The "Underclass" Debate: Views from History*. Princeton, NJ: Princeton University Press, 1993.

———. *Why Don't American Cities Burn?* Philadelphia: University of Pennsylvania Press, 2011.

Katznelson, Ira. *When Affirmative Action Was White: An Untold History of Racial Inequality in Twentieth-Century America*. New York: W. W. Norton, 2005.

Kaufman, Leslie. "Timeless Book May Require Some Timely Fact Checking." *New York Times*, January 30, 2013.

Kaufman, Michael. "In Street, Store and Subway, Rudeness Infects the Life of the City." *New York Times*, March 2, 1970.

Kaufmann, Stanley. "Midnight Cowboy." *New Republic*, June 7, 1969, 20.

Kazin, Alfred. "They Made It!." *Dissent* (Fall 1987): 612–16.

Kelling, George L., and James Q. Wilson. "The Police and Neighborhood Safety." *The Atlantic*, March 1982, 29–38.

Kessel, Dmitri, and Farrell Grehan. "A Newer New York." *Life*, August 10 1959, 56–67.

Kihss, Peter. "Upper and Middle East Side." *New York Times*, July 1, 1955. Article in a 20-part series, "Our Changing City," begun in the summer of 1955.

"The Kissing Sailor, or 'The Selective Blindness of Rape Culture'" at http://cratesandribbons.com/2012/09/30/the-kissing-sailor-or-the-selective-blindness-of-rape-culture-vj-day-times-square/ and "The Kissing Sailor, Part 2—Debunking Misconceptions" at http://cratesandribbons.com/2012/10/05/the-kissing-sailor-part-2-debunking-misconceptions/ (Aaccessed August 15, 2016).

Klemek, Christopher. *The Transatlantic Collapse of Urban Renewal: Postwar Urbanism from New York to Berlin*. Historical Studies of Urban America. Chicago: University of Chicago Press, 2011.

Klemestrud, Judy. "His Happiness Is a Thing Called 'Joe.'" *New York Times*, August 2, 1970.

———. "What Do They See in 'Death Wish'?" *New York Times*, September 1, 1974.

Knapp Commission. *Knapp Commission Report on Police Corruption*. New York: George Braziller, 1972.

Knowles, Scott Gabriel. *Imagining Philadelphia: Edmund Bacon and the Future of the City*. Philadelphia: University of Pennsylvania Press, 2009.

Kotcheff, Ted. *First Blood*. United States, 1982.

Kozak, Roman. *This Ain't No Disco: The Story of Cbgb*. Boston: Faber and Faber, 1988.

Kruse, Kevin M. *One Nation under God: How Corporate America Invented Christian America*. New York: Basic Books, 2015.

———. *White Flight: Atlanta and the Making of Modern Conservatism*. Princeton, NJ: Princeton University Press, 2005.

Kruse, Kevin M., and Thomas J. Sugrue, eds. *The New Suburban History*. Chicago: University of Chicago Press, 2006.

Lang, Robert. "Looking for the 'Great Whatzit': 'Kiss Me Deadly' and Film Noir." *Cinema Journal* 27, no. 3 (Spring 1988): 32–44.

Lassiter, Matthew D. *The Silent Majority: Suburban Politics in the Sunbelt South*. Princeton, NJ: Princeton University Press, 2006.

Le Corbusier. *The City of To-Morrow and Its Planning*. Mineola, NY: Dover, 1929.

Lee, Spike. *Do the Right Thing*. United States: Universal Pictures, 1989.

———. *Summer of Sam*. United States: Buena Vista Pictures, 1999.

Lefebvre, Henri. *Writings on Cities*. Translated by Eleonore Kofman and Elizabeth Lebas. New York: Blackwell, 1995.

"Letters to Fortune." *Fortune*, October 1964, 84.

Levy, Ellen. "Individuals and Autonomists: 1970s Group Theater and 1980s Performance Art." *Dissent* (Fall 1987): 585–92.

Lewis, David Levering. *When Harlem Was in Vogue*. New York: Oxford University Press, 1979.

Lewis, Sinclair. *It Can't Happen Here: A Novel*. Garden City, NY: Doubleday, Doran, 1935.

Linkon, Sherry Lee, and John Russo. *Steeltown U.S.A.: Work and Memory in Youngstown*. Lawrence: University Press of Kansas, 2003.

Loewy, Raymond. "How I Would Rebuild New York City." *Esquire*, July 1960, 58–62.

"The Lonely Crimes." *New York Herald Tribune*, October 25, 1965. Article in a 5-day series, "The Lonely Crimes."

Lucy, William H., and David L. Phillips. "Suburban Decline: The Next Urban Crisis." *Issues in Science and Technology* (Fall 2000): 55–62.

Lumet, Sidney. *Dog Day Afternoon*. United States: Warner Bros., 1975.

———. *Network*. United States: Metro-Goldwyn-Mayer, 1976.

———. *Serpico*. United States: Paramount Pictures, 1973.

Lyne, Adrian. *Nine 1/2 Weeks*. United States, 1986.

Madriz, Esther. *Nothing Bad Happens to Good Girls: Fear of Crime in Women's Lives*. Berkeley: University of California Press, 1997.

Mahler, Jonathan. *Ladies and Gentlemen, the Bronx Is Burning: 1977, Baseball, Politics, and the Battle for the Soul of a City*. New York: Farrar, Straus and Giroux, 2005.

Mailer, Norman. *The Faith of Graffiti*. New York: itbooks,, 2009.

———. "'She Thought the Russians Was Coming.'" *Dissent* (Summer 1961), 408–12.

———. "Superman Comes to the Supermarket." *Esquire*, November 1960.

———. "The White Negro." *Dissent* (Fall 1957): 276–93.

———. "Why Are We in New York?." *New York Times Magazine*, May 18, 1969, 30–31+.

Mandell, Melvin. "'But I Wouldn't Want to Work Here.'" *New York Times*, November 28, 1971.

Manuel, Jeffrey T. *Taconite Dreams: The Struggle to Sustain Mining on Minnesota's Iron Range, 1915–2000*. Minneapolis: University of Minnesota Press, 2015.

Marshall, Penny. *Big*. United States: 20th Century Fox, 1988.

Mass, Peter. *Serpico*. New York: Viking Press, 1973.

Maurrasse, David. *Listening to Harlem: Gentrification, Community, and Business*. New York: Routledge, 2006.

May, Elaine Tyler. *Homeward Bound: American Families in the Cold War Era*. Revised and Updated ed. New York: Basic Books, 1999.

May, Lary. *Screening out the Past: The Birth of Mass Culture and the Motion Picture Industry*. Chicago: University of Chicago Press, 1983.

"Mayor Bloomberg and Police Commissioner Kelly Announce New York City Remains the Safest Big City in America According to FBI Uniform Crime Report." New York: New York City Mayor's Office, 2010.

McCann, Sean. *Gumshoe America: Hard-Boiled Crime Fiction and the Rise and Fall of New Deal Liberalism*. Durham, NC: Duke University Press, 2000.

McCormick, Carlo. "A Crack in Time." In *The Downtown Book: The New York Art Scene 1974–1984*, edited by Marvin J. Taylor, 67–94. Princeton, NJ: Princeton University Press, 2006.

McEnaney, Laura. *Civil Defense Begins at Home: Militarization Meets Everyday Life in the Fifties*. Princeton, NJ: Princeton University Press, 2000.

McEvoy, J. P. "How to Get Things Done—If You're Robert Moses." *Reader's Digest*, January 1957, 111–16.

McGirr, Lisa. *Suburban Warriors: The Origins of the New American Right*. Princeton, NJ: Princeton University Press, 2001.

McInerney, Jay. *Bright Lights, Big City*. New York: Vintage, 1984.

McNamara, Robert P. *The Times Square Hustler: Male Prostitution in New York City*. Westport, CT: Praeger, 1994.

McReynolds, David. "New Booze on the Bowery." *Village Voice*, March 21 1974, 84–85.

Menand, Louis. "Young Saul." *New Yorker*, May 11, 2015, 71–77.

Mennel, Timothy McKisson. *Everything Must Go: A Novel of Robert Moses's New York*. PhD diss., Minneapolis: University of Minnesota, 2007.

Meyer, Edith Patterson. *Not Charity but Justice: The Story of Jacob A. Riis*. New York: Vanguard, 1974.

Mills, C. Wright. *The Power Elite*. New York: Oxford University Press, 1956, 2000.

———. *White Collar: The American Middle Classes*. New York: Oxford University Press, 1951.

Mills, Nicolaus. "Howard Beach—Anatomy of a Lynching: New York Racism in the 1980s." *Dissent* (Fall 1987): 479–86.

Mollenkopf, John Hull. "The Postindustrial Transformation of the Political Order in New York City." In *Power, Culture, and Place: Essays on New York City*, edited by John Hull Mollenkopf, 223–58. New York: Russell Sage Foundation, 1988.

Mollenkopf, John H., and Manuel Castells. *Dual City: Restructuring New York*. New York: Russell Sage Foundation, 1991.

Monkkonen, Eric H. *Murder in New York City*. Berkeley: University of California Press, 2001.

Moody, Kim. *From Welfare State to Real Estate: Regime Change in New York City, 1974 to the Present*. New York: New Press, 2007.

Morton, Brian. "The Banker's Red Suspenders: Looking at Yuppie Anti-Yuppie Magazines (Manhattan, Inc. And Spy)." *Dissent* (Fall 1987): 574–79.

Moses, Robert. "Are Cities Dead?" *Atlantic*, January 1962.

———. "The Civil Defense Fiasco." *Harper's*, November 1957, 29–34.

———. "Indefinable New York." *Esquire*, July 1960, 52.

———. "Mr. Moses Discusses Planning Et Cetera." *New York Times Magazine*, January 18, 1959, 7.

———. "New York Has a Future." *New York Times Magazine*, January 30, 1955, 22+.

———. "Problems: Many—and a Program." *New York Times Magazine*, February 1, 1953.

———. *Public Works: A Dangerous Trade*. New York: McGraw Hill, 1970.

——. "Significance: What the City Means." *New York Times*, April 29, 1956.

——. "Slums and City Planning." *Atlantic*, January 1945.

——. "The Traffic Menace, in Both Peace and War." *New York Times Magazine*, April 29, 1951, 8+.

——. *Working for the People: Promise and Performance in Public Service*. New York: Harper & Brothers, 1956.

Moses, Robert, and Arthur Wallander. *New York City Civil Defense*. New York: Office of Civil Defense., 1951.

Moyers, Bill. *CBS Reports: The Fire Next Door*. 1977.

Moyle, Allan. *Times Square*. United States: Associated Film Distribution, 1980.

Moynihan, Daniel Patrick. "The President and the Negro: The Moment Lost." *Commentary* (February 1967): 31–45.

Mumford, Kevin J. *Interzones: Black/White Sex Districts in Chicago and New York in the Early Twentieth Century*. New York: Columbia University Press, 1997.

——. *Newark: A History of Race, Rights, and Riots in America*. New York: New York University Press, 2007.

Mumford, Lewis. *The City in History: Its Origins, Its Transformations and Its Prospects*. 1st ed. New York: Harcourt, Brace & World, 1961.

——. *Culture of Cities*. New York: Harcourt Brace, 1938.

——. "The Sky Line: Mother Jacobs' Home Remedies." *New Yorker*, December 1, 1962, 148–79.

——. *The Urban Prospect*. New York: Harcourt, 1968.

Murphy, Kevin P. *Political Manhood: Red Bloods, Mollycoddles, & the Politics of Progressive Era Reform*. New York: Columbia University Press, 2008.

Nader, Ralph. *Unsafe at Any Speed: The Designed-in Dangers of the American Automobile*. New York: Grossman, 1965.

Nagourney, Adam. "Giuliani Sells New York as the Town He Tamed." *New York Times*, October 15, 2007.

Nelson, Paul. "Valley of the N.Y. Dolls." *Village Voice*, 1975, 130–31.

Neumann, Tracy. *Remaking the Rust Belt: The Postindustrial Transformation of North America*. Philadelphia: University of Pennsylvania Press, 2016.

New York Herald Tribune Staff. *New York City in Crisis: A Study in Depth of the Urban Sickness*. New York: David McKay, 1965.

Newfield, Jack. *The Full Rudy: The Man, the Myth, the Mania*. New York: Nation Books, 2007.

Newfield, Jack, and Paul Du Brul. *The Abuse of Power: The Permanent Government and the Fall of New York*. New York: Viking Press, 1977.

Nichols, Mike. *Working Girl*. United States: 20th Century Fox, 1988.

Nickerson, Michelle M., Darren Dochuk, and William P. Clements Center for Southwest Studies. *Sunbelt Rising: The Politics of Place, Space, and Region*. Politics and Culture in Modern America. 1st ed. Philadelphia: University of Pennsylvania Press, 2011.

"A Note from the Editors." *Dissent* (Summer 1961).

O'Connor, Alice. *Poverty Knowledge: Social Science, Social Policy, and the Poor in Twentieth-Century U.S. History*. Politics and Society in Twentieth-Century America. Princeton, NJ: Princeton University Press, 2001.

Orwell, George. *Down and out in Paris and London*. New York: Harper & Brothers, 1933.

Osman, Suleiman. *The Invention of Brownstone Brooklyn: Gentrification and the Search for Authenticity in Postwar New York*. Oxford; New York: Oxford University Press, 2011.

Osofsky, Gilbert. "The Enduring Ghetto." *Journal of American History* 55, no. 2 (1968): 243–55.

——. *Harlem: The Making of a Ghetto, Negro New York, 1890–1930*. Chicago: Elephant Paperbacks, 1996.

Page, Max. *The City's End: Two Centuries of Fantasies, Fears, and Premonitions of New York's Destruction*. New Haven, CT: Yale University Press, 2008.

——. *The Creative Destruction of Manhattan, 1900–1940*. Chicago: University of Chicago Press, 1999.

Pakula, Alan. *Klute*. United States: Warner Bros., 1971.

Paley, Grace. "Somewhere Else." *New Yorker*, October 23 1978.

Palmer, Robert. "A New Life for the Bowery." *New York Times*, April 15, 1977.

Park, Andie. "Borders under Siege in Brooklyn Neighborhoods." *Brooklyn Ink*, September 7, 2011.

Parks, Gordon. *Shaft*. United States: Metro-Goldwyn-Mayer, 1971.

Parks Jr., Gordon. *Super Fly*. United States: Warner Bros., 1972.

Patterson, James T. *Freedom Is Not Enough: The Moynihan Report and America's Struggle over Black Family Life from LBJ to Obama*. New York: Basic Books, 2010.

Peiss, Kathy. *Cheap Amusements: Working Women and Leisure in Turn-of-the-Century New York*. Philadelphia: Temple University Press, 1986.

Pells, Richard H. *The Liberal Mind in a Conservative Age: American Intellectuals in the 1940s and 1950s*. New York: Harper & Row, 1985.

Perelstein, Rick. *Nixonland: The Rise of a President and the Fracturing of America*. Reprint ed. New York: Scribner, 2009.

Petrie, Daniel. *Fort Apache, the Bronx*. United States, 1981.

Petrus, Stephen. "From Gritty to Chic: The Transformation of New York City's Soho, 1962–1976." *New York History* 84, no. 1 (Winter 2003): 50–87.

Phillips, Gene D. *John Schlesinger*. Boston: Twayne, 1981.

Phillips, Wayne. "Walk in the Dark—on West 46th Street." *New York Times Magazine*, September 13, 1959, 25+.

Phillips-Fein, Kim. *Invisible Hands: The Making of the Conservative Movement from the New Deal to Reagan*. New York: W. W. Norton, 2009.

Podhoretz, Norman. "The Article as Art." *Harper's*, July 1958, 74–81.

Pogrebin, Robin. "Sing of the Master Builder." *New York Times*, January 12, 2011.

Polsky, Ned. "The Village Beat Scene: Summer 1960." *Dissent* (Summer 1961), 339–59.

Porter, Russel. "Along Manhattan's West Side." *New York Times*, July 4, 1955. Article in a 20-part series, "Our Changing City," begun in the summer of 1955.

Pritchett, Wendell E. *Brownsville, Brooklyn: Blacks, Jews, and the Changing Face of the Ghetto.* Chicago: University of Chicago Press, 2003.

Putnam, Robert D. *Bowling Alone: The Collapse and Revival of American Community.* New York: Simon & Schuster, 2000.

Rand, Ayn. *Atlas Shrugged.* New York: Random House, 1957.

——. *The Fountainhead.* New York: Bobbs Merrill, 1943.

Ramones (Musical group). *End of the Century.* New York: Sire Records, 1980. Sound recording, 1 sound disc: analog, 33 1/3 rpm; 12 in., SRK 6077 Sire Records.

——. *Ramones.* S.l: Sire Records, 1976. Sound recording, 1 sound disc: analog, 33 1/3 rpm, stereo.; 12 in., SASD 7520 Sire Records.

——. *Road to Ruin.* New York: Sire Records, 1978. Sound recording, 1 sound disc: analog, 33 1/3 rpm; 12 in., SRK 6063 Sire Records.

Reed, Rex. "A 'Cowboy' Walks on the Wild Side." *New York Times*, May 25, 1969.

Reitman, Ivan. *Ghostbusters.* United States: Columbia Pictures, 1984.

Rieder, Jonathan. *Canarsie: The Jews and Italians of Brooklyn against Liberalism.* Cambridge, MA: Harvard University Press, 1985.

Riesman, David, Nathan Glazer, and Reuel Denny. *The Lonely Crowd: A Study of the Changing American Character.* Garden City, NY: Doubleday, 1953.

Riis, Jacob. *How the Other Half Lives.* New York: Penguin Classics, 1997.

Robbins, Jerome, and Robert Wise. *West Side Story.* United States: United Artists, 1961.

Robin, Corey. *Fear: The History of a Political Idea.* Oxford: Oxford University Press, 2004.

——. *The Reactionary Mind: Conservatism from Edmund Burke to Sarah Palin.* New York: Oxford University Press, 2011.

Robinson, Layhmond Jr. "Harlem Now on the Upswing." *New York Times*, July 8, 1955. Article in a 20-part series, "Our Changing City," begun in the summer of 1955.

Rockwell, John. "The Artistic Success of Talking Heads." *New York Times*, September 11, 1977.

——. "Bowery Is 'Home' to Young Bands." *New York Times*, 1975.

——. "Cbgb Club Is Hub for Bands Playing Underground Rock." *New York Times*, January 24, 1976.

——. "Patti Smith Plans Album with Eyes on Stardom." *New York Times*, 1975.

——. "Speculations about Rock Spectacles." *New York Times*, May 16, 1975.

——. "Where to Plug into Television." *New York Times*, 1977.

Rodgers, Daniel T. *The Age of Fracture.* Cambridge, MA: Belknap Press of Harvard University Press, 2011.

Rome, Adam. *The Bulldozer in the Countryside: Suburban Sprawl and the Rise of American Environmentalism.* New York: Cambridge University Press, 2001.

Root, Robert L. *E. B. White: The Emergence of an Essayist.* Iowa City: University of Iowa Press, 1999.

Rose, Tricia. *Black Noise: Rap Music and Black Culture in Contemporary America.* Music/Culture. Hanover, NH: University Press of New England, 1994.

Rosenthal, A. M. *Thirty-Eight Witnesses.* New York: McGraw-Hill, 1964.

Ross, Herbert. *The Secret of My Success.* United States, 1987.

Rotella, Carlo. *Good with Their Hands: Boxers, Bluesmen, and Other Characters from the Rust Belt.* Berkeley: University of California Press, 2002.

———. *October Cities: The Redevelopment of Urban Literature.* Berkeley: University of California Press, 1998.

Rowland, Roy. *The Girl Hunters.* United States, 1963.

Sacks, Alan, Eric Cohen, George Yanok, Gabriel Kaplan, Marcia Strassman, John Sylvester White, Robert Hegyes, et al. *Welcome Back, Kotter: The Complete First Season.* Burbank, CA: Distributed by Warner Home Video, 2007.

Safford, Sean. *Why the Garden Club Couldn't Save Youngstown: The Transformation of the Rust Belt.* Cambridge, MA: Harvard University Press, 2009.

Salinger, J. D. *The Catcher in the Rye.* Boston: Little, Brown, 1951.

Salisbury, Harrison E. "The Manhattan Midtown Area." *New York Times,* June 27, 1955. Article in a 20-part series, "Our Changing City," begun in the summer of 1955.

Sandercock, Leonie. *Towards Cosmopolis: Planning for Multicultural Cities.* Chichester, England: J. Wiley, 1998.

Sandercock, Leonie, and Peter Lyssiotis. *Cosmopolis II: Mongrel Cities in the 21st Century.* London: Continuum, 2003.

Sante, Luc. *Low Life: Lures and Snares of Old New York.* New York: Vintage Books, 1991.

———. "Unlike a Virgin." *New Republic,* August 20 and 27, 1990, 25–29.

Schaap, Dick. "The Fun City." *New York Herald Tribune,* January 7, 1966.

———. "In the Courts." *New York Herald Tribune,* October 25, 1965. Article in a 5-day series, "The Lonely Crimes."

———. "In the Streets." *New York Herald Tribune,* October 26, 1965. Article in a 5-day series, "The Lonely Crimes."

Schaap, Dick, and Jimmy Breslin. "The Lonely Crimes." *New York Herald Tribune,* October 29, 1965. Article in a 5-day series, "The Lonely Crimes."

Schlesinger, Arthur M. *The Vital Center: The Politics of Freedom.* Boston: Houghton Mifflin, 1949.

Schlesinger, John. *Midnight Cowboy.* United States, 1969.

Schneider, Eric C. *Smack: Heroin and the American City*. Philadelphia: University of Pennsylvania Press, 2008.

———. *Vampires, Dragons, and Egyptian Kings: Youth Gangs in Postwar New York*. Princeton, NJ: Princeton University Press, 1999.

Schoener, Allon. *Harlem on My Mind: Cultural Capital of Black America, 1900–1968*. New York: Random House, 1968.

Schrader, Paul. "Notes on Film Noir." *Film Comment* (Spring 1972).

Schulman, Bruce J. *From Cotton Belt to Sunbelt: Federal Policy, Economic Development, and the Transformation of the South, 1938–1980*. New York: Oxford University Press, 1991.

———. *The Seventies: The Great Shift in American Culture, Society, and Politics*. New York: Free Press, 2001.

Schumach, Murray. "Southeastern Brooklyn Area." *New York Times*, July 29, 1955. Article in a 20-part series, "Our Changing City," begun in the summer of 1955.

Schwartz, Joel. *The New York Approach: Robert Moses, Urban Liberals, and Redevelopment of the Inner City*. Columbus: Ohio State University Press, 1993.

———. "Robert Moses and City Planning." In *Robert Moses and the Modern City: The Transformation of New York*, edited by Hilary Ballon and Kenneth T. Jackson, 130–33. New York: W. W. Norton, 2007.

Scobey, David M. *Empire City: The Making and Meaning of the New York City Landscape*. Philadelphia: Temple University Press, 2003.

Scorsese, Martin. *After Hours*. United States: Geffen Co., 1985.

———. *Mean Streets*. United States, 1973.

———. *Taxi Driver*. United States, 1976.

Scott, James C. *Seeing Like a State: How Certain Schemes to Improve the Human Condition Have Failed*. New Haven, CT: Yale University Press, 1998.

Seidelman, Susan. *Desperately Seeking Susan*. United States: Orion Pictures, 1985.

Self, Robert O. *All in the Family: The Realignment of American Democracy since the 1960s*. New York: Hill and Wang, 2012.

———. *American Babylon: Race and the Struggle for Postwar Oakland*. Princeton, NJ: Princeton University Press, 2003.

———. "Prelude to the Tax Revolt: The Politics of the 'Tax Dollar' in Postwar California." In *The New Suburban History*, edited by Kevin M. Kruse and Thomas J. Sugrue, 144–60. Chicago: University of Chicago Press, 2006.

Seligman, Daniel. "The Enduring Slums." In *The Exploding Metropolis: A Study of the Assault on Urbanism and How Our Cities Can Resist It*, edited by *Fortune Magazine*, 92–114. Garden City, NY: Doubleday, 1957, 1958.

Severo, Richard. "Mickey Spillane, 88, Critic-Proof Writer of Pulpy Mike Hammer Novels, Dies." *New York Times*, July 18, 2006.

Seyfried, Vincent. "Kew Gardens." In *The Encyclopedia of New York City*, edited by Kenneth T. Jackson, 698. New Haven, CT: Yale University Press, 2010.

Shenker, Israel. "18 Urban Experts Advise, Castigate and Console the City on Its Problems." *New York Times*, July 30, 1975.

Shermer, Elizabeth Tandy. *Barry Goldwater and the Remaking of the American Political Landscape*. Tucson: University of Arizona Press, 2013.

———. *Sunbelt Capitalism: Phoenix and the Transformation of American Politics*. Politics and Culture in Modern America. 1st ed. Philadelphia: University of Pennsylvania Press, 2013.

Shkuda, Aaron. "The Art Market, Arts Funding, and Sweat Equity: The Origins of Gentrified Retail." *Journal of Urban History* 39, no. 4 (2013): 601–19.

Sides, Josh. *L.A. City Limits: African American Los Angeles from the Great Depression to the Present*. Berkeley: University of California Press, 2006.

Siegel, Don. *Dirty Harry*. United States: Warner Bros., 1971.

Silet, Charles L. P. "Mickey Spillane." In *Speaking of Murder: Interviews with the Masters of Mystery and Suspense*, edited by Ed Gorman and Martin H. Greenberg, 113–25. New York: Berkeley Prime Crime, 1998.

Sklar, Robert. *Movie Made America: A Cultural History of American Movies*. Revised and Updated ed. New York: Vintage, 1994.

Sleeper, Jim. "Boodling, Bigotry, and Cosmopolitanism: The Transformation of a Civic Culture." *Dissent* (Fall 1987): 413–20.

———. "Boom & Bust with Ed Koch." *Dissent* (Fall 1987): 437–50.

Smith, Erin A. *Hard-Boiled: Working-Class Readers and Pulp Magazines*. Philadelphia: Temple University Press, 2000.

Smith, Neil. *The New Urban Frontier: Gentrification and the Revanchist City*. London: Routledge, 1996.

Snyder, Robert W. "Crime." In *The Encyclopedia of New York City*, edited by Kenneth T. Jackson, 329–30. New Haven, CT: Yale University Press, 2010.

———. "Kitty Genovese Murder." In *The Encyclopedia of New York City*, edited by Kenneth T. Jackson, 702. New Haven, CT: Yale University Press, 2010.

Soffer, Jonathan. *Ed Koch and the Rebuilding of New York City*. New York: Columbia University Press, 2010.

Solomon, Barbara Probst. "The Person Alone." *Dissent* (Summer 1961), 404–7.

Sontag, Susan. *Illness as Metaphor*. New York: Farrar, Straus & Giroux, 1978.

Sorkin, Michael. *Twenty Minutes in Manhattan*. New York: Reaktion, 2010.

Southern, Terry. "An Investigation of the Mid-Century Literary Phenomenon in Which Mr. Spillane, a Popular Novelist of the Day, Chooses to Assay the Role of His Hero . . ." *Esquire*, July 1963, 74–76, 112.

Spillane, Mickey. *The Big Kill*. In *The Mike Hammer Collection*. Vol. 2, 175–346. New York: New American Library, 2001.

———. *The Body Lovers*. New York: Signet Books, 1967.

———. *The Girl Hunters*. New York: Signet Books, 1962.

———. *I, the Jury*. In *The Mike Hammer Collection*. Vol. 1, 1–147. New York: New American Library, 2001.

———. *Kiss Me, Deadly*. In *The Mike Hammer Collection*. Vol. 2, 347–517. New York: New American Library, 2001.

———. *My Gun Is Quick*. In *The Mike Hammer Collection*. Vol. 1, 149–344. New York: New American Library, 2001.

———.*One Lonely Night*. In *The Mike Hammer Collection*. Vol. 2, 1–174. New York: New American Library, 2001.

———. *Survival Zero*. New York: Signet Books, 1970.

———. *Vengeance Is Mine*. In *The Mike Hammer Collection*. Vol. 1, 345–513. New York: New American Library, 2001.

Squires, Gregory D. "Partnership and the Pursuit of the Private City." In *Urban Life in Transition*, edited by Mark Goettdiener and Chris Pickvance, 123–40. Newbury Park, CA: Sage Publications, 1991.

Stahl, Jason M. *Right Moves: The Conservative Think Tank in American Political Culture since 1945*. Chapel Hill: University of North Carolina Press, 2016.

Stange, Maren. "Jacob Riis and Urban Visual Culture." *Journal of Urban History* (May 1989): 274–303.

Stansell, Christine. *American Moderns: Bohemian New York and the Creation of a New Century*. New York: Owl Books, 2001.

Starr, Roger. *The Rise and Fall of New York City*. New York City: Basic Books, 1985.

Steffens, Lincoln. *The Shame of Cities*. New York: McClure, Philips, & Co., 1904.

Stern, Michael. "Rep. Koch Finds 27 Major Companies in Midtown Area Are Weighing a Move from City." *New York Times*, November 3, 1971.

Stern, Robert A. M., Thomas Mellins, and David Fishman. *New York 1960: Architecture and Urbanism between the Second World War and the Bicentennial*. New York: Monacelli, 1995.

Stone, Oliver. *Wall Street*. United States: 20th Century Fox, 1987.

Sugrue, Thomas J. *The Origins of the Urban Crisis: Race and Inequality in Postwar Detroit*. Princeton Classic ed. Princeton, NJ: Princeton University Press, 2005.

Sullivan, Robert. *Rats: Observations on the History and Habitat of the City's Most Unwanted Inhabitants*. 1st U.S. ed. New York: Bloomsbury: Distributed to the trade by Holtzbrinck, 2004.

Susman, Warren, with the assistance of Edward Griffin. "Did Success Spoil the United States? Dual Representations in Postwar America." In *Recasting America: Culture and Politics in the Age of Cold War*, edited by Lary May, 19–37. Chicago: University of Chicago Press, 1989.

Swados, Harvey. "Nights in the Gardens of Brooklyn." *Esquire*, July 1960, 124–44.

Taylor, Marvin J. "Playing the Field: The Downtown Scene and Cultural Production, an Introduction." In *The Downtown Book: The New York Art Scene 1974-1984*, edited by Marvin J. Taylor, 17–39. Princeton, NJ: Princeton University Press, 2006.

Taylor, Marvin J., Grey Art Gallery & Study Center, Fales Library, Andy Warhol Museum, and Austin Museum of Art. *The Downtown Book: The New York Art Scene, 1974–1984*. Princeton, NJ: Princeton University Press, 2006.

Taylor, Monique M. *Harlem between Heaven and Hell*. Minneapolis: University of Minnesota Press, 2002.

Teaford, Jon C. *Cities of the Heartland: The Rise and Fall of the Industrial Midwest*. Bloomington: Indiana University Press, 1993.

Tennant, Andy. *Sweet Home Alabama*. United States: Touchstone Pictures, 2002.

Thomas, Piri. *Down These Mean Streets*. New York: Vintage, 1997.

Thompson, Howard. "'Joe,' an East Village Tale, Arrives." *New York Times*, July 16, 1970.

Thurber, James, and E. B. White. *Is Sex Necessary?* New York: Harper & Brothers, 1929.

Tochterman, Brian. "Theorizing Neoliberal Urban Development: A Genealogy from Richard Florida to Jane Jacobs." *Radical History Review* 2012, no. 112 (Winter 2012): 65–87.

Turner, Frederick Jackson. *The Frontier in American History*. Project Gutenberg, 1920.

Tyler, Gus. "A Tale of Three Cities: Upper Economy, Lower—and Under." *Dissent* (Fall 1987): 463–70.

U.S. Office of Policy Planning and Research, U.S. Department of Labor. *The Negro Family: The Case for National Action*. Washington, DC: Office of Policy Planning and Research, 1965. Microform.

Vaïsse, Justin. *Neoconservatism: The Biography of a Movement*. Cambridge, MA: Belknap Press of Harvard University Press, 2010.

van den Haag, Ernest. "Notes on New York Housing." *Dissent* (Summer 1961), 277–81.

Van Dover, J. Kenneth. *Murder in the Millions: Erle Stanley Gardner, Mickey Spillane, Ian Fleming*. New York: Frederick Ungar, 1984.

Vernon, Raymond. *Metropolis 1985*. Cambridge, MA: Harvard University Press, 1960.

Victor, Phil, and George White. *My Gun Is Quick*. 1957.

von Hassell, Malve. *Homesteading in New York City, 1978–1993: The Divided Heart of Loisaida*. Westport, CT: Bergin & Garvey, 1996.

Wakefield, Dan. "Good-by New York: New York Prepares of Annihilation." *Esquire*, August 1960, 79–82.

———. *Island in the City: The World of Spanish Harlem*. Boston: Houghton Mifflin, 1959.

———. *New York in the Fifties*. Boston: Houghton Mifflin, 1992.

Wald, Alan. *The New York Intellectuals: The Rise and Decline of the Anti-Stalinist Left from the 1930's to the 1980's*. Chapel Hill: University of North Carolina Press, 1987.

Weegee. *Naked City*. New York: Da Capo, 1945.

Weise, Andrew. *Places of Their Own: African American Suburbanization in the Twentieth Century*. Chicago: University of Chicago Press, 2004.

Wertham, Fredric. Letter to Randall Larson. July 12, 1975. Wertham Papers, Library of Congress, Box 96 Folder 10.

Whalen, Richard J. *Catch the Falling Flag: A Republican's Challenge to His Party*. New York: Houghton Mifflin, 1972.

———. "A City Destroying Itself." *Fortune*, September 1965, 114–23.

———. *A City Destroying Itself: An Angry View of New York*. New York: Morrow, 1965.

Whisnant, Rebecca, and Christine Stark, eds. *Not for Sale: Feminists Resisting Prostitution and Pornography*. Melbourne: Spinifex Press, 2005.

White, E. B. *Essays of E. B. White*. 1st ed. New York: Harper & Row, 1977.

———. *Here Is New York*. New York: Harper & Brothers, 1949.

———. *The Lady Is Cold, Poems*. New York: Harper & Brothers, 1929.

———. *One Man's Meat*. Harper's Modern Classics. New York: Harper, 1950.

———. *Poems and Sketches of E. B. White*. New York: Harper & Row, 1981.

White, E. B., and Dorothy Lobrano Guth. *Letters of E. B. White*. 1st ed. New York: Harper & Row, 1976.

Whyte, William H. "Are Cities Un-American?." In *The Exploding Metropolis: A Study of the Assault on Urbanism and How Our Cities Can Resist It*, edited by *Fortune Magazine*, 1–31. Garden City, NY: Doubleday, 1957, 1958.

———. "Introduction." In *The Exploding Metropolis: A Study of the Assault on Urbanism and How Our Cities Can Resist It*, edited by *Fortune Magazine*, vii–xx. Garden City, NY: Doubleday, 1957, 1958.

———. *The Organization Man*. New York: Simon and Schuster, 1956.

———. "Urban Sprawl." In *The Exploding Metropolis: A Study of the Assault on Urbanism and How Our Cities Can Resist It*, edited by *Fortune Magazine*. Garden City, NY: Doubleday, 1957, 1958.

Wilentz, Sean. *The Age of Reagan: A History, 1974–2008*. New York: HarperCollins, 2008.

Williams, Raymond. *Keywords: A Vocabulary of Culture and Society*. New York: Oxford University Press, 1976.

Wilson, James Q. *Thinking about Crime*. Revised ed. New York: Basic Books, A Member of the Perseus Books Group, 2013.

Winner, Michael. *Death Wish*. United States, 1974.

———. *Death Wish 3*. United States, 1985.

Wolfe, Tom. *The Bonfire of the Vanities*. New York: Farrar, Straus and Giroux, 1987.

Wood, Robert C. *1400 Governments: The Political Economy of the New York Metropolitan Region*. Cambridge, MA: Harvard University Press, 1961.

"A Word to Our Readers." *Dissent* (Winter 1954), 3–4.

Wright, Frank Lloyd. "Broadacre City: A New Community Plan." In *The City Reader*, edited by Richard T. LeGates and Frederic Stout, 325–30. New York: Routledge, 2003.

Zevin, Robert. "New York City Crisis: First Act in a New Age of Reaction." In *The Fiscal Crisis of American Cities: Essays on the Political Economy of Urban America with Special Reference to New York*, edited by Roger E. Alcaly and David Mermelstein, 11–29. New York: Vintage Books, 1977.

Zipp, Samuel. *Manhattan Projects: The Rise and Fall of Urban Renewal in the Cold War*. New York: Oxford University Press, 2010.

Zoll, Stephen. "The West Village: Let There Be Blight." *Dissent* (Summer 1961), 289–96.

Zukin, Sharon. *Loft Living: Culture and Capital in Urban Change*. New Brunswick, NJ: Rutgers University Press, 1989.

———. *Naked City: The Death and Life of Authentic Urban Places*. New York: Oxford University Press, 2010.

Index

Abel, Lionel, 102, 104, 109, 112, 114–20, 158, 199, 224

Advocacy planning, 91–92

After Hours (Scorsese), 177

Agnew, Spiro, 6, 10

Allen, Woody, 31–34, 177–78

Anderson, Martin, 96, 131, 223 (n. 34)

Angell, Katherine, 21

Angell, Roger, 24

Annie Hall (Allen), 31–32

Architectural Forum, 67, 85–87

Atlantic, The, 24, 66, 77

Atlas Shrugged (Rand), 42

Atomic bomb, 7, 17, 23, 29, 71

Auletta, Ken, 142

Austin, Joe, 187–89, 212–13 (n. 23)

Authoritarian high modernism, 62, 75, 82, 96, 117, 220 (n. 20)

Baldwin, James, 74, 83–84, 92, 116, 131

Bambaataa, Afrika, 191–93

Banfield, Edward C., 2–3, 109, 140–41

Beame, Abraham, 169–70

Beauregard, Robert, 59, 140

Bell, Daniel, 102–4, 109–13, 120, 199, 224 (n. 1)

Bellow, Saul, 103, 117–18, 224 (n. 1), 228 (n. 67)

Bender, Thomas, 17, 28–29, 205–6

Benign neglect, 140–41

Berger, Meyer, 73, 230 (n. 18)

Berman, Marshall, 9, 199, 206, 210

Beyond the Melting Pot (Glazer and Moynihan), 125

Big (Marshall), 173, 178, 198

Big Kill, The (Spillane), 37–38, 48–49, 54

Black Mask, 41

Blight, 4, 7, 48–50, 59–66, 133, 175, 227 (n. 53)

Blondie, 180–81, 184, 192–93

Bloomberg, Michael, 198, 203–8

Blue Bloods, 208–9

Body Lovers, The (Spillane), 50, 56

Boston, 4, 7, 89

Bourne, Randolph, 28–29

Bowery Mission, 127–28, 180

Boyle, Peter, 159–61

Brathwaite, Fred (a.k.a. Fab Five Freddy), 193–94

Breakfast at Tiffany's (Edwards), 31

Breslin, Jimmy, 14, 124, 135–37, 147, 170

Broken windows theory, 11, 188–89, 198

Bronson, Charles, 147, 153–55, 162

Brown, Claude, 108

Buckley, William F., Jr., 94, 103

California, 5, 7, 114

Canby, Vincent, 147, 153–63

Cannato, Vincent, 145, 211 (n. 2)

Caro, Robert, 59, 70, 72, 96, 170

Carson, Rachel, 85

Carter, James (Jimmy), 170–71, 190

Catcher in the Rye, The (Salinger), 34

Catholic Worker Movement, 84, 113, 127–30

CBGB, 180–84, 193, 197

Chandler, Raymond, 44–45, 56

Chase, Edward T., 104–6

Cheever, John, 74, 118

Chronopoulos, Themis, 65

Cities and the Wealth of Nations (Jacobs), 95

City Destroying Itself, A (Whalen), 124, 138–40

City in History, The (Mumford), 3, 77, 119

Clark, Kenneth C., 123, 125, 133

Clark, Mamie, 133

Cold War: containment of communism, 38; and the "do-it-yourself" ethic, 46–47, 54; fears of the atomic bomb, 6–7, 18, 23–24, 70–71; gender and sexuality, 44–45, 54, 220 (n. 19); and the passage of the 1949 Housing Act, 4–6; political culture, 43–44, 80, 101–3; tensions between the United States and U.S.S.R., 8, 18

Collins, Max Allan, 41, 43

Columbia University, 109, 120, 125, 224 (n. 1), 227 (n. 53)

Coming of the Post-Industrial Society, The (Bell), 110

Commentary, 101, 103, 118, 128, 224 (n. 1)

Committee on Slum Clearance Projects, 63–64, 128

Communism, 4, 44, 53, 224 (n. 2)

Communitas (Goodman and Goodman), 104–5

Conference on Urban Design (Harvard University), 86

Conservatism: and anti-urban jeremiads, 103, 114, 121, 124, 139–40, 201; ideology in New York City films, 159–62; relationship with postwar New York City, 1–10; and the underclass debate, 13; and the writings of Jane Jacobs, 82, 93–95; and the writings of Mickey Spillane, 41

Cook, Fred J., 75–77, 82, 84, 88

Coser, Lewis, 103–4

Council for Public Safety, 8–9, 145–46

Cowie, Jefferson, 159

Crime fiction genre. *See* Pulp fiction genre

Cross Bronx Expressway, 62

Cruising (Friedkin), 175

Culture industry in New York, 6, 12, 20, 145–47, 175–80

Culture of fear, 14, 170

Culture of poverty, 107, 122–34, 141–42

Cuordileone, K. A., 44

Cycle of poverty, 3, 131, 135

Daly, Carroll John, 41, 45

Dark Ghetto (Clark), 125, 133

Davidoff, Paul, 92

Day, Dorothy, 113, 127

Death and Life of Great American Cities, The (Jacobs), 3, 50, 77, 81–97, 112

Death Wish (Winner), 54, 147, 153–70, 200, 208

Deindustrialization, 4–6, 109–11, 176, 201

Delany, Samuel, 204

Demographic change, 5, 10, 26–28, 50–51, 82–84, 106–7

Department of Cultural Affairs (DCA), 176

Desperately Seeking Susan (Seidelman), 182–83

Detroit, 12

Diaz, Eileen, 107

Dickens, Charles, 71

Didion, Joan, 119–20

Dinkins, David, 203–7

Dirty Harry (Siegel), 54, 158–59, 164

Disco, 174–75

Dissent: founding of, 101–4; Summer 1961 issue, 101–21, 128; Fall 1987 issue, 199–206

Do the Right Thing (Lee), 209

Echols, Alice, 174–75
Economy of Cities, The (Jacobs), 95
Eisenstadt, Alfred, 17
Ellis Island, 25
Ellison, Ralph, 33–34
End of Ideology, The (Bell), 109–10
Esquire, 74–75, 83–84
Exploding Metropolis, The (Fortune),
    61, 80–82, 86–87, 96–97

Faith of Graffiti, The (Mailer), 187–88,
    205
"Farewell to the Enchanted City"
    (Didion), 119–20
"Fifth Avenue, Uptown" (Baldwin),
    83–84
Film noir, 46–47, 55, 157
FIRE (Finance, Insurance, and Real
    Estate) sector, 109–10, 197–98,
    202–7
Fire Next Door, The (Moyers), 189–90
Fiscal crisis, 1–12, 196–97, 200–206, 211
    (n. 2)
Flamm, Michael, 155
Florida, Richard, 97, 207–8
Ford, Gerald, 1, 147, 169–70
Fordham University, 63–64
Fortune, 80–86, 124, 139–40
Fountainhead, The (Rand), 42
Freedgood, Seymour, 80–81
Freedman, Doris C., 176–77
Freeman, Joshua, 160–61, 211 (n. 2)
Friedan, Betty, 85
Friedman, Milton, 2–3
Fun City, 11, 145–46, 173, 176, 183–84,
    192–96
Funnies, Inc., 40–41

Galbraith, John Kenneth, 2, 125
Gans, Herbert, 89, 102–5
Gansberg, Martin, 137–38
Gay Activist Alliance (GAA), 174–75
Gay Liberation Front, 174

Geary, Daniel, 133
Geddes, Patrick, 3
General Motors (GM), 22, 61
Genovese, Katherine "Kitty," 14, 124,
    137–38, 153, 201, 232 (n. 49)
Gentrification, 12, 87, 92–98, 105,
    173–79, 197, 207, 209
George, Nelson, 191–93
GI Bill, 18
Girl Hunters, The (book), 55–56
Girl Hunters, The (film), 38, 43, 55
Giuliani, Rudolph, 10, 142, 185, 203–7
Glazer, Nathan, 2–3, 103, 118, 125, 141,
    188–89
Gleason, Gene, 75–77, 82, 84, 87–88
Goetz, Bernhard, 162, 200–202
Goldwater, Barry, 101, 168
Goodman, Paul, 104–6, 108, 113, 204,
    224 (n. 3)
Goodman, Percival, 104–6, 113, 204,
    225 (n. 21)
Graffiti, 142, 172–73, 186–96, 209
Grand Central Station, 9, 26, 148
Grandmaster Flash, 191–96, 239
    (n. 54)
Great Society, 11, 103, 120, 133
Griffin, John Howard, 85

Hammett, Dashiell, 44–45
Hannah and Her Sisters (Allen) 177–78
Hardhat Riot, 160–61
Harper's, 18, 21, 61–62
Harrington, Michael: at the Catholic
    Worker, 113, 127–28, 229 (n. 14);
    coining neoconservative, 103; at
    Dissent, 101–4, 108, 199; influence on
    policy, 120, 141; and the New Left, 2,
    13, 113; *The Other America*, 122–33,
    181, 230 (n. 15, 17); and the "under-
    class debate", 3, 13, 141–42
Hartman, Andrew, 117
Harvey, David, 97, 203
Hentoff, Nat, 108

Here is New York (White), 8, 17–19, 24–36, 70
Hip-hop, 172, 189–98, 200
Hofstadter, Richard, 85, 224 (n. 1)
Holiday, 8, 17, 24
Homesteading, 172, 181
House Un-American Activities Committee (HUAC), 23
Howard, Ebenezer, 67, 88
Howe, Irving: autobiography, 114; co-founding and editing *Dissent*, 101–4, 199–200; in Greenwich Village, 92; memories of "The Movement" in 1930s New York, 112–14, 120; on New York City in the 1980s, 203, 205–6; with the New York Intellectuals, 101–3, 224 (n. 1, 3); tensions with the New Left, 101, 103–4, 224 (n. 2)
How the Other Half Lives (Riis), 66, 123, 126–27
Huxtable, Ada Louise, 203–5

I, the Jury (Spillane), 37, 41–42, 52–54
International Style, 60, 87
Invisible Man (Ellison), 33–34
Island in the City (Wakefield), 84–85
Is Sex Necessary? (White and Thurber), 21

Jacobs, Jane: activism, 87, 175; biography, 10, 85–86; cited by William F. Buckley Jr., 93–94; criticisms of, 3, 122; *Death and Life of Great American Cities*, 3, 50, 87–92; "Downtown Is For People", 80–82, 86–87; gentrification, 92–93; legacy, 95–98, 105; on urban economics, 2, 94–95; vs. Robert Moses, 13, 72, 95–97
Jameson, Frederic, 44
Jane Jacobs Medal, Rockefeller Foundation, 96
Jarrell, Randall, 60

Jeremiads (urban), 10, 77, 106, 114–21, 124, 138–41, 201
Joe (Avildsen), 159–61, 164, 202
John F. Kennedy (JFK) International Airport, 9, 150, 169
Jones Beach, 76
Juilliard School, 64

Katz, Michael, 132, 141
Kelling, George L., 11, 142, 195
Kiss Me, Deadly (book), 38, 49–55
Kiss Me, Deadly (film), 41–43, 153
Klan Fantasy, 45–46, 54
Knapp Commission, 154–55, 197, 235 (n. 34)
Koch, Edward, 11, 142, 165, 170, 196, 199–207
Kool Herc, 191–92
Kristal, Hilly, 180–83
Kristol, Irving, 13, 103, 116, 140–41, 224 (n. 1, 3)

La Guardia, Fiorello, 5–6, 116
La Guardia Airport, 9
Lavender Scare, 48
Le Corbusier, 59, 62, 67, 79, 86–90, 106, 223 (n. 23)
Lefebvre, Henri, 14, 172–74
Levitt, William "Big Bill," 6, 18
Levittown, NY, 4–6, 18, 51, 71
Lewis, Oscar, 122–23, 132–33
Life, 17, 27, 72–73
Lincoln Center, 34, 63–64, 81, 87, 158, 225 (n. 21)
Lindsay, John: creating the Department of Cultural Affairs, 176–77; creating the Mayor's Office of Film, 145–46; liberal credentials, 155–57, 221 (n. 1); Norman Mailer's criticisms of, 187–88; projecting an image of "Fun City", 11, 145–46; struggles with public agencies, 151, 169, 234 (n. 20), 235 (n. 34)

Loewy, Raymond, 74–75

"Lonely Crimes, The" (Schaap and Breslin), 14, 124, 135–37, 147

Look, 82–83

Los Angeles, 6, 31–32, 89, 120, 146, 190

Lower Manhattan Expressway Plan (Lomex), 87, 106, 129, 175–76

Luce, Henry, 17, 72, 81, 139

Macy, William Kingsland, 76

Mafia, 38, 51, 164

Mailer, Norman, 104, 107–8, 114, 187–88, 195, 205, 238–39 (n. 35)

Manchild in the Promised Land (Brown), 108–9

Manhattan (Allen), 32–34

Maurin, Peter, 127

Mayor's Office of Film, Theater, and Broadcasting, 145–46

McCann, Sean, 45–46

McCarthy, Joseph, 23

McCormick, Carlo, 196–97

"Message, The" (Grandmaster Flash and the Furious Five), 195–96

Metropolitan Life Insurance Co. (MetLife), 62, 75–76, 83

Metropolitan Opera, 64

Midnight Cowboy (Schlesinger), 146–53, 165–67

Migration into New York City, 4–5, 8–10, 25–28, 40, 85, 106, 125–31, 179, 183–84

"Mike Danger" (comic), 41

Mike Hammer (television series), 42–43

Mike Hammer. *See* Spillane, Mickey

Mills, C. Wright, 101, 113, 125

Milwaukee, 4, 157

Minneapolis, 4, 165

Moseley, Winston, 137–38

Moses, Robert: arterial plans, 5, 87, 106–7, 175; as author, 10, 59–79, 88, 102; blamed for New York City's decline, 59, 91; and the cancer of the slums, 4, 70–71, 105, 122; as City Construction Coordinator, 49–50, 63–65, 81, 87; and civil defense, 70–71; criticisms of in media culture, 61–62, 74–76, 82–84; endorsements of in media culture, 73–74; interest in pulp fiction, 70; and modernism, 1–2, 62, 82, 94, 203; opposition to public transit, 106, 129; popular resistance to, 75–76; revision of legacy, 95–96; vs. Jane Jacobs, 13, 72, 95–97

Moss, Jeremiah, 209

"Mother Jacobs' Home Remedies" (Mumford), 3, 91, 118–19, 122

"Moving Out" (Cheever), 74, 118

Moynihan, Daniel Patrick, 123, 125, 133–34, 140–42, 190

Mr. Sammler's Planet (Bellow), 117–18

Mumford, Lewis, 3–4, 77, 86, 91, 118–19, 122

Municipal Assistance Corporation, 1, 196

My Gun Is Quick (book), 38, 52, 55

My Gun Is Quick (film), 41–42

Nader, Ralph, 85

Nation, 74–75

National Review, 103, 227 (n. 45)

Necropolis: coined by Patrick Geddes, 3; defined by Lewis Mumford, 119

"Negro Family, The" (or Moynihan Report), 125, 133, 231 (n. 39)

Neoclassical economics, 2, 11, 95

Neoconservatives, 9–13, 101–3, 108–21, 125, 141, 187–89, 224 (n. 1), 226 (n. 33)

Neoliberalism, 2–3, 10–12, 92–97, 109–11, 116, 142, 147, 151, 165, 170, 173, 179, 185–86, 197–98, 201–10

New Deal, 4, 44, 59, 75, 116, 141, 164, 211 (n. 2)

New Haven, 4

New Jersey, 11, 40, 53, 60, 182, 202

New Left, 13, 96–98, 101–4, 110–14, 133–40, 199, 211 (n. 2)

New Right, 10–11, 93–94, 101–3, 111, 124, 139–42, 155, 224 (n. 1)

New Urbanism, 94

New Wave music (a.k.a. punk), 172, 180–86

New York (magazine), 179

"New York City: A Remembrance" (Abel), 114–19

New York City boroughs: Bronx, 5, 76, 112–13, 135, 170, 172–73, 189–97; Brooklyn, 5, 40, 46–48, 64, 76, 92–93, 135, 172, 189, 201, 207–8; Manhattan, 5, 9, 11, 27, 30, 37, 46–53, 62–64, 74–78, 81, 106, 111, 115–18, 135, 139, 160, 169, 180–86, 208; Queens, 5, 46–48, 64, 76, 137–39, 159, 184, 200–202; Staten Island, 5, 111, 209

New York City Housing Authority (NYCHA), 64, 127

New York City in Crisis (Herald Tribune), 124, 134–35

New York City neighborhoods: Bowery, 29, 39, 47, 127–31, 172, 180–84, 230–31 (n. 17, 18, 26); Brownsville, 120, 136, 201; Carroll Gardens, 92; Cast Iron District/SoHo, 87, 173–86, 193–197, 208; Central Park, 24–30, 52, 114, 151; Chelsea, 175–81, 192–93; Cobble Hill, 92; East Harlem/Spanish Harlem, 83–90, 107, 127, 134–35, 142; East Tremont, 76; East Village, 159–60, 164, 179–84; Gashouse District, 63, 75; Greenwich Village, 21–28, 48, 76, 85–94, 101–3, 112, 115, 174–79, 181, 208; Harlem/Central Harlem, 20, 34, 50–51, 62, 66, 72, 74–77, 83–84, 89, 107–9, 123, 128–35, 196, 207; Hell's Kitchen, 49; Howard Beach, 200–202; Kew Gardens, 123, 137–38; Kips Bay,

64; Lincoln Square, 63–64, 82, 189; Lower East Side, 47, 66, 70, 74, 126–28, 179–84, 192–96, 208; Lower West Side, 89; Midtown, 25, 40, 50, 72, 81, 165, 178, 185; Morningside Heights, 64; South Bronx, 170–73, 189–96, 201; Sutton Place, 118; Times Square, 17, 28, 52, 149–52, 184–86, 193, 204–5; Turtle Bay, 22–23, 29, 35–36, 49, 63; Upper East Side, 32–34, 159, 208; Upper West Side, 64, 116–17; Washington Square South, 64; West Village, 87–93, 105, 120, 181, 210

New York Daily News, 1, 169–70

New Yorker, The, 18–24, 91

New York exceptionalism, 6, 24–29, 205

New York Herald Tribune, 23, 85, 123–24, 134–37, 145

New York Intellectuals, 13, 101–3, 114, 117, 224 (n. 1, 3)

New York Journal-American, 75

New York Mattachine Society, 174

New York Metropolitan Region Study, 77, 109–10

New York Police Department (NYPD), 53–54, 75, 135, 154–70, 204–9, 235 (n. 34, 36)

New York Times, 1, 6, 35, 40, 42, 62, 69, 73–79, 123, 137–38, 147, 150, 161, 165, 178–79, 181–84, 187, 207

New York Times Magazine, 61–62, 69–71, 88

New York University (NYU), 64, 224 (n. 1)

9 1/2 Weeks (Lyne), 178

1939 World's Fair, 22, 61

Nixon, Richard, 23, 54, 103, 139, 141, 148, 155, 159–60

Ocean Hill/Brownsville School Board, 120

Old Left, 101–3, 109, 121

One Lonely Night (Spillane), 38, 47, 52–53

Organization Man, The (Whyte), 80, 125

Orwell, George, 85

Osman, Suleiman, 92–93

Osofsky, Gilbert, 133, 230 (n. 16)

Other America, The (Harrington), 3, 13, 108, 122–34

"Our Changing City" (*New York Times*), 73

Out of Towners, The (Hiller), 147–48, 150–55, 165, 177

Paley, Grace, 173, 195

Partisan Review, 101, 103, 224 (n. 1)

Patterson, James T., 133

Pei, I. M., 64

Pennsylvania Station (N.Y.), 9, 26, 48, 73

Perelstein, Rick, 160

Philadelphia, 4, 85–86, 89

Pittsburgh, 4, 164

Podhoretz, Norman, 60, 78, 84, 103

Port Authority Bus Terminal, 9, 148, 151

Power Broker, The (Caro), 59, 70, 72, 96, 170

Progressive Era, 65–66, 127, 220 (n. 19)

Public Interest, 103, 188, 226 (n. 37)

Pulp fiction genre, 7, 37–39, 41–46

Queer culture, 48, 172–75

Quinones, Lee, 193–95

Race Williams, 41, 45, 54

Ramones, The, 180–84

Rand, Ayn, 42, 45

Reader's Digest, 73

Reagan, Ronald, 101, 139, 142, 173, 190, 197, 202

Redlining, 48, 201

Riesman, David, 125

Right to the city, 14, 172–75, 181, 189–93, 197, 206

Riis, Jacob, 10, 65–66, 123, 126–27, 142

Riverton, 66, 83–84

Rockefeller Center, 81

Rockefeller Foundation, 87, 96

Rockwell, John, 181

Rosenthal, A. M., 137–38

Ross, Harold, 21–23

Rural crisis, 12

Rust Belt, 6–7, 96, 209

Saarinen, Eero, 87

Salinger, J. D., 34

Schaap, Dick, 14, 124, 135–37, 145, 147, 158, 201

Schlesinger, Arthur, Jr., 44

Scorsese, Martin, 146, 156–58, 164, 177

Scott, James C., 62

Secret of My Success, The (Ross), 197–98

Seduction of the Innocent (Wertham), 52

Seligman, Daniel, 81

"Shame of New York, The" (Cook and Gleason), 61, 75–78, 84, 96

Shkuda, Aaron, 178

"Simple Art of Murder, The" (Chandler), 45, 56

Sleeper, Jim, 201, 206

Slum clearance, 4, 11, 13, 19, 30, 42, 49, 55–56, 60–86, 102, 111, 127–32, 176–77, 204

Slum designation, 7, 49, 59–67, 84–86, 122–33, 140

Smith, Alfred E., 59, 62

Smith, Patti, 180–83

Soffer, Jonathan, 203

SoHo Weekly News, 179

Solomon, Barbara Probst, 107

"South Bronx Subway Rap" (Grandmaster Caz), 195

Spillane, Mickey: biography, 12, 37, 40–41; and Cold War ideology, 43–44, 46–47; in film, 42–43; friendship with Ayn Rand, 42–43;

Spillane, Mickey (cont.)
image of New York City, 7, 10, 46–52;
influences, 41; legacy in New York
City media culture, 38–40, 60–61,
68–70, 119, 136, 140, 153, 174, 201–2;
and Mike Hammer, 37–56; novels of,
37–56; place in pulp fiction genre,
44–46; religious hiatus, 55; and
vigilantism, 53–55; working class
identity, 216 (n. 8)
St. Louis, 4, 86, 127
Stonewall Inn Uprising, 48, 174–75
Students for a Democratic Society
(SDS), 101, 224 (n. 3)
Stuyvesant Town/Peter Cooper Village,
62–63, 66, 83, 89–90
Suburbanization, 4–13, 18, 25–26,
51–53, 60, 71, 80–81, 109, 118, 125,
128–30, 167–69, 182
Summer of Sam (Lee), 170
Sunbelt, 6–7, 10, 165–69, 206
"Superman Comes to the Supermar-
ket", 108, 238–39 (n. 35)
Survival Zero (Spillane), 50
Susman, Warren, 46
Swados, Harvey, 74

Taft, Robert, 63
Talking Heads, 180–83
Tangle of pathology, 123, 133–34
Taxi Driver (Scorsese), 31, 147, 156–58,
163–65, 169, 177, 185, 234 (n. 27)
Television (band), 180–83
That Girl, 31
"Three Faces of New York, The" (Bell),
110–12
Thirty-Eight Witnesses (Rosenthal),
138
"37 People Who Saw Murder Didn't
Call the Police" (Gansberg), 137–38
Thurber, James, 31
Times Square (Moyle), 184–86, 204
Times Square Show (Colab), 183

Title I of the 1949 Housing Act, 4, 13,
59–77, 80–86, 96, 104, 131, 168, 177,
179
Tourist-focused development, 12, 179,
204
Triborough Bridge, 48–49, 76
Triborough Bridge and Tunnel Author-
ity, 63
Trilla, Dr. Francisco, 134–35
Trilling, Lionel, 103, 224 (n. 1)
Turner, Frederick Jackson, 167

Underclass, 13–14, 40, 51, 56, 123–24,
132–42, 148, 159, 191, 195, 201–2, 231
(n. 39)
Underclass Debate, The, 142
Unheavenly City, The (Banfield), 3, 109,
140–41
United Nations, 22–23, 29–30, 44,
48–49, 63
Urban crisis, 4, 54, 80–81, 101, 105,
108–9, 127, 138–42, 159, 162, 165,
168–69, 173, 188–90, 199
Urban renewal, 3–4, 11, 19, 30, 49–50,
54–56, 59–91, 96–97, 102–5, 121–34,
141, 176–77, 203, 207

van den Haag, Ernest, 111, 227 (n. 45)
Vengeance Is Mine (Spillane), 37–38,
47, 52
Vernon, Raymond, 109
Village Voice, 87, 179, 184, 200
Vital center, 41, 69, 96, 103, 115
Vital Center, The (Schlesinger), 44

Wakefield, Dan, 84–85, 107, 127, 229
(n. 14)
Wald, Lillian, 66
Walt Disney Company, 204–5
War on Poverty, 124, 141–42, 196
Washington Square Park, 87, 89, 223
(n. 30)
Weegee, 53, 218 (n. 58)

Welcome Back, Kotter, 189
"Welcome to Fear City", 8–9, 11, 145, 178
Wertham, Frederic, 52, 153–54, 162–63
Westchester County, 20, 53, 60, 118
West Side Story (Robbins and Wise), 5, 189
White, E. B.: appeals to revise Here is New York, 35–36; cosmopolitan vision of Here is New York, 8–10, 13–14, 17–20, 24–31, 39–40; early life and career as essayist, 20–24; enduring themes in postwar New York media culture, 31–34, 47, 51, 70, 74, 106, 120, 131, 158, 198, 203–206, 210; on postwar internationalism and the United Nations, 22–23, 29–30, 44
Whitman, Walt, 25, 28
Whyte, William H., 80–82, 86, 91, 105, 125
Wild Style (Ahearn), 190, 193–95
Wilkins, Roy, 3
Wilson, James Q., 11, 140–42, 195
Wood, Robert C, 77, 109
World War II, 17, 23, 40–41, 116, 151
Wright, Frank Lloyd, 67, 71

Yamasaki, Minoru, 86

Zipp, Samuel, 96, 127
Zoll, Stephen, 105, 120

MIX
Paper from
responsible sources
FSC
www.fsc.org   FSC® C013483